R. F. Delderfield's Novels as Cultural History

PETER LANG
New York • Washington, D.C./Baltimore • Bern
Frankfurt • Berlin • Brussels • Vienna • Oxford

Victor J. Lams

R. F. Delderfield's Novels
as Cultural History

A READER'S COMPANION

PETER LANG
New York • Washington, D.C./Baltimore • Bern
Frankfurt • Berlin • Brussels • Vienna • Oxford

Library of Congress Cataloging-in-Publication Data
Lams, Victor J.
R. F. Delderfield's novels as cultural history:
a reader's companion / Victor J. Lams.
p. cm.
Includes bibliographical references and index.
1. Delderfield, R. F. (Ronald Frederick), 1912–1972–
Criticism and interpretation. I. Title.
PR6007.E36Z73   823'.912–dc23   2011045103
ISBN 978-1-4331-1395-6 (hardcover)
ISBN 978-1-4539-0527-2 (e-book)

Bibliographic information published by **Die Deutsche Nationalbibliothek**.
Die Deutsche Nationalbibliothek lists this publication in the "Deutsche
Nationalbibliografie"; detailed bibliographic data is available
on the Internet at http://dnb.d-nb.de/.

The paper in this book meets the guidelines for permanence and durability
of the Committee on Production Guidelines for Book Longevity
of the Council of Library Resources.

© 2012 Peter Lang Publishing, Inc., New York
29 Broadway, 18th floor, New York, NY 10006
www.peterlang.com

Printed in Germany

ad deum qui laetificat juventutem meam

ACKNOWLEDGMENTS

Grateful acknowledgment is made for the following:

By permission of McBooks Press, Inc.

Extracts from SEVEN MEN OF GASCONY.
Copyright 1949, 1976 by May Delderfield

Extracts from TOO FEW FOR DRUMS.
Copyright © 1964 by R. F. Delderfield

By permission of Harold Ober Associates Incorporated
Extracts from works subject to copyright as follows:

FAREWELL THE TRANQUIL MIND
Copyright 1950 by R. F. Delderfield

THE AVENUE STORY: THE DREAMING SUBURB.
Copyright © 1958 by R. F. Delderfield.
Copyright renewed 1986 by May Delderfield, P. A. Delderfield, V. A. Persse

THE AVENUE GOES TO WAR.
Copyright © 1958 by R. F. Delderfield.
Copyright renewed 1986 by May Delderfield, P. A. Delderfield, V. A. Persse

THE CRADDOCK TRILOGY: A HORSEMAN RIDING BY comprised of:
LONG SUMMER'S DAY.
POST OF HONOUR.
Copyright © 1966 by R. F. Delderfield

THE GREEN GAUNTLET.
Copyright © 1968 by R. F. Delderfield.
Copyright renewed 1998 by V. A. Persse and Paul Delderfield.

TABLE OF CONTENTS

INTRODUCTION

In *What is Cultural History?* (Cambridge 2004) Peter Burke explains what cultural historians do, whether they favor the internal approach, which brings to light "something at once elusive and important," or the external approach which "connects the rise of cultural history to a wider 'cultural turn' in political science, geography, economics" etcetera. Burke notes that these historians are of several minds about the method of inquiry they should adopt. As it becomes "increasingly difficult" to say what does or does not "count" as culture, some of them "see their aim as essentially descriptive" while others believe that cultural history "can and should be presented as a story" (1–3). While not a cultural historian, R. F. Delderfield is a novelist with an ear cocked toward the realities which they address. And it is where cultural history merges with and melds into story that his best and most distinctive novels operate.

Above all, Delderfield seems committed to preventing the past from sliding out of our social memory. As Burke points out, the history of memory is "currently enjoying a boom" among the New Cultural Historians, which is "probably a reaction to the speeding-up of cultural change" which threatens to divide "what we are from what we were." As they recede, events tend to lose their specificity and come to resemble "the general schemata current in the culture," his illustrative example being Paul Fussell's observation that British memories of the Great War "were shaped by recollections of" Bunyan's *Pilgrim's Progress*, which was still "widely read at that time" (Burke, 65–6). In the same vein, though with a more positive and forward-looking cast, William Doyle in his short introduction *The French Revolution* (Oxford 2001) draws attention to contemporary endorsements which demonstrate that the French experiment is a paradigm which has not lost its mobilizing power.

Poles, who first sang the *Marseillaise* in 1794 as they resisted the carve-up of their country, sang it again in 1956 in revolt against Soviet tyranny. In 1989, as France commemorated the Revolution's 200th anniversary, the same anthem of defiance was heard in

Beijing among the doomed student protestors in Tianamen Square. Few countries have failed to experience some sort of revolution since 1789, and in all of them there have been people looking back to what happened in France then and subsequently for inspiration, models, patterns, or warnings (3).

Delderfield would not be surprised at these expressions of solidarity with the French of the Napoleonic era, for, as his five books about Napoleon and his three related novels picturing the experience of ordinary citizens of that time demonstrate, he differed from many other English people in seeing the French Revolution not as a *Tale of Two Cities* horror story, but as genuinely liberating in both intention and effect, and long overdue.

Once again, Delderfield was a novelist rather than an historian and he contributed nothing original to our store of information about Napoleon and his influence. Rather, he evaluated and re-presented the wealth of information he had accumulated by immersing himself for forty years in the large shelf of histories of the period and the many memoirs of eye witnesses. The case is different as regards his Avenue novels (*The Dreaming Suburb* and *The Avenue Goes to War*), focused upon the period from the Great War's end to the defeat of Hitler and set in the London suburb to which Delderfield's father moved the family in 1917 [a safer home than the London then being bombed by German Zeppelins], and his Craddock trilogy (*A Horseman Riding By*), whose action is located in the Devonshire to which he relocated in later childhood and lived for the remainder of his life, with the exception of his service as an R.A.F. officer. In these novels Delderfield acts as a cultural historian presenting "as a story" (Burke) the realities that he knows intimately from personal observation, from direct experience. His two Diana novels and *To Serve Them All My Days* are altogether a different kettle of fish, for in them the cultural history involved is more diffuse, their action being less well described by this book's title.

· 1 ·

DELDERFIELD'S
NAPOLEONIC *OEUVRE*

In Doyle's recounting of events, the crisis which led to the *ancien regime*'s collapse was "financial overstretch" (19), which was not ameliorated by Louis XVI's efforts to prevent national bankruptcy. What made reform impossible was the glaring inequality "in the structure of privilege and exemption" by which the heavy weight of taxation "fell disproportionately on those least able to pay," while parlementary magistrates "were all nobles and represented nobody but themselves," whom they exempted (26). The pre-revolution, as Doyle calls it, occurred when Calonne, "the financial minister appointed in 1783" to halt the impending disaster, attempted to "float new loans" to fund "lavish expenditures in the hope of sustaining confidence." Being resisted in this attempt by the Paris parlement, Calonne next presented the king with a plan for "comprehensive reform" which involved a "new, uniform land tax, with no exemptions," to be overseen "throughout the kingdom by provincial assemblies elected by all prominent landowners." In his third attempt, Calonne imagined that "a handpicked Assembly of Notables" whose "approbation would powerfully influence general opinion" would have the desired reformative effect. But general opinion was powerless to moderate the excesses of entrenched wealth and privilege, so this plan like the others offered no hope of correcting the problem. Push having come to shove, "as crowds came onto the streets to cheer for the Estates-General, the Parisian magistrates were sent into exile" (34–5).

However, the Estates-General, which had not met since 1614, was a "massive disappointment" when it met, since it was an outdated political instrument which guaranteed that the nobility and clergy would overwhelm the reform efforts of the third estate. There was a ray of hope, though, one which emanated from the third-estate's deputies, who "made it clear that they would transact no business as a separate order." Their appeals to the nobility and clergy "to unite with them" were ignored, and a six-week stalemate followed, "during which bread prices continued to rise, public order began to break down in many districts, and the widespread hopes of the spring began to sour." Then, Sieyès proposed that the third estate "begin proceedings unilaterally," and after "an overwhelming vote in favour," they invited the other orders to join them, and three days later a handful of parish priests did so. The dam had sprung a leak, which widened as "other clergy trickled in over the next few days, and a body that was no longer just representative of the third estate recognized that it now needed a new name."

> Once again at Sieyès instigation, on 17 June [1789] it chose an ominous but uncompromising title: the National Assembly. Immediately afterwards it decreed the cancellation and then re-authorization of all taxes. The implication was clear. The assembly had seized sovereign power in the name of the French Nation. It was the founding act of the French Revolution. If the Nation was sovereign, the king no longer was. (Doyle, 39–40)

At that point "certain regiments" began to converge at Versailles, and when more troops joined them, the "nervous assembly" begged the king to withdraw those forces, which Louis argued were necessary "to secure the public order." Predictably, "Paris exploded with a mixture of fear and indignation," and members of the Paris garrison of "French guards began to desert," while bands of "hungry insurgents were ransacking strong points in the city for arms, powder, and hoards of flour." Then on 14 July they descended upon the Bastille, the prison "which commanded the entire east end of the city with its guns," and with the assistance of "military deserters" they seized the fortress. "A counter-revolution had been defeated. The National Assembly had been saved" (42). Without tracing the enabling events in specific detail, what followed was "Civil war and terror" (52), which exascerbated the latent hunger for effective leadership of the country—a leadership not committed as the *ancien regime* had been to crushing ordinary citizens while profiting an exalted minority. The stage is now set for Napoleon to take control, to unite and lead the nation.

This is an appropriate juncture at which to discuss one of those cultural historical studies which brings to light "something at once elusive and important," namely Lynn Hunt's *Family Romance of the French Revolution* (U.Cal Press 1992). While Freud's family romance "was located in the individual psyche," Hunt uses the expression to signify "the collective, unconscious images of familial order that underlie revolutionary politics," especially (as I see it) the politics which led to the enthusiastic acceptance of Napoleon to govern France. As Hunt puts it, "the ideology of absolutism explicitly tied royal government to the patriarchal family, and the use of the term *fraternity* during the French Revolution implied a break with this prior model." Hunt does not mean that the French "were acting out of some pathological fantasy rooted in warped individual psychologies," but that they were engaged in "creative efforts to reimagine the political world, to imagine polity unhinged from patriarchal authority" (xiii-xiv). Now the killing of King Louis XVI "was the most important political act of the Revolution and the central drama in the revolutionary family romance." It was *through* the king's execution that kingship itself died, because "the government which ordered the execution of the former king was a republic whose legitimacy rested on popular sovereignty" (2–3). Hunt illuminates the restiveness of the French people regarding the rule of no fathers or bad fathers by teasing out the implications of the popularity of Saint-Pierre's novel *Paul et Virginie*, published in 1788 and "reprinted more often than any novel published during the revolutionary decade; thirty separate editions appeared between 1789 and 1799."

> What is perhaps most remarkable, however, is how much of the action of these novels [Marivaux's *La Vie de Marianne* was also one of the most influential eighteenth-century French novels] takes place in the absence of the father. In a sense, then, the eighteenth-century French novel predicts the fate of the king; it might even be argued that the novel produces the fate of the king in that the spread of the ideal of the good father and the father's subsequent effacement fatally undermined the monarchical regime. (*Family Romance*, 29–34)

Further, Hunt points to the French Salon paintings of the second half-century, which "seem increasingly preoccupied with figures of old men who had trouble holding onto their powers," the "status of the father" being "particularly ambiguous" in Jacques-Louis David's best-known paintings of the prerevolutionary decade (37).

In terms of the political paradigm at stake, if the bad old king could no longer rule, who would replace him as the icon of a post-absolutist form of government based upon the consent of the governed? Not even the good father, but no father at all, for "the killing of the political father enacted a ritual sacrifice and opened the way to the band of brothers," the first of these being Napoleon, who became the first among equals since he inspired, and rewarded, the diligent and successful enterprise of the officers and men he commanded. As Hunt puts it, tyranny was replaced by the "authority of affection that the laws cannot command." In this paradigm "liberty would guarantee individual autonomy, and love would provide familial solidarity" (64–5). That Napoleon would attempt to replace the *ancien regime* with a family dynasty not unlike the absolutist configurations he displaced is irrelevant here, where the point is to picture the palpable alternative to the crushing system the French had previously endured.

Delderfield's Napoleonic Engagement

I use the term in the *engagé* sense meaning "to involve oneself in or commit oneself to," to which Delderfield's authorship of *Napoleon in Love* (1959), *Napoleon's Marshals* (1962), *The Golden Millstones* (1965), *The Retreat From Moscow* (1967) and *Imperial Sunset* (1968) bear sufficient testimony. His passion for things Napoleonic developed out of an adolescent enthusiasm which fed upon Lockhart's *Life of Napoleon*, which he chanced upon in Appleby's bookstore and read until lunch time, "was there again the next day," and finally bought, for "it was, after all, marked down to sixpence." Earlier than that his imagination was captured when he was "shown his Waterloo coach in Madame Tussaud's, a relic unfortunately destroyed in the great fire at that Museum." Napoleon's coach and Lockhart's biography acted upon Delderfield as Edward Casey's "commemorabilia," i.e., the "texts and artifacts which are the souvenirs" of the dead that help others recall them (*Remembering*, 1987, 159).

Another instance of the commemorabilia that eventually came to occupy "three long shelves" in Delderfield's study is Baron de Marbot's *Memoirs* (two volumes, Longman's Green, 1892), an account of this sublieutenant who rose to become a full colonel in Napoleon's army. In reading Marbot, says Delderfield, "the armchair strategist can partake of every kind of adventure and narrow escape," and, in his imaginary company, "march and fight alongside the veterans of the Grande Armée throughout the period of fifteen years when they dominated the Western world." Nor did his enthusiasm for Marbot's *Memoirs* disappear with his adolescent reading, for when Delderfield was sent out by the R.A.F. with a crew of photographers and camera men in three small aircraft to compile "a review and assessment of the damage to French and Belgian targets [by Allied bombing] prior to the D-Day assault in June," he took Marbot's reminiscences along with him.

> With Marbot's book in my pocket [A. J. Butler's translation, issued by Cassels in 1929 in "a pocket edition" (*Retreat from* Moscow, p. 238)] I travelled over some of the same roads as those along which he had ridden in the company of men like Ney, Lannes and Masséna but thank God I was never called upon to face his personal risks, or exercise his daring or ingenuity. For all that he was a kind of patron saint for me when I crossed France and Belgium in the final stages of World War II, and I thought of him—indeed, I almost saw him in the flesh—when De Gaulle walked down the Champs Elysees surrounded by cheering Parisians. How Marbot would have cherished that moment of liberation! And how proud he would have been of that section of the French nation that had kept its courage and will to resist during the German occupation. (*For My Own Amusement*, 274-5 and 342)

Delderfield's first attempt to present the material he had become familiar with, *Napoleon in Love*, is tangential to this study because it examines personal, not cultural, history. That the great leader had "two wives and at least a dozen mistresses" while at the center of the world stage (11-12) has little bearing upon his ambitions and career. Its bearing is limited to his having two wives: Joséphine Beauharnais, the thirty-two-year-old courtesan and widow who was the love of his life, so far as he had one, and Marie Louise of Austria, the bovine eighteen-year-old woman descended from seven centuries of "every reigning house in the Western world" (203), whose purpose was to provide the heir who would carry forward the line his father intended to establish. That Napoleon's siblings hated Joséphine and tried their best to get her out of the family, in part to enhance their own dynastic aspirations, is interesting for the light it throws on human nature, but that is a separate topic. One senses that Delderfield hoped to write a book which had not been written before, a book that a general readership would find interesting.

Similarly, *The Golden Millstones* is focused on family and dynastic matters rather than cultural history. After Napoleon became the head of the Buonaparte family at age sixteen when his father died, he attempted to direct his four brothers and three sisters this way or that the better to fulfil his own dynastic aspirations. But except for Joseph (and even he was not "the dull, clumsy fellow of Napoleonic legend"), his siblings "possessed considerable individuality and an exceptionally strong character" (7). Herding cats would have been easier. Says Delderfield, "this book is not an attempt to trace the military and political history of Napoleon," but rather "to follow the careers of the seven millstones Napoleon chose to hang around his neck during the twenty-one years separating the siege of Toulon from the final disaster at Waterloo," and so it is not the great man's story "but an attempt to tell seven almost parallel stories over a period of sixty-odd years" (11). That being the book's focus, one does better to concentrate upon Delderfield's other three volumes of Napoleonic history; these contain concentrated, definitive passages which capsulize his convictions about Napoleon's importance as an element of change in European political culture, from which there has been no going back.

The March of the Twenty-Six: The Story of Napoleon's Marshals (1962, reissued as a "Military Classic" by Pen & Sword Books in Yorkshire in 2004) tells their story, says Delderfield, "for the average reader who may want to know more of the brave, ambitious men who sustained the weight of Napoleon's throne—how they began, how they reacted to power, how they met their several ends, what kind of employers they seemed to the men who followed them and how they behaved to the man who had elevated them from stable boys and travelling salesmen to places in history where their names became legends in their own lifetime" (11). In Delderfield's book-blurb prose one can hear echoes of Henry V encouraging his troops on Crispin's Day: "Then shall our names,/ Familiar in his mouth as household words,/ Harry the King, Belford and Exeter,/ Warwick and Talbot, Salisbury and Gloucester,/ Be in their flowing cups freshly remembered" (IV, iii, 53-55). This is the "we few, we happy few, we band of brothers" theme which is endorsed by the staid *Columbia Desk Encyclopedia* when it summarizes the key reasons why Napoleon was able to quickly transform his "starving and ragged army" into a first-class fighting force. His success resulted not only from his supply system, which permitted troops to "live off the land" instead of depending upon "the financially exhausted Directory," nor only from using "speed and massed surprise attacks by small but compact units," but above all by "his magic influence over the morale of his soldiers" (p. 1878). Could such a "magic influence" constitute cultural history? It could, and it always has done. *The March of the Twenty-Six* highlights Napoleon's ability to inspire enthusiastic popularity in the men under his command and illustrates the general historical truth that love of comrades and faith in one's commanders is more efficacious toward inspiring self-sacrificial efforts on the battlefield than imprisonment in the hulks or the pain inflicted by the bloody lash.

> By May 1798, when the Egyptian adventure was well advanced, [Napoleon] had gathered about him a group of talented officers who took his luck for granted. Their confidence in it, plus their faith in his ability, seeped downward through the ranks of junior officers, sergeants, corporals, to the ranks. Today, we should call this confidence *esprit de corps* and the attitude of the men of the British Eighth Army towards Montgomery, or that of the American troops toward Patton, are examples of what collective confidence can do for a fighting force. The German Africa Corps felt this way about Rommel and in Napoleon's own time the Peninsular [Spain and Portugal] veterans acquired the same faith in Wellington's luck. (*March of the Twenty-Six*, 65)

Moreover, what is true of a nation at war will also be true in peacetime, for the same psychology operates in both venues. Delderfield nicely juxtaposes the band of brothers solidarity which Napoleon had activated against the foolish arrogance of the Bourbon émigrés when in the spring of 1814 they returned to France "after twenty-two years of exile." Headed by Louis XVIII, who had been advanced to the throne by the aristocracy following Napoleon's exile to Elba, they "had everything in their favour" and had they been tactful, the bourgeoisie and working-classes would have been content to support them. How did the Bourbons conduct themselves? "One of their first public acts was to parade the statue of the Virgin Mary through the streets" as though it signified the delight of Kingship Above at the return of a Bourbon to France's throne. King Louis "pretended that the Revolution and Empire had never existed at all" and dated documents as if he had "mounted the throne in the twenty-second year of his reign." Under Napoleon "honours had to be won," but "now they were for sale." One could purchase "the coveted ribbon of the Legion of Honour" for "about twenty pounds," and in the period "between August and December 1814, the Bourbons made more Legionaires than Napoleon had made in the twelve years of his reign!" Was it any surprise when "within six months of the restoration the popularity of the exile in Elba was increasing at a rate that thoroughly alarmed" men who saw where this could lead? By March 1815, the exile had returned from Elba, Louis XVIII had fled, and Napoleon began his rule of a Hundred Days until he was stopped at Waterloo. The Bourbons had virtually *demanded*, by their attempt to reverse French history, that Napoleon reinstate what the émigrés thought they had rooted out.

> Inconceivable errors of judgment stemmed from the new government. Injured pride and a spirit of malice dictated its every gesture for the returning exiles had come home determined to exact revenge for twenty years' penury and obscurity in Britain and elsewhere. They wanted more than obedience. They demanded grovelling subservience. These vain and rather pitiful men and women cared nothing for the glory won by French arms against successive coalitions. They only remembered that they had been bundled out of their homeland by the uprising of a rabble they considered less than human and forced thereafter to live on charity, or on their wits in foreign lands. Here, for the first time in their lives, they had to earn their bread and watch their country march to triumph after triumph under the man they had once hoped would restore the privileges they and their kind had enjoyed under Louis XIV and XV. Their outlook was still entirely feudal and they tried by every means in their power to re-rivet feudal fetters upon a people to whom Napoleon had given cohesion and boundless opportunity. (*The Twenty-Six*, 232–33)

Moreover, Louis mistakenly supposed that by honoring the marshals he was "automatically enlisting the support of the army." This was for him an inevitable error since "he had no conception of the warm relationship that had been shared by senior officers, junior officers, N.C.O.s and men during twenty years in the field." To Louis XVIII and his friends "an officer was a professional brute" and the men under him "dumb, patient serfs, ready to be flogged into obedience as the Prussian armies were driven" (233).

Delderfield continues and amplifies in *Imperial Sunset* the contrast he earlier drew between the feudal outlook of the terminally intermarried European ruling class and the brave new world which the Revolution had brought to birth.

> They could not or would not bring themselves to understand that the French Revolution, and its greatest single gain, the opening of avenues of advancement by merit rather than birth, was an international event of tremendous significance and not the product of a large scale riot initiated by the rabble of the Paris slums. For the most part their hired and conscripted soldiers fought without enthusiasm and without any prospect of political or material rewards. They were there in the field by royal decree, and fear of the firing squad or the lash, while enough to keep them at their posts, was not sufficient to enable them to compete on equal terms with Frenchmen who could expect to share in the glory of a victory, who could win promotion to the highest ranks in their new profession and also share in loot made available by conquest. In the armies of Napoleon were men who had risen from the status of farmhand and apprentice journeyman to that of duke in ten years. They had no equivalents in the musters of the Habsburgs, the Hohenzollerns, the Romanoffs or, indeed among the British where the social structure was equally rigid. It is this, as much as the technical ability of their chief, that explains victories like Marengo, Ulm, Austerlitz, Jena, Auerstadt, Friedland and Wagram. (*Imperial Sunset*, 10)

Delderfield estimates that in the Russian campaign alone the French had lost "probably about 150,000 trained soldiers (exclusive of allies)," who were but a small part of "the sacrifice Frenchmen had made to overthrow their own autocracy and spread the Revolutionary creed across Europe" (32). Now France in 1813 had been almost continuously at war since 1792, and war weariness was apparent. And yet, despite what that sustained conflict had cost every family in the country, the fact that Napoleon could create another army "throws into sharp relief the astonishing popularity of a man who had raised France to the position of the most dominant and aggressive Continental power since the days of Charlemagne" (32).

> To appreciate this is to understand why, after so many sacrifices, France was willing to make still more to preserve the dynasty, one has only to read a report made to the Legislature by Montilivet, Minister of the Interior, on February 25, 1813. It goes some way towards banishing the popular conception of Napoleon as a military bully preoccupied with blood and conquest, and substituting, in place of this cartoon figure, an administrative genius whose achievements in the civil sphere were far superior to those of any previous despot. Montilivet declared "Notwithstanding the immense armies which a state of war has rendered necessary, the population of France has continued to increase; French industry has advanced; the soil was never better cultivated, nor our manufactures more flourishing; and at no period in our history has wealth been more equally diffused among all classes of society."
>
> It would be easy to dismiss this as the lip service of a political puppet were it not for facts quoted in later stages of the report, or contained in a survey of civic achievements during the last decade-and-a-half. From the anarchy of a revolution that had bedeviled the population from July, 1789, until November, 1799, the hand of Napoleon had produced a modern state that compared with the most progressive in the world, not excluding her nearest rival across the Channel, untouched by war and civil strife. Rotation of crops was studied, cattle multiplied and their breed improved, feudal tenures, tithes, mortmains, and monastic orders that had kept small farmers in a state of subjection for centuries were suppressed, the processes of law were not only simplified but speeded up, money was lavished upon buildings, seaports, docks and harbors, new roads ran right across the country, new bridges were built by the score, and millions of francs went into canals, embankments and drainage. "These miracles," says a contemporary writer, "were effected by a steadiness of purpose, talent armed with power, and finances wisely and economically applied." These achievements after centuries of oppression by a dissolute aristocracy, are an indication of why France was willing to renew the interminable war in 1813. (*Imperial Sunset*, 32–3)

Delderfield's Napoleonic Novels

Before we focus upon *Seven Men of Gascony* (1949), *Farewell The Tranquil Mind* (1950) and *Too Few For Drums* (1964), his novels dealing with the Napoleonic period, it is useful to draw attention to a phenomenon important for cultural history, i.e., the transmission of past events with the intent of making them present-to living audiences. The Bayeux Tapestry—unsuited for hanging in a church but just right for being mounted at eye level upon the interior walls of a great hall, such that the ambulatory viewer can peruse up close a continuous sequence of pictures that tell in living color how the unworthy King Harold was overcome by William of Normandy—is the outstanding exemplar of the transmission of past events so as to make them present-to the living. Similarly, it is the pungent immediacy of the memoirs written by Napoleon's marshals and their retentive wives that fascinated Delderfield, a personal response to which the "Sources" sections that conclude *The March of the Twenty-Six* and *The Retreat From Moscow* testify ("the wealth of memoir that flowed from European presses during the long peace that followed Waterloo," *Retreat*, 237).

But his last Napoleonic history, *Imperial Sunset*, does not end with the selective bibliography which one expects. Instead it *begins* with an "Acknowledgements" section which, although it does list selected books in categories such as memoirs and history-commentaries, does not *open* with those descriptors. Instead, the "Acknowledgements" section opens with the heading "Fiction." Now to use fiction as a basis of history is sufficiently unexpected that the writer finds it appropriate to explain what he has done.

> It is not usual, in a history, to quote fictional sources but I make no apology for using background material contained in that excellent book *History of a Conscript of 1813* by MM. Erckmann-Chatrian [the pen name of Emile Erckmann and Louis Chatrian, who collaborated in writing both *Histoire d'un Conscrit de 1813* (1864) and *Waterloo* (1865)]. I first encountered this as a French exercise at school. It can be read in English, excellently translated by Russell Davis Gillman [Everyman's Library, London:Dent, and New York:Dutton, 1909. It contains both the *Conscript* and the *Waterloo* texts]. As stated, the authors collected all their material from Napoleonic veterans and if one compares their work with contemporary accounts it will be seen that they have written with a very careful eye on the truth. Theirs is a moving account of what it was like to be a private soldier in the Grand Army. (*Imperial Sunset*, ix)

Delderfield should have put it "to be a private soldier *in the final stages of Napoleon's career*," after former allies turned against him and the ideals of freedom that the great leader formerly espoused were defended by his enemies. It is within that late-Napoleonic time frame that Gillman can accurately say "Here we see the intense aversion felt by young Frenchmen to fight after the Emperor had abandoned his earlier ideals" (*Introduction*, ix).

One can find in these data the chronological sequence wherein an original event (Waterloo) occurs, after which it is commemorated and thus brought to life for new readers, then *re*-presented again, and yet again. In my *Introduction* I have said that "above all Delderfield seems committed to preventing the past from sliding out of our social memory." And in the particular case of Napoleonic history he was not the first to put his hand to the effort, the necessarily collaborative effort, of recovering not simply the facts or lessons of the Napoleonic era, but the *drama*, the living texture of past events. Here is the chronological sequence of the collaboration, the history of its re-presentations:

- Waterloo, the event itself.
- Fifty years later, the narratives recounting the event, i.e., two volumes by Erckmann-Chatrian published in 1864 and 1865.
- Forty-plus years later, Gillman's translation of Erckmann-Chatrian is published in 1909.
- Forty-more years later *Seven Men of Gascony*, dramatizing Napoleon's declining fortunes in the field over half a dozen years, as observed from a rifleman's perspective, is published in 1949.

Here, then, we have a chronological line of descent in the collaborative sequence, the re-activating iterations of the cultural history of French conscripts in the Napoleonic wars, the re-presentations of historical viewpoints as they have been typified by fictional characters.

Delderfield found in the Erckmann-Chatrian volumes not only what the late-Napoleonic French foot soldier thought about the task he had been conscripted to perform, he found as well the precedent for presenting an accurate historical record within a fictional construct that makes it "a moving account." Baron Marbot's *Memoirs* are accurate and moving, but he was bred up to be a military leader like his father, a professional soldier, so his perspective is significantly different. In *Seven Men of Gascony*, Delderfield utilizes both viewpoints: in some measure that of Napoleon and his lieutenants, but overwhelmingly that of French infantrymen, fictive persons who give a local habitation and a name to the variable and shifting attitudes of a close-knit group of comrades—men who argue within themselves and with one another regarding the aims and the costs of what they are doing. Erckmann-Chatrian's hero, Joseph Bertha, a young fellow with a limp who does his best, is, says Delderfield, "more surely than any other figure in the literature of the period, the prototype of the French conscript of the Napoleonic wars and his wry comments on military discipline will find an echo in the hearts of millions of men of later generations who were encouraged by armchair patriots to seek glory in Flanders and the jungles of Vietnam and Malaya" (*Imperial Sunset*, 44). That is true enough, yet Bertha is rather too much of a hook to hang set-speeches on; his *representative* function overshadows the distinctive personality traits which make for more interesting reading. Bertha models how it might be done but *Seven Men of Gascony* does it better.

Seven Men of Gascony

A river is a natural boundary. Many rivers help to define the limits of countries which they border, for they seem to say "thus far shalt thou go and no farther." This is particularly true because on the other side of the wide water live folks who take the position "this close shalt thou come and no closer without a fight." I still remember word-for-word a sentence from a summary paragraph in a high school history book which read "Having crossed the Rubicon, Caesar returned to Rome and began civil war with Pompey and the Senate." I had no idea what the fuss was about, but it was crystal clear that crossing the water was equivalent to throwing down a gauntlet. Washington crossing the Delaware has taken on the same symbolic meaning, and knowing this about rivers, Delderfield uses six of them to provide the structure of *Seven Men of Gascony*. That novel consists of six "parts," each of which is given a river's name, i.e., the Danube, the Tagus, the Otter, the Niemen, the Elster, and the Sambre. The Otter, a Devonshire river, is included because it signifies the pastoral interlude that his French riflemen (British prisoners of war doing construction work for the English locals because the war has resulted in a manpower shortage) enjoy, before they escape back to France to rejoin the Grand Army, cross the Niemen, and by invading Russia seal Napoleon's fate.

Whether Napoleon's military career lasted for fifteen years or for twenty depends on when it begins. If we count from March 1796 when he left for Italy, transformed the army, crossed the Alps to Vienna, and by early 1797 had become the idol of half of Europe, then he enjoyed a twenty year career which ended at Waterloo in 1815. At some point his rising fortunes levelled off and began to fall, but in so complex an action as the Grand Army's attempts to bring more and more of the western nations under his control it is impossible to say just when that point might have been. It is sufficient to say that Delderfield opens his novel at the point when Napoleon's fortunes had passed their apogee, and what remained thereafter was the six year slide from 1809 to Waterloo. The point Delderfield selects to begin *Seven Men of Gascony* is the 1809 Battle of Wagram, fought on the banks of the Danube from Napoleon's headquarters on the island of Lobau, over unstable bridges into towns such as Aspern, Essling and Enzerdorf across the river, and back from there ten or twelve miles into Wagram. The Austrians had challenged Napoleon's dominance, and he came not simply to subdue the city but to claim the Austrian Marie Louise as his second wife. Her function would be to provide him an heir to his throne, i.e., Napoleon II (1811-32), the boy who never ruled and died of tuberculosis at age twenty-one.

Delderfield says in an introductory note that "most of the incidents recorded in the following pages" are episodes written down at the time or afterwards by officers and men of Napoleon's Grand Army. The novel's chief characters are "typical infantry men in the years of the First Empire's decline." His purpose in writing was "to commemorate the gallantry and the hardihood of a million unknown men who marched, fought and died during the years when France challenged a continent" (*Gascony*, 7-8). The fictional representatives of those men are the seven members of "the Eighty-seventh Regiment of the Line" (25), conversationally known as a "file," which is also called a "line regiment" (32). Of these seven characters, three are very important because the intellectual evaluation that goes on within the file is concentrated in and between them, the others having the functions of dramatiz-

ing the variety of backgrounds, temperaments and talents of the young men serving Napoleon, and of being picked off one by one by the accidents of war until
only one member of the file remains alive, Gabriel. While not the narrator, he is
the most narrator-near file member and he gets the "I-alone-survive-to-tell-thee"
role. We begin our cast of characters with this newest recruit to the Eighty-seventh
Regiment, which has recently lost one of its men and needs a replacement before
the Battle of Wagram begins.

Gabriel, who was raised by his putative "Aunt Marie," a pastry maker and con-
fectioner in a French village, is in fact the bastard son of an Italian painter hired
by the de Courcey family to repair one of the estate's chapels, his mother having
been a de Courcey maid. This young fellow's talent for drawing enables him to create a visual record of the file's final six years of service. Finding himself in a town
where all the eighteen year olds had been called to the army, and the shoemaker's
son "was already back with an empty right sleeve and a distressing habit of drib-
bling," Gabriel chose to enlist since he needed "the companionship of other young
men" and decided to go where they could be found. When the recruiting sergeant
learned that he had previous experience with firearms and saw him score "eight
hits out of ten" on the firing range, he was quickly packed off to join "a company
of *voltigeurs*, sharpshooters just then going into action south of Vienna" (18–25).

Footsore but eager, Gabriel searches for the Eighty-seventh Regiment and finds
it just as "the Grand Army was pouring down the Danube Valley, its chief seeking a major action and a Habsburg bride." Napoleon's soldiers have an audience,
because both "the great and the defeated stood by watching, watching Spain and
the Danube, hoping that the roar of battle would not end once again in a fanfare
of Imperial victory trumpets and the boom of triumphant salvoes from the Paris
depots," sounds which for too long "had been the final notes" of every attempt
of France's neighbors to stop "an annual extension" of the Napoleonic empire. It
was the third week of May, 1809, and the Grand Army "was enjoying one of the
last of its victorious sweeps across hostile territory, driving all before it" (26). This
is the point at which *Seven Men of Gascony* intersects with Volume II, Chapter 1
of Marbot's *Memoirs*, which begins "By the end of June I was well enough to join
[marshal] Masséna's headquarters on the isle of Lobau," of which more later.

The second important member of the file, Jean Ticquet, is approaching fifty
and had been fighting since he was twelve. He is the file's leader, the experienced
soldier who knows how to do things. For example, there is no food? Jean will disappear for a while, returning with something unpalatable but edible. Yet at this
moment, as he marches "across the flimsy bridge," leading the other voltigeurs in
the file "to take up positions in the granary of Essling," Jean feels some trepidation.
"He had not served in fifteen campaigns and as many major engagements without
learning how to draw conclusions from the close observation of facts." Ticquet,
illiterate but not stupid, is the man to follow if your life depends upon it, which is

why "what was left of the file" after two campaigns in Spain and the present conflict on the Danube "worshipped him," for "there was not one whose life he had
not directly or indirectly saved during the last eighteen months" (33-4). Today, in
his unsettling ruminations, he

> paid particular attention to the haphazard structure of the floating bridge stretching
> from the bank to the island. It looked to him, an expert layman in bridge-building,
> far too light a contrivance to provide the only thread between the main battle and the
> reinforcements. He said as much to Nicholas, the big man at his side (36).

Nicholas was the other member of the file blessed with both intellect and experience, with whom he conferred whenever a critical situation required joint assessment to be properly understood and dealt with.

A former schoolteacher, Nicholas is the most troubled member of the file. He
carries heavy emotional baggage, "old wounds that had ached intermittently ever
since he had slipped out of the lodging the night when Old Cicero found him in
Camilla's arms." He had come to Old Cicero straight from university and almost
penniless, but his generous host spent many hours of "extra tuition" with him. If
only the student had resisted that voracious woman until her husband had expired,
"the house, the school, the beautiful inlaid Italian furniture, all would have been
his." Turning from that sordid disaster to reflect on his file-mates, Nicholas contemplates Jean, "looking as if his doglike faith in the Emperor's tactics had been
shaken"; then Claude, who "still insisted" that Napoleon's mission was to "impose
liberty, equality and fraternity upon everyone. The naïveté of the man!" Nicholas
munches his meat ration as he then studies Manny, the Jewish acrobat and the file's
cut-up; Louis, the coachman's son, who loved horses and "seldom thought of anything else"; and Dominique, the half-wit who played the fiddle and danced when
not simply obeying orders. At that point, the Emperor appears before them in the
night, as he often does to enhance his popularity with the soldiers.

> Deep in the shadow Nicholas ground his teeth. "That's how he does it," he hissed to
> himself, "a gold piece, an assumed interest, a small avalanche of accurate detail. Suppose
> he had stood in my shoes three years ago, would he have had Camilla, house, property,
> and all, without being discovered in bed with the woman?" *Gascony*, 48-53

Though not a member of the file, the cantiniere of the Second Battalion—
who supplies everything from brandy to hospital transportation if a wounded officer can afford the service—must be mentioned. Old Carla knows she is dying and
informs her sixteen-year-old daughter, Nicholette, that she will need a husband to
look after her; when Carla dies, Jean accepts from Nicholette the "jug of Bordeaux
wine" and pockets "the small plug of tobacco she gave him," tells him "I'll have the
curly-headed one!" [Claude Dupont], and Jean reciprocates by ensuring that when
he offers the men his handful of straws Claude will draw the short one—there is
to be no "frantic dispute" because the matter was so fairly managed. "The can-

teen wedding was held in the company's glade within a few hours of Carla's burial"
(56–63), and Nicholette will be a fixture in and around the action from then on,
as time and chance ravage her along with the rest.

Part I: 'The Danube'

The first contact between French and Austrian troops was a two-day exchange,
the first day saved for Napoleon by "Nansouty's cuirassieurs, big men on huge
horses, a torrent of steel, their crested helmets dipping left and right as their long,
straight swords flickered" among enemy columns which they "rolled up and hurled
back, their furious charge having been a measure of desperation," as "a huge floating mill" set on fire by Austrian troops up-stream had "drifted down and crashed
through the frail bridge to Lobau." The Frenchmen who were able "limped back,"
leaving "two-thirds of their number dead or prisoners." The fight continued on
the next day, but again it was a draw in which "Aspern had been retaken five
times, Essling six" (46, 55). Clearly, a continuation of such killing would not settle
the matter.

"There was to be no repetition of the slaughter opposite Aspern-Essling."
Instead, for a month and longer Napoleon's forces "transformed" Lobau "into a vast

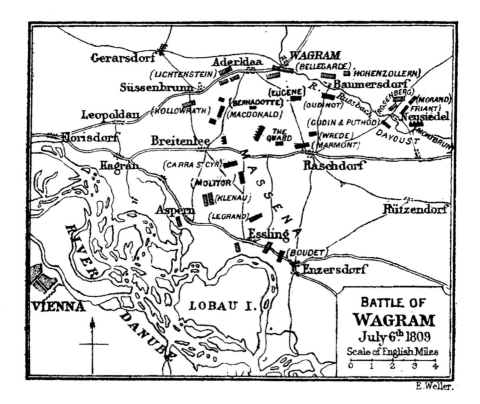

E. Weller.

fort, bristling with nine hundred large-calibre guns, hedged round with rampart, redoubt and complicated systems of abbatis." During this time the voltigeurs were employed as a construction crew, working with mattock and wheelbarrow on the gun emplacement. Jean had wondered "What in God's name was the Grand Army coming to that it should need naval men [in boats, clearing away debris upstream] in the field? Were the old days of infallible victory receding? If so, it was because men like himself were becoming used up. Dead of plague on the Jaffa road, or of cold and hunger in the Spanish mountains; and in their place were mere children like this new recruit, [Gabriel], who had never heard a shot fired save at a brace of pigeons" (36-7). Toward the end of that long construction period—in which the cannon that would decide the conflict in Napoleon's favor were hidden away, out of sight of the Austrians, who would only sense their presence when they began to fire—Gabriel "painted his first portrait group of the file," six men "grouped against a background of summer foliage," three standing, the others sitting or kneeling. "The sketch is dated July 3rd, 1809" (71-4).

With the decisive troop encounter in the offing, it is useful to follow the battle from Napoleon and his marshals' viewpoint, which Baron Marbot narrates masterfully. During the month before the July 6th battle, Napoleon has been planning how the conflict might go; when the configuration of troops on the ground is right, he issues the orders and his marshals vigorously perform the complex movements he requires, at the precise times when they are to be enacted. Early skirmishes had suggested that "the chances of either side seemed to be about equal."

> Really, however, they were all in favour of Napoleon—in the first place, because it was unlikely that the village of Neusiedel, where the only means of resistance was afforded by an old fortified tower, would hold out long against the attack which Davout was delivering with his usual vigour; and it was easy to see that when this was taken, the Austrian left, being outflanked and without support, would retreat indefinitely and get separated from the centre, while our left wing, though beaten at the moment, was in its retreat coming nearer to the island of Lobau, the powerful artillery on which would check the Austrians, and prevent them from following up their success. Secondly, Napoleon, acting on inner lines, could hold a great part of his troops in reserve, and yet show a front in different directions; while the Archduke, being obliged to extend his army, in order to execute his great movement on an outer line with the view of surrounding us, was not in force at any point. The Emperor, observing this mistake, was perfectly calm, though he could read in the faces of his staff the anxiety caused by the conquering march of the enemy's right, which, always driving Masséna's corps before it, had already reached the battle-field of May 22, and after crushing Boudet's division by a formidable charge of cavalry, was threatening our rear. But the success of the Austrians was short-lived. The hundred heavy guns with which Napoleon's foresight had armed the island of Lobau opened a scathing fire upon the enemy's right, and it was compelled, under pain of annihilation, to halt in its triumphant course, and retire in its turn. Masséna was then able to reform his divisions, which had lost heavily. We thought that Napoleon would profit by the disorder into which the cannonade had thrown the enemy's right wing to

attack with his reserves; Marshal Masséna, indeed, sent me to ask for instructions on this point. But the Emperor remained impassible, his eyes ever fixed on the extreme right, towards Neusiedel (which lies high and is surmounted by a tall tower, visible from all parts of the field), waiting to hurl himself upon the enemy's centre and right until Davout had beaten the left and flung it back beyond that village. A valiant defence was being maintained by the Prince of Hesse-Homburg, who was there wounded; but at last we suddenly saw the smoke of Davout's guns beyond the tower. Beyond a doubt the enemy's left was beaten. Then, turning to me, the Emperor said: "Quick! Tell Masséna to fall upon whatever is in front of him, and the battle is won." At the same time the aides-de-camp from all the other corps were sent off to their chiefs with an order for a simultaneous attack. At this supreme moment Napoleon said to General Lauriston, "Take a hundred guns, sixty from my guard, and crush the enemy's column." As soon as their fire had shaken the Austrians, Marshal Bessières charged them with six regiments of heavy cavalry, supported by part of the cavalry of the guard. In vain did the Archduke form squares; they were broken, with the loss of their guns and a great number of men. Our centre advanced in its turn, under Macdonald, and Sussenbrunn, Breitenlee, and Aderklaa were carried after a smart resistance. Meanwhile Masséna had recovered the ground lost on our left, and was pressing the enemy hard, forcing him back beyond Stadlau and Kagran; and Davout, calling Oudinot to his support, occupied the heights beyond the Russbach, and captured Wagram. This decided the defeat of the Austrians: they retreated all along the line, retiring in very good order along the road to Moravia. (*Memoirs*, II, 18–20)

Being a novelist rather than a military historian in *Seven Men of Gascony*, Delderfield's narrative is different from Marbot's, yet he too gives us the large picture rather than descend to the particulars of his characters' actions in the battle. He focuses upon one of the more colorful of Napoleon's generals, Masséna, doing his part along with the other marshals, yet in Delderfield's prose entertaining the reader rather than describing the battlefield's complexity.

On the French left, where the voltigeurs fought alongside Boudet's infantry of the line, old Masséna slowly yielded ground to the enemy's main attack, sitting all day in an open carriage amid a tempest of shot, calmly directing a withdrawal to lure the enemy within range of the Lobau batteries...Vainglory, obstinacy or both had caused him to choose four white horses for his carriage, well knowing that such an entourage would attract fire. The marshal sat there...rubbing his chin and screwing up his one sound eye, as though he were turning over a gardening problem in one of the ornate summer-houses on his country estate. The issue of the battle was never in doubt. It was combat after the old style, stirring the veterans' memories of Marengo, Austerlitz, Jena and Friedland, but the artillery fire was weightier and more destructive than in any of these battles, and the losses, on both sides, were proportionately heavy" (*Gascony*, 75)

Small, compact units of soldiers attacking swiftly are now in the past, because Napoleon has fewer soldiers to carry out such tactics. The big guns take up the slack, but they cannot take the place of enthusiastic men like Jean Ticquet in the old days. Thus the victory of cannon-fire at Wagram is also the clear sign that Napoleon is trending downward.

While they awaited the peace treaty's signing, the voltigeurs were "under arms every other night," the rest of the time being their own. Gabriel explored Vienna with Manny, who knew the city intimately, and they walked among Viennese people "who seemed to bear the French no grudge on account of the recent campaign or their defeats and humiliations of the past fifteen years," as though what the generals did was no business of theirs. Word circulated that Napoleon would soon marry an Austrian princess, which distressed Jean Ticquet because "like most of the veterans he was attached to" Joséphine, regarding her "as a symbol of victory, dating back to the early Italian campaign" when their leader was "an experimental general of twenty-six." The two voltigeurs eventually go their separate ways, Manny to "sample the Viennese brothels," the young artist to walk the city's streets, "storing up impressions for the future" and occasionally drawing, sometimes attracting "a crowd of curious urchins to his sketch book."

On one lovely day, Gabriel hired a punt and poled up the Danube, exploring "one of the many backwaters that flowed into the main stream above the bridge." It was on this occasion that he found Karen, an eighteen-year-old blond-haired farmgirl who had driven her small herd of cows into the water, where "their stumbling hooves" stirred up the mud and sent out "a ring of gentle ripples that splashed softly against his punt," while the artist, hidden by the low-hanging leafy branches on the bank where he sat, observed the young woman

> dabbling her feet in the stream and humming to herself as she leaned on her hands and watched the cows drink their fill. There was a pastoral perfection about the scene that delighted Gabriel. Its appeal lay in its very ordinariness, the contented cattle revelling in the cooling ripple of the water, the dappled pattern of sunlight on the still leaves, the girl's relaxed contentment as she wriggled her pink toes in the stream. *Gascony*, 83-5

Gabriel draws a remarkable memorial of this scene before he announces himself, and the delighted girl takes him to her father and sister on their nearby farm. A lovely bucolic relationship develops between them which opens toward the future—but there is a hitch, or rather two hitches.

One problem is that Karen has an older sister who some years back had a child by an unknown father, but she still has no husband and this young fellow, being seduced, might do. Yet no crisis develops because Gabriel summons Manny, who fellowships with her in the hayloft. "The sun-drenched landscape of the Danube Valley inclined a man towards lotus-eating," and things continue until the Eighty-seventh receives its orders to move north-west, "where Masséna was assembling a vast army for the Spanish Peninsula." Gabriel must comply, but what brings down the curtain on the sunny interlude is the return of Karen's brother Karl, discharged from the Austrian army with one thigh ending "in a knot of dirty bandages" where his right leg had formerly been, and mentally disturbed. The ever-observant Manny says "there's murder in that fellow," and that night the returnee fires the house and barn, which go up in flames. While escaping the hayloft, Manny brings out Gabriel's sketchbook, and its owner is struck by the strange "incongruity of Manny's act of salvage. Two women and two men burned to death," along with the farm and livestock, "yet here was his sketchbook, not even soiled" (92-7).

Part 2: "The Tagus"

The Tagus, a major river in the Iberian Peninsula, flows from the west-central portion of Spain into Portugal, debouching into the Atlantic at the port of Lisbon. A gull travelling in a straight line from Madrid to Lisbon would approximate the direction if not the ragged course by which the Tagus traverses that mountainous terrain. One could plausibly see the river as the objective correlative of the tortuous course of Napoleon's effort to subdue the British. Early in his career the Emperor hoped to raise an invasion force which would cross the English Channel and overwhelm his most formidable competitor in Europe, but that had not been possible. This newest attempt to get the edge over the English by driving them out of Lisbon will also fail, because Wellington holds the winning hand, though his cards remain secret.

> Nobody in the French army...had the slightest inkling of the presence of vast lines of fortifications, erected by the British with Portuguese labour, in the area of Torres Vedras outside Lisbon. Every pass, every gully had been blocked and fortified. The Mountains bristled with guns. A chain of small forts, each of which would have defied the assault of an army corps, ran like a granite necklace round the lower slopes of the bare hills" (133-34).

The impossibility of capturing Lisbon will be revealed only after Masséna's army suffers terrible hardships and losses.

Part 2 of the novel, "The Tagus," is the story of that failure, which does not feature great battles like that on the Danube, whose purpose was to solidify Napoleon's union with the Austrians by marrying one of them for the dynastic purposes which had not entered his mind as a young officer. The Emperor is not even *in* Spain but off somewhere with the Archduchess Marie Louise, engendering Napoleon II while his weary marshals are not cooperating in a military action but arguing with one another: "It was common knowledge in the army that Masséna was at loggerheads with his lieutenants, Ney, Reynier, Foy and Junot. Rumors of furious quarrels trickled down to the ranks through the gossip of staff orderlies and headquarters guards. Ney was said to have insulted Masséna's mistress in front of the junior staff officers." The first or Danube Part of the novel contains seven chapters, "The Tagus" only three because the story of an extended attrition—the commander absent, his marshals arguing, while men like Jean "who were the barometers of the battalions who now distrusted their commanders," were "sapping the confidence" of the soldiers who trusted their judgment (119)—all that does not require a long telling.

"The Tagus," Chapter 1, does two things: it describes the savage conditions the French soldiers experience and it dramatizes the degeneration of the band-of-brothers spirit that Jean Ticquet laments the loss of. The "fierce African sun" of the Iberian Peninsula is the natural background for a campaign in a country where "no loot was to be had," and "an hour's lagging behind the column meant almost certain death" suffered "with the refinements of Oriental torture." Food was scarce, draught animals "almost unattainable and beyond the reach of any but high-ranking officers with money to burn" (102–03). Worse than this, leadership of the ranks collapsed in the proportion that the quality of their soldiers plummeted. Captain Vidal became vicious as "would-be deserters," rounded up after "individual attempts to evade service," were being kept "under close guard" at night until "they could be absorbed into regiments where they would be under permanent observation." Men like that would *never* be absorbed, yet attempting to make soldiers of them turns the army into a reformatory. Captain Vidal, the company's senior officer, "a ruthlessly efficient soldier" who after twenty year's active service had won the Legion of Honor, would if given his way "have shot the prisoners en masse before they left France." Coddling a group of men who had done their best to evade service "in the slender hope that one or two" might become genuine soldiers "seemed to him the outside limit of idiocy" (106).

Manny will become the file's first casualty when he foolishly puts himself in the center between Captain Vidal and one of the prisoners they are guarding, i.e., Andreas, "a kinsman of mine," as he tells Gabriel. Manny passes to his kinsman "a farrier's file," and by morning Andreas has gone missing. Vidal, "already a day's march behind the main column," which puts all the men under his command in jeopardy from lurking assassins, is shown "the neatly filed links of the gipsy's chain," while Manny, who with Gabriel had been guarding that group, "stood by expressionless" and his artist-companion "made himself scarce at the far end of the column" (110–11). Anybody "less resolute" than Vidal would have been happy to see the last of Andreas, but the Captain aims his full-bore determination towards recovering the escapee. "Take eight men and keep out of sight," he directs, and the first person assigned to the search patrol is Manny. Before long the voltigeurs of the Eighty-seventh "were marching back over the road the guard company had travelled," and one hour before sunset "on the second day" (which dramatizes how far Vidal's troops have strayed from an army's core task of finding and defeating an enemy) they found the massacre scene.

> On a flat rock, where the shelf widened, the voltigeurs found their comrades, six of them, with bullet wounds and throats cut, spread naked for the mountain eagles and laid in a neat row, as though the Spaniards had planned an obscene parody of parade-ground precision.

One of the patrol is not there, "The Jew, Jacobsen!", cries Vidal, and further search discovers him, dead, nailed naked to a tree "by his hands, through which had been driven two strong nails, his ankles roped a few inches above the ground." Does that conclude the matter for Captain Vidal? Not at all, for they then proceed to a nearby village where they go house to house, dragging "men, women and children into the street" in order to hear Vidal say "I shall give you one minute to hand over the guide who led my detachment across the mountain path!" After one minute, he will shoot "all the men present, one after another, until there is no male Spaniard in the square!" Having stated with precision what he intends to do, the Captain sets about doing it.

> Gabriel's senses reeled with the horror of the scene. The whole agony of the human race seemed to rise from the little mob enclosed in the hollow square. Vidal, calmly priming his pistol, looked like a uniformed demon. As the first wave of horror passed, Gabriel felt curiously alive to the ghastly symbolism of the picture—a whole people crucified, nailed, like Manny, to a tree in the wilderness. He looked left and right for some answering feeling in the eyes of his comrades, but found none. *Gascony*, 113.

"The Tagus," Chapter 2, dramatizes the continuance of the band-of-brothers ethic in that "happy few" who have not let the pressures of combat transform them into Vidal-style killers. On a sunny day in September of 1810, "the French army halted beneath the towering escarpment of Busaco," the strategic high point above the Mondego Valley in northern Portugal which the British occupy. Jean Ticquet knows that if French troops attempt to take Busaco "without any effort to turn the enemy's flank," as Napoleon had so effectively done outside Wagram, they must rush "headlong up the slopes of Busaco ridge, right onto the bayonets of the redcoats." But the attack order is given and the result is inevitable.

> Urged on by Marshal Ney himself, hatless and clambering from rock to rock as the voltigeurs prised the British riflemen from the hillside, Jean, Nicholas, Dominique and Gabriel gained the summit, only to receive the full blast of a point-blank volley fired by English guards who rose up from ambush immediately in front of them. The head of the French column withered away under a deadly and accurate fire. Gascony, 119–20

When Jean goes down with a bullet in his thigh, Nicholas flings his rifle to Gabriel and carries the wounded man "down the steep slope on his back, rolling him behind a boulder in the valley and returning to keep the cautious pursuit away from close range." Cautious Redcoat "pursuit" notwithstanding, "five thousand killed and wounded out on the sunny slopes" was enough carnage, and "at midday the attack was called off." Louis, who knew how to doctor dogs and horses, heated a knife and dug out the bullet in Jean's thigh, then went to the cavalry lines for water, returning with "more bad news" (120–21).

Nicholette had struggled into camp though one of her horses had broken its leg, and without a replacement animal the wagon would have to be abandoned, and Jean's chances of survival would be negligible since her wagon was the file's ambulance when that was needed. What to do? The Carolini brothers, a rival can-tiniere family, are nearby, but they hate Nicholette and don't need the money, so they refuse to sell her one of their animals for any price. In the dark of the night the enterprising Nicholas strangles a sleeping Carolini with a cord around a wagon-wheel spoke, steals a mule, and Louis brands its shoulder as proof of ownership. In the morning Gino Carolini bursts onto the scene seeking justice, and while he is shouting "A group of brilliantly dressed officers" reined in behind the wagon upon which the dispute is centered.

> One of them, a red-headed middle-aged man in the uniform of a marshal, edged his horse forward.
> "What's the trouble?" he asked.
> The soldiers in the group immediately recognized Michael Ney and were silent. Once more Gabriel thought: "This is it; this is where Nicholas leaves us." *Gascony*, 129

Ney listens to the enraged Gino's story and then has him escorted to his canteen, promising that "You'll get justice all right. I'll investigate the matter myself." Then his eyes "roved over the file and finally settled on Nicholas," a sound choice because he is the man to deliver a reliable report succinctly, his weak point being the cho-leric temper which has Gabriel worried.

> "Are you in charge?"
> "I suppose I am, the sergeant's out of it for a spell!"
> "Come into the wagon," said Ney, and swung himself from the saddle, tossing the reins to the single aide-de-camp who had remained.
> The marshal and the corporal climbed the tailboard and sat facing one another on the lockers, with the pallid Jean between them. The sergeant was lying on a truss of straw stolen from the cavalry lines by Louis during the night. Jean was conscious and recognized Ney with a quiet smile.
> "This is a bitch of a campaign; what's happened to us lately?"
> Ney grinned and a current of sympathy seemed to pass between the two men. Nicholas noted it and hoped. He said: "The sergeant was at Hohenlinden."
> "We fight better in low temperatures," the marshal said, and scratched his chin. He turned from contemplating the sergeant to Nicholas again.

Ney is an experienced interrogator. He goes straight to the pivotal questions that will get him quickly to the heart of any matter.

> "Why didn't you buy that mule?" he asked. "The girl has money; all these people have money."
> "She offered him eleven thousand and all her stock," growled Nicholas.
> Ney looked incredulous. "She did? Why?"
> "Her mother was an old friend of the sergeant's. She's like that—one of us."
> Ney nodded. After sixteen years' continuous warfare he knew all about canteens and canteen rivalry. He recalled Old Carla, and his mind went back to an evening more than five years ago, on the night after Elchingen, when he had dismounted outside this

same wagon to chat with a dying man, an old friend of his boyhood, to whom Carla
was giving wine. He did not tell Nicholas that this was the reason why he had stopped
after recognizing the wagon by its bizarre tailboard decorations. The marshal had a
memory for that sort of detail.

All he said was "Eleven thousand and stock!" And then, "Wounded were to
be abandoned!"

Nicholas blazed out and Old Jean stared at him incredulously. There were times
when this ex-schoolmaster addressed officers as if they were stupid children.

"Go on, then, arrest me and the girl, arrest the lot of us. Six men who win your
battles count for less than an Italian civilian's mule! That's justice! Give him back his
mule and leave a man like Jean, good for a hundred more fights, to be cut to pieces by
the Portuguese! That's logic, that's about all the logic you get in the army nowadays.
No wonder things aren't going so well with us!"

Ney's initial astonishment gave place to amusement. He suddenly bellowed with
laughter and stood up…"You found the mule straying," he said quietly, "An English
mule, perhaps, that broke loose during the battle. The English artillery mules have a
distinguishing brand, a crown over a blank scroll. Much the same as our Westphalian
Hussars, I believe!"

He winked down at Jean and, climbing out of the wagon, swung himself into his
saddle again and spurred down the bank, calling to the provost and his aide-de-camp
to follow. *Gascony*, 130–31

Taking the hint, Louis "went over to the Hussar's horse lines," where he found
and borrowed the branding iron that Ney had described. Old Jean smelled the
"singed hair" and heard Gino's mule braying in protest against "the indignity of
two brandings within six hours." The band-of-brothers ethic is not entirely extinguished, even in this army which has fallen upon hard times.

"The Tagus," Chapter 3, narrates the events leading to the file's exit from
Portugal and relocation to England as POWs. Old Jean was taken to the hospital at Coimbra, about five miles south of Busaco and thirty-five north of Lisbon,
as I read the map. Ignorant of the British fortifications around Lisbon, Masséna
"hurled his advance guard" southward to maintain contact with the British rearguard, "hoping to wipe out earlier failures by a grand coup which would result
in expelling the British Forces from the Peninsula." That was impossible, but the
British guaranteed the safety of their French enemies, since except for "the presence of an English commander," many wounded soldiers like Old Jean would have
been dragged from the hospital and slaughtered in "an orgy of throat-cutting" the
moment that Masséna's soldiers got south of Coimbra (132–33).

During the early days of autumn the voltigeurs lived in small towns along the
banks of the Tagus, a countryside which had been "rich and fertile" but was now
unproductive. "Millions of plovers soared over the rotting olives. Vines had been
stripped and the figs shrivelled on the trees," while in the little river towns there
were "no sheep, no goats, no chickens, no men and no women." When the weather

improved Gabriel took his sketchbook into the countryside in order to render "the sweep of orange trees, lemon groves and oleanders, under a vivid blue sky."

> But by far the most interesting page in this section of his book is a lively sketch of the barriers, where the hostile camps merged...The relationship between the infantry of both armies was cordial. The British did not want to come out, not, at least, until Masséna's troops were sufficiently thinned...and the French were resigned to their role of simulated seige...A sort of careless stupor descended on the victors of Austerlitz and Friedland...The British soon showed themselves ready to live and let live...Gabriel's sketch shows a grinning British sergeant, his flesh straining at the buttons on his red tunic...handing a bottle to a melancholy sergeant of the Eighty-seventh whose blue great-coat hangs on his shoulders as upon a peg. The sketch is entitled "Villafranca, October, 1810"...Manny might have called it "The Taking of Lisbon," but Manny was dead and lay in his shallow grave high up on the slopes of the bleak sierra. His lighter suggestions are missing from the later pages of the sketchbooks. *Gascony*, 134–36

Now this is how the surviving members of the file came to be working to clear away the pebbles in the Otter River in Devonshire in the attempt to render it again navigable for trading vessels. A lucky French hit had sunk a British gun-boat, which went down in "fairly shallow water" in the Tagus. Part of the wreck could be seen "lying exposed" at low tide, its crew having gotten safely away. Now Captain Tinville, "a good-natured but somewhat stupid successor to the ruthless Vidal, decided that an attempt should be made to salvage anything of value on the gunboat," and ordered "an obtuse Breton named Soutier, to detail a reliable file to punt out to the wreck at low tide, employing home-made rafts for the journey." Nicholas and his campanions were given that task. Unfortunately, "Soutier was no Sergeant Jean," and the foolish fellow, given an order, corrupted it by contributing a *Catch-22* provision of his own creation. In this case Soutier changed Tinville's "at low tide" into "before nightfall," forgetting (if he had ever observed it) that "this particular hour the full tide would be sweeping downriver," whereas if the work were left until morning "the incoming tide would greatly reduce the force of the current," enabling the salvage job to be done "without risk or difficulty." When Nicholas pointed this out to Soutier, he "shrugged his shoulders."

> "Orders," he explained.
> Nicholas pointed to the current racing past the half-submerged gunboat.
> "We'll never anchor these rafts in that flood," he told Soutier.
> "Orders!"

An hour before sunset they poled out to the wreck, and, as Nicholas had predicted, "it proved almost impossible, once they approached midstream, to check their prog-ress down the river with the makeshift anchors supplied" (137). Without giving the full dramatic account, suffice it that Nicholas, "his free hand straining at Claude's collar," was unable to keep the thrashing fellow from slipping loose and drown-ing, rising once or twice, but "finally sinking to be tumbled along the muddy bed

by playful undercurrents and flung at last on the wrinkled flats of the left bank"
(139). The other four voltigeurs survived, but left the water on the British side of
the Tagus and were taken prisoner.

The English routinely brought shiploads of stores to Lisbon and on their return
to Plymouth took back shiploads of prisoners. As the four voltigeurs were being
escorted to the loading wharf, Louis noticed "a half-naked and badly wounded
man being trundled along" by guards and wondered out loud "where are they
using grapeshot?", for he had not heard any artillery. Nicholas explains that "the
man has been flogged, practically to death I should say," which prompts Gabriel's
"Why didn't they hang the poor devil?" That is the opportunity for Nicholas, a
character in a cultural history novel, to display his skill as a cultural historian on
his own. "The British are great believers in discipline and they've only two methods of enforcing it, the noose and the lash," and this man's offense "was not a capital one." During their voyage to England his three comrades will discover that
Nicholas, who "had specialized in English literature at his university," knew a surprising amount about "the strange inconsistencies of the race," and he gives them
a seminar on that topic.

> He knew, for instance, that an island that had fought against France for seventeen years,
> in defense of freedom of the seas and constitutional government, still kept many of its
> children at work for sixteen hours a day, sometimes for a weekly pittance, often enough
> for nothing at all but a few meals and a communal bed. He knew that the sailor who
> leaped the bulwarks of the French men-of-war, wielding a cutlass against what he consid-
> ered the intolerable tyranny of the French Emperor, whom he knew from his cartoons
> and broadsheets as "Bony, the Robber Baron," had most probably been torn from his
> native village by the press gang and flogged into becoming one of the finest seamen
> in the world. He knew also that in England a standard of living far higher than that
> enjoyed by the wealthiest aristocrat who fell by the guillotine during the Terror could
> flourish side by side with abject poverty and semi-starvation. Nicholas spoke much of
> these things, but he did not neglect to remind his friends that the very men who were
> born and reared under these conditions possessed an independence of spirit and a con-
> sciousness of race superiority exceeding that of an Imperial Guardsman. He accepted
> this as part of the explanation of the continued survival of Britain against the orga-
> nized might of a Continent dominated by a plump little man who had jocularly asked
> after their wine on the island of Lobau.

A word of explanation. During preparations for the Battle of Wagram, Napoleon
had visited the file as they sat eating "their midday soup" and had asked the voltigeurs whether the wine is "good" since he had ordered the distribution of four
thousand bottles "only yesterday." Nicholas answered "It's gone the way of most of
our wine, sire." Two days after that, "four commissary officials were found guilty
of misappropriation and shot.... Nicholas volunteered for the firing party. Louis
and Dominique went over to see the fun" (72-73).

> Kept informed by Nicholas's flow of laconic comment, and directed by the schoolmaster's unusually strong powers of observation, Gabriel, Louis and even Dominique rapidly adjusted themselves to their new surroundings. In this way Nicholas partially filled the vacancy left by Old Jean, whom they had all loved as boys in their teens will love and admire a wise old uncle who shares in their games and their adolescent enthusiasms. *Gascony*, 142–43

When Nicholas abandons the cause he has been fighting for, which he eventually will do, the loss of his intellect will rob the remainder of the file of the contrarian analysis he had provided—and after that loss how can the center hold?

Part 3: "The Otter"

"The Tagus" contains only three chapters since no more than that are required to narrate a military stalemate, yet "The Otter" is shorter still, two chapters, since it is in essence a holding-action interlude, a pastoral diversion. Its military usefulness is that the file will be restored to health by food and sinews-building exercise so that they can return to Napoleon's ranks ready for service. The star player in this Devonshire drama will be Louis, the self-effacing, horse-loving youth whose concern for equine well-being captures the heart of Lucy Manaton, who precipitates the file's sudden departure back to France, of which more later.

The new prison at Dartmoor "specially built to receive French prisoners of war" was full even before the building was finished, the result of English efficiency in flooding POWs into the country. As circumstances would have it, the influx was balanced-out by the impressing of young men into the English military "and the constant migration of rural populations to the manufacturing towns," which drained the farms and "the smaller coastal communities" of manpower. Landowners in the west country had "asked if they could engage paroled prisoners [those who promised not to attempt escape] for routine work on their estates" and the military commissioners were given discretion to grant such requests (151–52). Lord Rolle, a powerful landowner of East Devon, wrote just such a letter to the commissioner soon after the new shipload of prisoners had been discharged, requesting two hundred men, in particular engineers with experience in dyke-building, and though there were no more than a dozen of these specialists, many prisoners were "anxious to give their parole."

Old Jean, now in good health and restored to the file, had lengthy arguments with Nicholas upon the subject. Jean was determined to escape the moment he found a chance, but Nicholas told him escape was "practically impossible," that Spain had depleted their "enthusiasm for a military life," and that "the humane treatment of the British up to this point encouraged them in the belief that there were far worse fates than that of a prisoner of war in England—the fate of a free man in front of Torres Vedras, for instance" (152). The voltigeurs' leaders reached a compromise which permitted the group to help erect "a long, curving bank at the mouth of the River Otter,"

> a shallow stream which had once seen a considerable amount of wool and wine trading to and from the Continent...Until comparatively recent times, both [Otterton and Budley] had been important centres for wool distribution, while returning vessels imported Continental wines. Now the villages were dwindling...their decay being due to the accumulation of a vast pebble ridge which all but sealed the mouth of the river. In summertime the stream was unnavigable for vessels of more than a few tons burthen. *Gascony*, 153

Mr. Duke, the local landowner, convinced Lord Rolle that clearing the river's mouth could restore prosperity to the area. He planned to build "a large earthen breakwater" to "confine the tidal water to a limited area," which he hoped would deepen the estuary, thus "opening it up once again for larger vessels." That was the plan, and the voltigeurs who had spent time with mattock and spade building cannon emplacements on Lobau would hardly find the construction of the Devon breakwater an unusual task. That the locals who lived in the area were "more skeptical" than the landowner is not surprising, since hands-in-the-pocket folks are much alike everywhere—skeptical when ventures are being made, but proprietary when they succeed. As for human relations, the instinctive fear that the newcomers might steal their sheep or molest their daughters was alleviated by the facts that the workers would be remotely housed and fed, as well as properly supervised. Moreover, were the locals given an opportunity to meet and interact with the Frenchmen, they would find them likeable fellows. The best fear-dissipator is the passing of time without unpleasant incident, which was what happened. In early spring of 1811, the file began what would be a stay of nearly two years in England, their life there being a "pleasant, humdrum" one. In that summer they "arranged concerts," which were sometimes attended by Lord Rolle and Mr. Duke, "rapidly becoming" a Francophile, since his project was going forward smoothly. Dominique, who lost his fiddle, made another, and "scores of curious cottagers came into the barn and guffawed uproariously when he capered a Gascon dance to his own accompaniment." All in all, Gabriel considered these months "the most contented of his life."

But Ticquet felt restive, being "starved for the sound of a cavalry trumpet." The narrator, who alternates with Nicholas in evaluating the veteran's feelings, says "to know Jean was to understand the years of success that attended French arms up to that unlucky day on the banks of the Danube in 1809," the defeat lessened only by the large-bore cannon which overwhelmed the Austrians when Napoleon's Grand Army couldn't prevail in its usual manner. "Nicholas put it into words," the narrator says, preparing to stand aside for his file spokesman. When Gabriel interrupts the ex-schoolteacher—"Jean doesn't identify himself with the Revolution. He despises it!"—Nicholas clarifies what he had attempted to express.

"He identifies himself with Bonaparte, and that's the same thing under an imperial mantle. Every man in Jean's generation feels that he shares personally in the glory of conquest. Don't ask me to explain their idea of glory. Perhaps it's a substitute, in men like Jean, for the land-hunger of mediaeval Jacks, for education or for avarice. I don't know; I only know that there have always been Western Europeans who have grown up and grouped themselves round a lucky adventurer. Caesar had his tenth legion; Gustavus Adolphus his pikemen; the English despot Cromwell had his psalm-singing cavalry; Bonaparte his Old Guard and the grognards, like Jean. Napoleon knows all this. He knows that this Empire of his is a thing of gilded tatters, held together by one thread. When the thread wears thin and breaks, as it must sooner or later, the whole thing will fall to pieces in less than a year. I advise you to stay here and watch the climax from a safe distance. Then you can go home and help to gather up the pieces, if the Habsburgs and Romanoffs leave any lying about!"

Nicholas spat onto his leathery hands and swung his pick into the soft red earth. *Gascony*, 156-57

As we see, even this pastoral—more accurately, georgic—interlude is punctuated by cultural-historical exposition precisely like that we have seen in *Retreat from Moscow* and *Imperial Sunset*.

Jean's hankering for the military lessened as he began taking "professional interest in the technical aspects" of their work: "penning the floodwater into the bell-mouth of the little estuary" (157). A pleasant autumn followed the dry summer, and when Mr. Duke's "affable stewards" read the Continental news to them, "they heard of Masséna's retreat into Spain and of the birth of Napoleon's son, the King of Rome." Jean was gratified by the news, but Nicholas failed to share that feeling, observing grimly that "We'll be here for the rest of our lives!" However, that would not be the case, and of all people it was Louis "who ultimately cut the cable that bound them to this soft landscape" (158). After nearly a year in England, Louis fell into a different employment, the care of horses. One day at the beginning of a hunt, Lucy Manaton's mare hurt its foreleg, and Louis instinctively came forward to calm the mare and bandage her leg, expertly and tenderly. As the months went by, Louis, who relocated from the construction site to the Manaton's stable, cared for her distressed or injured animals. Lucy began spending more and more time with the sensitive boy, which her lawyer warned her "could not continue" (165). In the end, a friendship which proved the prelude to intimacy took possession of Lucy. When Louis tells her "You've been very kind to me, madame!" Lucy replies "Don't ever go back, Louis, never, never!" (170). And that is where the opening chapter of "The Otter" puts the matter to rest temporarily.

The last chapter of "The Otter" is less concerned with cultural history than with pulp-fiction melodrama, although cultural considerations apply. Lucy Manaton has involved herself in a love affair with a French POW—[Louis' "shy, inexperienced lovemaking had stirred in her a physical appetite which she had thought Vince had killed during the first ugly week of their marriage"], and when her estranged

husband hears about it the vicious brute will rush back to triumph and to punish. Here is the scene.

> A sallow, elegantly dressed young man stood on the threshold of the room, regarding
> her with an unpleasant crooked smile. She started back against the fluted bedpost.
> "Vince!"
> He strolled into the room and she stared at him. All her contempt and loathing
> for the man, blunted by nearly two years' separation and thrust into the back of her
> mind by the happiness of the past few weeks, flared up again, like a smouldering fire
> fed with pitch. He stood there a moment longer, enjoying her utter dismay. Then he
> flung a single word at her.
> "Whore!" *Gascony*, 173-74

When the intruder began beating her with his riding-switch, the pain-aroused
woman "groped for" and found "the empty ewer that stood on her marble-topped
wash-stand." Swinging it "like a flail" by its "long, curved handle," Lucy struck him
"with shattering force on the right temple" and he went down with a yelp, "like
a puppy crushed by a blundering foot." She had killed him, and when the village
people learn what she has done, "they'll take Louis" (174). Indeed they will, unless
she can disappear him immediately. Now Lucy knows a local seaman in the smuggling trade along the Devon coast who for a commensurate fee will spirit her French
lover across the Channel, but Louis will not leave without his friends, so Lucy seeks
out Old Jean and shares the situation with him. When Jean realizes that before
the dawn breaks he will be back to fighting Napoleon's battles, his heart leaps up
like Wordsworth's. "Be there at eleven tonight, all four of you," she instructs him.

At this juncture the narrator provides a situational analysis that reaches well
beyond Vince-got-what-was-coming pulp fiction, a commentary that one recognizes
as cultural history, a comparison of the sexual mores of two different nations.

> To Louis, and to all of them, she had remained a British aristocrat, with her full share
> of civic rights, whereas they, as alien prisoners, had no rights at all. Jean said that from
> what he had seen of her he judged Lucy Manaton capable of steering herself clear of
> trouble. He knew nothing at all of the harsh inconsistencies in the character of the
> local squirearchy, where a woman might command the respect of her neighbors under
> almost any circumstances except that of preferring a foreigner to an Englishman as a
> bedfellow. Nicholas, who knew the English, had a vague suspicion that all would be far
> from well with Lucy if it once became known that, in addition to taking a Frenchman
> for a lover, she had engineered their escape, but he kept his thoughts to himself. It
> would do no good to worry Louis at this stage and make things more complicated for
> them all. *Gascony*, 182

As the initial half of the novel concludes, the emotional transition is made from
pebble-clearing in Devon back to the military routine which Old Jean hankers to
recover. As the voltigeurs wait for the smuggler's boat that will take them back to
France, they lie stretched out in a thicket trying to sleep. "It was astonishing how

naturally they slipped back into the old campaign routine," as if nearly two years in England had been a day, "and now they were back in the vanguard, the army's feelers for an enemy lying out in the boisterous darkness ahead" (183).

...

In *Seven Men of Gascony* Delderfield divides the period of 1809 to 1815 into symmetrical halves, BOOK ONE narrating the file's experience from the Battle of Wagram to their POW detention in Devon, BOOK TWO presenting the precipitous slide of Napoleon's fortunes from the Russian debacle of 1812 to his Waterloo exit from the world stage. Following Erckmann-Chatrien, who created the fictional Joseph Bertha as their eye-witness participating in historically accurate events, Delderfield writes the cultural history of the Napoleonic wars in a manner which re-presents those events for readers too far removed from the original actions to apprehend them even marginally through the waning cultural memory still available to them. It is helpful here briefly to review Peter Burke's *What is Cultural History?* in order to reflect upon what Delderfield is doing in his Napoleonic histories, as well as his Napoleonic novels.

Burke says there are two "approaches" to answering the question that is posed by his book title, only one of which is applicable to Delderfield, the "internal approach." That strategy seeks to correct the oversights or exclusions of earlier historians who, having had different aims, bypassed things not relevant to those aims. In Burke's words, these "approaches to the past...left out something at once elusive and important" whereas the cultural historian "gets to parts of the past that other historians cannot reach" (1). He points out that there has in recent years been "a shift," among a minority of scholars at least, "from the assumption of unchanging rationality...to an increasing interest in the values held by particular groups in particular places and particular periods" (2). I take the term "rationality" to be the synonym for an Olympian view, standing in sober contrast against the smaller matters—in warfare, for example, homesickness, terror that the wounded leg will have to be amputated, or perhaps the disturbing suspicion that the commander one trusted has lost his grip and become more committed to preserving his Empire than to defending values he had once championed. For the cultural historian, the emotional realities which color one's views and energize one's actions are not so peripheral that they can be ignored in any history aiming at completeness.

Writing that aspires to both delight and inform its readers must have them in mind from the outset, which calls for skill in estimating audiences responses. Early in his career Delderfield served a "long apprenticeship in writing plays," which supplemented his years of newspaper reporting before that. He eventually wrote "a commercial hit, *Worm's Eye View* (1944)," which proved "a phenomenal success," what none of his later plays did (Sternlicht, 21). However, the experience taught him things which the future historian and novelist needed to know. How could he effectively present the Napoleonic material he knew so intimately? Repetition being out of the question, he would need a strategy for bringing alive for his audience the pulsating drama coldly contained in all those volumes they would never peruse. A voice was needed, something akin to Shakespeare's "We few, we happy few, we band of brothers," which injected new fire into a battle nearly two hundred years after it was fought, in 1415.

If we glance quickly at Delderfield's second and third Napoleonic histories, *The Golden Millstones* and *The March of the Twenty-Six*, we see him succeeding in finding a slant which breathes unexpected life into scattered material that is only infrequently brought together. Reading *The Golden Millstones* in preparation for writing this book, I admit to being impatient with the Bonaparte family's long, eventful history because that was not what I was looking for at the time. But in retrospect, it truly is an interesting story. Fugitives from Corsica in 1793, a time when "the future of the young Republic was desperately uncertain and that of Madame Letizia Buonaparte and her family almost hopeless" (3), we read how this plucky woman, her husband having died leaving her indigent with seven children, the oldest only sixteen, held the family together. Against the odds, they not only survived but prevailed, disagreeing violently and yet never severing their mutual ties, which makes for an interesting saga. Consider, too, *The March of the Twenty-Six*. The marshals' names appear in histories of Napoleon's wars, but their conduct as the ambitious and resourceful soldier-leaders they were deserves the focal attention they receive in Macdonnell's *Napoleon and His Marshals* (1934), and in Delderfield's equally fine analysis *The March of the Twenty-Six*: two instances of the process of re-presentation which keeps the past alive despite time's obscuring effect.

But it is Delderfield's fourth Napoleonic history, *The Retreat From Moscow*, which is most helpful for our purpose as BOOK TWO begins, because here we have the juxtaposition, or rather the layering of one version of Napoleon's Russian adventure upon the other. Putting the history alongside the novel, one can appreciate the reciprocity between the two, since their cultural history is mutually reinforcing. In the early pages of *Retreat From Moscow* one finds what can be described as the "premonitory history" of Napoleon's Russian adventure, the intuitive anticipation of the future event, for what Napoleon hoped to do had been tried before. The setting [Delderfield opens with a dramatic encounter] is Vilna, then the capital of Russian Lithuania, the date is June 30th 1812. Diplomatic discussion is under way. A single Russian is discussing the case with five Frenchmen, one being Bonaparte, who asks him a number of questions, including how many people lived in Moscow, and how many churches it had. Told there were 340 churches, Napoleon scornfully retorted, "people nowadays were not religious."

> The Russian, General Balachov, demurred. 'It varies,' he said, quietly, 'they may not be religious in Germany or Italy but they are in Spain and Russia!'

It was a barbed gibe. At that moment a hundred thousand Frenchmen were being herded back across the Spanish peninsula by a small British army and the world was laughing into its sleeve. One of the main reasons for the French failure in Spain was the fanatical religious faith of the Spanish peasant. Balachov was implying that Napoleon was opening another running sore in the East before there was any prospect of the wound in the West being healed, or even staunched.

Napoleon was silent for a moment, measuring his man and perhaps his chances. Then he asked, abruptly, "Which is the way to Moscow?"

This time it was the Russian who considered. "I find that a puzzling question," he said at length. "In Russia we say, as you do, that all roads lead to Rome. The way to Moscow is a matter of choice. Charles XII was going by way of Poltava."

Charles XII had been a King of Sweden who invaded the realm of Peter the Great one hundred and four years before. At Poltava, a town in the Ukraine, he had been disastrously defeated and had fled back across the River Niemen almost alone." *Retreat From Moscow*, 14

Having wittily implied that Napoleon is undertaking a foolish course of action, one which always fails no matter who attempts it [Hitler could not resist opening a Russian front, which likewise proved disastrous], Delderfield a few pages later presents another facet of his brand of cultural history in describing the collapse of the military spirit in men like Old Jean, who could not fight whole-heartedly for a leader who had abandoned the noble goals they earlier shared. That is intuitively correct, of course. But it is not quite *history*, it is *cultural* history, which takes into account emotional facts, how soldiers feel and think about what they are doing. *Psychological* history I take to be a distinctive reality that psychoanalysts care about, which is not my focus. I would rather not worry the terminology too much, for as Samuel Butler says "all a rhetorician's rules/ Teach nothing but to name his tools" (*Hudibras*, 89–90). Yet since I wish to be understood about the theme of this study, I offer here a second example of Delderfield's cultural history in operation.

Since nobody kept a tally of the casualties on either side, "All that can be said without fear of contradiction" is that of the hundred thousand who went, "fewer than ten thousand returned and with them perished the legend of Napoleon Bonaparte's invincibility."

Never again, despite many victories obtained against impossible odds, did the veterans of Egypt, Austerlitz, Jena, Friedland and Wagram, or the conscripts of 1813 and 1814 who replaced them, fight with the elan that had made post-Revolutionary France the most formidable military power in the world. The heart had gone from the senior commanders, the faith from the junior officers and old moustaches. With very few exceptions all ranks had entered Russia confident of victory on a grand scale. The stragglers who survived carried the virus of defeat into the newly-raised armies that were to fight holding actions against a confederation of European powers during the twenty months before Parisiens watched Cossacks ride down the Champs Elysees. They marched in as conquerors. They returned knowing that the Empire was doomed. *The Retreat*, 16

Returning to the novel, "The Niemen" consists of seven chapters whose action shifts nimbly from here to there, as battlefield reporting must to project a sense of the whole picture. Chapter 1 is in part the heart-warming reunion of the soldiers just back from Devon, and their cantiniere, Nicholette, who in their absence had not attached herself to any other group "although she had several offers." She chose this unit "because she knew that the retreat would be a difficult one, and the Guard seemed the safest bet under the circumstances" (197). Nicholette does not say she had been missing them, but they know that and the affection is mutual. Yet the reason she gives is situationally shrewd, for Nicholette understands wagons, mules, roads and weather conditions, as well as ill considered military decisions—but Napoleon had not asked her advice before setting out. Something between experience and a premonition enables this woman to intuit what the men suspect but cannot foresee so surely. The narrator observes that "the voltigeurs did not know what was happening behind them," were ignorant of the "long, burdened columns" dragging toward the starting point "days behind schedule, their strength already reduced by a strange sickness among the horses, due to the use of unripe rye as fodder." Had they known, "they might have wondered if this were to be another Portuguese debacle...on a much vaster scale" (192). Nicholas, too, can extrapolate from what he knows to what he fears. "'If we're with Ney we're for it again,' was [his] comment when the batallion received orders to dismiss" (194), for he remembers Ney's furiously scrabbling up "the towering escarpment of Busaco" on the day Jean took a bullet in his thigh, and he realizes that where Ney is positioned the fighting will be fierce.

However, the first chapter is not entirely preoccupied with premonitions of disaster, for Nicholas and Nicholette "were married by a priest in Konigsberg," which surprised none of the others because were she to stay with them "she would have to marry someone, and Nicholas was the senior after Old Jean," a confirmed bachelor (198). The truth is, though, that Nicholas had long thought himself best suited to be her husband, and after marrying Claude when a girl of sixteen, she was now nineteen yet "looked a mature woman of thirty and in some ways seemed even older than Jean" (199). It was a love match on both sides, and when Nicholas tells himself that

> she was a habit, prevailing, established, in the customary scheme of things like the smell of wood smoke, the champ of the horses in the cavalry lines, the rumble of artillery caissons, the rattle of musketry, the deeper chorus of fourteen-pounders,

he is in effect confessing with Henry Higgins that he has "grown accustomed to her face," which he tells her as soon as they are alone.

> "I've always wanted you, Nicholette, all my life."
>   She said quite simply, "We ought to have known it before, Nicholas."
> *Gascony*, 200-01

The second chapter is notable for its long dialogue, primarily between Nicholas and Napoleon. It had thus far been an uneventful campaign, little fighting, "the Russians retreating as the English had done," strategically burning the countryside as they fall back. However, there was "one sharp engagement" in which the voltigeurs had distinguished themselves "under the eyes of the Emperor and the entire army," and the following day there was a reward ceremony to honor them. Making small talk in his usual way afterward, Napoleon recollects that "One of you played the fiddle," scarcely able to disguise "the triumph in his voice at such a brilliant display of memory." Yes, Dominique the half-wit played the fiddle, which he thought he had lost, but has just found in Nicolette's wagon, wrapped carefully for safekeeping. Napoleon continues, and by doing so begins a dialogue which is important enough to the novel as cultural history to be quoted at some length. First Jean, and then Nicholas, address the Emperor.

> "And where have you been since Busaco?"
> "In England, sire. We were captured in the Peninsula, myself at Coimbra, the others on the Tagus."
> Napoleon's eye gleamed and the staff officers edged nearer.
> "You escaped?"
> "We came back on a smuggler's fishing boat, sire! He was bribed."
> "How much?"
> "We never knew, sire. The money was not paid by us."
> Napoleon nodded. It was obvious that he was deeply interested. Possibly his brain was turning over the possibility of organizing large-scale escapes among the fifty thousand soldiers and seamen held by the British. The exchange system had broken down long ago. It had no chance of success whilst the British held twice as many men as the French.
> "Can you write, Sergeant?"
> "I regret, not, sire, but my corporal writes well!"
> Nicholas gave Jean a sour look, but it was too late.
> "I would like a report upon the circumstances of your escape; see that I get it tonight!"
> The Emperor and his staff moved on and the companies were dismissed. Nicholas spent two hours in the wagon laboriously compiling a report of their sojourn in England and their ultimate escape. It was years since he had written more than a couple of lines, and the effort made him sweat. He cursed Jean at the completion of every laboured sentence. A grenadier of the Guard was waiting to conduct them into the Presence. Jean was fidgety, Nicholas pretended to be bored.
> The grenadier handed them over to a staff colonel at the entrance of the Imperial marquee. After a brief delay they were conducted into Berthier's tent, used as an anteroom.
> "Straight through, Sergeant!" said the red-headed Chief of Staff, without looking up from the immense map he was studying. They passed through the silken hangings and found the Emperor lying back in a deep-seated chair. Constant, his valet, was shaving him. For an instant even Nicholas felt a trifle awed.

"Read it, Corporal!" said Napoleon, without a glance in their direction.

Nicholas read the manuscript. It was blunt and factual, giving brief particulars of the capture, of the Lisbon compound, the voyage and general treatment of prisoners, the Otter Bank breakwater construction, Louis's engagement as groom and the incident that led to their escape. The only fact withheld was Louis's association with Lucy Manaton. Nicholas tried to give the impression that the incident had been due to a ridiculous fit of jealousy on the part of the returning husband.

The Emperor mused for a while. There was no sound in the marquee except the steady rasp of Constant's razor on his master's bluish bristles.

Presently Napoleon said: "How is it that men like this smuggler Rattenbury are willing to transport enemies of their country out of captivity?"

Jean looked at Nicholas, and the corporal shrugged. It struck the sergeant as extraordinary how composed Nicholas could be in the presence of exalted rank. He seemed to mind Napoleon no more than he minded Sergeant-Major Soutier.

"Well?"

"I can only express an opinion, sire!"

"And what is your opinion?"

"Men will do most things for money. This man was well paid by an old customer."

"Is that all, Corporal?"

"No, sire, the smuggler was a deserter from the navy and like most of the pressed men he had been barbarously treated by officers. He had had his patriotism flogged out of him!"

Napoleon sat bolt upright with disconcerting suddenness. Constant, accustomed to his Imperial master's nervous movements, made a deft sidestep, raising the lather-crusted blade level with his shoulder.

"Yet their navy continues to win victories. It beats our navy off the seas! Can you explain that Corporal?"

"By another opinion, sire," said Nicholas doggedly.

"Come, come—I'm asking you!"

Jean held his breath and felt his palms sweating. Roustam, the Emperor's gorgeously attired Mameluke, came in with silent tread and stood behind his master's chair, his white eyeballs gleaming in the light of the hanging lamps.

Nicholas spoke slowly, as though considering every word.

"The English are a family, and families quarrel furiously until one of their number is attacked by somebody outside the circle. Pressed men hate the service until they are within range of an enemy vessel. Then the habit of discipline and their own temperament are too strong for them. They fight as well as anyone in the world. Afterwards, if they survive, they persuade themselves that they share the glory with their officers."

Napoleon was silent for a moment, ruminating. Finally, he said: "I shall want you to return to Paris and take up duties in the Intelligence Section of the Marine Office. Summon my secretary, Roustam!"

Nicholas set his jaw. Old Jean wished that he could faint.

"With your permission, sir, I would prefer to stay with my company."

A dark cloud seemed to settle on the Emperor's face. The lather dried and flaked on the side that Constant had yet to shave.

"You're a fool," he barked. "I need intelligent, educated men. Thousands of ex-peasants can do your work in the skirmishers' line!" He broke off and studied Nicholas closely. "The transfer would mean officer's rank and a special rate of pay!"

> "Both of us have previously refused promotion, sire!"
>
> A tired secretary came in, giving his black breeches a perfunctory dust as he crossed to the desk.
>
> Suddenly Jean spoke up, his voice nervously high-pitched, "We are a unit, sire. We have been together a long time."
>
> His words sounded lame enough, but the shaft was well aimed. Jean might have been illiterate but he understood Napoleon's psychological make-up as well as Berthier, Chief of Staff. The cloud on the Emperor's round white face disappeared, chased away by a warm smile. Nicholas recognized the transition, knowing that diplomats from all over Europe and the East had been fascinated by that rapid change of expression.
>
> "Go back to your company, both of you. Roustam!" The Emperor settled back in his chair and by a swift gesture of his right hand indicated that Constant could resume shaving. "Give these men ten napoleons apiece!" *Gascony*, 206-10

The voltigeurs did not participate in the battle of Borodino, which Delderfield may have shied away from since Tolstoy's narrative had been sufficient. They were "held in reserve with the Imperial Guard" not in order to be sent into battle but to take part in Napoleon's triumphal entry into Moscow, the "advance bands" playing "The Marseillaise" while a drum-major headed each regiment. It was a "hollow triumph" because the streets were empty, except for French soldiers transformed into looting savages. Nicholas falls into a deep depression over "the abysmal folly of it all," marching that far to "occupy an empty city," and once there to "run about the streets like greedy children" stealing whatever they can. What really troubles Nicholas, however, is that Nicholette is going to have a child before long, in that toxic environment or something even worse. A red glow spreads across the sky as unseen persons methodically begin "firing the city." Of course "a gutted city" would provide neither food nor shelter were they to remain there during the winter. Without taking a bullet, Nicholas has become a casualty, for "he was out of reach of their comradeship and conversation." Yet Napoleon is still in command and "after five weeks of waiting for peace terms that never arrived the Emperor had ordered a general retreat" (211-24).

A "general retreat" means that the Grand Army, having arrived in Moscow, must turn around and go back the way it came, which Chapter 4 begins narrating. French conscripts carry loot instead of food and clothing, the folly of which becomes clearer as the winter worsens. Napoleon's Staff "decided to attempt a more southerly route passing through districts unwasted by the army's advance," but their enemy foresaw the strategem. "A strongly reinforced Russian army barred the southern route and turned them back onto the old road. The French gave way reluctantly" and soon arrived at the site where the battle of Borodino had been fought two months earlier.

> Seventy-five thousand corpses lay there, for the most part unburied, many of them gross and bloated in the mud which the rains had washed from their shallow graves. Others had been half-eaten by wolves and birds of prey. The stench was indescribable. *Gascony*, 227-28

Gabriel thought of the battle scenes he had seen in the art galleries of Vienna, and reflected that whoever had painted them "must have had a limited experience of war."

Napoleon's troops realize that a general retreat means it's now every man for himself. Collaboration with others is increasingly difficult given the scarcity of food and temperatures plummeting far below zero. Nobody gives the order that hundreds of shivering wretches should be crammed into a carriage way-station, an empty barn in the Russian wilderness. And nobody can say who kindled the little fire in that barn hoping to warm themselves, but that is what happens, and when the fire torches the barn and hundreds are incinerated, who can be blamed? Chapter 5 narrates how vicious these starving soldiers had become. Now Louis, the horse-lover who some time before the march into Moscow had transferred into the cavalry, has been able to steal enough hay to feed his mare, Roxy, by creeping into Russian camps at night. But during the last few days he "had not been unconscious of the looks given him by stragglers as he picked his way carefully along the road that ran through the endless birch forest" (238). At this stage in the retreat the supplies of horseflesh were giving out,

> and, to make matters worse, men were getting into the habit of killing horses on the spot for the sake of their blood. He saw one wretched animal slaughtered in this fashion by a party of Polish lancers, horsemen who should have had more sense. The same night he shot the gunner who tried to steal Roxy whilst he was collecting wood for a fire. *Gascony*, 243

Eventually it was bound to occur. As Louis approached a party of infantrymen, the "steep banks inches thick with ice" on both sides of the road making avoidance impossible, he was asked "Got anything to eat, brother?" Shaking his head no and attempting to pick his way through the group was fruitless. Louis and his horse were both killed, and later on Jean pointed out to the scandalized Gabriel that "Louis ought to have got down and handed over the horse. He could have fought for his share of it." Reflecting that in all the years he had known Jean the veteran "had never been wrong about anything," Gabriel eventually became quite sure that he himself "would have been a party to shooting the rider and eating the horse." Louis's death, he came to see, had been his own fault, "like Manny's, who had stayed behind to search for a man whose escape he had engineered, and was crucified for his pains" (266–68).

In the context of this general collapse of civilized behavior, Delderfield provides a contrary example in which character prevails over distress. That counterinstance is Prince Eùgene, "one of the few personalities around the Emperor who had earned Nicholas's respect," for although he was the Viceroy of Italy and "the Emperor's stepson by Napoleon's first marriage," he did not give himself airs as did some other officers. When the army was disintegrating around him and many other officers were "cooly shifting for themselves," Eùgene stood firm.

They had all expected Eùgene to sulk when his mother, Joséphine, had been cast aside for the Habsburg woman, but when summoned for the Russian campaign Eùgene rode up from Italy with a full complement of men and guns, and displayed his usual cool generalship in all the minor engagements along the road to Moscow.

Watching the Prince dismount and harness his magnificent Arab horse to a floundering gun-carriage in a birch forest outside Smolensk, Nicholas pondered on the vicissitudes of all Frenchmen of his generation. Sixteen years ago Eùgene de Beauharnais had been an orphan of the Terror; his father was a victim of the guillotine, his mother the mistress of a corrupt politician. Nicholas wondered if the man's startling change of fortune was due to his mother's sound judgment in marrying Napoleon when the latter was an obscure, hysterical general, or to Eùgene's own talents and integrity. He did not pursue the query, his reflections being cut short by the necessity of climbing down from the box and helping to lever a dismounted gun clear of the road. *Gascony*, 249

Not long after that, Nicholas had buried in a shallow grave Nicholette's stillborn son, which he had delivered in the cantiniere's wagon in the midst of a howling storm. As he patted down the snow covering the monkey-like corpse, he looked like "a primeval savage in the performance of a grotesque rite" (263). This was Nicholas's low point in the story. Michael Ney was directing the rearguard as they re-crossed the Niemen, and when one of the Germans dropped his musket, Ney picked it up and, "his cloak bellying in the wind," fired the final shot of the campaign toward the partisans who were fast closing in on the bridgehead, Ney's action being characteristic—"half genuine defiance, half bravado" (281).

Part 5: "The Elster"

The fifth segment of *Gascony* is titled "The Elster," that being the river near which the Battle of Leipzig was fought in mid-October of 1813. It narrates the experience of the surviving voltigeurs as they approach and are drawn into the combined onslaught of Russian, Austrian, Swedish and other Allied forces who know Napoleon must be stopped. The people in whose houses his troops are billeted ("every family had its quota") have grown unfriendly, and with good cause. The Prussians suppose that their aroused feelings are evidence of a "reawakened nationalism," but their real reason is commercial.

The exclusion of British trade was ruining the German towns, and the Grand Army, since its return from Russia, had degenerated into a diseased rabble. *Gascony*, 283

The disaffection of the locals matters in the novel because Nicholas—depleted by having nearly frozen to death on the night he buried his stillborn son, and further weakened by his habitual pale cast of thought when he reflects upon the folly of the Emperor—lies in a coma in the "sickroom" in the house of the surly Prussian silk-dealer who had already cost Nicholette "nearly a thousand francs" in order to "buy her way into" his house. This man is an immediate problem.

Because the silk-dealer was wealthy and had political influence, he was "excluded from the billeting list" and so Nicholette pays him privately. She consents to paying her landlord increasingly higher sums because her husband would die were she to put him in a hospital (283–84). When the coma lifts and Nicholas becomes aware of his surroundings, Gabriel, visiting him with Jean, explains that "Nico's been paying a ransom to keep you here all these weeks and now she's been told to move out by tonight" (291). Dominique, who can hear the landlord listening just outside the door, opens that door abruptly and the sordid wretch tumbles onto the floor, the question now being how to dispose of him. Jean has the solution, "a safer way than killing him." He will be put in prison "on a charge of robbery," Gabriel and Jean swearing him into the jailor's custody, where he will stay. Says Jean, "'the provost is an old comrade of mine, and nothing this hog says will get any farther than the gaol door'" (292–93). They do that, after the extortionist has returned to Nicholette the money he took from her.

That bit of unresolved business having been concluded, Chapter 2 shifts away from private concerns to the overall military situation, in which the French were attacking, but with "barely fifteen thousand cavalry," across bad terrain, and "against the most powerful international alliance since the Crusades." Many of the marshals were there, those who had not died, been badly wounded or joined Napoleon's foes, but after "nearly two decades of unremitting service," they were worn out. The Emperor was there, "tense and eager for decisive battles," as always.

> But the day of decisive actions had passed and the men who had established Napoleon were dead, gone to gild the eagles of half-forgotten triumphs...There is a limit to any nation's exertions, and some said that the limit of Bonaparte's France had been reached on the far side of the Niemen the previous autumn. Napoleon, however, did not think so and in those hot, sunny days of late spring [April, when his opponents were in the process of marching to oppose him] it seemed as if he were right once again. *Gascony*, 295

Yet the Emperor's "initial spurt" did not last long, and as the coalition opposing him grew stronger, "France and the men of the West were outnumbered by four to one, and by ten to one in cavalry" (296).

Shifting back to Nicholas and Nicholette to finish the second chapter, the two of them decide to defect and go to Switzerland, posing as watch merchants at the border when they are questioned. They share this plan with the others, and Sergeant Ticquet, who should arrest him for desertion, gives Nicholas a "six hours' start" before he reports him, along with this last bit of advice: "Don't try to take that wagon any farther than the army lines." Border guards who "won't bother a man and woman walking" would want to know what's in Nicholette's wagon and when they look inside, the game would be up. That is precisely how their flight ends, because Nicholette cannot part with either her money or her property (299–301).

Chapter 3 is focused at the outset on Jean, answering the question of how this veteran who long fought for love of the idea that Napoleon represented, can remain faithful to the Emperor when his idol is fallen. How can Jean cope? That summer, he "got a good deal of gloomy satisfaction out of the muddled compaigning," and his "reasoned pessimism became a byword in the ranks." For example, when recruits were ordered to march "five leagues in the rain to make a feint at a village" held by twice as many Prussians, they told one another "Sergeant Ticquet says that we always win if we don't start fighting until we're exhausted." As time went on Gabriel wondered whether such sophistry "was Jean's method of keeping the youngsters comparatively cheerful," which is the *Catch-22* formula for maintaining army morale: keep them laughing with "the Soldier in White." When the order came down to "shoot one out of every ten men caught away from the regiment," it failed to lift the conscripts' morale. Ticquet's genial contempt of the army's leadership was more successful in keeping the young fellows chuckling.

Yet the order had been given, and one of the first men caught in its mesh was Nicholas, apprehended at the border and returned to his regiment, where, just before resumption of hostilities between the two armies, Jean was summoned to identify a deserter. He asks permission to speak privately to the file's resident philosopher, historian and all-round intellect. "The two men regarded one another silently for a moment. Finally Jean said 'What happened, Nicky?'". He tells Jean what had happened at the border and asks him for a favor, that the voltigeurs who remain alive volunteer for the firing squad, because, as he puts it, "I'd like to be shot by somebody who can hit a cow at ten paces. Those conscripts you've got would puncture me in half a hundred places." After the execution, Nicolette puts his body in her wagon, and when Jean, knowing that the army is the only life she'd be comfortable with, suggests that she return to the bivouac, Nichollette "spat into his face," hitting him "just above the mouth" (316). Sometime later on, Gabriel, the recording angel of the diminishing file, sketched "a memory impression of Nicholas before the firing-squad," an odd piece of work that was left "unfinished."

> The artist has shown the five musket barrels radiating like the spokes of a wheel, while the man in the hub of the picture has no features to identify him as Nicholas. The only clear part of the sketch is the background, showing the spires and battlements of Dresden. It is difficult to understand why Gabriel left it in the book. The sketch has a laconic title—"Dresden Parade." *Gascony*, 319

As a sharpshooter Gabriel has the clear eye and steady gaze needed for that role in the military. Yet the eye that had focused upon the "clumsy rosette" Nicholas pinned above his heart as a target refuses to assist the artist in depicting those features that would "identify him" as an individual. The friend he helped kill becomes Everyman, representative of the general condition. "Parade" in the sketch's title suggests Napoleon's penchant for public self-advertisement, implicitly assigning blame for Nicholas's death, while also calling to mind Thomas Gray's reflection that "the paths of glory lead but to the grave." Why did Gabriel keep this painful sketch in his book? Whatever the answer, it could not be far removed from Pascal's insight that the heart has its reasons that the reason cannot know.

Chapter 4 begins with "the Grand Army at bay on the outskirts of Leipzig," the French resembling "a maimed bear striking blindly at a pack of lithe wolves." A majority of the recent conscripts had disappeared, "gone home," many of them, "with the instinct of homing pigeons", not challenged by military police, who were "swept into the firing line." Even the conscripts "eager for glory soon decided that one cannonade is very much like another." To Gabriel, the slow whittling down of their own group—Manny crucified, Claude drowned, Louis killed for his horse, Nicholas executed as a deserter—seemed "symbolic of the process that was going on in every battalion." The "old spirit of unity" had not crossed the Niemen along with the straggling survivors who did, and the Grand Army was "awaiting extinction" (317-20).

Finding themselves soundly whipped by superior forces at Leipzig, the survivors began "filing through the narrow streets towards the single bridge over the Elster." Foot soldiers, artillery and baggage moving slowly "like a ghost of the ragged cavalcade that had recrossed the Berezina less than a year before." They inevitably obstructed each other's progress as the swelling multitude headed towards a single narrow exit. Jean made the decision for Gabriel and Dominique. "We'd better get out of here. Alone!" Gabriel cannot believe that Jean is willing to leave "the wretched conscripts" but they have no hope of surviving in any case. "How long do you think they'd last?" says Jean, answering Gabriel's unspoken thought. "Let's move!" he said, and the three voltigeurs "left the boulevard and crept cautiously along the river bank" towards the column nearest "the first span of the bridge." So many men struggling to advance but blocking each others progress led to stasis; then an hour before dawn "the voltigeurs heard a deafening explosion." The French engineers, "alarmed by the rapid advance of Austrian and Prussian skirmishers, had blown the bridge." When the smoke cleared, the French troops on the Leipzig side of the river saw the "ragged gap in the centre of the structure" (322-23).

Dominique remembers then that when he had been staying in this location earlier he had walked up river looking for fish, and was told that there were fish "up by the ford!" How far up asks Jean, a short march replies Dominique, and Jean broadcasts that information: "March north to the ford! Get to the ford, all of you!" Searching to find the place, Dominique stopped a ways above "the second curve beyond the bridge," for he had seen the ford when the water level was low, but now the river is full and the current is powerful. The first few men who entered where the ford had been "were swept off their feet and only two strong swimmers reached the farther bank" (324).

> Suddenly there was a burst of firing from houses close to the river, and a body of horsemen forced their way through the indecisive crowd to the water. Gabriel recognized two of the marshals, Prince Poniatowski and the Scotsman Macdonald. Poniatowski had

been wounded and was supported in his saddle by an aide-de-camp. A troop sergeant of the Polish lancers rode up to Jean.

"How deep is the river at this point?" he demanded.

Jean shrugged. "My comrade here says there is a ford, but several men have been drowned trying to cross."

"It's either that or the Prussian bayonets," said the lancer, turning back to the two marshals. After a moment's deliberation the group moved forward, coaxing their exhausted horses into the stream. At the same instant volley-firing commenced from the houses about half a musket shot along the embankment, scattering the fugitives between the river and the town in all directions. The horsemen launched into the stream, the two marshals and their staff in the lead. Jean chewed his moustache for a moment, glancing upstream and then towards the town. He made a rapid decision.

"Into the water, both of you, and get hold of a tail!"

The three of them plunged into the current. Several of the horses, terrified by the uproar immediately behind them, reared in the shallows, resisting the shouts and spurs of their riders. The three voltigeurs seized a tail apiece, other infantrymen followed their example, and the struggling mass blundered forward. Jean and Gabriel were lucky in their choice. Their horses fought the current to midstream, then settled down to swim diagonally across. Dominique's horse floundered and lost way, but the farm boy hung on, turning and twisting in an effort to dodge the thrashing hooves. *Gascony*, 325-26

When the rider lost his seat half-way across, the horse, freed of his weight, recovered "and finally struggled up on the far bank." When Dominique staggered from the shallows, he collapsed, mortally injured. "He had been kicked twice, once in the shoulder and once in the chest" (326).

Jean, cursing the medical orderlies for not being there and the engineers for blowing the bridge as they did, "abandoning a third of the army to the enemy's bayonets," and cursing Nicholette as well for driving off as she did with a dead man's body "when her wagon would have been of inestimable service to the living." They had no bandages, no salves, no hope of getting the wounded man onto his feet to march to Erfurt (327). Even while alive, Dominique was already a dead man. After jolting him along for five days in "a two-wheeled cart of the type used by German farmers for the transport of pigs and manure," Jean and Gabriel had to abandon him in a barn already "crammed with wounded." As they walked away together, Jean spoke what amounted to a brief epitaph: "He might have been short of wits, but he was a damned good soldier" (328-31).

The last chapter of "The Elster" finds the remaining two voltigeurs camping out in the woods of Fontainbleau. "It was twenty years since a battle had been fought on French soil," and the curious thing was that they had "won half a dozen victories in a row." But although the small French army "tumbled the invaders out of town after town," they never obtained a decisive result, and Old Jean had "no illusions" about how it would all end. Indeed, the end had come, for "one morning early in April" of 1814, orders came "to parade for an Imperial review" and most of the soldiers realized that they were unlikely to have another chance of cheering the man who was "still popular with every one of them." The review proved to be "a parting ceremony," and Gabriel's fingers "itched for pencils and brushes." They marched "towards the incomplete Arc, raised to commemorate twenty years of unbroken triumphs," the bourgeois staring at them "as if they had been a circus troupe," and Jean noticed that all of the onlookers "sported a white cockade, emblem of the Bourbons" (332–38).

Part 6: "The Sambre"

As Peter Burke instructs us, some cultural historians believe that "cultural history, like political history, can and should be presented as a story" (3), and *Seven Men of Gascony* demonstrates that Delderfield embraced that view. Napoleon's career ended at Waterloo, near Charleroi on the Sambre river in southern Belgium. Having escaped from Elba in February of 1815, he entered Paris on March 20, gathered his troops and set out for the confrontation at Waterloo on June 12, was decisively defeated, and signed his second abdication on June 22. That is the brief political history of how the French Emperor was removed from the scene. But the backwash, the oscillation produced by his exit from and sudden return into French politics, was as much cultural as political. Napoleon could not have lightening-bolted back from Elba to confront the coalition of European powers had his popularity within France not been vigorous, which it was. And for that he was indebted to the Bourbons, who had "made every mistake it was possible to make." Delderfield specifies a number of those errors in a long passage which, given the focus of this book, ought to be quoted at some length. What did the Bourbons do?

> They renamed the Imperial Guard the Royal Guard and forced soldiers, most of whom had never been to church in their lives, to attend mass every Sunday. They distributed the cross of the Legion of Honour, coveted by every veteran who had the luck to win it, to unblooded young popinjays of ancient houses who gaily donned the brilliant plumage of the Household troops. They were miserly with pensions for the crippled and the orphaned. They placed thousands of the finest officers in Europe on half-pay, standing by when returned émigrés sneered at soldiers who had marched into half the capitals of Europe during the last twenty years. They imported a glut of English goods, throwing whole populations of manufacturing towns like Lyons out of employment. Despite all this, the ageing King Louis had good intentions, but he could do little to curb the arrogance of the aristocrats who had sulked in exile whilst Frenchmen were tumbling down autocracies north, south, east and west.
>
> Even so, the Bourbons might still have been welcomed had it not been for the action of the Allies in sending home one hundred and fifty thousand prisoners of war within a few weeks of Napoleon's abdication. From the Allies' viewpoint it was a stupid policy; from the point of view of the Bourbons it was suicidal.
>
> The freed veterans tramped and begged their way to the frontiers from every direction. They came from the fortesses of Germany and Austria, moved like a tide of scarecrows across Central Europe from Russia, marched down from the north with Davout's

hardbitten infantrymen and up from the south with the wreck of Soult's Peninsula divisions. They came in by boat from the English hulks, with old scores to pay and plenty of questions to ask. When they met and mingled with the men who had fought in the final campaign, the sum total of their conversation over the café tables was, "Ah, but this could never have happened if we had been there!"

Gabriel, a realist by now, knew that it would have happened in any case. Six corps of veterans could not have expelled the invaders from France whilst there were traitors like Talleyrand and Marmont scheming in Paris. But Gabriel knew better than to contradict the veterans, especially when Old Jean endorsed their arguments. It was a difficult summer for the men of the Grand Army. *Gascony*, 339–41

Gabriel and Jean found employment in a bakery run by "an active Bonapartist" whose shop became the rendezvous of a group of old soldiers who gathered to discuss old times. "There was no real treason talked in Grinard's bakery, but the latest Bourbon outrage was the topic of every session," and when the baker disappeared and his shop was closed, the "painstakingly active" secret police of the Bourbons might have been responsible. Next, Gabriel took a badly-paid job with a coach-maker and got Jean hired as a night watchman. The life was boring enough, but then suddenly in March "an incredible rumor circulated the cafes. Napoleon was said to have left Elba and landed at Cannes," and Paris was in turmoil as soldiers were instructed to present themselves "at the Guard's barracks in the Ecole Militarire" (341–45). Whereas the army of two years earlier "had been composed of conscripts," the army of March 1815 were "veterans to a man," happy for the opportunity "to teach the enemy that they had not yet forgotten how to use the bayonet" (349).

The two armies faced one another "across the shallow valley" near the farm and chateau of Hougemont, occupied by the English. The battle began with "a murderous artillery duel," in which Jean was wounded, though not mortally. The battle "rolled past them" while the voltigeurs "crouched in the trench" which provided them cover (351–59). Jean had "picked a lively place to get a ball in [his] leg," for after the cannonade ended, they listened as "five thousand hooves" thundered through. The two men "cowered under the wheels" of an abandoned gun while "an avalanche of cavalry swept over them." These were the combined remnants of much larger numbers of French horsemen from earlier years.

Milhaud's cuirassiers, Lefebre-Desnouette's chasseurs, Piré's and Jacquinot's lancers, mounted grenadiers of the Imperial Guard, a sea of blue, red, yellow and green uniforms, as they crouched over their horses' necks, heading directly for the squares [of allied infantry], overturning everything in their way until they recoiled from the wall of bayonets jutting from the square or piled up under the volleys discharged at point-blank range by men who seldom missed at a hundred paces.

It was the last suicidal charge of the too-small remnant of Napoleon's Grand Army, a contest of weight and speed against stolidity, of impotent sword and ill-aimed pistol against the steady crackle of musketry, wave on wave of the finest cavalry in the world hurling itself upon the most dogged infantry in the world.

Gabriel and Jean remained where they were, "in comparative safety," and watched as the French cavalry battered itself to pieces against the squares (362–63).

Some staff officers around Napoleon would have held back the Imperial Guard to cover a retreat, but the Emperor saw clearly that "the chance of a decisive victory was so slim as to be no real chance at all" (366), and while the French forces melted away all across the battlefield, the Imperial Guard, in the early twilight of Waterloo, claimed their right "to stand to arms throughout a battle and then march forward at the final moment to gather the first fruits of victory" (365)—though now they gathered not the victory, but annihilation. When Napoleon's special troops advanced, Jean wrenched his musket away from Gabriel, who tried to keep him out of the fighting, and Sergeant Ticquet died, "transfixed" on the point of a bayonet (369). He had not wanted it any other way.

Coda

Delderfield opens *Seven Men of Gascony* with a Prologue which has not been mentioned earlier, this being the proper time to introduce it. It narrates an event that took place in December, 1840, a quarter-century after Waterloo, a time when the report was spreading by rumors and newspapers that Napoleon's remains have entered Paris to be re-interred at the Invalides. "He's come home," said Father Pavart to an old acquaintance of his, a man who "might have been any age between fifty and seventy" (9). This was Gabriel, who had made a pact with the wife he had buried a year or two ago [Nicholette] "to forget the past" as their "only chance" to survive those memories (12). Gabriel has taken on some of the traits of the Ancient Mariner, i.e., age made uneasy by disturbing memories of past events which haunt him. Yet despite his "air of brooding and his large, sad eyes," he feels no compulsion to *tell* what is disturbing him. Father Pavart, the only man in the village who has not been wholly "discouraged by the veteran's incivility," was asked by his cousin, "the editor of a Rennes newspaper," to get from the old fellow his eye-witness account of Napoleon's campaigns.

> "My cousin in Rennes wants you to write about him.
>   The old man spun round and stared into the priest's eyes.
>   "Me!"
>   Pavart affected not to notice the old man's agitation. He shrugged his shoulders.
>   "Why not? You could do it as well as anyone I know. You were there, were you not?"
>   "There are dozens of veterans in Rennes. There are one or two here, so I've heard."
>   "The men here are conscripts, Leipzig and Waterloo men. My cousin wants something better than that. I told him about you when we met during the summer. He is an unrepentant Bonapartist and often asks after you." *Gascony*, 11

The priest had never seen Napoleon, and "it gave him a pleasant shock to realize that the gaunt, nondescript man standing on the hearthrug had marched with the Emperor across the Danube plains and through the icy pine forests from Moscow to the Nieman." Pavart, possessed by a greedy curiosity, makes his pitch by instructing the veteran that accurate history is important if generations to come are to profit from the experiences of their forebears.

> "The First Empire is already a legend," he began. "It does not matter whether your memories are painful or pleasurable. Nothing can alter the attitude of the average Frenchman today or that of succeeding generations tomorrow, to the man who made that Empire and sustained it for nearly twenty years. People who were in exile like me, or those that were born after he went away, cannot be expected to measure the good or the evil of his influence on our country or on Europe. History a century hence may decide upon that, or again it may never arrive at a conclusion. What is important is that we Frenchmen build up truthful records from the testimony of men such as you. Whether you regard Napoleon as a living force or as a fiend now in his master's keeping is incidental. The fact remains that he and his generation belong to us, to France. New dynasties, new invasions, new theories, cannot influence that fact, much less alter it. It is for men like you to tell us what you yourselves know of those years. History is only important if, by surveying it, we are able to account for the past and shape the future. If you have suffered in the past, as I presume you have, then it is your duty as a Frenchman—"
>
> Father Pavart broke off and coughed, feeling suddenly embarrassed. The man opposite was still looking towards him, but his melancholy eyes were quite vacant. Pavart knew that he was no longer listening to a word of the lecture. His unlighted pipe was still clutched in his hand. *Gascony*, 13

After the priest had gone, the veteran stirred up the fire, crossed over to his bed, pulled an old trunk out from under it, opened its battered lid and, carrying the sketch books it contained over to the table, he lit his oil lamp. Then, "drawing a chair up and leaning forward on his elbows he opened one of the books and flicked the first few pages." Each page featured a crayon sketch, "but he did not examine any of them until he came to [one] labelled "Lobau, June, 1809," a portrait group of six men, three sitting and three standing" (14). Gabriel is examining the "commemorabilia" [Edward Casey] that help one to remember, to call the past into present attention—as Delderfield had done when as a schoolboy he had been fascinated by Napoleon's coach in Madame Tussaud's museum, and by Lockhart's *Life of Napoleon* when, as a teenager standing in Appleby's bookstore, he had read it for hours until the proprietor pointed out that, at only sixpence, he could afford to buy it.

Farewell The Tranquil Mind

Seven Men of Gascony is a fully satisfying novel whose infantrymen represent the entire class of those who see war from the foot-soldier's point of view—following the model of Erckmann-Chatrien for Napoleon's wars and Remarque's *All Quiet on the Western Front* for the Great War. *Gascony* and *Western Front* are successful as cultural history not only because they are historically accurate but because they are successful as novels, whereas Delderfield's *Farewell The Tranquil Mind* is not completely successful, and that for a reason which Aristotle explained long ago. In his *Poetics* this shrewd observer pointed out that while plot, character and thought [or theme] are necessary elements in a drama, plot is more important than the characters who enact it. Plot is the core, the heart, whether in Aristotle's time or our own. But in *Farewell The Tranquil Mind*, plot is either secondary or absent, its role being usurped by thought or theme, i.e., the events of the period 1792–1794, chiefly in Paris. These events—which do not constitute a plot but only an unfolding—are more important than David Treloar. His role in the middle portion of the novel is simply to be an observer-participant in events; he is purely a reactor. It is this usurpation, this encroachment or enfringement by theme upon the centrality of plot and even character which is the book's weakness.

To be fair, Treloar is a successful novel character in about one-third of *Tranquil Mind*, i.e., the early action in Devon before he flees to France to avoid the false charge of murder that would otherwise be brought against him, and the closing action in which, no longer merely the observer in a theme-dominant animated-history lesson, he flees *from* France to escape from Revolutionary hit-men pursuing him. And to give credit where it is due, Delderfield's attempt to turn a source document into a cultural-historical novel is energetic if not wholly successful. For he did have a source text, one that must have had a tar-baby plausibility for him. David Treloar was an historical resident of Devon who in the spring of 1792 fled to France to avoid a false murder charge, and in 1794 fled from France to avoid a true one. How convenient is that? This *tabula rasa* outsider comes at just the right moment to observe and reflect upon Historical Events unfolding in Paris, then is intercepted, with his French wife, as they attempt to sail to safety in America. Returned to Devon by the English authorities, he cools his heels in jail waiting for his trial to come up, where he writes a full account of the frightening events he had been caught up in, a document he hopes will exonerate him but which his jailor takes to be a confession, for that is all that is needed or wanted.

The "Author's Note" prefacing the novel discusses the source he used and his modifications of it. "Only about one-third of David Treloar's story has been reproduced in anything like his own words," for what David wrote was "set down" later by his grandson, although whether with David's collaboration or not is unknown. The grandson's revision was "less than half the length" of Delderfield's novel, and "there were several gaps in the narrative" (ix), which is why the novelist had to exercise "editorial despotism" to make the story coherent, complete—and appropriate for his purpose. And yet, historical accuracy was his goal, which raises the question of how he could approximate accuracy working from the defective written document. The answer is that he consulted the oral traditions of Devon, unwritten knowledge of the past which cannot be dismissed as hearsay, though in a print culture one inclines to pooh-pooh that as unreliable. Yet that is not a reasonable position to take, as Benjamin Franklin's brief essay "Concerning the savages of North America" testifies. He remarks that the business of the Indian women in public councils "is to take exact notice of what passes, imprint it in their memories, for they have no writing, and communicate it to their children. They are the records of the Council, and they preserve tradition of the stipulations in treaties of a hundred years back; which, when we compare with our writings, we always find exact" (179). Likewise, that more recent work, Alex Haley's *Roots*, informs us that the tribal historian in Africa, who was born long after Kunta Kinte went missing from his native village, provided the evidence which solved the puzzle about how the young African had arrived across the ocean in Annapolis. Kinte's American descendants knew, and gave accurate witness despite their imperfect knowledge of the English language. Human memory as the guarantor of accurate knowledge of the past was operating as effectively in Devon when nobody was writing things down.

But when a novelist begins reshaping David's imperfect autobiography, is not accuracy the loser? Not necessarily. Sir Walter Scott's *Minstrelsy of the Scottish Border*, long taken as a collection of authentic historical material, was altered by its collector. As Sir Walter "himself admitted, half apologetically, half proudly," he could "never retell a story without decking it out 'with a cocked hat and a sword.'" As his editor puts it, although "he had a hand in polishing or in retouching most of the forty odd ballads first printed by him, let it be remembered that...his 'improvements' were true to the spirit, if not the letter" (7). Delderfield's situation and conduct parallel those of Scott, and as a final evidence of the historical accuracy of *Tranquil Mind*, I quote again from his "Author's Note."

> To remedy these and other minor discrepancies I had to rely on my old friend Frank Treloar, who, until his death just before the Second World War, returned each summer to spend a holiday in Devon.
> Frank was a lovable character, naively proud of his smuggling ancestors. I suspect that his reverence for the shadier members of the East Devon Treloars was considerably greater than that he entertained for the hero of his book. It was Frank, of course, who first introduced me to the Devon Treloars, the family having left Cornwall thirty years before I settled in the west...I need only add, in closing, that the bulk of this narrative is based upon hearsay; stories such as this exist in most old-established West Country families, and I have heard Devon yarn-spinners tell far more improbable stories than that of David's flight across Revolutionary France, or his clever French wife's brazen blackmail of the Naval Commissioners at Plymouth. *Tranquil Mind*, p. x

Tranquil Mind begins with a brief cultural history of smuggling in Devon, the illegal exchange of goods between Brittany and Cornwall/Devon that had flourished long before David Treloar had been born. It was an honored tradition kept alive by young men like Saul Treloar, who, twenty-five years earlier, "was known by sight and reputation to every exciseman west of Plymouth," an undesired popularity which made "a change of scene imperative," the more so since Saul had "lost most of his relatives and business associates in the customs operations" of 1772 on the Cornwall coast, from which they operated. A few members of the Trevannion gang "were hanged," because they were "a murderous lot, but the majority were transported" and Saul never saw them again (7). After that disaster, he and his French wife, pregnant with their son David, relocated to Devon and settled in a hamlet "midway between the fishing village of Exmouth and the declining wool port of Budley Haven at the mouth of the pebble-choked Otter," the river that the Gascony prisoners later helped to make navigable for deeper-bottomed vessels. There, "they were offered Westdown, a derelict farm of something under a hundred acres," which Saul acquired on "a long lease from Saxby, Squire Duke's agent," who as chance would have it was a bosom friend of the writer Tom Paine. Saxby taught young David to read and write, skills which he needed in France, along with fluency in the Norman French dialect he and his mother habitually used with one another.

Now David's father and mother had different views on how life should be lived—Saul always looking for the main chance that would make him rich, his wife carefully socking away small amounts of cash, so that when push came to shove the money would help David, who loved farming, to transform Westdown into the best farm in the area. The three younger boys, attracted by the adventurous style of Saul, followed their father's lead. Says David,

> Saul, my father, had been reared in the trade and could never regard farming as anything more than a convenient cloak for the running and distribution of contraband. My mother, the daughter of a Norman father, was aware of this when she married him, for they had met and courted during my father's weekly cross-Channel trips when he was hardly more than a boy. Her family was closely connected with the export side of the trade and her brother was at that time dragging a shot in the Brest galleys for his share in a raid on the Cherbourg customs house.
>
> She saw nothing wrong in smuggling and even applauded it when it was safe and profitable, but I don't think my father ever understood that she regarded contraband running as a prank or, at best, a spare-time occupation to help tide over a bad harvest. She never confused it with the real business of life, the cultivation of land and the care of beasts.
>
> With my father it was very different. During the twenty years he was at Westdown he came by considerable profits but he never put aside more than an odd guinea or two. The greater part of his income was devoted to buying half-shares in galleys, speculating big sums on Virginian tobacco run in by Savannah crews and, more often than not, watching his vessels rammed and sunk by patrol cutters, or his hogsheads located and hauled up by the revenue officers who were always combing the shallows of the cove for our market buoys.
>
> Saul didn't talk much and I never had an opportunity of discovering his reasons for preferring uncomfortable nights at sea, and the constantly increasing risks

of his profession, to regular hours of sleep and a modest living on the farm, for he might have had that and more if he had spent the profits of an occasional enterprise on Westdown and reclaimed some of the cliff-edge land that had gone back to gorse and thistle. Perhaps the pull of his Cornish seagoing folk was as potent as that of my mother's land-hungry peasant ancestors. Their dispute continued through the whole of their married life...*Tranquil*, 9

The triggering event which precipitated David's sudden relocation to France was a crisis in his father's smuggling business. Surprised by an exciseman's cutter one night, he and his fellows were obliged to "swim for it" to save their lives. They got away in the dark, but their cargo, "forty-four casks of cognac and seven chests of Indian tea," had been confiscated and "locked up in the customs depot at Teignmouth," yet the outraged smugglers were determined to "attack the depot" and recover the goods (13). To succeed, Saul would need lots of helping hands, but other members of the smuggling ring, more diffident in their commitment to their leader's conception of economic justice, understood that circumstances made that attempt foolhardy. "Somewhere between Beer and Torbay were five naval cutters and six troops of dragoons, in addition to a full establishment of excisemen," and these were prohibitive odds against them. Ben Cheetah, "a truculent fellow, said bluntly that it was sticking one's neck in a noose and he would have none of it" (15). Undeterred by wiser counsel, Saul decides to run the operation with whomever will join him, which turns out to be mainly his three younger sons. He and his three boys will be killed on the night after the excisemen are alerted to the action by Mrs. Treloar, who expects that her husband and sons will be captured and sentenced to prison to teach them a lesson. The best laid schemes even of smugglers and their wives oft go much a-gley, as they do that night.

Recognizing that the hour she had feared for twenty years has come, Mrs. Treloar gives David the bag of money that will help him improve the farm. And that night, while her husband and three other sons are being shot down at the seashore, knowing "there was no point in her fleeing from authorities with whom she had entered into alliance"(29), she tells David [his shirt bloodied by carrying from the beach his mortally-wounded youngest brother] to escape in the short time left while she secures the house—blasting out exciseman Vetch's stomach with a shotgun at point-blank range, buying time for David to get away as the house goes up in flames. It is Vetch's killing for which David would be convicted and hanged if he failed to escape from Devon.

Needing immediate concealment, David spends the night in a badger earth he knows, then in the morning crawls out to discuss his situation with old Jake, a neighbor who explains that "the Georgies" would not be looking for him "so close to home." He's safe for the moment, but needing a permanent solution, David trusts to Saxby, who points out that boarding a ship going towards "Georgia or Virginia" is not really a good idea. English frigates routinely stop ships bound for America in order to remove young men trying to escape from military service. The Press Gang see to it that these unfortunates spend the remainder of their lives unwillingly serving in England's navy. Saxby's experience dictates his advice: "Your father and brothers averaged two cross-Channel runs a month" and seldom even saw a frigate. "If you run for France," Saxby explains, "you can cross in the dark," and he knows someone who could smuggle him over, a man who "has not lost a cargo in years" (32–26). Well paid for his service, Muttford transports David to France, then up the Seine to Rouen, after which David finds his own way to Paris. Now, the long middle of the novel begins.

Chapter Four of *Tranquil Mind* opens with David walking in Paris, reflecting that he had never before felt "so free and elated" as in his earliest hours in that capitol during the summer of 1792.

> I sensed the current of vitality that eddied about those narrow streets like a south-easterly breeze soughing across the high plateau of Westdown. There was something in the step and bearing of every individual I passed that proclaimed the Revolution. Perhaps I noticed it the more because I had lived all my life in the feudal atmosphere of a Devon village where, despite obvious points of contact that existed between squire and tenant, tenant and labourer, smallholder and shopkeeper, the stamp of patronage and condescension is discernible to the casual onlooker and this will always estrange human beings and sour their relationships.

In Paris during that summer, class privilege seemed to have been swept away, "leaving an impression of easy fellowship" (51). Yet that impression of freedom and ease did not last for long since David was soon engulfed by a mass of elderly women who began shoving him toward the table where young fellows could sign up for the "volunteer force"—an honor which only a coward or "a counter-revolutionary" would seek to avoid. At that critical juncture, Andre appears, Andre Lamotte, who will introduce him into his family and act as his companion-guide during the middle portion of the novel. "Limp away, you idiot, you're a cripple" he mutters, under cover of the volley of abuse which the crones are shouting. Those accusers were not at all shamefaced at having berated a cripple, but laughed at David and looked about for "other reluctant protagonists of liberty" (53). Just that quickly David realizes the difference between the apparent freedom and the underlying compulsion of Revolutionary Paris. It is a city ready to run mad at a moment's notice.

But Andre's open-heartedness is real. He is a young doctor, a man who behind his posture of ironic indifference is compassionate towards others. Knowing that David needs help, he offers it, yet without appearing to be charitable. David could not have had a better guide, one who explains what is happening when events turn dangerous, who analyzes the motives and the probable fortunes of the various groups and individuals vying for power in an unstable and shifting public scene. Papa Rouzet, who deals in perfumes and hair-styling, had adopted not only Andre and his sister Marcelle after their parents died, but another niece too, Charlotte, who becomes David's wife. Delderfield's cultural-history novels always hinge upon small groups of representative men and women whose attitudes and experiences are typical of a city, a profession or a nation, the role which is performed by those who congregate in Papa Rouzet's house. Charlotte quietly does the housework, while her cousin Marcelle hosts the group of rising politicians, as fine a set of "barnyard roosters" as could be desired, who argued pointlessly, all of them having read too much and experienced too little, many of whom are engaged in writing epic poems. Meanwhile, Marcelle sings the "Marseillaise" at their request and with annoying frequency. These roosters belong to the Girondist faction, which will scatter like roaches when Danton takes command and the guillotine becomes warm from revolutionary friction. And thus David finds himself positioned not only in Paris, but in a house where he cannot help but become increasingly knowledgeable about the political situation by simply watching and listening.

In retrospection, David recognizes that "Brunswick's manifesto," a "frightening document couched in the most imperious language," was "the greatest stimulus that could have been given to the Revolution," converting most of the "waverers" to the republicans, for those in the middle "now saw that a victory for the émigrés," the privileged class who had fled from France, "would mean the loss of every privilege won" since the Bastille was destroyed three years before. What was Brunswick's document like? It threatened "instant death and confiscation of property" the moment the émigrés "had re-established themselves and their foreign allies in Paris" (73–74). In this retrospective analysis, David Treloar the twenty-year-old farmboy from Devon sounds distressingly like Delderfield the student of Napoleonic history, which is an aspect of theme's dominating effect on plot and character, which is not a strong point in a novel. As that commentary continues, Brunswick's manifesto proved to be "the king's death warrant and the elimination of what remained of the constitutional party" (74). Says David as on-site historian, "Gone were the flamboyant exchanges of greeting, citizen to citizen," as "mutual distrust replaced bonhomie." Andre helps start the local action moving again after this evaluative interlude, by telling David that they should both sign "a contract for temporary enrolment in the Cordelier battalion of the National Guard" (76), which will put them in position to be shot at, enter the royal prison and visit the King and Queen, and watch the guillotine in action—that sort of thing.

"They'll have their precious republic before sunset!" Andre prophesied, as the bells, "increased in volume every minute" with "the shouts of a wildly excited multitude" who were "pressing down towards the Pont Neuf and Pont Royale," a human flood "in the area around the Tuileries" not easily overlooked. Entering onto the street, Andre and David were "swept along on the tide of revolutionary fervor." Danton had apparently planned the rising, "with the tacit support of the Girondists and a majority of the Assembly" (82–83). Confusion maintains for some while, and "this is only the beginning," says Andre grimly, for the best men are at the frontiers and "only the windbags and thieves have been left behind," that being "the usual course of revolutions" (92). In this crisis, it was "the giant revolutionary Danton" who emerged "head and shoulders above" everyone else, standing boldly, "jaw thrust forward, chest flung out, like a figure out of some heroic legend of the past" (98). Danton is the central figure in this political theatre, when nuance must give way before the loudest voice, the widest shoulders and the terror which most terrifies, which must be obeyed. If one is looking for cultural history in a book such as this which purports to find it in Delderfield's novels, one must attend to the following three paragraphs. They are rather familiar, since we have heard sentiments very like them in the novelist's historical volumes about Napoleon.

> The revolution was less than four years old and the common man was still near enough to feudalism to recall the sanguinary penalties meted out to recalcitrant peasants. They recollected systematic hunting down and execution of casual poachers, mutilations for the slightest infringement of the game laws, the monstrous inequalities of taxation which kept the peasant in a hovel and the townsman in a slum, and they knew that there was not one of them who had not openly rejoiced at the turn of events that made them masters and the nobles despised exiles.
>
> Nor were these fears of restoration confined to the lower classes. The Revolution had, for the first time in the history of the nation, thrown open avenues of advancement to the middle classes, previously held back by the place-hunters of the privileged. Out on the great plain west of Paris men who had inherited the conditions of mediaeval serfs were now tilling their own land, wrenched from a corrupt Church or a *seigneur* who spent two-thirds of his year fawning and intriguing at Versailles. In Paris, and in all the great towns of the departments, younger sons who would have lived their lives as half-starved clerks and copyists were now making their way as advocates and independent merchants. In the fourteen armies of the republic, volunteers who would have been fortunate to aspire to a sergeant's cane under the old regime were leading divisions in the field.
>
> In a thousand Government offices up and down France men were showing that a bureaucracy is only cumbersome and inefficient so long as the men who staff it are prevented from exercising imagination at their desks. All these Frenchmen, and the bulk of their womenfolk, dreaded a return of a regime that showed by its manifestos that it had learned or forgiven nothing and, if it regained power, would clamp down even heavier shackles upon the will and energy of an imaginative people. The knowledge made them desperate and the measure of their desperation was the ammunition of the men who led them, men for whom, almost without exception, there could be no turning back. *Tranquil*, 102–03

If they intend to be man and wife, David and Charlotte will need to share their opinions with one another, and the occasional breathing space from the public events going on about them makes that possible. One night, "sick from the scenes and stench of the city," David describes for her his "bouts of homesickness for Devon, of the smell of the sea on the plateau, and the leafy solitudes of Hayes

Wood in the summer." To this Charlotte responds that Paris used to be "neighborly," a place where nobody "went short of food or logs to burn," but she seconds David's love of the earth saying "Every word uttered here isn't worth a single turnip from one of your fields. You can't eat proclamations," to which he adds his Amen. Charlotte is moved to declare her love, and David reciprocates, but they postpone telling the others until "there isn't so much to think about" (120-26). Nearing midnovel, it's high time for them to get that far at least. But then, the fact is that their relationship is peripheral to the novel's central focus and purpose.

With that behind them it's back to business for David, whose narrative impulse is to correct an inaccurate British notion of how and why the Revolution occurred. He writes

> To my mind, the peoples of Europe, and more particularly those of Great Britain, are being gravely misled by statesmen and journalists, most of whom have never set foot in France, much less witnessed the Revolution at close range as I did. The impression that the overthrow of the old regime was accompanied by violent repressions and indiscriminate slaughter was current in England even before I set foot in Paris. *Tranquil,* 130

Delderfield published that paragraph in 1950, yet precious little effect it had since in the bicentennial year of 1989 the British royal family "refused to attend any celebration of a regicide revolution," and Margaret Thatcher, attending only in order to beat the Dickens into the French, "gave Mitterand a lavishly bound copy of *A Tale of Two Cities*" (Doyle, 17).

As a personal friend of Saxby, David is introduced to Tom Paine, in Paris to do what he can for liberty, and the two Englishmen hit it off very well. Paine, however, can neither read nor write French, so David peruses the current opinion journals and summarizes them for his new friend. Moreover, the farm boy from Devon explains to Paine what is going on in Paris, surprising himself by "the accuracy" of his own "day-to-day political sense." The Girondins are "honest, decent fellows" he informs Paine, but few of them are "men of action capable of standing up to leaders like Danton, or even Marat." There is a bright spot, though, he says: at least in America "your gospel has succeeded." But Paine replies, sadly, that there is "no parallel."

> America is new territory, unencumbered by the traditions of a thousand-year-old feudalism. It is a land where the brave and the steadfast can carve for themselves free acres out of God's wilderness and, having wiped the sweat from their eyes, can shout: "This is mine and my children's! I made it, I own it!" And there is none to march in with hired soldiers and take it from them!

When David reminds him that King George had tried to do it twenty years before, Paine answers, yes, but his "uniformed serfs" were obliged to "sail three thousand miles" in order to march through endless forests and "grapple with an enemy they seldom saw," and indeed, "You can fight tyrants under those conditions,

Mr. Treloar" (*Tranquil*, 138–41). As the conclusion of this round-robin cultural history symposium, Andre Lamotte adds his reflections upon the general subject of revolutions, their various modes and styles. Says Andre to David,

> I believe more in the revolution in your country than I do in ours. You think you haven't got one over there but you have, and it's the only sort of revolution that works; a passion for everyday justice married to a love of law and order! You're slow to act, you chuckleheads across the Channel, but the best of you think and read, and then go on biding their time and touching your cap when the squire trots past. You're building up a new class over there, people who own industries and whose sons won't be able to make them show a profit if they don't take their labourers into their confidence...Most of them are traders, with one eye on their balance sheet and the other on a comfortable seat in paradise, they'll vote for reform. *Tranquil*, 159

Most of the document's cultural historical reflections having been presented, David can get on with his individual future. Andre is looking that way too, since he asks David to get money from Saxby in order to bankroll their escape to America. David is willing, but their "little plan" will probably founder, for Charlotte refuses to consider leaving Papa Rouzet behind, or Marcelle and her newborn infant, or her husband Biron—a Brissotin rooster who will infallibly be guillotined should he be discovered in Bordeaux. With Paine's assistance they obtain passports, two for David and Charlotte, two for Andre and Lucille Souham, the innocent girl who hangs herself in prison to free the compassionate doctor from his self-imposed obligation to save her. Andre gives his passports to Biron before he flees to Bordeaux to hide from his pursuers. One can see that David's task has been worsening by the hour. "I only know how I'd feel," says Charlotte, "if we left [Marcelle] alone with the baby and she and Biron never saw each other again" (228). In the midst of indiscriminate slaughter of whole populations, this vexing woman demands the happy endings that reasonable persons—and she is one—would immediately know cannot be had. But David does what he must. He takes Marcelle and her baby to Bordeaux to reunite her with Biron, leaving the ineffectual pair to figure out how to get aboard the vessel on which they'll perhaps be sailing to America. David's chances of ever committing his adventures to writing are becoming slimmer by the minute, Charlotte's recalcitrance being the plot-horse Delderfield drives onward mercilessly to produce the harrowing cliff-hanger effect he intends to achieve. David understands the situation.

> Even the people one loves can be maddeningly stupid at times and the vague, unsatisfying term "arrange something," together with the cool proposal that I should make a leisurely journey to and from Bordeaux before I set out getting her and Rouzet out of the doctor's clutches, was uncharacteristic of Charlotte's practical self. Then I perceived that her sangfroid was assumed and that she was deliberately placing Marcelle's welfare before her own and had doubtless discussed the whole thing with Rouzet, if not Andre.
> "Let Marcelle look after herself," I said. "She and that damned husband of hers are partly responsible for all the trouble we're in. If Biron had—"

> "She's got a child," Charlotte interposed, and for a moment her eyes were hard.
> *Tranquil*, 227

Soon after that David and Charlotte get married. They have a lovely wedding in Dr. Germaine's *maison de sante*, a private insane asylum which advertises itself as "the most secure retreat in Paris," where those who can afford to buy concealment can stay hidden for as long as they pay for it. The proprietor will have forced Charlotte into an unwilling concubinage and sent Rouzet to the guillotine before David returns to fetch his bride, but his immediate task is his coach trip to Bordeaux. David rides outside and Marcelle inside the coach, past the country fields that look "sadly neglected" and villages "pillaged by the hungry republican battalions marching due west to finish the civil war now ravaging La Vendee" (235). They come to Bordeaux and find Biron and his companions still lacking all self-discipline, "still ready to bicker and argue amongst themselves" even in the shadow of the guillotine, still indecisive as they "continue to wrestle with the theatrical fatalism that had been one of the principal causes of their overthrow" (241). David gives Biron the ultimatim "You've got four minutes to make a decision" and the poor man collapses into a decision he never could have reached without compulsion. David is now ready to take "the northbound coach" and return to find Charlotte, but another adventure will intervene during the journey. For he shares a coach with General Fournayville, who is the "embodiment of active, aggressively vindictive republicanism," so vicious that "he soon reduced the other two inside passengers to a state of terrified silence" (247). They get off at the next stop, leaving the general and David alone inside the coach.

Fournayville is a character so pitilessly malevolent, so self-dramatizing in his brutality to virtually everyone that "long before he had finished the account of his youth [David] had come to regard him with a loathing disgust that [he] found difficult to hide, but by this time a vague plan had begun to form in [his] mind" (248). David jollies the general to assure him of his docile delight in his lurid tales, the plan being to murder the general by strangling him while he is asleep during the night, dress himself in the dead brute's uniform and accoutrements, tumble the huge body out of the coach into the roadside birches, then roll himself out, collect his wits, and continue back to Paris. Hiring a "two-horse chaise" in a small town he reaches at sun up, David "bowled into Versailles in the early afternoon" and caught a public coach to Paris, where he "flourished his general's papers" and was directed to a good hotel, within easy walking distance of Germaine's *maison de sante*. After a good sleep, the dutiful bridegroom will be ready for the shootout at the *second* villain's corral (247-55).

Chapter 18 is the tipping point in this 22-chapter novel, the pivotal moment in David's adventure which sends him on his way back home. In Paris again, he takes stock of his position and discovers that events have been moving quickly during his absence. An old journal tells him that a girl called Corday has killed the demagogue Marat "with the deliberation of a professional assassin," and David has "no means of knowing how this would affect Germaine's power to sell his prisoners." But this much was clear, it would be folly "to march up to Germaine's establishment as plain Mr. Treloar, a man for whom a warrant had already been issued." Happening to glance into the hotel mirror, David hardly recognized "the bearded ruffian" he saw there, and mixing "dye from wine dregs" and "a pot of blacking" which he found in the general's portmanteau, he managed to worsen his appearance considerably and left the hotel (256–57).

> I soon noticed that my uniform was the best defence I could have selected, for I now represented the military arm of the all-powerful Committee of Public Safety, and almost every person I encountered skipped out of my path as though I was a wild beast. After a while I began to enjoy myself and went out of my way to glare at homegoing linkmen, street porters, National Guardsmen, and other pedestrians I passed on my way up to the *maison de sante*. It was not until the door of the establishment had been opened to me by the rapacious drab who collected the meal tribute, however, that I congratulated myself on the excellence of my disguise, for the woman's face turned the colour of a cod's underbelly when I brusquely demanded to examine her prison register.
>
> She tried to slip off and get Germaine, but I knew that the key of the hall cupboard hung from her belt and made a grab at it, standing over her threateningly while she fumbled in the cupboard and handed me the book.
>
> I thumbed through the pages until I came to the original entry relating to Rouzet, Charlotte and Andre. Against the names of Papa and his nephew were two notations, but the doctor's handwriting was so bad that I had to ask his jailor to interpret them.
>
> "What does this mean?" I demanded, pointing to the scrawl.
>
> The woman hesitated. Sweat began to show on her forehead and she fidgeted with her key-chain.
>
> "The girl is still here but the two men have gone," she said reluctantly.
>
> "Gone where?"
>
> "Don't distress yourself, General," she went on hurriedly. "The old man went to the Conciergerie and is probably buried by now, and the younger one was transferred to the Bicetre at his own request."
>
> "The Bicetre! That's a hospital, you liar," I growled.
>
> Her face began to twitch and she looked despairingly into the back of the hall, hoping desperately that Germaine would appear.
>
> Nobody came out of the cardroom, however, and it occurred to me that the place was far less crowded than when I had left it on my wedding day. Possibly the Committee, maddened by Marat's death, had made a clean sweep of the majority of Germaine's paying guests. *Tranquil*, 258

Hearing from a "seedy little priest" who was also an honest one that Charlotte was tricked into "moving into Germaine's suite" by the false promise that Rouzet would be saved from the guillotine, the mock-general enters the room adjoining the dining room and, "using Germaine's gold-tipped quill," writes *The bearer has authority to convey the subjects named below...* . He then enters the dining room where he discovers the proprietor finishing his chicken, while Charlotte at the other end of the table is ladling out the sweet; she has aged five years, her mouth is "set in a sour line, and her large eyes had blankness beyond that of misery" (261). Germaine pretends he is dealing with a real general, though he immediately recognizes David—and then suddenly, the *maison's* owner is pointing a pair of pistols at his visitor, who "grinds his teeth with rage" (261–64). Though he wholly controls the situation, Germaine at last makes one mistake. Says David,

> I heard the bell jangle in the hall and saw his left hand let go the tassel and grope for the other pistol which he had laid aside on an occasional table close by.
>
> It was then, while his attention was fixed wholly on me, that Charlotte acted. One moment we formed a tableau, Germaine and myself facing each other, with the table between us, and Charlotte sitting perfectly still at his end, the next we were in a thrashing heap on the floor, with the table and its contents overturned and Charlotte lying half across the prostrate doctor plunging away at his exposed side with a fruit knife she had somehow contrived to slip into her lap whilst he approached the bureau for his pistols.
>
> She seemed to extract a fiendish delight out of killing him and, during the brief instant it took me to join them after I had overturned the table, she must have stabbed him half a dozen times, for when I turned him over blood was gushing from his mouth and he was all but dead.
>
> I had to drag her back from his twitching body and strike the knife from her hand, and I think her exultation was the ugliest thing I had ever seen, for notwithstanding the fact that her spring had saved our lives, her behaviour momentarily placed her on a level with the murderers of the Swiss Guardsmen in the Tuileries and the unhuman monsters who had perpetrated the massacre at the Abbaye.
>
> "Have done, for God's sake, Lotte!" I begged, but she flung herself on her knees beside him again and began fumbling in the bloodstained folds of his cravat.
>
> "He keeps his key here," she exclaimed breathlessly. "We can get some of our money back. I know where he—"
>
> I took her by the hair then and dragged her to the door by main force. All I wanted at the moment was to be out of that evil house and I didn't care what risks we took in leaving. *Tranquil*, 264–65

The "seedy little priest" became a "sly old fellow" in David's narrative when he shrewdly helps the fleeing couple by coaxing the avaricious doorkeeper to take the cash: the priest will hand the key Charlotte found to the doorkeeper "and urge her to decamp with the money," keeping her mouth shut about how she acquired it, ensuring that David and his wife "had a fair chance of getting away without a hue and cry" (267). His confidence in his disguise being shaken by Germaine's recognizing him he asks Andre's advice, who says that "in a country at war it is always safer to travel in uniform." And Charlotte's concern that Andre go with them? Tell her that "I'm travelling after you alone," and if you make it to Philadelphia, that's "time enough for the truth" (272). If their flight is to succeed, the attempt must be made, and *"Time and chance..."*, you know the rest. But perspicuous thinking can minimize the untoward influence of chance by favoring the prudent, including David, who "sat down to consider the most promising means of getting to the coast."

> At first glance the successful accomplishment of a long-distance flight across land and sea appeared a sheer impossibility. France was at war with most of Europe and I knew that the Channel was certain to be thickly patrolled by British naval craft and privateers, so that the northern ports were closed to me.
>
> If I attempted to leave France by the south the chances of capture by the British were just as numerous as would be run on the coast of Normandy, particularly as the port of Toulon had just been surrendered to them and was at that time the principle venue of the Mediterranean squadrons. If I turned east I would have to cross a frontier into hostile territory, and would almost certainly be arrested as a spy. Quite apart from these contingencies any move to the east would necessitate passing through the cordon of the republican armies where, even in the guise of General Fournayville, I would have no possible explanation of my presence, for the general's commission explicitly drafted him to the war in the west. My only chance then, and that a slim one, appeared to be a variation of my original plan, namely to push into the heart of the western provinces and flourish my commission under the noses of any military authorities who challenged me. This course also carried with it grave risks, particularly if any of Fournayville's personnel had arrived in the area and knew the general personally. I would probably get as far as army headquarters without much difficulty but after that our final bid for the coast would depend on luck. If I did get through the republican armies I thought I might count on being received as a royalist fugitive and getting a ship for Philadelphia or some other American port, but in any case I would have to run the gauntlet of the blockading British frigates even though they were far fewer on this coast than in the Channel or on the Mediterranean, owing to the difficulties of maintaining station in the face of the frequent Atlantic gales. *Tranquil*, 276-77

David and Charlotte set out for France's west coast and "almost enjoyed it" for they were "travelling alone for the first time and faced every hardship together", their love turning "danger shared into privilege." Fournayville had given David a military uniform to wear as his personal aide—too small for him but just right to fit Charlotte, who, to curious eyes, became the general's concubine in her fetching disguise. Dodging past places where troops would be congregated, tending in a south-westerly direction, they came on the third day to Angiers, eighty miles north-east of the island of Normoutier "a short way south of the mouth of the Loire," which was "still held by the royalists" and where David guessed American shipping would be found. But two problems still faced them. First, how could they get through the republican lines "without a guide"? (279-85), and secondly, how might they neutralize the threat posed by Carrier in Pellouaville, the town near Angers where they would soon confront him.

Their travelling companion, Houdier, knows the fellow. He tells them that Carrier is "the most ruthless party man in the Convention," who has been sent south "in the hope of terrifying the district into giving up the struggle." This man will be upon them almost immediately.

"Why don't we move on?" [David] suggested.
"Too late now," [Houdier] grunted. He'll have heard we're here and if we decamp
he'll take it as an insult and lay for us at Nantes. Keep your little poppet out of the
way, I've heard he's partial to young women. Watch out, here he comes." *Tranquil*, 287

Carrier immediately gives the mock-general an assignment. On their way to
Pellouaville his entourage has "picked up a prisoner in the woods," and Fournayville
has "one hour" to beat certain useful information out of him. Going to the harness
shed where the prisoner is guarded by two fellows who could easily be dealt with,
David and Charlotte reflect that just inside the shed is "a local man as desperate as
ourselves and if we could free him" which they do, "and get but a brief start," which
they also do, "we all three stood a good chance of threading the republican lines
and getting unharmed into coastal territory" (290). In fact, they have an excellent
chance, since the prisoner is a Vendean who knows the country well enough to
run through the thick forest at top speed in the dark when he leads them through
the republican lines. As David reflects on the experience, it was "like my father
and brothers playing hide and seek with Portsmouth dragoons on our own slopes
at Westdown" (295).

The following day the final stage of their flight was arranged. Several American
ships had unloaded cargo at the island of Nourmoutier recently, and Yankee skip-
pers "would probably agree to take off two passengers if they were paid in advance,"
their informant thought. Discarding all their disguises, "plain Mr. And Mrs.
Treloar" set off with their "more or less genuine" American passports, anxious to
board *The Pennsylvanian* the following Sunday (304–05). They got away smoothly,
but then a shot was fired across the ship's bow, "an order to heave-to and await a
boarding party", and David felt apprehensive. The British intention was to stop
"persuasive Paris representatives" from arguing their case to the Americans, yet
any technical charge would be enough to transfer David and Charlotte onto the
British ship, and David from there to an English jail (309–10). The crisis seemed
to have passed when Treloar was unexpectedly greeted in a brogue he had not
heard since leaving Devon.

"Why Lor' bless us if it bain't Maister Davy!" he roared, wringing my hand and execut-
ing half a horn-pipe. *Tranquil*, 311

It was Charlie Venn, youngest son of old Jake, their carter at Westdown. David tries
to talk his way out of their fix, and nearly succeeds, save that General Fournayville's
boots tumble out of Treloar's valise—boots that had developed a small crack which
let in water, until Davy plugged the hole with a small wad of paper, which, removed
and unfolded, had proved to feature words printed upon letterhead stationary,
words which implied that Treloar might in truth be a French agent. Thus in the
final stage of his return to Devon, David was sent to prison to await trial on whatever charges might be brought against him.

Chapter 22 concludes the novel with *deus ex machina* decisiveness and brevity. While David writes his memoirs in Exeter Castle awaiting trial for murder, Charlotte has been working to get him released by bartering the document she holds—"a detailed survey of the republic's military strength in the west, together with its current facilities for establishing depots for remounting and revictualling its divisions along the vital stretch of river road between Nantes and Saumur" (322-23). This document which she found among Fournayville's papers, Charlotte concealed "about her person" before her baggage had been searched, knowing that the British would be delighted to peruse it. All that she needed was patience and the powerful argument "No!" every time the authorities demanded that she turn it over without expecting them to pay the price she asked. She eventually won that contest of wills.

> At last the Admiralty agreed to obtain king's clemency for [David], in exchange for the documents, but here the Customs and excise had to be dragged in, for Charlotte's cool request for an impounded farm and livestock (or compensation in lieu of) was quite outside the Admiralty's power to grant. By this time, however, the naval men had crossed the floor and taken up the battle on Charlotte's behalf, and after frequent exchanges between Plymouth, London and Bristol a compromise was agreed upon, the terms of which were that I was to go free under a Royal Pardon, that the farm was to be restored to me as my father's sole heir, and that the Admiralty was to pay over the sum of 200 pounds for the dispersed or slaughtered stock. *Tranquil*, 324

Meanwhile, Saxby has contrived that the Treloar's farmhouse and out-buildings would be reconstructed, and when David is released from jail, returns home and sees Charlotte sitting in his mother's corner of the kitchen, "holding the handle of a large, shining frying pan," we see that all losses are restored and sorrows end.

Too Few For Drums

In overview summary of Delderfield's three Napoleonic-era narratives, *Gascony* is the most satisfying as a novel and the richest in explicit cultural history; one-third shorter than *Gascony*, *Tranquil Mind* combines the story of David Treloar's situational problems with the newsreel-like play-by-play of Revolutionary events in 1792-94 Paris; one-third shorter than *Tranquil Mind* and less rich in explicit cultural history than its two predecessors, *Too Few For Drums* is a small portion of the story of Napoleon's final Peninsular campaign as seen from the contracted viewpoint of the nineteen-year-old British Ensign who leads a file of seven men and one boy—supplemented by the addition of a Welsh "camp follower" from the 43rd Highlanders, interrupted as she buries her third husband in the church where Keith Graham and his men will in minutes find themselves attacked by Polish light cavalry working for the French in Portugal. Although *Too Few For Drums* contains cultural history, it is less explicit than in the two other novels, more interwoven with the file's actions, and assumed rather than focalized.

What most sharply distinguishes *Too Few For Drums* from the other two is this novel's genre. It is a *bildungsroman* focused upon the protagonist's development from a nineteen-year-old boy who has had military training in England but lacks any conception of war beyond daydreams sparked by his boyhood play with lead soldiers—airy narratives about the military glory which he assumes will be his lot now that he is serving under Captain Sowden in Portugal, just after the British victory at Busaco and a subsequent retreat towards the safety of Lisbon. But when Sowden is killed by the sniper's bullet shortly before the bridge is prematurely blown, putting the file on the wrong side of the river, and Graham in command, his lead-soldier glory dreams evaporate. He finds himself without even a map, and with absolutely no experience in evaluating situations, let alone dealing with them. All he has is the file's confidence that because he is in command, he will lead them competently. That, along with the awareness that he is utterly unprepared to fulfil his responsibility. It might be better to call the novel a *bildungsconte*, a mini-*bildungsroman* or a *bildungsromanette*, because the time span which is involved is only a matter of weeks, while one supposes that a genuine *bildungsroman* is a longer, more imposing more majestic proposition altogether.

The narrative which comes to mind as being generically identical with *Too Few For Drums* is Joseph Conrad's story *The Shadow Line*. In his prefatory "Author's Note" Conrad says that his intent was to examine "the change from youth, carefree and fervent, to the more self-conscious and poignant period of maturer life" (viii). That description well describes the alteration that must perforce take place within Keith Graham if he is ever to command. As Conrad continues, the "privilege" of early youth is to enjoy "the beautiful continuity of hope which knows no pauses and no introspection." As time goes on, however, "one perceives a shadow-line warning one that the region of early youth, too, must be left behind" (3). For Graham, the sniper's bullet that fells Captain Sowden shrinks to a single moment that shadow-line's onset. What can any young man *do* when faced with the need to act properly yet with no formative experience in doing so? Conrad's narrative solves his ship captain's lack of experience by having him lean on Ransome, a crew member who "needed no direction" since "he knew what to do" in every situation. Ransome's example works magic on *The Shadow Line*'s protagonist. Conrad's "Secret Sharer" is equally pertinent to Delderfield's narrative because it too features a ship captain given command "only a fortnight before" he must act effectively in a difficult situation. What the protagonist of this Conrad story "felt most" was his "being a stranger to the ship," and "if all the truth must be told, I was somewhat of a stranger to myself" (93). Ensign Graham's difficulty cannot be better described than by borrowing Conrad's articulation of like situations.

Too Few For Drums takes shape as a sequence of ten chapters, each headed by a descriptor identifying a person, place or thing which epitomizes the action of that segment. Thus "The Bridge" is the appropriate descriptor for Chapter 1, because its destruction before the last of the British troops had crossed to the British side of the river creates the problem sequence which follows from that circumstance. Now Sergeant Fox, whose long experience makes him competent to command though the British caste system does not permit that, grasping the situation perfectly, helps Ensign Graham by telling him in private what needs to be done. Before long, Graham begins "getting himself in hand," assisted by Fox's presence "and his own raw pride" (22). He does not yet know how to command but he can imitate the assurance of authority by making the correct noises. Thus, for example:

> "Sergeant Fox?"
> "Sir?"
> "I shall lead with Private Lockhart. Space the men in twos at intervals of twenty paces and bring up the rear yourself."
> "Sir!" And as Fox wheeled about and began pairing the men Graham could have sworn that there was a twinkle in his eye, as though he were watching a child take its first, staggering steps across a floor and make a grab at the nearest piece of furniture. *Drums*, 25

Before long they are able to get across the "torrent", and this time Graham "took the initiative" for lengthening the twelve-foot rope "another seven feet" by knotting "all the crossbelts" together. His men see that and appreciate his initiative, which "gave him right of entry into a new world where men were measured by what they did rather than by their social caste" (28-9). In short, "The Bridge" reduces to Graham's terror, his first baby steps, and then, by God, his unleashed initiative in a pinch—getting them over one river, not the big one, but at least a beginning towards rejoining the main body of the British Army.

The Church

Graham is now giving commands such as "we must bear left and go on down until we can find the smaller river again," making it sound "very definite, as though he personally had knowledge of the crossing" when he was in fact relying on Fox's guess (31). Such borderline pretense is a stage in this leader's discovering how to lead and it has already changed Graham's situation importantly, because bonding has taken place. That night he lies awake not from pain caused by the cheek laceration suffered in the river crossing but from the "strangeness" of his new situation,

> cooped up in a cave beside a tumbling Portuguese river with a group of men who at sunrise that morning had been no more than a file of blank, stupid faces but were now, by some extraordinary chance, linked to him and his future more closely than were his brothers at home or the junior officers with whom he drank and gambled and boasted in the depot at Hythe. *Drums*, 35

About midday on the morrow, the leading pair in the file came to a crossing with "horseshoe scars" in the mud, which Fox recognized as French, made by horses that passed within the last 48 hours. Learning this, Graham sees that "they were now faced with two choices," either backtrack on the hoofmarks hoping to find a village and food, or press forward around the shoulder of the mountain "in the general direction of the big river." But "this time he did not ask Fox's advice and the sergeant offered none." They press on and in early afternoon emerge into a "little valley" with a town and "a square around the church" beside a river that ran between "flat meadows" (42). Entering the town, they hear a "high-pitched wail" from inside the church, alerting them into cocking their firelocks, but it was no enemy. It was a camp follower wearing "a quasi-uniform," keening over her dead husband, the Highlander whose corpse was stretched upon the floor, she having been too weak to shove aside the stone slab covering the burial chamber. The woman had not been taken by the lancers when they galloped into the town, because she "took refuge in the belfry loft" which they did not examine before they left. The narrator observes that

> She was obviously a woman well accustomed to the hazards of war, the type of camp follower who would soon choose a successor from among her late husband's comrades and trudge along with him, cooking his meals, mending and washing his clothes and possibly bearing his children until he was killed in action or completed his term of enlistment. Already he [Graham] was familiar with such women…"He said suddenly, 'Bury her man, put him inside the tomb and then scatter and search the houses for food. We shall bivouac here for the night!'" (46). Graham's order cutting abruptly across the narrator's backgrounding information so jarringly emphasizes the fact that a habit-of-command has already begun taking hold of him. And this new woman is no feeble butterfly, but a reliable soldier. "She said softly 'you will be glad of another musket,' adding casually 'The French are not far away'" (48). She invites herself into membership in Graham's file, and just in time, for at "that precise moment" the lancers attacked and the file began the counter-attack from inside the church. After a short pause the lancers regrouped and once again dashed down the street at them. As Graham's hand groped for his sword, the angry Fox, who has no patience with folly under attack, barks at him:
> "Don't draw, use the pistol, man! as though the ensign had been a particularly obtuse private of the line. Graham had been on the point of asking how many lancers had galloped across the square, but the sergeant swung away, forcing Lickspittle and Watson down on one knee and taking his place behind them with musket leveled. Already the girl was crouching behind Lockhart, her musket barrel steadied on his shoulder. *Drums*, 50

This "girl" in her early twenties is a seasoned veteran who can foresee what the surviving lancers will do now that five of their comrades lie dead in the road. Form another charge? No. "They won't come again until dark and then on foot!" (52). As Sergeant Fox draws Graham deeper "into the gloom of the big building" out of the other's earshot, the girl joins them uninvited because she belongs to the circle of leadership experience, a troika for the time being given Graham's situation. "'We can get out of here without them [the lancers] knowing,' she said calmly. When Fox stared at her unbelievingly she added 'There is a crypt below with a passage leading up on the hill'" where at one time a now-ruined monastery had been erected. Fox wavers between suspicion and trust, saying "You are sure of that?" (53). Oh, yes. She explored the premises along with her husband, who "went down there searching for rings" on the fingers of long-dead corpses. Fox verifies the camp follower's report by exploring the tunnel himself, and when he returns gives Graham his orders:

> "You must lead the file out through here the moment it is dark," he said. "I and one of the others will stay on and hold them off. That way you can get clear and can wait for me back in the hills. That's no kind of country for cavalry and they won't follow armed men up there. We can be deep in the woods by the time they discover we're gone!" *Drums*, 54

When the firing broke out down at the church, those on the hill heard "one or two isolated shots, then a long, ragged volley" (56). They waited until they heard someone struggling up the gradient, Lockhart as it proved, carrying four muskets and breathing hard. "The sergeant's done for" he told them, "we downed two of 'em before he tells me to run and I don't doubt but he got another with his bayonet come to the last, sir" (56). With misery in his heart, the ensign "gave the order to move towards the woods" (57).

The Camp Follower

Graham knows the file will be safe only if they travel where cavalry cannot follow, but moving in the dark on broken ground is not only hard but dangerous since they insensibly travel downwards towards the lancers. He called a halt until the moon rose. It was clear to him that Fox had "deliberately sacrificed himself" to give the file a chance of escaping safely, since they needed muskets to form a rearguard. But the narrator knows Fox's thinking better than Graham, and what the ensign understands is not "the whole truth." After the skirmish with the lancers, Fox had felt elated. "Five with nine balls!" he chanted, with "the ebullience of a schoolboy engaged in some kind of prank at the expense of authority" while he moved about the file banging the men on their shoulder, his eyes "sparkling with excitement" (52). He loves the danger, the adrenaline rush of face-to-face shootouts. What Fox does *not* like is war as the British Army Commanders conceive of war. They whip the French decisively at Busaco and immediately slink away to the safety of Lisbon, where the beef and beer of England await them. For seventeen years he has fought and beaten the French—the only foreigner "worthy to engage his professional skill"—and for seventeen years has been ordered to retreat from these victories like a whipped dog. He is now too weary of the shameful charade to take part in it any longer. Yet here he was "on the run again, plodding across the mountains to the sea and toward the inevitable British Navy" (60). Waiting in the church for the lancers return Fox decided he would rather die than escape only to keep on escaping. He knew this was not a professional attitude, but at this moment he "wanted to think of himself as a fighting man answerable to no one but himself." He had his bayonet—the "long, needle-sharp" blade he carried about for years—and with it "grasped tightly in his right hand he remained in the porch waiting, feeling as he did so a wonderful sense of elation and irresponsibility," and "he had not long to wait" before the lancers returned.

And yet, we ought to suspect that Fox would only have decided to go out in a blaze of glory, his bayonet gleaming in the moonlight as he cashiered more of his worthy foe, if he were assured in the depths of his own awareness that his incompetent charge, Graham, would not be left without sound guidance. But such guidance the woman is fully competent to provide him, Fox knows. The hand-off to Graham's new leadership instructor having tacitly taken place, the old soldier can now act as irresponsibly as his heart desires.

Having told us much about Sergeant Fox, the narrator, who will in a leisurely roundabout describe the characters and backgrounds of all the file members, turns attention to Graham, who knew that his older brother would inherit the family estate and fortune, and who therefore decided early on to seek the next-best career path. His idyllic picture of the military life had been "tarnished" by the long march and the confrontation with the lancers, but it had not been wholly obliterated. Now that Fox was dead, Graham did not know how to get through the mountains. Yet because at the roots of his awareness he feared death "at the hands of the savage little men" who attacked them at the church, he was happy to "seek refuge" from that terror by pondering how to get through the Sierra and over "the seemingly unfordable river." In desperation, he remembered the camp follower, who must know something about the geography of this awful place. "Post a sentry and ask the woman to come with me!" he ordered Lockhart, the ex-gamekeeper. The collaboration between he who holds the leadership position and the woman with the knowledge and skills he lacks has begun. Summoned to him,

> She said flatly, "You are lost?"

Well of course he is lost and hates to admit that, but they will all die unless he does so. Finding it humiliating to confess, he does that indirectly, by asking her a question.

> "Do you know what direction we should take to find the left bank of the Mondego and cross it after the rearguard?"

The file has a chance to succeed, for she understands her own importance for Graham's success and the file's safety. She knows far better than he what he will need, and for the first time since Fox's death, Graham "felt that he was not alone." Quietly, he asks her another question.

> "What do the men believe? Do they think we shall find a way out of here?"
> "They still have you to lead them," she said, with a note of surprise, "and you are an ensign!" *Drums*, 63-7

Graham was "disappointed" in her remark, because she ought already to have "satisfied herself regarding his unfitness for the task of leading men out of this wilderness." He has given up on himself, but *she* has not, since she would in some degree have trained-up her three husbands and knows that it can be done. Belatedly recognizing the uselessness of the sham battles the officer trainees had fought on the downs of England and lacking a map to guide him, "All I can do at the moment" he admits, knowing an officer is supposed always to *know* what to do, "All I can do is guess." Then comes the pivot, the turning point which changes everything for himself and the file he fecklessly commands.

> "Can you help me to guess?"
> At that moment the moon sailed out from behind a bank of cloud, its light flooding through the aperture and striking her face slantwise so that she looked for a moment exactly like one of the stone goddesses beside the lily pond in his father's Italian garden in Kent. He was astonished at the classical regularity of her features, but even more by her expression of serenity. He knew, in that instant, that his life and the lives of those other men would depend upon this woman whose instincts were so much more developed than theirs, and he wanted instant assurance of this. He said urgently, "Forget that I am an officer! This is no time for courtesies of rank. It is different for the men. To them I must remain the leader and if they have no trust they will break away and try to make their way back individually. The sergeant was very insistent about us keeping together, and he was a good soldier. They must believe that I know the way home and that I have a plan. If you think you can find the way back it is you who must lead through me, it is you who must make up for the map and the compass, do you understand?"
> She got up and without answering walked into the open, holding the folds of her dress with both hands like a woman crossing a muddy street. Wonderingly he followed as she moved across the heather to the edge of the escarpment and stood there, her head raised like that of an alerted animal, scenting the keen, rain-laden breeze from the valley.
> "Well?" he said expectantly. "What can you tell me?"
> "The west is there," she said, pointing, "and the big river runs through that valley to the south," and she pointed once again, swinging her body around in a slow, graceful movement.
> "How can you be so sure?"
> "I can smell the rain," she told him, "and the rain comes from the west. Besides, I can see the river in the moonlight. If it were not the big river, then it would not gleam, for the small rivers run through deep ravines with trees growing close to the banks!"
> "Suppose we followed the slopes of the mountains until we could go down into the valley, would the French have occupied all the crossings?"

"I told you, there are no crossings below here," she said patiently, "therefore there will be very few French, only an odd foraging party. Masséna and the main body are already on the far side of the river. He would have rebuilt the bridge your people destroyed and crossed over by now. The French are very good at bridge building. They are a clever people indeed!"

He was impressed by her confidence and the certainty with which she seemed able to draw credible conclusions from her experience. *Drums,* 66–68

The "Camp Follower" chapter ends with a shocking shift from the sublime of the woman's looking like a goddess in an Italian garden to the depravity of Lickspittle's attempt to rape her. The assailant does not recognize that she and others like her live by a strict code of morality. Seeing her stripping to wash herself, he presumes the woman is a slut and refuses to be persuaded otherwise. They struggle, her thumbs attack his eyes to good effect, making him "cry out with pain and relax his hold," thus permitting her to "regain her feet and kick with great precision." When at this juncture Graham arrives to see what is the matter, she "snatches at his pistol," cocks it, swings around, and with equivalent precision transforms Lickspittle's face into "a mask of blood." He falls dead. Unrepentant, the woman is persuaded that such men should be hanged "as they come ashore from the transports," before they can infect better men. She and Captain Vidal agree on the irreformability of hardened ne'er-do-wells.

The Crucifix

The novel proceeds as a chronological problem-solving sequence, for the most part uninterrupted by cultural-historical asides or inserts. At the moment the file's problem is food since they must eat to live, and Portugal has repeatedly been stripped of consumables by the French, who are now scrounging to fill a food depot Masséna hopes to create. Lockhart is a good shot and the goat, "an easy target, obligingly stood still between two rocks while they deliberated, weighing the risks of alerting the enemy against the certainty of starvation" (81). The goat was killed and cooked and the file ate heartily. The abundance of nourishment and the pleasant lassitude of a full stomach provided Graham an opportunity to "talk awhile" alone with the woman. He does not want to discuss their situation but wishes to know how she acquired her "instinctive knowledge of men and mountains" (83). She obligingly tells Graham of her youth in the Welsh mountains, where she had married her first husband, a carpenter who "went for a soldier" and she went with him. Having listened to her history, Graham is still curious to discover how she came by her independent, confident spirit, and she replies "it is difficult to say in English words." He listens to the musical Welsh words she "rattles off" expressively but cannot get their drift.

"What does that mean?" he asked, fascinated.

> She shook her head and replied, "I told you, it is hard to explain in your language,
> but it has to do with the age of my people and the kind of people they were before the
> English king came over the mountains to build the castles!"

At that point, Graham reflects upon what she has attempted to tell him in light of what he knows about the Irish, the Scots and the Welsh in relation to the English, and this is one of the cultural-historical inserts that Delderfield has introduced—a passage "inserted" since it is pertinent not only to the Portugal campaign, but to the British Army over centuries. Her account "was not in any way a satisfactory explanation,"

> yet it helped him to grasp something of her approach to the profession of arms. Graham
> remembered talking to one of the surgeons on board the transport, an officer attached
> to a Welsh regiment, and he recalled the man saying that all Welshmen claimed descent
> from kings. They were a people, he reflected, who had never quite lost their separateness
> or sacrificed their spiritual independence, and in this they were like the Irish and the
> Scots who contributed so much to the offensive spirit of the British Army. Recruited,
> bullied and led by mahogany-faced Englishmen from the shires, they yet infiltrated into
> the higher echelons of every expeditionary force sent out by England to fight its battles.
> Crauford, Graham's own divisional commander, was a Celt, and so was Picton, whereas
> Wellington, the Commander in Chief, was an Irishman. *Drums*, 86–87

Before she leaves Graham for the night, she asks "You want me before you sleep?" He stammers a shamefaced "No," but asks her name. She tells him that it is "Gwyneth", and as she pronounced it "slowly and carefully like a school dame teaching a child his letters,"

> he lifted his hand and touched her cheek very lightly with his forefinger. Again it was
> the act of a child seeking reassurance in physical contact with someone he needed and
> trusted. *Drums*, 88

Graham's need for reassurance increases to a crisis point as they traverse the Portuguese landscape in the wake of butchery so fresh that the gathering vultures have not yet descended upon the remains. Gwyneth guides him through a Dantesque Inferno of mutually inflicted brutality, and it is the cumulative depressive effect of seeing such savagery as the French and the Portuguese work upon one another that brings Graham to his knees. That is particularly the case because the killings have been orchestrated for rhetorical effect. The corpse they encounter in the deserted village square, for instance, the remains of one who died from the weight of the boulder laid upon him when alive and well, crushing the wretch with "agonizing slowness," his outflung hands grey with the dust he clutched, "his elbows pressing into the ground as though he had exerted a tremendous effort to draw himself from under the stone." He had been executed to make a point in a game of kill-and-tell: "You see what happened to him? Worse will happen to you if you resist."

Herself hardened by long exposure to this rhetoric of war, Gwyneth calmly explains what Graham is too shaken by the novelty of such slaughter to grasp clearly.

> "A convoy passed through not more than three days ago," the woman said impassively. "They were Ney's men, most likely, for the Second Corps are a hard-bitten lot and this they did as a warning to other Portuguese. I saw it in the north once, near Astorga.
> "How could men calling themselves soldiers do a foul thing like that?" Graham demanded.
> But the woman shrugged and replied, "Clearly you do not know what the partisans do to French stragglers they catch. This man died within an hour. Some of the French conscripts watch the sun around the sky before they are dead." *Drums*, 90-91

Another scene they stumbled upon was announced by two dead mules and the sprawled bodies of men "shot down in flight" before their killers had the leisure for staging executions with dramatic effect. It was on "the far side of the oak" that a kill-and-tell scene had been conceived and enacted.

> Here were three more Frenchmen, two privates of the line each hanging upside down from one of the lower boughs and a middle-aged officer nailed by his hands to the main trunk, his feet not more than a few inches from the ground.
> They stood around in an awestruck group, as they watched, the officer's eyelids flickered and the body twitched so that Graham shouted hoarsely, "Take him down, damn you, take him down from there."
> Lockhart at once began to prize at the blunt nail driven through the man's right hand while Croyde, white-faced, hacked at the rope securing the officer's ankles.
> "Shoot him," the woman said calmly. "There is no life left in him!" But Graham snarled around on her and tried ineffectively to wedge the hilt of his sword under the head of the nail pinioning the officer's left hand.
> "You let me attend to that, sir," Lockhart said gently, "I'll have him down in a trice."
> He managed at last to draw out the nail on which he was working so that the man's hand dropped suddenly and Watson shied away in alarm. The others stood back, huddled in a group, but Graham moved to take the weight of the man's body as the rope fell away and Lockhart chipped away at the bark to expose an inch or so of metal and get a purchase on the second nailhead. When the left hand was freed they lifted the body clear and Graham, tearing open the tunic, laid his ear to the Frenchman's breast, but could come to no conclusion as to whether the man was alive or dead. The wounds in each palm welled a trickle of blood and Graham took the woman's canteen, holding it to the officer's lips and watching the water trickle down the dark beard.
> Then, unexpectedly, the man gave a long shudder and Gwyneth said, "He's dead, Mr. Graham, as dead as the others! Leave him now, he feels nothing." *Drums*, 96-97

The descent from the cross. A favorite theme for Christian artists, enthusiastically adopted by Portuguese Catholic partisans who crucified the French Catholic officer. They foresaw that their rhetorical gesture would be understood, would *carry weight*. Graham feels its force, falling into a swoon that made him "stagger and clutch wildly at Curle, who was nearest to him. As through a red mist he saw

Lockhart run to catch him and then, as though watching a distant explosion, the whole slope of the mountain seemed to heave…" (97).

Graham is revived by the goat stew Gwyneth brings him, and the brandy she found concealed in the "ditched wagon's" flour bin, flour she is using to set bread to baking in her improvised dutch oven. But he is far from well despite his having eaten. He felt "a nag of depression" caused by "an awareness of the uselessness of a war fought on behalf of bigoted peasants who answered cruelty with cruelty, so that the wheel of horror turned faster and faster in and about their bleak, savage mountains." Despondency weighed upon him "like the stone on the breast of the peasant" (101). Understanding the distraught state of mind which has fallen upon the file's leader, Gwyneth undertakes to save him and the file from the destructive effects of that despondency.

> "You must put it all from your mind, Mr. Graham! Only this way can you play a man's part in our business, for, see now, it is not good to change places with the dead in your thoughts. That way is death itself, but before that, madness, you understand?" *Drums*, 102

A pertinent aside occurs to me here. Could anybody better describe what ails the Hamlet who wishes that his too solid flesh might melt, thaw and resolve itself into a dew? How does Ophelia react to her depressed admirer's conduct? She obeys her father, gives back Hamlet's love tokens, throws flowers roundabout as she drowns, and follows Yorick into the rotting grave. Gwyneth has not read Shakespeare, but she emphatically does not intend to play Ophelia's part. Not being evasive in her approach to serious matters, she boldly decides to physic what ails their depressed leader.

> "You must not be afeared of me, Mr. Graham," she counseled earnestly. "It is to make you a man fit to lead that I can do, for now you are a boy like the little drummer [Curle] yonder. If you take me you will feel yourself a man, and think of better things than a man nailed to the tree. I tell you this, Mr. Graham, because you must think a man's thoughts if you are to lead us to Lisbon!"
>
> Her voice, he thought, was like the murmur of a mountain rivulet laving his self-doubts and misgivings. He lifted his right hand and touched her wrist, finding it cool and firm under the tatters of the sleeve. The touch of her flesh had an immediate effect upon him, releasing him instantly from the bonds of diffidence that had restrained him. He swung around to face her…*Drums*, 102–03

Having come to the Shadow-line he crosses it, which pleases Gwyneth because "it adjusted the balance between them and she said, unemotionally, 'Ah so, you shall be master now if you are quiet inside. I am not to be taken roughly, you understand?'" (103). As the chapter ends, the Ensign who commands the file in name is now able to do so in reality.

> His grasp of the situation was a man's grasp, a deliberate weighing of risks, an estimation of unpredictables—the weather, the food supply, the likelihood of a French punitive column's arrival, the nearness and approachability of the irregulars. He considered

these things as a soldier and no longer a panic-stricken youth shrinking from reponsi-bilities that he yearned to put upon other shoulders. The fear had left his belly and the uncertainty his brain. *Drums*, 105

And not a moment too soon, for this is the mid-point of the novel, and beyond this point he has serious work to do.

The Renegade

This chapter's title refers to Herve de Dieu Castobert, a man who "incorpo-rated within him most of the vices of the French feudal families whose degeneracy had brought France about their ears, but he possessed also a redeeming streak of obstinacy that had kept him in the field when most of his relatives had scampered abroad" (112). Long before the war in Portugal and the atrocities that so appalled Graham, the man had been "roasting French republicans alive and pegging out prisoners for the birds and dogs that followed the path of the Vendeans and their equally savage opponents" (113). A thoroughly vicious man, Castobert is a fat-bel-lied glutton, although agile and very strong—a duelist no challenger who valued his life would cross swords with. *The Renegade* is a practical seminar in military com-mand for Graham, for although he is no longer the frightened boy he had been, he has no experience that would prepare him to deal with this Goliath, the initia-tor of the contest between them, whose pretense of friendship is intended to lure the file into his camp in order to take their rifled muskets. "Come into my parlor" says a smiling Castobert to the boy who commands these few British troops in the Portuguese wilderness.

Graham's first thought upon seeing the irregulars at a distance at dawn was to confer with Gwyneth, but on second thought "he preferred to take the initia-tive" and came down nearer them. Still too far away for voice messages, Graham mimed his identity and friendly purpose with arm gestures. Satisfied that he has made contact with friends, he informs the woman that "We have made contact with the partisans," and she says, "I hope they are local men." He is curious to know why, and she replies that if they are not locals,

"one and all they are brigands and there is hardly a soldier among them! [Moreover,] the fact that they are loose in the mountains means that they are nothing more than deserters. To get help from them you must impress them with your authority, you are someone of importance, you understand?"

"They will believe anything I tell them?"

"If you believe it yourself, Mr. Graham. It would be very foolish to admit the truth, to say we are stragglers cut off crossing the Mondego. You must think of something bet-ter or they will take our muskets and cartridges and go." *Drums*, 109–110

At a loss how to present himself, he asks the woman for a strategy, a plausible untruth that he can back up with his best performance as an unpracticed liar. She has an idea.

> "You are behind the lines on the orders of General Crauford and are here for the pur-
> pose of estimating the enemy's strength. You have completed your mission and all you
> need from them is a guide or a route to the Tagus, where you have a rendezvous with
> the gunboats. If you do not report in three days, then your kinsman Crauford will send
> out a strong force of cavalry to search for you." *Drums*, 110

This subterfuge is nicely focused upon precisely what they need from the irregulars, and having been told how the script should be played, Graham sets about
giving his best imitation of a British officer barking at his soldiers and presuming
superiority over the strangers he is addressing, whose privilege it is to aid the British
Army. Castobert understands the situation, listened attentively, and, as if to reas-
sure his visitors, he "smiled, put out his hand and administered a series of short
pats on Graham's shoulders." Suggesting another scenario entirely, he tells Graham
"You will be safe enough here, my young friend" (112-14). No, Graham replies,
for he must be at his rendezvous with the gunboats on time, to which Castobert
replies winningly, "We will discuss that after we have eaten" (115).

As the file walk down the slope towards their affable host's camp, Graham,
whose command instincts are developing quickly, observes the bolt-hole they may
need, and imagines how that narrow path might be utilized by a group as small
as his. No longer Pinocchio walking between The Cat and the Fox, Graham has
become Leonidas at Thermopylae. As he moves towards the camp, he "spotted a
zigzag path"

> rising from the rock plateau immediately behind the pines, crawling uncertainly up the
> steep face to disappear in the canopy of mist that hung low over the valley. Without his
> understanding why, the path became for him the focal point of the camp and he noted
> everything about it, its nearness to the largest of the cabins, its tree-masked approach,
> its steepness and narrowness as it followed the broader contours of the mountain. A
> column of men, he thought, would be obliged to use such a path in single file and one
> man might hold off any number of pursuers providing he had ample firepower. It struck
> him as odd that he should be considering the means of retreat while entering the camp
> of an ally, but there was something about the place and the men who inhabited it that
> encouraged him to anticipate the worst. *Drums*, 115-116

When the column reached level ground, Graham drew Lockhart aside and whispered, "Don't let the file disperse and don't on any account lay aside your arms!";
Lockhart nodded his assent, for he shares his leader's suspicions. Graham now
trusts his hunches, which sharpen his observational powers as he foresees possible
futures that will go badly unless he is able to anticipate what might happen. As the
camp closes down for the night, Graham announces that "We march at first light,
so I bid you good night, sir" (115).

Surprised at his demonstration of firmness, their host agrees that he can "smell
his way" through the mountains if he wishes, but "In any case, you will leave the
woman behind!" (118), which initiates verbal sparring between the Frenchman and

the English Ensign until Gwyneth enters the conversation. She joins Graham and becomes the co-leader. Knowing that Castobert's followers are deserters who have no allegiance except to themselves, she has undertaken to break that weakest link in the chain with which their host expects to hold them captive. She has bribed Pedrillo with a gold piece from the money belt that Croyde salvaged from the corpse of his companion Lickspittle, and Pedrillo seems to have absconded from the camp with motives unknown to but deeply feared by Castobert. The woman has him by the short hairs, almost entirely by bluff. Where is Pedrillo now?

> "He is well on his way south with a message for General Craufurd, the kinsman of the officer you are threatening, but I do not think you will do more than threaten, because although you are a dirty ruffian you are not as stupid as the men outside."

Why did she choose to bribe Pedrillo?

> "He seemed to me the least stupid of the band, having just enough brains to desert with a gold guinea in his pocket and the promise of four more when he reports the whereabouts of this detachment."

What will Castobert do now?

> "You play chess, Capitano?" she said at length when Castobert stopped stuggling for words that would not come. "This is checkmate, but you will think of a move sooner or later and it will be our business to be gone from here before you do!"...She turned abruptly to Graham. "You can put up your pistol, Mr. Graham. He will not dare to attack us yet, he is far too uncertain of his men to risk his life for a woman and half a dozen rifled muskets!" *Drums*, 120-121

And that is where things stand for the time being, and the file bed down beyond the camp, keeping careful watch to ward off a surprise attack. But when Tam Strawbridge—the huge Kentish farm laborer who, thrashed for stealing beans, ran off and enlisted, loving the Army life which he shared with Brown Bess, his treasured musket—turned back to the tree against which he had leaned Bess for half a minute and found it gone, like an enraged elephant trumpeting threats, he attacked the camp below, "plunging down the slope with great, loping strides and splashing across the stream into the heart of the sleeping encampment," where he recovered Bess. But the enemy awakened and fell upon Strawbridge, as he struck out against them until overwhelmed by the numbers of his assailants (124-29). When it became clear to Graham that Strawbridge has raised the whole camp and by now would have been killed for his pains, the rest of the file head towards the zigzag path. Lockhart knew that they would not be pursued "so long as the French are below" (134). And he is right about their being there, since from the top of the summit they had climbed Gwyneth pointed to "a rift in the woods" far below them, the rippling sparkle of which Graham mistakes for a river, when in fact it was Masséna's massive army marching south (135).

The Torrent

When the file descends from the granite mountains to levels where abundant vegetation reminds him of his home, Graham finds "the first of his new confidence" (136). He earns his sense of personal power by a double-barreled performance: preparing for Wellington an accurate, eye-witness report on the size and state of Masséna's army marching to Lisbon, and leading his file across the torrent they must cross if they are to reach the British line. The narrative of these exploits is enriched by the cultural-historical insert where Graham and Gwyneth discuss whether Napoleon is a force for good or for evil, Gwyneth endorsing Delderfield's view that Bonaparte's effect is liberating.

Reconnoitering their whereabouts, Graham has the group make camp in a clearing while he pushes on, "threading a dense spread of undergrowth until he reaches the lip of an almost precipitous drop of about a hundred feet where the timber fell away to begin afresh on a lower shelf, masking the road" (136). From there he could hear the "steady roar" of Masséna's army, shouts of teamsters urging their mules up inclines, "the harsh rattle of ammunition cassions above the deeper rumble" of the cannon. Scrambling down further to see what he hears thundering past, he was amazed by what he saw, an army so vast that it stretched from east to west, which gave him "a unique opportunity to estimate the fighting strength of Masséna's cohorts" (137).

> Hour after hour he lay there, noting and scribbling, while Masséna's army filed below, three entire corps comprising about seventy-five thousand men if one took into account the corps that must have passed earlier in the day...This was the army, he remembered, that the British had mauled at Busaco, a month ago, but there was nothing about the endless columns to suggest that Masséna had taken the check very seriously...His horizon widened and he remembered that all his life the French Emperor had been marching and countermarching these same men about Europe, overturning everything that lay in its path. Where, he wondered, did the man recruit and train such splendid battalions? *Drums*, 138-139.

These are questions that Graham will discuss with the woman when leisure for conversation becomes available.

The file's immediate difficulty is ameliorated when Lockhart, to avoid firing a tell-tale shot, snares a rabbit for food. Without any preamble Gwyneth observes that after Masséna's army passes they must still get over the river, if Wellington is to profit from Graham's report. But where there is a river crossing, "there will be French," so the file must cross where the enemy could not get their baggage and gun teams over the water. "You say you can swim, and we have a rope," which can be lengthened, and "who knows?" Problems can be solved. If the French march through the night, they will "pass quicker and leave the road free for us to cross," though we'll have to look out for stragglers lagging behind (141-42). At this point Graham voices the question which has been nagging at him, thus initiating the discussion about Bonaparte's influence on Europe.

"Where does he find so many men?" Graham asked suddenly.

She replied, shrugging, "From every village and hamlet in Europe. The price he asks the bourgeois for government is their young and strong to fight his wars. It is not so difficult. Before he came the kings and emperors took the men just the same, but they did not give anything in exchange."

He was interested in her defense of Bonaparte and asked, "What does he give apart from wounds and medals?"

She looked at him unsmilingly. "If he was left alone he would give a great deal," she said. "He offers roads, bridges, good harvests, a thriving trade, manufactories, aye, and something more, I think, judging by what I have heard from French prisoners in Lisbon. He gives them something no other ruler ever gave them, a share in his glory. In our army it is very different, Mr. Graham."

"Tell me, Gwyneth!"

"The French are all one, you understand, the rich and the poor, the officers and the rankers. There is no flogging in the French Army and the provosts do not hang a man for looting. The rank and file are encouraged to loot and live upon what they find, wherever they may be. They made a revolution in France and it will never be the same for them again. Perhaps one day we shall make a revolution, but I think not. We sing that we are never slaves but it is not really so, because in England property is everything and a man is judged not on what he is but on what he owns...That sergeant of ours, the one who died back at the church, he would have been a major or a colonel in the French Army, and you, when you got back with what you have written down today, you too would be promoted and wear gold lace!"

"Perhaps I will," he smiled, but she went on, earnestly.

"No, Mr. Graham, it is more likely that you will be reprimanded for losing your regiment."

He realized that he was always learning from her, and here were things never to be forgotten, the true difference between imperial France and her opponents, the one fighting as a tribe, the others under a rigid caste system, yet he was unable to abandon all his prejudices without argument.

"Napoleon enslaves people wherever the Grand Army marches," he argued.

"He has no other choice," she said simply. "From the beginning he has been ringed by enemies." *Drums*, 142-143

The marching French became "more scattered" and there were "moments when the road is almost quiet." Thirty-six hours later they found the church belfry with its bell rope intact, twenty feet of cord "as thick as a man's thumb" (144), which they will use to cross the water. "There was no way of telling whether it was a tributary of the Mondego or the Tagus" but in either case it presented "a formidable obstacle," and to succeed in their attempt, various members of the file contributed to the group's effort. Because no timber grew there, they could not fell or find a tree for a bridge as they had done at the outset of their trials, and worse still, the bank where they hoped to cross was yellow mud. When Watson "sank to his armpits" in it, "screaming with fear when he could find no bottom," Lockhart noosed his length of rope and dragged him free (145-46). Turning from the bank problem to the rope situation, they found a church with the bell rope "passing through a hole in the belfry floor," but getting to the belfry had required the ladder which has since been carried away.

> "We need every inch of that rope," Graham said. "Watson can go outside, climb up and break through the tiles of the roof to the belfry."
>
> "The risk of being seen on the roof is greater than the advantage of another foot or so of rope," she said shortly and then men waited, uncertain whom to obey. *Drums*, 146–47

Though Graham felt a "spurt of irritation," he mastered it and, working through the situation mentally, realized that Gwyneth was right, for "the tower was the single landmark in a flat, featureless landscape and anyone clambering on the roof could be seen from the ridges above." So he told Watson, the ex-chimneysweeper, to "take a knife and see what you can do." What he could do was to scramble up the buttress "using his toes like a monkey," hoisting himself up to within fifteen feet of the bell rope, and from there over to the rope itself which— snugging it under his chin to secure it—he gradually sawed through with his knife. Twice the invisible clapper "complained, its harsh note booming through the tower and causing Lockhart to curse softly." But at last the rope snaked down to the floor and Watson began his "perilous retreat," delighted to have contributed something to the group's progress, celebrating himself on his victory, and drawing welcome agreement from the others.

> "It was a good climb," the woman said, and Lockhart added, "Arr, it were that" and fell to examining the rope with professional thoroughness. *Drums*, 148

Then it is Lockhart's turn to make his contribution by reconnoitering the bank for a mile upstream and finding the site of "the original footbridge," destroyed by either the British or the locals as the French approached. Here, the river was perhaps twelve yards wide, ten feet deep and very fast-running, "but because of the height of the banks at this point there were no shallows at either side" (149). It was better than the quicksandy spot they had earlier had in mind, and Graham estimated that, with luck, the file might "cross singly, clinging to the rope and being hauled up the bank by whoever had gone over first." But Lockhart adds a perfecting amendment to that assessment.

> "No matter how strong a swimmer you be, sir, you'll not make yon bank with a heavy rope attached to 'ee, for when her's wet her'll weigh considerable. Still, mebbe we can get over that if us makes a guide rope to carry the big 'un. Seed it done, I have, when I was a little lad!" *Drums*, 149

As the time for action approaches Graham reflects that every crisis they passed since Sowden's death had been met "by one of the others," Strawbridge helping them with his huge bulk to scale the rock face, Fox's "reckless courage" covering their escape from the lancers, Gwyneth charting a course, and Watson's agility securing the rope. "But now at last he was about to do something that no one of them could attempt and the knowledge steadied his nerve and lifted his spirits" as he stripped down to swim across the water, having instructed the others to roll their shoes and clothes into "bundles that could be maneuvered along the downward slant of the rope when it was made taut," their muskets to come over the same way (151).

Graham swims for it, reaching the other side "capering and slapping himself like a boy on a frosty morning." The gamekeeper signalled him to pull on the guideline, the rope slid into the water, and he "pulled it in hand over hand, bracing himself against the rock to counter its drag." The single spike embedded where the bridge had been anchored is the post around which he "knotted the sodden rope," and the file are ready for the touch-and-go effort to get over, one after another. It is sometimes frightening but other times delightfully funny for the other file members—seeing, for example, Gwyneth's broad buttocks getting dunked and wetted as she tries one maneuver after another, combining Graham's suggestions with her own notion of what might work best for getting herself over. But they all cross the water safely, except for Croyde. Having retrieved Lickspittle's money belt from his companion's corpse, he cannot give it up even when terrified of "being left behind to fend for himself." Torn thus, Croyde is doomed when halfway across the water "he saw the drifting log bearing down on him," not a large log, but a branchy tangle coming at him fast. The weight of the driftwood piling up behind the rope along with the drag of the current "tore his right hand from the rope and sent him rolling over and over in the brown flood." Recovered years after the war, when a string of dry summers "reduced the torrent to a trickle," that money belt enabled the purchase of "materials for a strong metal bridge" at the very spot where Croyde had "fought his losing battle with the piece of flotsam" (155–58).

The Convent

The file's greatest disappointment comes when they collect themselves after having crossed the river and witnessed Croyde's drowning. They reflect sourly upon "the blamed vool's" death, Watson observing that Curle, who had lost a shoe in the yellow mud that almost took his own life, "could have 'ad one of his brogues, for the boy's in rare need o' shoe leather." Graham "said nothing, for the sense of failure had come down on him again," thwarting his "unspoken boasts to get home without losing another man," even though it was Croyde's own "greed, hesitancy and crass stupidity" that caused his death (159). Suddenly he noted "a swirl of movement in the reeds" and the French hussars were upon them, men pouring into the rock basin "like a mob of boys on a playing field" while Lockhart was on his hands and knees "with his head bowed and blood pouring from" the bullet wound in his leg. The miraculous appearance of the French had been "the result of military prescience on the part of the Irish mercenary" leading them (160–61).

How had the French contrived to be lying in wait for them the moment they succeeded in the most difficult of the group's efforts? The French crossed the river on hastily built bridges, half a day's march above the point where Graham anchored the rope, their mission being to find food.

> It was no miracle that had filled the marsh with dismounted hussars but rather the prosaic report of a sharp-eyed troop sergeant who had seen half-clad figures running along the riverbank and had deduced from this that there must be a village close by. As a village meant, or might mean, mules, pigs, grain or even vegetables, he lost no time in reporting the presence of the file to his colonel. *Drums,* 161

That colonel was Michael Dillon, an experienced soldier whose presence there "led all the way back to the abortive Irish rebellion of '98" when he had "escaped from Kerry with a price on his head and enlisted in the French Army as a sublieutenant of light cavalry." The fourth generation of professional soldiers in his family, Dillon progressed rapidly through the ranks until "at the age of thirty-five" nothing could surprise him. This was his third Peninsular campaign and from his long experience he knew what Napoleon seemed not to know,

> the hopelessness of waging war in the Spanish Peninsula with armies of more than a few thousand men, for where a division could barely exist a corps began to starve in two weeks and most armies began to disintegrate a few days after they left their base. Yet Dillon's Irish sense of humor made him a good commander of light cavalry, and somehow, by exercising ingenuity and forethought, he had kept his men moving and his horses shod. *Drums,* 162

Graham hesitated, remembering the notes he had made, which, before swimming the river, he had stuffed into his boot, where "he could feel them with his great toe." What to do? He decided that "the only way" to keep the French from finding the papers "was a show of complete frankness, for they would be more likely to search truculent prisoners and the discovery of the papers could easily lead to all five of them being shot out of hand." Such thinking is not that of the lead-soldier incompetent who saw Sowden killed and the bridge blown weeks before. "With the determination to bluff this suave, gentlemanly captor a little of his courage returned and he said, with a smile," that getting over the torrent had been easier than what came before, and he describes in detail what they had gone through. He was wise to have done so because Dillon had been aware of their presence in the area. When General Reynier heard from the surviving lancers what had happened, two squadrons of light cavalry were sent to hunt them down, for "We were under the impression that there was at least a company of the Fifty-first in our rear" (165–66).

Needing advice and realizing that Dillon could provide it, Graham asks whether it would be "within the laws of war to ask" what he ought to do given his situation.

The Irishman nodded gravely and Graham was suddenly aware of a great liking he had conceived for the man, so great that he felt ashamed of the bulge he could feel in the toe of his boot. It was as though by concealing the papers he was betraying the confidence of an enemy who had become a friend. "In my position, what course would you adopt, sir?"

"As a field officer old enough to understand the absurdity of jingling across a depopulated country, I would be inclined to give my parole and sit out the dance in some tidy provincial town, but how old are you?"

"Nineteen, and this is my first campaign," Graham told him.

The Irishman knitted his brows and drew in his cheeks, as though giving the matter serious contemplation. Finally he looked up and smiled. "That alters things. At nineteen I daresay I would withhold my parole and stay with my men!"

"Thank you, sir, Graham said quietly, and it was almost as though the man beside him knew all about the papers in his boot. *Drums*, 168–69

It is "almost as though," and not out of character for an Irishman with wide experience and a sense of humor, i.e., a sense of proportion about serious things.

What happened thereafter was that the major in charge sent Lockhart, whose wound was "painful but not serious," to the hospital, "locked the three sound men in what had been a wine cellar of the convent, and gave the woman the run of the camp" on the condition that she wash the clothes of officers stationed there. From his observations of the French soldiers being carried into the hospital every day, Lockhart understood that Masséna's army "had fared little better than had the file," for they were gradually starving to death. Lockhart is free to move around, as is Gwyneth, and therefore they can support their imprisoned comrades in various ways, Lockhart by helping them escape from the wine cellar prison. He describes the layout of the areas around the convent, and he steals a blacksmith's file to help them cut the bars of the little window they will escape through. Though he had handed Graham the file and suggested its use, even more important, the touch of Lockhart's hand "relit in Graham's heart a flame of hope that had been all but extinguished when Dillon's men had swarmed out of the marsh and taken" the sword that to him was "a symbol of authority and freedom of action"(169–76).

Before Lockhart arrived at the prison window, Graham's mental state had been bleak indeed. The door to their cell was massive, their one window was secured "with inch-thick iron bars," and even if they got out, they were "in an area heavily patrolled by French troops." He knew also that "the north bank of the river was picketed along twenty miles of its length" by Masséna's soldiers, but that the southerly bank was held by the British. Yet crossing over the river was not possible, for even if they broke out and found "an unguarded spot," there were no boats. Wellington had destroyed "every river craft" before he "retired behind the lines around Lisbon" (177–78). Watson was cheerful and Graham did nothing to disillusion him. But Curle's health was rapidly declining because of the prison diet of "beans and new wine," as well as the foot problems brought on by walking with a single shoe. Graham's sense of abandonment extended to Gwyneth as well, and it seemed to him that their close comradeship throughout the march over the mountains and down to the plains was something that had uplifted him a long time ago, belonging to the golden period of his boyhood in the woods and fields of Kent. He was aware that both Watson and Curle in their differing ways continued to look to him for encouragement and inspiration, but he had none to give them. He thought of himself as a failure, and because he had failed them he could now regard their future with indifference.

Then, in the blackness of the night, with the wind soughing through the grille and little spatters of rain driving into the cellar, Watson had gripped him by the shoulder and whispered that Lockhart was there, Lockhart the steady, the imperturbable, the silent, tireless man who walked on ahead with his firelock in the crook of his forearm, his searching gaze sweeping the peaks and valleys for the gleam of enemy metal. Graham's response to the summons was instantaneous. He sprang up like a man told that the house was on fire and heard himself babbling directions to Watson to make a back that he might reach the grille and project himself from past to present at a bound. Physical contact with Lockhart was a powerful restorative, and news that Gwyneth was still free made his heart soar, for, with this news and possession of the file, his mental vigor leaped within him. *Drums,* 179–80

But Graham's enthusiasm dropped like a shot bird when he began filing the iron bars and realized that cutting the central bar was wasted labor because "it would be necessary to cut the iron clamps at each corner where the frame was bolted to the stone" (180) and that could not be done. But while he battled disappointment, Curle spoke up and asked "Might I take a look at it, sir?" And there was "the same incongruous note of confidence in [his] voice when he said "We broke out of a window like that before, sir! First we pulled the tops off the bolts, then Lieutenant Peterson used his belt, sir!" (180–81). The boy was impatient and his commander baffled as they continued talking at cross-purposes, until Watson suddenly realized what the boy was saying and shouted "Jesus, he means a capstan."

> "I seen it done, sir. The boy's right about it, sir! You ties the belt to something as can't move and slips in a capstan bar, anything as'll twist round and round an' tighten up gradual like! Then she gives all of a sudden but it's like I said, sir, wi' the file we c'n weaken them clamps so as they'll come away easy like!" They were like three boys now who have found an unexpectedly easy means of reaching a bird's nest. *Drums,* 181–82

They finished the job, staying in the cellar to get a good night's sleep, since "we shall need it if we are to get to the Tagus by this time tomorrow." Graham thought, as they lay down to rest and he drifted into sleep, "Surely a man couldn't wish for better comrades, a gutter rat and a waif, with the courage of lions and the patience of starving cats at a mousehole!" (183).

The Tagus

Escaped from imprisonment and joined by Gwyneth, the four of them head for the Tagus, hoping to strike it midway between the two towns where French troops are clustered. Gwyneth's contribution at this stage is the information gleaned from a Portuguese woman she talked to, that "underground grain stores" are regularly spaced along the riverbank, marked by white stones set to form a Maltese cross. This Portuguese had also seen that British gunboats regularly "sailed up the estuary and warped inshore to pepper the French concentrations." In Gwyneth's view, the only hope of their success is if Graham watches for the opportunity to "swim out and persuade the naval commander to make a landing and bring them off under the noses of the shore patrols" (184-85).

They travelled easier without the muskets, although Curle was too sick to walk and had to be carried, and in that fashion they went forward until reaching "the welcome cover of the ditch" near the spot where they hoped to sight the gunboat. The ditch, an irrigation channel thick with weeds growing on either side and with three inches of water at its bottom, flowed swiftly, and because he could "hear the roar of its outfall at the far end" Graham knew that the Tagus was close by. The ditch ended at a brick tunnel carrying water up to his waist, but it provided excellent cover. Suddenly Watson "bobbed up from ground level" snug inside one of the grain storage funnels, chirping "Dry as a bone down 'ere, sir, an there's grain enough to make porridge for a regiment" (186-91).

How much water would the British gunboat draw, Graham asked the one-time chimneysweep.

> "Not above six feet," Watson said. "I watched 'em sail close in when we was took ashore through them breakers at Lisbon. "Andy little craft, they are, an' them Jacks can 'andle 'em smart as you'd like."
>
> "Well, then," she said, drawing her brows together in a way Graham had noticed when she was considering tactical problems, "they will surely haul over to the far shore the moment they stand off, so as to sail home out of range of fixed batteries. That means you will have the better part of a mile to swim, Mr. Graham."
>
> "I could swim to the farther shore if I had to," Graham said.
>
> "Then perhaps it is your duty to do that and we need not concern ourselves about the gunboat," she said quietly. When he looked at her in astonishment she went on, "You have information of value, more value than Watson and me and that drummer-boy yonder" (192).

They discuss further whether Graham ought to forget about the three of them and narrow his problem to simply swimming across the Tagus with the notes he has taken on the size and condition of Masséna's army, so that his report gets to General Wellington, the British commander at Lisbon. When Watson suggests that if he gets across he could "still send a boat for us," Graham says slowly, thinking his way ahead as he speaks,

> "If I got ashore over there it might be days before I could get inside the lines…Besides, if they once got my notes how much would any of them care what became of you?"

It surprised him to hear himself saying this, to learn that the bedraggled trio with whom he had shared this odyssey now meant much more to him than the approval of the High Command, more indeed than the outcome of the war, for during the past weeks his entire conception of the enterprise in which they had all engaged had undergone so many radical changes that it was difficult to regard it as anything more than a background to the personal survival of these few human beings. It was as though every man and woman he had known in the years up to the moment the shot from the hill laid Captain Sowden dead were anonymous strangers passing the window of his consciousness and only the members of the file, both dead and living, had the substance and reality of fellow members of the human race. Their survival, and a justification of their trust in him, had become far more essential to him than the approval of beings as far removed from him as, say, Wellington, and at the same time more important than his personal survival because their needs reached out beyond his estimate of himself as a soldier and embraced everything that governed his understanding of manhood. *Drums*, 193

Having reviewed his own feelings and come to understand the relationship between himself and the file he has learned to lead, he speaks to them, explaining what he intends to do.

"If, for some reason, I fail to stop the gunboat, then I will swim back to you and we will try some other way. Whatever we do now we will do together, the way we have come this far."

The woman flushed as he said this and the flush proclaimed her pride in him. She had found him a boy and now he was the only type of man she could understand and value. He had learned all the lessons she had read him since the night that they had been deprived of the sergeant's leadership. Now he could wear the badge she had sewn for him, and the knowledge that this was so filled her with the deepest kind of satisfaction. She watched him draw off his cracked and broken boot and extract from it a hard-packed roll of paper covered with writing now blurred by water that had leaked in at the toe. He did not know if the notes he had made were still legible or could be made so and he did not attempt to unroll the papers.

"Keep it for what it is worth," he told her, "and if they are against coming ashore for you, than I shall have something to tempt them." *Drums*, 194

The evening before Graham will swim for the gunboat, he and Gwyneth talk about their futures. He asks whether she will take another husband if they get back safely to the regiment. "Why, surely! What other way is it possible for a woman to follow the drum?" Although there was never a moment when he failed to grasp "the impermanence of their association," Graham, feeling a stab of jealousy, told her "I have no intention of devoting my life to the Army...I have seen too much bloodshed and misery to encourage me to soldier until I am retired on half pay!" Astonished by this declaration, Gwyneth asks "What else can a man like you do" after you have been trained so well? "For men such as you, Mr. Graham? No, there is nothing, not once it is well begun as you have begun it" (198-99). He will become a magnificent officer. Yet knowing that Graham can profit from snuggling "as his blood quickened to her challenge," she carves out a "shallow excavation" for them to spend the night in together, out of the weather and mutually warmed.

> Above them the rain-laden wind came searching down the mountains; behind, the big river warbled over a million stones on its way to the Atlantic. But he forgot mountains and river in the sanctuary of her strong, wholesome body, and this was not because of the physical protection it offered but because she was willing him warmth and comfort with the whole of her being, drawing upon the reserves of countless Celtic ancestors, each a woman whose usefulness had been measured by the solace she could offer a mate. *Drums*, 198–201

The Gunboat

Can Graham prevail in what is essentially a boy's adventure story featuring a callow youth who shows his mettle and makes good? Indeed he can, and the military context within which he succeeds has an impeccably accurate cultural-historical basis. He will make it to the gunboat while the French threaten his friends, but the British Navy will beat them back, and Wellington will be happy they did. One does not take kindly to surprises after so many trials overcome, and this wholly conventional plot always pleases.

> There was no time to deliberate, for it was approaching at a spanking pace and even as he stripped off his tunic and breeches the sun caught its brass deck cannon and threw diamond-hard rays of light, advertising the vessel's purpose there at that early hour. He said as they scrambled down the bank, "will you wait in the tunnel?"
>
> But she replied, "No! It's all or nothing now, Mr. Graham! I'll fetch the others as soon as I can and we must take our chance in the open. If you reach it and the captain will heave to, then our chances are good, for there is nothing here to fire at them. Go now and God give you strength!" *Drums*, 202

If he misjudged the distance or failed to maintain his pace, he was doomed, for once in the water he knew that he lacked the endurance to swim back and the "slow current" would carry him past the bend into the hands of the French. Graham struck out "using the crawl kick that his father's gamekeeper" taught him, "keeping his head down but raising himself every few strokes" in order not to lose sight of the gunboat's prow. When he came to himself on board the ship, he heard his teeth "clattering against the neck" of the bottle they were holding up to his mouth. He managed to gasp "British stragglers on shore—through the lines—vital information—Lisbon!"

> "Stragglers you say? How many? Where did you come from?...Hard to starboard! Ease her off there!" as the boat shuddered around and the jibs cracked like a salvo of cannon shots above their heads. *Drums*, 202–04

Graham has done his part and now it is up to the gunboat's captain to manage getting the rescue craft to shore, while gunning down the French cavalry who will soon appear on the scene to threaten the three stragglers still on the shore.

He saw a little cloud of horsemen jostling down the gulley higher up the beach and he
swung his telescope down like a flail, screaming the news to the group beside the cannons. But the gunners had already seen them and Graham's warning shout was lost in
the roar of the guns. *Drums*, 207

The scene then changes from the deck of the gunboat to the shore, where
Graham's comrades could yet be killed in the last moments of being rescued. They
have work to do, stepping and fetching to be ready for rescue, for just then "a minia-
ture landslide of mud and stones" caused confusion among the slithering horses as
the troopers struck at them "with their long, straight swords." During that interval,
Watson and Gwyneth got to the tunnel, "where the water rose to their waists and
no horse could follow them." When the leading cuirassier swung down from his
saddle and "entered the tunnel," he quickly realized that "his heavy top boots and
spurs" immobilized him, and he went back to assist his comrades get their "excited
horses" onto firmer ground. As push comes to shove, Gwyneth takes charge.

"Come," she said, seizing her end of the pole [onto which Curle has been belt-strapped],
"we must chance their fire. We are lucky they are cuirassiers, they have no carbines,
just pistols." And together they lifted the drummer and set off to the water's edge as
the boat swung around and shot inshore.
    They heard the roar of the guns, and to Gwyneth, slithering across the last few
yards of beach toward the knot of sailors, the sound came as the final salute of the
campaign. A moment later the seamen had them and Curle had been dragged into the
boat, and as the sailors thrust off with their long sweeps she caught a fleeting glimpse of
horsemen scattering beyond the rim of the dunes and busied herself unbuckling Curle
from the pole, chafing his wrists where the leather had bitten into the flesh. *Drums*, 211

Vale

The novel's good-bye is a brief document which seems to be concerned only
about reuniting Graham with his three comrades a month after the *Prometheus*,
the gunboat that had rescued them from the French, disembarks them in Lisbon
where their good-bye takes place. But it undertakes more important work as well.
This codicil is important for a study of Delderfield's novels as cultural history
because it concludes what I have called a boy's adventure story not from the boy's
perspective alone, but from the narrator's cultural-historical standpoint. That view
reaches into the future by recording the impact of Napoleonic-era "just-now" events
upon the future's "not-yet," when, for example, the rigid class distinctions that earlier prevailed will become gradually ameliorated. What we saw earlier on, when
Graham and Gwyneth discussed Napoleon and whether his influence is towards
good or towards evil is here reiterated, indirectly but unmistakably.
    The British authorities were eager to wrest from the ensign his detailed account
of the file's march south from Coimbra. They "pestered him mercilessly" concerning his recollections as they studied his "almost illegible notes," which had been

copied out under the direct supervision of Crauford himself. Graham waited until they had finished to make "personal pleas" regarding Watson and Curle and it was regarding "those two applications" that he found the two in their wretched quarters. Watson was frying a pan of salt beef and mashed vegetables when Graham found him and he sat on a tub quietly until he finished his cooking. Wearing a lieutenant's chevrons now, Graham offers him a place.

> "As a lieutenant I can have a permanent soldier servant. I came down here to tell you that you can be my servant if you wish. You would have better quarters than this and as much food as you can eat, so long as we are in garrison." *Drums*, 214–15

The young officer from the wealthy family in Kent offers the gutter rat the best he has to offer, and Watson is glad to retreat from being his companion in arms and occupy once again a socially inferior place. "Graham smiled, finding that the sweep's lively acceptance of the post renewed his faith in the future, inasmuch as it offered some kind of continuity" (216). Yet the "future" and its "continuity" is a desideratum that Graham finds more comforting perhaps, than would the narrator, who tactfully does not interfere with his characters' dialogue by pointing out that Watson is taken care of at the cost of continuing the caste system that Napoleon's armies had done their best to smash. For what difference is there between the British Parliament and the Bourbon's similarly-structured designs for governance?

As for Curle, Watson reports that "He's still in sick quarters over beyond the slaughter house." But when Graham shares his information that the drummer, the son of a camp follower who has never known anything other than a military life, has gotten his discharge papers and will be "going home soon," Watson looked startled.

> "'Ome? Curle fer 'ome, sir?' Wot 'ome's he got, barrin' the regiment?"
>
> "My home," said Graham,"
>
> who has written his father clearing the way for the boy to live nearby the family mansion in Kent. He tells Curle
>
> "You will live with Rowley, the keeper, and he will teach you to trap like Lockhart. To fish too, perhaps, in the river where Rowley taught me to swim." *Drums*, 216

But the more Graham explains, the less the boy understands, whereupon Watson translates the lieutenant's crude efforts to be helpful into language Curle can comprehend, which is not soaring in its expectations about the life Curle will enjoy, when in sober truth the boy cannot live much longer. Watson stresses regular food, a dry bed, and being out of the rain. "Besides, you got no choice, 'ave you? You bin discharged, son, just like Mr. Graham says!" (217–18).

The offer the lieutenant puts to the recently crippled teenage boy—whose foot could not endure their long march in the mountains and the physical damage caused by losing a shoe, which caused the infection now creeping through his body—is his attempt to give a sick soldier the formative experience of the life that had blessed him on his father's estate in Kent. But Graham's friendship, his gratitude for the boy's endurance and invaluable assistance in the escape from the convent prison, cannot mask the fact that from the outset Curle has been a worth-less human creature judged by the social structure. Worst of all, the pointing finger of blame cannot point toward anything in particular. From his conception Curle has been a casualty of war, and Lieutenant Graham, although he has survived, has not been untouched by its tragedies. As Samuel Johnson puts it in his *Vanity of Human Wishes*, "...nor think the doom of man reversed for thee," which reminds us that the revolutionary improvements Delderfield sees as being jump-started by Napoleon's effort have a limit. Sober probability endorses only a qualified and imperfect hope of providing the world a paradisal drift through an organizational restructuring of its constituent elements.

The novel's good-bye has a third file member in store for Graham to meet and part with, the woman whose influence upon him has been so overwhelmingly all-embracing that one could think of her as the tale's main character—a distaff Pygmalion who carves a genuine soldier from a lead-soldier youth and brings him to life. At the camp ground where he had been "tying loose ends" regarding Watson and Curle, he unexpectedly bumps into the woman.

> She at once assumed command in the way she had made decisions during the march, taking him by the hand and leading him through the gate to a steep cobbled street that sloped down to the Waterfront. As he glanced at her he was struck once again by her essential freshness and bloom, suggesting a background infinitely remote from that of a squalid camp teeming with unwashed men and rank with the stink of wood smoke and cooking fat. *Drums*, 219–20

Now and always, Gwyneth is Wonder Woman with a bloom on her cheek, her raggedy clothes concealing her astounding power. Once again in the force field of her commanding femininity, Graham attempts to claim her as his wife on the grounds of his own dependency.

> "I need you now and always, Gwyneth!"
>
> But she shook her head. "No! You understand nothing of women, not even women of your own kind, but because of me you will learn when you go among them again. Do you think that a word from you could change me into the kind of wife you will need when you rise in rank or live among civilized people once more? What would I do in a great house such as yours, with servants to scold and linen to count? And if, so be it, I found myself in such a place, do you think for one instant I would be content to stay there whilst you were away somewhere campaigning? No, Mr. Graham, you cannot play the rich young suitor with me, and you cannot pack me off home like the sick drummer-boy yonder! This is my place and in your heart you know it to be so. All else is no more than a boy's fancy!" *Drums*, 221

Graham reflects that "for the first time since he had seen the woman kneeling beside her dead Highlander he came close to understanding her true nature."

> She was something out of the long-distant past, when tribes lived out their short, dangerous lives in forests where death lay in wait for the unwary and the weak, where a cleft in the rocks was hearth and home, and a man's family was fed in relation to his prowess with bow and spear. He saw this as something revealed by a flash of light on a dark night and ceased, in that instant, to quarrel with its finality." *Drums*, 222

· 2 ·

THE *AVENUE* NOVELS

England as Neighborhood

Seven Men of Gascony's Nicholas, the college-educated voltigeur who comprehends pivotal subtleties in the manner of a cultural historian and who understands the psychology of its people by having studied English literature, replies to Napoleon's question in this way.

> The English are a family, and families quarrel furiously, until one of their number is attacked by somebody outside the circle. (*Gascony*, 209)

Napoleon's question had been about the British Navy, the reason for its stunning superiority, but Nicholas's answer, foreshadowing the country's response to Hitler at Dunkirk and the Battle of Britain, goes to the heart of the matter. It is not individuals but the people as a whole that is strong. And when Churchill tells the hushed crowd "This is *your* victory…!", their response indicates that he has spoken a truth they intuit but cannot express that simply. The people erupt into "the wall of sound" that "rushed down Whitehall and was taken up by thousands too far away to see the balcony, or to know what was happening there" (*The Avenue Goes to War*, 601). Churchill articulated the heart of the matter, Nicholas tried to explain it to Napoleon, and Delderfield's *Avenue* novels are about that heart.

Part I: *The Dreaming Suburb 1919–1940*

The first *Avenue* novel opens with a statement that the families living on the fictitious "Manor Park Drive" typify "the lives of any suburban dwellers, on the outskirts of any large city in Britain." They are "for the most part unsung,"

> even though they represent the greater part of Britain's population. The story of the
> country-dwellers, and the city sophisticates, has been told often enough; it is time some-
> body spoke of the suburbs, for therein, I have sometimes felt, lies the history of our
> race. (Author's note prefixed to *Contents*)

The gauntlet has been thrown down. Stand back, Hardy and Galsworthy! For the
Carvers, Friths, Fraziers and Cleggs who represent the multitudes carrying forward
"the history of our race" are coming front and center onto Delderfield's stage. His
success as a cultural historical novelist will be measured by his accuracy in presenting their thoughts, emotions and actions during a tumultuous half-century.

Delderfield was born two months before the *Titanic* hit the iceberg and went
down in 1912, which shook the nation because the English *knew* that Britannia
ruled the waves, whether in peace or war. It was therefore foolish for the Germans
to challenge her naval superiority by building up their own fleet. Yet little boys see
things more nakedly, without benefit of knowing the outcome before the contest
begins. And that small boy's London neighbors shared his trepidation when their
city was bombed by Zeppelins, "the first time in human history that a civilian population was bombarded from the air." The effect of such attacks upon Londoners
was "frantic terror," the city being "absolutely defenseless" against the night raid-
ers that were picked out by searchlights illuminating the Zeppelins in the darkness
overhead (*Own Amusement*, 24).

Delderfield's father moved the family out of London to a nearby suburb to
increase the margin of safety, thus the novelist knew his characters well by having lived with them in childhood. A passing remark in the novel concerning the
family relocation suggests the accuracy of his fictional neighborhood: "I did not
know the Avenue until the Spring of 1918, so my story begins shortly after that
season" (*The Dreaming Suburb*, 3). The novelist does not figure in the story beyond
that remark, but it is enough; he lived in the suburb he wrote about. A more substantive testimony to the accuracy of *The Dreaming Suburb* and *The Avenue Goes To
War* as cultural history can be established by turning to his eye-witness accounts
of the attitudes and conduct of those suburbanites in his collected essays.

> The impact of my transition from central London to what was then a semi-rural suburb
> was considerable. All my very earliest impressions were of drab streets, strident Cockney
> voices, khaki, naphtha flares, Zeppelin raids and fog, of maroons exploding neighbors
> into panic, of pinched, wartime expressions in butter queues and of the firelit security
> of a home dominated by a noisy, extrovert father. But on a showery day in April, 1918,
> all this disappeared and in its place were rows of trim terrace houses lurking behind

hedges of clipped privet, flocks of rosy-faced children who inhabited them, clumps of towering elms and meadows bordered by flowering hawthorn but, above all, acres of buttercups and daisies, with here a rush of bluebells and there a rank of foxglove. The freshness, color and variety of the scene enchanted me. (*For My Own Amusement*, 17)

Perhaps no area in outer London has changed more dramatically than Croydon has changed over the last half-century. Today its southern boundary is a wilderness of housing estates and shopping centres but in the spring of 1918, when the British army was battling to plug the gaps torn in its line by Ludendorff's final offensive, Addiscombe was as pastoral and peaceful as is most of the West Country peninsula today. But although my imagination was deeply stirred by the rural aspects of the shift the social implications had an even stronger effect. It was here, at that time, that I came to sense and ultimately to understand, the subtle undercurrents of the English class system. We Avenue dwellers were all conscious of having a great deal in common and an obligation to conform. We revelled in it and went out of our way to emphasize the subtle distinction between the ranks of the carefully graded society in which we found ourselves. (*Amusement*, 58)

I have been back several times in the last few decades, and on every occasion the place seems to have sloughed off a little more of its identity. I may be wrong, but I have a feeling that the spurious but highly prized gentility of our suburb was destroyed by an assortment of factors. By the onslaught of the Luftwaffe, by the creation of the Welfare State, by the ball-and-chain tug of our economic malaise, by the loss of the Empire and also by the forest of TV masts that now weave a crazy pattern along the rooftops. A majority, perhaps, will view this demise as a significant social advance, but I am not convinced of this. The egalitarianism that has replaced it is as featureless as a Government White Paper and for the incurable romantic the suburb had a flavor that has disappeared as surely as flavor disappears from the prepacked meal. Whenever I wander up Shirley Road today and poke about among the new roads, I seem to be remembering a time as distant as Agincourt, but the song of the suburb, although considerably muted, is still to be heard. A whirr of lawn mower at Number Twenty-three. The slow castanet of hedge clippers at Seventy-three. And the scent of the suburb lingers too for those who inhaled it fifty years ago. (*Amusement*, 62)

I follow this lengthy meditation on the loss of a cultural environment with two less-all-embracing instances of rapid change experienced by his society in the twentieth century. First, the invention-driven death of the piano lessons that the Avenue mothers insisted upon providing their children.

There is a curious parallel between the efforts of early-twentieth-century children to learn to play the piano and the disasters that overwhelmed the British canal companies of an earlier generation. The canals were put out of business by the railways before their courses were half completed. The piano practice of my generation was rendered vain by the invention of the crystal set, the portable Gramophone and the talking picture. All that we later victims of circumstance and maternal Mozart-fixations had to show for our lost hours of childhood was a thin smattering of "theory" and the ability to stumble through half of "The Hunting Song" or "The Merry Peasant Returning from Work." (*Amusement*, 64)

Second, the sudden onslaught of the talking movie, with the widened response-scale, the new vulnerability to thundering emotional agitations which delighted Delderfield along with Edith Clegg, the middle-aged spinster who cannot get enough of the cinema, who played piano accompaniment at the movies to supplement her income earlier on, and whose passion was re-ignited when the talkies came along.

> It had been one thing to see puppetlike figures crumple in the dust of Main Street, Hicksville, epitaphed by the subtitle *"There's only one kinda law around Big Bull Creek, Bonzo!"* but quite another to hear the crackle of gunfire and the screams of the dying. It was the same with the crowd scenes in the new epics. To the stirring strains of *William Tell* I had watched fleets of galleons heel over and sink without a qualm. Now I was caught up in the fury of the wind and the crash of green seas pounding the superstructure. I did adapt, however, just in time for the spate of gangster films, when the tires of touring cars screamed round the streets of Cicero, and the stutter of the Thompson machine gun was as essential to the story as had been the ripple of Handel's "Water Music" in silent-picture river scenes. (*Amusement*, 96)

Delderfield's comedy *Worm's Eye View*, which satirized the conduct of some English citizens during the Second War and was "the longest running play to its time" (Sternlicht, 24), was an early version of the same theme in *The Avenue*. Millions of civilians had worked tirelessly to help the war effort on the home front.

> But there remained the uncommitted, a remarkably large minority in a country that was fighting for its life, and the uncommitted were the group that prompted me to write *Worm's Eye View*. Among them were many landladies, but they were not exclusively landladies. There was the midlands butcher who, in the winter of 1940, refused to accept service meat coupons issued to living-out personnel on the grounds that the services wasted food. There were grocers who practically lived under the counter. There were thousands of bureaucratic bullies who made a kind of hobby of persecuting men and women in the King's motley, and there were many insignificant and extremely tiresome little bastards who threw their weight about in bars, cinema queues, fish-and-chip saloons, and even omnibuses, people who would have proved invaluable to Hitler had he succeeded in getting a footing in the island. These were the minority who worked tirelessly at sapping public morale, hauling old ladies off to jail for showing a sliver of light through their blackout curtain, preventing soldiers and sailors burdened with kit from getting on a bus, sometimes with ironic witticisms, such as "Sorry, mate, war workers only". These people had no face, were of all ages, and spoke with a hundred different accents but they had about them a common expression. The hostile stare they reserved for junior N.C.O.'s and rankers somehow reminded one of a face on a tarnished Roman coin.
>   There were pockets about the country where you seldom found such persons. In my experience Edinburgh was such a city, and Scotland generally had a hospitable reputation among servicemen. So did some of the small coastal towns that were being hammered in hit-and-run raids, and I met plenty of kindly folk in remote villages in the Pennines. (*Amusement*, 279–80)

Because *The Dreaming Suburb,* which opens the two-novel set, is largely devoted to showing the shifting political stances of its characters, Delderfield's own altering views as an individual and a newspaper reporter are pertinent for testing his cultural-historical credentials. He does it in the essay "The Left and the Right of it," from which I now quote, with silent abridgements to move it nim6bly forward.

> Right and Left were labels not often displayed in the shires until the early 'thirties and they emerged not from the Slump, and the terrible social inequalities of the post-war period, but from the postures adopted by the Dictators in Europe. The real watershed in British politics was not the Spanish Civil War of 1936, as is generally believed, but the invasion of Abyssinia in the previous autumn, resulting in the collapse of the League of Nations. What really occurred, I think, was that the arrogance and menace of the two Dictators compelled the local Left to mature, and maturity on their part caused the local Right to take them far more seriously than during the seventeen years that had passed since the Armistice.
>
> Something along these lines was happening all over the country at that particular time. Until then the small but always vocal Left of provincial Britain had been obsessed with domestic issues, like bad housing, unemployment and, later on, the Means Test. But the Spanish Civil War caused the entire political scene in Britain to turn a somersault. It was so sudden and so complete that it left most people breathless and bemused. Looking back, it is interesting to isolate the events that brought about this all-change on the part of one's neighbors. The first, I think, was the burning of the Reichstag. The second were newsreels showing elderly Jews scouring the streets of German cities, with armbanded young thugs looking on. A third was Hitler's Night of the Long Knives, warning even those living in remote Devon villages that we were now confronted with a Continental Al Capone. Then came Mussolini's invasion of Abyssina and the tacit acceptance of naked aggression by the democracies, and after that the outbreak of the Spanish Civil War and the policy of non-intervention. Shame began to invigorate the local Left, who became convinced that the intervention of Germany and Italy in Spain was nothing more than a dress-rehearsal for the conquest of the world. The Local Right began to put it about that appeasement was a cunningly conceived policy designed to buy time in order that we could re-arm for the fight—if there was a fight. This justification of the craven behaviour of government did not fool any local Socialist or Liberal I interviewed during this period.
>
> By the time Hitler took office, driblets of news concerning the concentration camps reached the town, and I interviewed several Jewish refugees who confirmed the frightful truth. Now the pattern of Fascist intentions became clearer day by day and after I had digested Koestler's *Spanish Testament* I no longer had any doubts about the future. I executed my private somersault. From advocating disarmament I moved on to write banal leading articles urging the policy of rearmament upon the dithering Government, and I did not blame some of my local Conservative friends for thinking me weak in the head. We had bleated down the years, first to convert swords to ploughshares, then to convert the ploughshares back into swords. The only excuse I can find for us is that we had grown up in the aftermath of the Somme and Passchendaele. We had honestly believed that the 1914–18 war was a war to end wars. Nobody had told us that the Versailles Treaty was a blueprint for its successor. It was very difficult, growing

up in an English shire, watching how our sober elections were conducted, and how an unarmed police force went about their work, to conceive of whole nations succumbing to hysteria on the German and Italian patterns. No one had ever knocked on our doors in the middle of the night.

Munich demolished the last parochial railings that had isolated us through the years, when I was growing up in the little sea-coast town of Exmouth. After the ecstatic post-Munich honeymoon we knew, with complete certainty, that the roof would fall on us in one year or two. I shared in the general relief when Chamberlain stepped down from the plane waving his famous piece of paper. I was relieved but by no means reassured. I volunteered for the R.A.F. and stayed on the job awaiting a call-up until the spring of 1940, and bad as things were for everybody after that I don't think they were nearly as depressing as the eight months of the Phoney War. I would choose to relive any period of my life in preference to that interval of gloom, frustration, doubt and yammering boredom. When, at last, the Panzers began to roll westward, when Churchill took Chamberlain's place and the epic of Dunkirk was followed by the Battle of Britain, it was as though we had not survived a chain of frightful disasters, but had won a brilliant victory.

The alchemy of Churchill, months of brilliant sunshine, and the whiff of Gestapo breath in our nostrils, fused Left and Right in a way that would have seemed unimaginable a year before. Middle-aged men who had been calling one another rude names ever since the invasion of Abyssinia nearly five years before shared an amiable cliff-patrol in the Local Defence Volunteers, forerunner of the Home Guard. Younger men, who had been dragged apart by policemen at the Blackshirt scuffle on Chapel Hill, joined the same unit and travelled in convoy to military depots. People hoped and people grinned. People didn't give a damn about standing alone and fighting it out on the beaches. There was something else, too. Whenever I returned to Devon on leave I never once heard the words Left and Right bandied about. They cropped up again, of course, but not until around July 1945, when we all trooped off to the polls. (*Overture*, 118–127)

Before proceeding we must examine Delderfield's topsy-turvy attitude toward Aristotelian drama, which makes the reader transfer his attention nimbly in order to keep track of that number of characters clattering noisily about in that many subplots. In Chapter One, I criticized *Farewell the Tranquil Mind* because it violates Aristotle's maxims that plot is the key element of drama, that the characters serve the plot by enacting it, and that thought or theme emerges atmospherically as a backdrop to the plot. Such is not Delderfield's way. In one of his *Own Amusement* essays, he says "I have never been the kind of author who looks for his materials in terms of plot or even person." What does he do instead? He topsy-turvies Aristotle's scheme, giving precedence to drama's last element, the theme. "For better or worse I am far more deeply concerned with backgrounds. With me it is the canvas on which I am going to paint that is the essential piece of apparatus" (16). The poet W. H. Auden appreciated that preference for the larger picture, the potentially distracting background instead of a tightly focused plot. In *Musee des Beaux Arts*, Auden writes "when the aged are reverently, passionately waiting/ For the miraculous birth, there always must be/ Children who did not specially want it to happen, skating/ On a pond at the edge of a wood." He illustrates the generic point with a specific example. "In Breughel's *Icarus*, for instance: how everything turns away/ Quite leisurely from the disaster; the ploughman may/ Have heard the splash, the forsaken cry,/ But for him it was not an important failure." As presentational artists, what Breughel and Delderfield have in common is their preference for the larger picture, the broad canvas which contains various figures engaging in a range of actions which gather to a greatness when seen as constituent elements of a simple, bold design. Readers of Delderfield's *Avenue* novels must be alert to discover the simplicity of the action that emerges from the large number of subplots treading on one another's corns as they move forward together. How else could a writer proceed if he intends to make a small handful of families representative of the multitude which made England strong when the rest of Europe collapsed? This is how Delderfield concludes his (1958) Introduction to *The Dreaming Suburb: 1919–1940*.

> Life has moved at a terrifying tempo since the trench veterans came home to a land fit for heroes to live in after the 1918 Armistice, the real starting point of the story and in the decades that follow after the story ends Western Europe is still catching its breath in an attempt to keep up with the pace of events. I like to think of this book as a modest attempt to photograph the mood of the suburbs in the period between the break up of the old world and the perambulator days of an entirely new civilization ushered in by the bleat of Russia's first sputnik in the 'fifties. In the main, of course, the story concerns the personal lives of the twenty odd men and women who spent these years in the terrace houses of Manor Park Road but in a wider sense the mainspring of the book is the time in which they grew up, loved, laughed, despaired and had their being (ix-x).

Writing the usual reading of *The Forsyte Saga* would be less daunting than doing the same for *The Dreaming Suburb*, since there are fewer Forsytes, and their hopes along with their disappointments are more concentrated and less varied than the corresponding "dreams" of the Avenue dwellers. Were it attempted, a conventional reading would hop-scotch from this character group to that, in touch-and-go fashion, which is how the thirty-two chapters of Delderfield's novel are presented. Were it attempted, such a reading would be a kaleidoscope of colorbursting agitation, rather than a coherent commentary, or else it would be interminably long. What to do? I am going to provide a glancing summary of Delderfield's chapters, incomplete but nimble-winged, using his chapter titles as a walk-line enabling a rapid survey of persons and events. The first four of these walk-line sub-headings will be *The Avenue, Home-Coming, Prince Wakes Beauty,* and *Miss Clegg Takes A Lodger,* which demonstrates the touch-and-go hopscotchery of the novel's progress. The second volume, which will cover much less time and involve characters who by then will be very familiar to us, will be differently managed. Let us begin.

The Avenue

This story is an account of the lives of five families out of the hundred houses where four hundred people lived. It is the tale of "twenty-odd people," which began in the middle of World War I and ended, "again as a group, when the sun was high over the beaches of Dunkirk, and dreams were cast out by stark incredulity and fear." It begins when "men like Jim Carver were drifting home from hell to look for work" (3).

Home-Coming

Ada Carver had struggled for four years on a low diet and fatigue but did not succumb until Spanish 'flu and the disappointment of Jim's reassignment to the Army of Occupation in Germany in Spring 1919 sent her over the edge. She had moved the family to the Avenue when she knew for certain that she was pregnant again, and with her 19, 17 and 8-year-old children Louise, Archie and Judith, the twins Bernie and Boxer, and the new baby on the way, they would need more room. Her exhausting work routine was typical of many women serving on the home front.

> All through the war the Carvers had been a bare inch or two above subsistence level. Soldiers' wives, and 'teenage girls like Louise, could earn good money in munitions, but if they had gone into factories there would have been no one to care for the younger children, and Archie, now turned seventeen, was himself at work all day as a shop assistant.
>
> So Louise and Ada took shifts of part-time domestic work, office-cleaning, milk deliveries, and long hours at the camouflage-net yard. The war seemed to go on for ever and the children, apart from Archie, seemed never to grow beyond the jam-smearing stage. The moment Ada returned from her stints Louise began hers, and she took over the cooking and housework. Usually, her day began at dawn, and ended around midnight.
>
> Under these conditions it was not surprising that she succumbed so swiftly to the epidemic. What was surprising was that she had held out for more than four years. Even the veterans of the front-line trench system were pulled out every now and again, and sent into the rest billets. There were no rest billets available to women like Ada Carver in 1918—just Spanish influenza, at the end of the line. (*Suburb*, 5–6)

When Jim arrived at the house he had not seen before, summoned by Louise's message about Ada's declining health, he is a stranger to children who have been without him so long that they're not sure how to deal with him now. After kissing his wife's brow and touring the upstairs rooms, Jim is called down to the kitchen by Louise for a family meal.

> "I've made a stew, Dad. You must be hungry!"
>
> He clumped into the tiled kitchen, and found the children crowded round three sides of the table, with Louise already ladling from the saucepan.

He sat down, and for a moment nobody spoke. He realized they were waiting for a lead, and the awkward silence embarrassed him. He tried to think of something to say, but the utter inadequacy of family small talk kept him silent. Louise concentrated on the plates, and even Archie avoided his eye.

Suddenly Judith, the eight-year-old, burst into tears, and pushed her plate away. The odd tension broke as Louise's arm shot round her.

"Try, Judy—please try," she pleaded. "Daddy won't like it if you don't; Daddy wants you to try!"

The child's puffy face, framed in dark curls, touched Carver. He got up, and lifting Judith from her chair sat down in her place, putting the child on his knee. He spooned a slice of dumpling into her mouth and was absurdly gratified when she swallowed it, and smiled suddenly, nestling closer to him. He noticed then that she had brown eyes, like his own, and that her hair was deep chestnut, like his mother's. His contact with her melted something, far down in his breast, and he felt his eyelids twitch. Unable to speak, he twisted his mouth into a smile and immediately, to his intense relief, a ripple of smiles answered him from all sides of the table.

He cleared his throat and spooned up a mash of carrot and onion—there was barely a shred of meat on the plate.

"It's all right now," he told them; "I'll be home very soon and everything's going to be all right." (*Suburb*, 9)

The ice being broken, Jim and the children talk for a while. He tells Louise "I expect you'll need this," giving her two folded pound notes, and he hands new sixpence coins to the twins and Judy. At this, Archie suddenly rose, lit a cigarette, and blew smoke through his nose as he tossed some small change on the table-cloth for the kids to share. Jim perceived "something aloof and vaguely contemptuous in Archie's attitude," as though after being man of the house for four years "he resented his father's return, and was by no means ready to abdicate" (11-12), telegraphing clearly the difficulty they will have in trying to get along.

By the bye, Ada's pregnancy resulted in twin girls who were taken into care temporarily by the District Nurse; they became the war-brides of two American Army soldiers.

Prince Wakes Beauty

Eunice Frazier and her son Esme moved into the house next door to the Carvers the week after Ada died, and from his mother's bedroom eight-year-old Esme had "watched the funeral party leave" for the churchyard. Eunice had married into old money, but when Granny Frazier died her Kensington house was sold—on the advice of Mr. Harold Godbeer, representing the solicitors who "administered the estate"—and the widow let herself be persuaded that the sensible thing was to find a smaller house in "a pleasant outer suburb, something not too far from his own bachelor lodging in Addiscombe" (12-13). The young woman was "petite, flaxen-haired, blue-eyed, utterly trusting, and quite stupid." Her husband had adored her because she exemplified "the feminine helplessness sought after by the chivalrous." Lieutenant Frazier, who died on the Marne in 1914, had been "blown to pieces by a grenade, whilst kneeling to hold a water-bottle to the mouth of a wounded enemy," because in that autumn "there were still men who saw war in terms of Rupert Brooke's poetry." These being his parents, Esme possessed a romantic outlook, "part inherited, part cultivated by the bed time stories of his gentle mother, and the nineteenth-century romances he pored over in his grand-mother's house, from the moment he could tackle three-syllabled words."

> Like his mother Esme was never really aware of the present, but unlike her his mind was not a comfortable vacuum. On the contrary it seethed with action, ranging from single-handed captures of Spanish settlements, to participating in thundering cavalry charges, alongside Rupert of the Rhine, and Warwick the King-maker. (*Suburb*, 12–14)

Esme disliked Harold, a "spare, eager, bespectacled, and physically frail" person who was also "fussy, pedantic, and inclined to be pompous" with the pomposity of a man unsure of himself. He was, on the other hand, "kind, amiable, and gen-uinely sympathetic" to Eunice, whose ignorance of money would lead her to the poorhouse unless someone as astute as he came to her rescue. But Esme disliked him, and Eunice so lacked decisiveness that her son's opinion would settle the mat-ter if it ever came up (15).

When the Fraziers arrived in the neighborhood, Esme immediately began exploring it, searching in the real world for the enchantments he found in read-ing, pushing along the paths leading into Manor Woods until he came in sight of the Manor itself.

> He stopped short against the crumbling stone balustrade that bordered the overgrown lawn. As he came upon it suddenly, from the deep shade of the woods, its impact was considerable, for it was huge, rambling, and awesomely empty. Once white, its porti-coed façade was now a dirty grey. Plaster was falling away from the cornices, and the wood-work of the window-panes was rotting. Some of its first-floor windows were bro-ken, and all were cob-webbed, and thick with grime. The outhouses were beginning to fall in, and some of the garden ornaments that bordered the terrace had been over-turned and chipped. Broken flower-pots littered the weed-sprouting drive, and festoons of ivy, honeysuckle, and red creeper were climbing right across its face, in some cases half obscuring the shattered, upstairs windows.
>
> There was a small lake within a stone's throw of the porch, its surface thick with water-lilies. In the middle of the lake was a tiny islet, studded with silver birches, and through them Esme could just glimpse the roof of a summer-house.
>
> What struck him most forcibly about the ruin was the quiet that surrounded it, a quiet so different from that of the woods, a quiet that seemed to have endured for a century, as though the last carriage wheels to crunch the weed-grown forecourt, were those in the days of the Prince Regent and Beau Brummel. It was an eerie, man-made quiet; sad, deliberate, and very frightening for a child of eight.

He was standing there wondering if he could ever have the courage to climb the balustrade, and peep through the windows, when he heard a twig crack immediately behind him. He wheeled around poised to flee, back through the woods, across the field, and into the Avenue, away from this eerie stillness to the safety of people and houses.

Then he relaxed, for it was only a child, a girl about his own age, and as she picked her way over the straggling briars towards him, he recognized her as the girl from next door, the girl whose mother's funeral he had watched a week or two ago.

Judy had followed him into the woods confident that he would welcome her company and be more gracious than Berni and Boxer, who "hardly ever let me play, except when they want a squaw." That is roughly what Esme has in mind since he does not wish to play house, which he rightly supposes "would involve dolls as its principal stage properties" (19–20). They have different dreams but Judy can play with him if she becomes Tonto to his Lone Ranger. He reads in Judy's eyes "her complete acceptance of him, not merely as a protective male, but as a hero, straight out of one of his books," and he orchestrates with her as an audience and minor participant the "sword-play" and "sudden ambuscades" he is determined to translate from the world of dreams into the real world. When Judy tells him the story of Sleeping Beauty, Esme is interested because it is new to him, and it may provide exciting opportunities for heroic action. When during her long sleep Beauty feels something brush her lips as Esme flourishes his crooked-branch-pistol over her head, she interprets that slight touch as an heroic lover's kiss. The fairy tale has come true, or rather, will become true. Prince has awakened Beauty.

> In kissing her he had transformed her into a real Princess. She knew now that she would marry him, would never contemplate marrying anyone else and she knew with an intuitiveness beyond her years, that this was not the time to tell him, but the time to tread warily, and let him realize he had a ready-made audience for any venture he might pursue in the future. How lucky it was that he lived next door, and because of today, no one else should ever have him, no one, boy or girl, never, never, never. *Suburb*, 24)

Miss Clegg Takes A Lodger

Edith Clegg and her sister Becky had lived in the Avenue since 1911, when most of the suburb houses had yet to be built. At first Edith had been homesick for the vicarage in North Devon where her father had been pastor for forty years until his death, but over time she came to prefer "the casual neighborliness of the suburb, and the undoubted convenience of the shops, to the stifling intimacy of the Devon village, and the wretched isolation of the grim old parsonage." And living in the suburb, Becky had fewer "spells." Twenty years before the Avenue story begins, Becky had confided in Edith that she was in love and "needed money to elope with Saul Cooper, the painter who had bewitched her." That ended very badly. Saul beat her savagely and terrorized her mentally; their bastard child had been still-born; and when Edith found her abandoned in a wretched London flat,

Becky had been reduced to a near imbecile. The older sister had to fight Parson Clegg along with the "parish busybodies" about bringing the poor girl home or "sending her to an institution" (25-28). Her mental age had since risen to about seven, but during her "spells" Edith had to watch her carefully. These could be provoked by anything upsetting.

Edith had another difficulty to deal with, i.e., her financial situation was becoming precarious.

> About the time Jim Carver came home, and Esme bewitched Judith in the gazebo of the old Manor, Edith Clegg received her first letter from the Barnstaple solicitors, who were executors of Parson Clegg's modest fortune. (*Suburb*, 31)

Edith lived frugally, but "she made no allowance for the rising cost of living after 1914", being barely aware of it until the Barnstaple solicitors' letter arrived, giving her "a severe jolt." She sought advice from the local bank manager, a sensible fellow who invested her thousand pounds "in gilt-edged" and, after questioning her closely for an hour, advised Edith to "set up as a music-teacher, and let one of her bedrooms", which was excellent advice. She soon attracted piano students burning to master "A Merry Peasant Returning from Work," the benefit for Edith being that it helped bring her "out of the tiny world in which she and Becky had been living since they left Devon" (31-34).

The arrival of Ted Hartnell, the lodger, "provided a sharper and more permanent break with the past." Ted was "probably about nineteen," sprightly and pleasant, and the two of them quickly discovered in one another the answer to their hopes. Edith had laid out nine pounds to prepare the room for him, and while everything was second-hand, she had got her money's worth. Concerned about the rent, Ted asks "How much in all?" But not having rented before, she has no idea, and asks him what the "usual" was. Delighted by the contrast between Edith's agreeableness and the rather different attitude of his earlier landladies, Ted gives her good advice and they soon come to a satisfying arrangement. Could he play music in the house? Edith thinks that would be fine, which delighted Ted because he had no interest in his job except that it paid the rent.

> He was a stonemason simply because a post at the stonemason's yard had presented itself the week he left school, more than four years ago. His mission in life was to play jazz tunes in public, or, if no such opportunity presented itself, to listen to them, hum them, beat them out with his chisel as he chipped marble gravestones, tap them with his feet as he munched lunchtime sandwiches, pick them out, chord by chord, on his wire-strung banjolele, or follow them, beat by beat, on his portable gramophone—now, alas, in a Hammersmith pawnbroker's window. (*Suburb*, 37-38)

Carvers, At Work And Play

Jim fought the Kaiser for four years, but, appalled by the death of a teen-aged boy sent into harm's way just moments before the Armistice took effect, by the stupidity of "a pot-bellied Major fresh from base," he "changed sides." In the future, "he was to fight his own people" (8). An excellent worker in robust health, he was competing for jobs against a million ex-servicemen, most "much younger than Jim," many with pre-war training to attract employers. Rather than "take refuge in the general bitterness that had soured the easy comradeship of the trenches by the time the first anniversay of the Armistice came around," Carver began relating "his personal problems to those of society" (39–40). Doing so made him a *de facto* cultural historian, evaluating contemporary phenomena on-the-spot, while England's post-war difficulties worsened.

Meanwhile, Archie Carver typified those males in the Avenue who had been too young for combat but old enough to be "men about the house," which he undertook as an errand boy in the provisioning, or grocery, trade. Observing that "some people were getting rich very quickly," Archie began to study that phenomenon "in relation to the people he worked among," like sixty-year-old Mr. Cole. This man, as Archie discovered, surreptitiously "added various packages to certain of the boxes" he personally delivered to certain houses, while the fully-alerted Archie observed "where the boxes were going," which satisfied his curiosity. Instead of telling the store manager about "the chief storeman's excessive zeal," Archie approached Cole with an alternative program. The aging storeman would remain in the cozy shop, while Archie would manage the deliveries—a piece of bold blackmail which Mr. Cole found acceptable.

This system worked well for Archie, who had taken his first step towards a career of marginal criminality, using wartime shortages of provisions to enrich himself and, more importantly, to boost his self-approbation, self-adulation in fact, which paid off in the sexual favors his under-the-counter women customers began providing between-the-sheets. Rita Ramage was the first of these, because her bed was not encumbered by her husband.

> She was the wife of an ex-officer in the Tank Corps, who spent most of his time in hospitals, undergoing a series of operations designed to make him walk again. So far, they had not succeeded, and his wife Rita had ceased to pretend to herself that they ever would. Being a realist she had come to terms with herself emotionally, and had decided that she was too young, at thirty-three, to enter the purdah reserved for the young wives of totally disabled veterans. She was a full-blooded, buxom woman, and she needed a whole man, not two-thirds of one. (*Suburb*, 45)

The tall, muscular under-the-counter delivery boy was ready to play. Rita remained his mistress until Spring of 1922. She became a habit, "like eating and shaving," which freed Archie's brain to focus upon "the more important matter" of getting his own shop, the better to work under-the-counter for himself alone. Outraged by his neglect, Rita quarreled with him; he "consoled himself with the red-headed cashier, Lorna," who had not before been able to catch his wandering eye. So far, very good. But when Rita began periodically invading Mr. Brooks's store, astonishing his customers by berating her errant lover, demanding an immediate return to the bedroom, Brooks ordered her from his place of business. Rita answered him by screaming at Archie "I wonder if this little bastard knows how much you've had out of the till during the years you've been working here," and the Carver who had been a thief as well as an adulterer was dismissed. Being out of a job meant putting his mind to the problem of finding another way to get on board the gravy-train, more profitably this time, and more securely.

Mutiny At Havelock Park

Boxer and Berni, the Carver twins, were the neighborhood pranksters. They employed the string-and-wallet trick to mislead the unwary, hooting with delight when the victim looked around furtively upon seeing the purse at her feet, bent down to claim it, then quickly recovered herself, and walked past with as much dignity as she could manage. They did nobody any harm and the Avenue chuckled over their roguery. They were "the inseparables," the bond between them having been established the day Boxer fell through the ice on a duckpond and Berni barely managed to save him: "With the speed of a young baboon, he flung himself at the elm branch immediately above him, and swung out, hand over hand, to the spot were Boxer was shoulder deep in jagged fragments of ice..." (59). Boxer lived, and Berni's "dream" came into being. His mission would be "to make sure that Boxer survived, nothing else was of the smallest importance." Thus, when Boxer was in danger of a beating by Mr. Little at Havelock Park Elementary School, a beating with a cane that the vicious disciplinarian whipped "from his trouser-leg", for an offence the boy had not been guilty of, Berni "in a flash seized the cane from behind, wrenched it from the headmaster's grip, and flung it high over the railings into Cawnpore Road," his action provoking the "long drawn-out gasp" of the other students. Berni was adamant in his defense: "Boxer wasn't moving. He stopped, soon as the whistle blew. Soon as he could!" Mr. Little went into retirement, Boxer and Berni were transferred into another school, and the rest of the Havelock Park faculty, along with "the women of the Avenue," deeply impressed by the boys' mutual devotion and their honesty under pressure, rejoiced at the return of civility to the school (56–71).

Archie Takes A Holiday

By autumn, 1923, the families of the Avenue had finished grieving for the deaths of their soldier relatives and "adjusted themselves to patterns they were to maintain throughout the decades between the wars" (71). Jim Carver did not seek another wife because Louise tended to the family and "he was now wedded to politics." A fellow moving-company driver persuaded him to join the Labour Party, and Jim applied himself to the Party's public awareness activities "with the same quiet doggedness that characterized everything he did" (71–72). His domestic distractions were few because Louise was a better housewife than Ada had ever been, and Jim was undistracted from "his dream of the Brotherhood of Man", his gaze being fixed on the day Labour would "obtain a majority at Westminster." That would be the time to enjoy life, not now (73).

Archie, meanwhile, was occupied with his own dreams, "and these were of a somewhat more practical nature." Working in grocery stores since the age of fourteen, he had become convinced that "to make money *all* the time, one must deal in food." Quick returns could be had elsewhere, but few lines of work yielded "steady profits come war come slump" (73–74). His experience with Rita Ramage "whetted his appetite for women," but as someone else's employee "he could never have the means to buy their company for long enough to make them need him for his own sake," as Rita had done. That being his goal, Archie toured the area looking for "a derelict business he could buy for fifty pounds or less," and could stock with provisions acquired on credit. He would not waste his youth on employment that "led but to the grave, via retirement, at sixty-five, on a four-pound-a-week pension" (74–75).

But Archie's compulsion to enjoy women on his way to wealth nearly capsized his long-term planning, for at this time his girl-friend was Edna Gittens, whose father was "a diabetic tram-conductor" and Edna's siblings "innumerable." Nineteen and "incurably lazy", she regularly copulated with Archie in "a grassy hollow bordering the golf-links." When Archie bought that "battered side-car" for his motorcycle in which camping equipment might be stowed and invited Edna to enjoy the wide outdoors, she agreed, with the proviso that her twenty-one-year-old sister Hilda should accompany them. "The camping holiday was a great success," and before long Archie learned that he had impregnated both the Gitten girls. Mr. Gittens located him, introduced himself, and said, civilly, "You must be t'lad who's put both my girls in t'family way." What could be done in this dilemma which thwarted Archie's dreams? Then out of the blue, the worried father-of-his-town was visited by Toni Piretta, who owned "the corner shop" where most of the Avenue residents brought groceries. Toni, too, had a dream, which was that his homely daughter secure a husband and provide him with grandchildren to tumble with, while he enjoyed retirement. Archie would become the owner of his store. There must be a divinity which shapes the ends of idiots and overreaching whoremasters who endanger their own rough-hewn schemes, and advances them despite their own folly.

New Worlds For Edith

When Ted Hartnell was sacked for spoiling the gravestone he was inscribing by "Red, red, robining" with his chisel, "bob-bob-bobbing long after he should have laid aside his tools, and shifted his position to begin another line" (84), Edith almost lost him and with him a close companion who made Becky's life more cheerful. Mr. Foster, the "ardent churchgoer" who had employed him, was "profoundly shocked" by the funereal blasphemy which Ted visited upon the stone. With his parting pay, he gave him sound advice: "Get yourself a job in a jazz band, lad. Maybe somebody will pay you to bob-bob-bob from morning to night!" Although an edge of sarcasm was probably intended, it was the nudge Ted needed, since until then "it had never occurred to him to try and convert his obsession into a means of livelihood" (85). His future lies that way.

Hartnell returned to the Avenue and fretted about his disemployment, but Edith quickly came to a decision about him and her own household.

> "I've decided, Teddy; you mustn't leave here. It would be very bad for Becky; besides, wherever you go, they won't let you play your gramophone. I'm going in to talk it over with Mr. Carver! Go down now, and play something for Becky. She's in the kitchen shelling peas." (*Suburb*, 86)

In recent years Edith had made a habit of consulting Jim about practical matters, for she trusted his judgment ever since the day he took her to see the Unknown Warrior's tomb in Westminster Abbey and explained to Edith its cultural significance. "Touched by this twittery little spinster's eagerness to identify herself with the national symbol", he was "gentle and mildly gallant towards her that day," which turned him into "a sage" in Edith's mind. Jim advises her that Hartnell will have to go find other employment, since he can't stay without a job, and "you'll have to let his room to someone else, won't you?" Yet Edith considers the matter "as good as settled" because Mr. Carver had taken an interest in it.

"In the event it was both Edith and Ted who found jobs." Jim got Ted part-time work as an auction hand, and since he was home half the week, Edith could range farther and buy cheaper. On one of these shopping expeditions, she saw the advertisement on the cinema building: they needed a replacement pianist to accompany their silent movies. The proprietor was skeptical, but Edith, anticipating a gloomy dismissal, got her dander up and said with "a pertness that surprised" him, "I can play anything, and play it in the dark. Why don't you try me?" (91). He did, and she could.

> She sat down, cracked her finger-joints, and sailed into *Song of the Bells*, after which, without waiting for his comment, she played exerpts from all the scores he had mentioned...Thus began a new life for Edith, a warm, exciting life, that had little connection with Becky, or Ted, and all the habits that had fenced her round in the past. She acquired, almost overnight, a new personality. (*Suburb*, 92)

Elaine Frith And The Facts Of Life

These were Judith Carver's best years since she had Esme all to herself years before Elaine, of Number Seventeen, "moved between them" (93). Judy's family never learned about her diary or the "Esme-Box" she kept hidden under hair ribbons in the drawer she and Louise shared. They teased her, but did not grasp how serious her affection was. Nor did Esme, even as "the sorely-wounded Arthur" resting his arm on her shoulder while she assisted him "to the barge on the margin of the lake," suspect that Judy saw herself "cooking and sewing" for him, after he had "ducked laughingly beneath the shower of confetti and hustled her into a beribboned taxi" after their marriage (96). Her dream was completely private.

Now whereas most of the Avenue dwellers knew something of all their neighbors, "the Friths were the exception, for all that anybody knew about them was that they emerged at 10:15 every Sunday morning" and walked towards "a Methodist chapel in a neighboring suburb," the parental pair walking before, the two children behind. They were the unhappiest family in the suburb, and Mrs. Frith was the foundation and cause of their misery. Her cold tyranny poisoned the lives of her husband and children. Shortly before Esther Frith's aunt died, in 1907, the family's solicitors inventoried the books in the "vast, dingy mansion" where the aunt had lived as "a virtual recluse." Edgar Frith, employed by a local antique dealer and bookseller, was for weeks "perched on the high stools in front of the shelves," and Esther, who was driven by loneliness, started helping him, and a mild attachment developed (100). Such an attachment could not survive the marriage that followed. Edgar had gone in unto her as a husband will, and she conceived, yet was violently disgusted by that which had been done to her. She abruptly cut off Edgar's supply. As for the children, Esther

> regarded them as living evidence of the indignities she had suffered, as witnesses of the silent, stealthy affronts meted out to her by Edgar, during the first three years of their marriage. (*Suburb*, 103).

She distanced her offspring from "normal contact with other children," and "set out to regulate their reading matter, conversation, and thoughts" in her attempt to isolate them from the horrid contamination of sex" (104).

However, Elaine was a problem for she had spirit and, unlike Sydney, was not a hypocrite. Whipping her only made Elaine more determined to escape her mother's tyranny. One afternoon when she was twelve and had the house to herself, conjecturing that books "confiscated by her mother were not destroyed, but were secreted somewhere about the house," she began a careful search which ended in "climbing through the ceiling-trap" into the attic, where she found pay dirt: "a thin book wrapped in brown paper," Edgar's "honeymoon purchase, *The Art of Marriage*, long since abandoned and forgotten" (105). Coming to the diagrams, Elaine knew she had been on the right scent. "She did not understand much of what she read but it was at once obvious that she had stumbled on the key to something tremendously important" (106). Thrusting the book down the neck of her dress, she closed the trunk, stepped over the rafters to the aperture, and told Sydney, "There's nothing up here at all, just a pile of old junk." Elaine is now on a mission, one which will disclose the dream secreted in her dawning awareness. "She felt like a counter-spy who, after prodigious effort, has at last broken down the enemy's code" (107).

Alibi For Archie

Jim Carver and his eldest son have differing attitudes towards other people. Jim is revolted by the pot-bellied Major's sacrifice of the young soldier in hopes of earning glory and promotion for himself, while Archie and the Major are as alike as peas in a pod in their self-absorption. Archie does not want to be interrupted by Toni Piretta while he marinates in his paternity problem.

> Haven't I enough on my mind at the moment? *Both* of them. Edna, who must have been sound asleep when it happened, and that giggling sister of hers, who had it worked out from the beginning! Their fertility infuriated him. (*Suburb*, 109))

Maybe—although he is *more* infuriated by being outsmarted, being taken down the garden path by intellectual inferiors. But Piretta, patiently approaching this brooding solipsist, finally gets his attention. That is only possible because Toni addresses his auditor's self-interest, the infallible method for accessing his mind.

> "They tella me you a grocer-boy, hey?" he pursued cautiously.
> "I've worked in provision shops," said Archie, with dignity. "What of it? What's that to you, Toni?"
> Like most Englishmen of the suburbs, Archie was very proud of his nationality when he conversed with a Latin. Mr. Piretta ignored the snub, and became more earnest.
> "Then I maka da bargain with you!" he said flatly. "you worka for me, and I maka da bargain with you!"
> Archie was interested, in spite of himself. Slowly he shook off his mood of self-pity. At the prospect of a commercial deal he found he could forget the Gittens' girls, at least temporarily. It was whispered along the Avenue that Toni Piretta was rich, that he had done extremely well at the corner shop he had opened shortly after Italy joined the ranks of the gallant Allies, and, by so doing, released him from the crippling limi-tations of an alien in a country at war. What sort of "bargain" could the old boy be contemplating? Some sort of insurance wangle possibly. A fire? Surely not? A claim in damaged goods, that needed some sort of independent verification? Groping with vari-ous possibilities, Archie forgot the Gittens' girls altogether.
> "What are you getting at, Toni?" (*Suburb*, 110)

As he realizes that Piretta wants him to marry his daughter Maria, Archie turns his liability into an asset by bluntly admitting his situation. "It had one advantage, presenting as it did incontrovertible proof of the prospective husband's virility. It made the ultimate appearance of a Piretta grandchild almost a certainty" (113). As

Chaucer's Wife of Bath remarks, Everything's for sale, Whatever you have, put it on the market. Archie intuitively knows that and instinctively follows her advice. And his heart warms towards his father-in-law-to-be because he recognizes that Toni's proposal is "the final, triumphant unfolding of a long, carefully-planned campaign to secure a son-in-law, a lively young partner, and an heir at one stroke" (115).

In negotiation with the parents of the pregnant girls, Toni had the advantage of knowing the family personally. He knew that they "in their casual, indolent way, were realists and would assess the value of a lump sum far above an affiliation order," because such orders were difficult to execute "on a footloose young fellow like Archie" (115). He would offer the Gittens one hundred pounds, they would accept the offer, and the matter would be settled.

Harold As Giant-Killer

Though Eunice appreciated his ministrations, she never gave Harold Godbeer an opportunity to propose marriage. Had Esme been a girl, she reflected, the child "would have been quick to appreciate" Harold's "comforting knack of being in the right place when he was wanted, and of withdrawing the moment he was not." Esme, her son, was "a strange, proud, aloof little boy" rapidly growing into "an introspective young man, with his nose in a book." Eunice did what she had always done, namely, "she left the decision to somebody else," Esme as it turned out. But to persuade the strange boy of his worth, Harold would have to perform some heroic action as a rite-of-passage to the fair dame. An occasion arises when Esme and Judith are cheated at the Easter Monday Fair. Judy asks for "change" from the half-crown she had handed the dishonest old crone, which had immediately been dropped into her moneybag along with coins the woman had taken from earlier customers.

> The crone looked up, a trifle sharply.
> "Change, dearie! That was a penny!"
> Judith's stomach cart-wheeled, and Esme, sensing that something was wrong, came back to the stall.
> "It was a half-crown," whispered Judith: "You *know* it was a half-crown; you *looked* at it!"
> She turned desperately to Esme, beseeching instant corroboration. "I had a half-crown, Archie's half-crown, and she says it was a penny!"
> Shame and fear clutched at Esme. Like his mother, he hated a scene, any sort of scene, but his reputation was at stake. There was no evading Judith's appeal.
> "She *had* half-a-crown and a threepenny-bit; she didn't have a penny," he said hoarsely.
> Judith, immensely relieved, turned back to the woman. "You see, I had two-and-nine altogether. Here's my threepenny-bit," and she began fumbling with the tiny knot in her handkerchief.

The old woman looked at them bleakly, then she turned her head towards a bell
tent, pitched immediately behind her stall.
"Fred," she called, "come on out and get rid o' these bloody little shysters, will
yer?" (*Suburb*, 121)

Esme is not fit to deal with the emerging situation and the policeman he summons
to their aid, knowing precisely what has happened, also knew he "had not the
slightest chance of proving" it. Thus he took the line of least resistance and said,
"Run along kids, and don't get into any more trouble" (123). The blatant injustice
of what had been done to Judy struck Esme hard, but he could not see what to
do—until he saw Harold Godbeer nearby. "Very well," he said; "I'll fetch my lawyer!" which set the carnival crooks to laughing uproariously.

Harold came to their aid, told the young lady who had been victimized "Make
an apron of your skirt, Judith!" and began scooping bag after bag of the confetti the
crone had been selling, "smartly slapping at the claw-like hand of the old woman,
as she reached out to check him" (127). Esme's eyes widened with "undisguised
admiration" at this novel procedure for righting the injustice by taking out in trade
what had been stolen from Judy. When they arrived back home, Esme sought his
mother, brushing her hair at her mirror, and asked her quietly, "Mother, why don't
you marry Uncle Harold and be done with it?" (129). And so she did.

Jim Burns A 'Bus

The General Strike of 1926 is the historical occasion Delderfield employs to
illustrate the range of political attitudes that were being enacted in the England of
that time. He reduces the Strike's complexity to a neighborhood group flanked by
two individuals, Jim and Archie Carver. The Strike did not "seriously involve" the
Avenue "as a community," since few industrial workers lived there. Half a dozen
suburb dwellers took a few days off to march around "hoping to witness something
exciting," since they thought any work stoppage that large "should provide some
visual evidence of a real revolution." But "fiery talk" could not arouse the families
we have been becoming familiar with "to look upon the event as anything more
than a welcome break in the monotony of their everyday lives." One could sense
among them "a curious detachment" from the emergency (130-31). But with Jim
Carver it was not so, and Archie outraged him by adopting political convictions
which reduced to the desire to continue enriching himself. Jim Carver is a social
patriot, his son a profiteer.

Jim could see "no evidence of true political awareness in the suburb, no true
recognition of the class struggle, as set down in the pamphlets and statistical sur-
veys" he was now spending eighteen hours a day distributing as a Labour Party
activist, endangering his own employment by espousing views frowned upon by
his employers (131-134). The 'bus that became the focus of the potentially dangerous ruckus was driven by two university students, "each swathed in a colorful

scarf" as though they had dressed themselves for a sporting match. The vehicle was stopped by "a small road obstruction, set up by a picket under the leadership of a huge Clydeside docker." One of the students climbed down to remove the obstruction, looking for trouble he had not really expected to find. Jim was there, and suddenly found himself "hitting in all directions" as his coat was "ripped down from the lapel, and his tie was jerked into a choking knot." Then the smoke began rising all about them. Jim escaped the commotion only because he wished to save the dog, which "caused him to forget everything else." His instinct for cover returned after the lapse of eight years, and he dived "into a maze of empty side-streets," set down the dog and took stock of his minor injuries (135). And he reflected upon the harrowing experience.

He was "not a man to look upon a gaol-sentence as a badge of class loyalty," being too near "the era when such a thing branded a man for life." He felt "a sense of shame that he had taken part in destruction of public property," and had moreover "struck out at a uniformed policeman." Is Jim a revolutionary? If so, it is upon an English model of action which discourages flamethrowing violence. But there was something he had seen—"his own son, wearing the arm-band of the reactionaries, who were successful in breaking the strike." His son had taken the side of "a Government determined to starve the miners into abject submission. He had to know if the boy realized the enormity of his betrayal of their class, or if he had simply donned the arm-band for a lark" (136-138). When father and son could not avoid meeting as they walked towards the Avenue, they engaged in some "Oh, yeah? Yeah!" mutual insults which for Archie was simply a continuation of his teenage contempt of his father. But for Jim the situation was as serious as it could be. "From now on, Archie was not a son—just one of the enemy, and could be treated as such, impersonally, if need be, mercilessly."

> "Well," he said, with a bitterness that was uncharacteristic of him on public platforms, "I'll tell you one thing, Archie: "I'd as lief see you dead as wearing that arm-band. So, from today, don't show up at Number Twenty while I'm there, or I'll make sure you're kicked all the way from the front-gate to the feather-bed you've hooked for yourself with that Eyetie! If you don't think I'm capable of doing it, you're welcome to try me, son, any time you like; and if you've a mind to, right outside the front-windows of your bloody customers!"
>
> Under his father's calm gaze Archie lost the initiative, and fell back on bluster. He had never thought of his father as a political opponent, but simply as a well-meaning failure, whose principles—heard over the kitchen table *ad nauseam* during the first years of Jim's return home—would keep him poor, and shabby, for the rest of his life. Archie's politics were, and always would be, the short-term enrichment of Archie. His enlistment as a "Special," during this present ridiculous business, was an act of simple insurance, agreed upon with Toni, his father-in-law, as a step towards the preservation of law and order; and the rapid return to normal deliveries and business conditions. When he had presented himself at the police station, and volunteered to ride a 'bus

platform for an hour or so, he had never even thought of his father, only of the need for business-men to stand together against the *hoipolloi*, whose junketings were beneath notice until they caused a falling off of shop trade. He was shocked, despite his natural arrogance, by his father's forbidding him the house. (*Suburb*, 139)

Edith In Mourning.

Whenever Edith recollects 1926, it is not the General Strike that she thinks of but Ted being hired by a dance band, and the death of Rudolph Valentino. Hartnell's debut as a professional musician had been partly her own doing. When Mr. Billings, owner of the cinema for which she is the piano accompanist, describes the stunning visual effect of the silent *Ben Hur* he has just previewed, Edith reflects upon the limitations of the silent film. "I have always thought that it is such a pity we have to *see* things without *hearing* them," she tells Billings. "I can't do really con-vincing bangs, when buildings fall, and cannons go off." Having thought about it, Edith concludes that someone with Ted's talent could make the sleigh bells "tin-kle" as they ought to do when the sled's passengers are fleeing from "those terrible wolves." It would make "*such* a difference, now, wouldn't it?" (142). As accompa-nist for *Ben Hur*, Hartnell was "almost as sensational" as the movie itself. Yet the French Revolution picture *The Tragic Queen* was even more moving. Audiences heard galloping horses, salvoes of cannon, and "the clash of arms on the stair-case of Versailles." When Marie Antoinette attempted to make "a scaffold speech above the monotonous roll of drums," the effect was even better and the guillo-tine scene better yet.

> Urged on by Edith, who, with shining eyes, was thundering out the *Marsaillaise*, Ted flung himself into the business of producing an increasingly rapid tattoo on kettle and side-drums, the rhythm culminating in the final shattering "*kerlunk*" on the bass drum. This signified the fall of the knife, and produced gasps of horror from electrified audi-ences." (*Suburb*, 142–43)

Having learned that something interesting was going on at the cinema house, Al Swinger, who managed a dance band, came to investigate. He found Ted Hartnell, and auditioned him on the spot. The *Rhythmateers'* drummer had quit, and after Swinger had performed *Valencia* with the potential new drummer, tell-ing Ted "give it all you've got," he hired him. After that career change, Ted's hours were such that "there were no more front-room soirees, no long, gossipy meals in the kitchen, with Becky" (144–147). That was a serious loss for the two sisters who considered him family.

Still more crushing for Edith was the loss announced by the headline "*Valentino Dead.*" He was not just a Balkan monarch or a British Prime Minister, but an elec-trifying screen presence who so stirred Edith's imaginative capacity that she was shaken to her depths. She bought a paper to read all about it, knew that she could not go to work that day, sat on a "fallen elm" until she had gained "sufficient resolution" to read the headline, and found to her surprise that it said nothing about Rudy's death. It only announced that Germany had entered the League of Nations.

> She could not remember feeling like this before, not even when Becky ran away, or was found, reclaimed, and brought home to the vicarage, speechless, bruised, and half an idiot. On that occasion she had been able to act; to argue with her father and the Bishop, to nurse her sister, to throw herself into the desperate search for Becky's lost wits. This was very different. There was nothing whatever she could do.

Setting out towards the cinema to discuss Valentino's death with Mr. Billings, she felt light-headed and faintly sick. When Archie Carver came out of his shop "carrying a tub of apples" and greeted her pleasantly, "Lovely afternoon, Miss Clegg!", she "neither heard nor saw him" (147-149).

Schooldays For Three

"Bastion of Privilege" narrates Delderfield's own experience, which was typical of English education when he was a boy. His recollections illustrate "the vast distances we have moved towards the establishment of a permissive society" (*Amusement*, 146), which was hardly what the Left had in mind when it attacked the "privileged" system that favored children of the rich and suppressed the poor. Headmasters ranged from brutal disciplinarians, like the one the Carver twins bested in *Mutiny At Havelock Park*, to the genially avuncular headmaster of Delderfield's novel *To Serve Them All My Days*. Longjohn Silverton was one of those better teachers for Esme, the kind whose personality was "imprinted on a boy's mind for all time" (*Suburb*, 152).

Longjohn was not the avuncular type, but a hardbitten trench survivor who had been repaired by plastic surgeons as best they could, his eyes having "survived the blast of flame" that disfigured his face. He had further injuries which semi-crippled him, but "made very light of these, so light indeed that he drew no war pension after 1924."

> Silverton had that curious sense of peace and balance that was a legacy of front-line survival. Emotionally he was difficult to disturb, but he could pretend to cold, devastating anger if he thought anger served a good purpose. He had a deep love of scholarship, and a strange abiding tolerance with every living creature under the age of eighteen. Beyond that notch, humanity could go hang, collectively and individually. (*Suburb*, 151)

He is the ideal teacher for Esme Frazier, who himself is a cripple of sorts. He made no friends among the Avenue's children, Judith being less a friend than "a shield-bearing acolyte," and he took no pleasure in boys his own age, who were "lamentably lacking in imagination" and "dull partners in his eccentric games of make-believe." Other boys soon discovered "the real Esme," who when attacked fought back like a tiger. Bigger boys, like Boxer Carver, "feared his biting tongue more than his sudden rages" (151-52). Esme is near enough to a freak that Longjohn would eventually take him aside and guide his development, so far as the boy proved amenable.

The prelude to Silverton's taking him under his wing centered upon "the bargain between Esme and the twins." On the way home together one day, Esme addressed Berni saying "3-B for you and me next term." That comment touched "a hidden spring in Bernard's mind. He stopped short, and turned to Esme," desperation in his frown. "They're going to split us up, young Frazier. Boxer's going to 3-C. I saw the list" (153). But the Carver twins are known as "the inseparables." Will the school succeed in separating them because of their unequal academic abilities? Esme met the challenge, being a shrewd and observant boy, and a plan emerged for keeping all three of them at the same academic level. "They perfected their system throughout that first term, and by the end of the year it was very nearly foolproof" (155), the system hinging upon both in-class and at-home cheating, which on the face of it helped the twins, though in reality it harmed all three boys.

When a minor prank involving the Girl's Grammar School next door provides him the opportunity, Silverton makes his pitch. "'Sit down, Frazier,' he said shortly; 'it's time you and I had our first intelligent conversation. How old are you now?'" Fifteen, he replies, and a lengthy silence follows. Then Longjohn proceeds.

> "I've known all about your arrangements with the Carvers for some time past, Frazier. I tell you this straight away so that we can start on open ground. What I *am* anxious to know is how long do you intend to keep it up? Until you leave? Until you've failed School Cert., and throw away every opportunity you ever had of learning *how* to learn?

Silverton explains to Esme what he had actually been doing. He had been steadily "knocking-away footholds for the chap you think you're helping."

> "It's been going on for hundreds of years, and it's always disguised as comradeship. All his life now Carver One [Boxer] will have to rely on somebody else. That isn't your fault, not in the main, and it is difficult to blame his brother, either, but it's still a fact, and not a very pleasant one, is it?" (*Suburb,* 161)

Esme agrees, it is not a pleasant fact, and after allowing the boy time to collect himself, Longjohn continues:

> "It's like this, Frazier, the chaps here fall mainly into two streams, those who are going to have to earn a living with their hands...and the chaps who are able to *create* something out of themselves, chaps who can do something without big organizations, and lots of apparatus behind them. You're one of that minority. You might not know it yet, but you are, most definitely. In other words, you've got a spark, and all the time you've been here you've been doing your best to stamp it out. Do you follow me?"
> "Yes, sir," said Esme, almost inaudibly. (*Suburb,* 161)

A question-and-answer talk follows as Silverton asks about Esme's family background, and then he springs the *piece de resistance,* pulling from his files a paper Esme wrote over a year ago, four pages titled *Books I Enjoyed*—which had taken him ninety minutes though they passed like five. The shrewd instructor looks for the sentence: "A sentence here…where is it…listen…right at the end."

> The books I liked, I think, are the books that people liked writing. You can tell this somehow. It's like humming a tune, that sticks in your mind. You know that what they are writing about was in their minds a long time before it was written down.
>   "That's the spark I told you about, Esme. Stop treading on it and try blowing on it for a change." (*Suburb*, 163)

Silverton has not the "slightest doubt" that this fifteen-year-old will "arrive with drums in the end," and should he need any editorial advice along the way, he's available and can provide the blue-pencil that a budding writer may need.

The Ice Cracks At Number Seventeen

The narrator says that sometimes a decade would pass without anything "out of the ordinary" happening in some Avenue houses. The Frith's house was one of these, until "one October evening in 1928" the place "erupted" with activity, an ambulance was called, and Esther went into the hospital with acute appendicitis, which gave the other three residents the opportunity to get out from beneath her thumb before she returned six weeks later. Two of them took advantage of the opportunity. The third, Sydney, who had formed an alliance with his mother that "shut out Elaine and Edgar, throwing each of them back upon their own limited resources" (167), was still there to welcome his mother when she returned to Number Seventeen. The other two were long gone, having seized the chance when it was offered them. This chapter of the novel narrates Edgar's pursuit of a new life for himself, the next chapter shifting its attention to Elaine's use of her new freedoms.

Edgar had spent "practically all of his waking hours at home in his greenhouse," where he raised a variety of indoor plants "that must have given him, vicariously, some of the color and variety so lacking in his everyday life." Between his stamp collection and his greenhouse, Edgar had "effaced himself completely from the family circle," while outside the house he worked for an antique dealer who found in him "a good judge of current values, a stonewaller with dealers on the make, and a scrupulously honest handler of cash" (168). It had been on his employer's instructions that Edgar was obliged to leave "the Cherry Road Shop" and visit another branch three times a week to "see how Frances was getting on." A shy woman of about thirty, Frances was very like Edgar in important respects, and the two admired one another, then formed a close personal relationship that was based upon mutual support. Edgar "had never had much confidence in himself, but what little he had originally possessed had dissolved under Esther's acid," so initially he had approached Miss Hopkins "very gingerly, expecting rebuffs, and saying as little as possible." In scarcely a week he "began to enjoy her company," experiencing it as "a balm to his self-esteem that was very pleasant" (169). Can Edgar ever return to the Avenue? His wife will not grant a divorce when it comes to that. Esther refuses the divorce purely and simply to make her errant partner suffer at some distance what he will never again endure at closer range from that evil woman.

When the time comes for Edgar to tell Frances what his life had been like, "he found it impossible to relate the stark facts," but he did not need for, because "she already understood."

> "I think I know what your life has been, Edgar. I think I've known for a long time," she began, before he could exclaim, "I *knew* as soon as I met you that you were wretched, and lonely, and despairing, and I suppose I knew that because I was the same way for so long, before I got over it, before I won out by *making* myself get over it."
>
> In his amazement he withdrew into the chair.
>
> "That's impossible," he argued; "you've never even been married...."
>
> "I've had a child," she said, simply. "I've got a daughter. She's nearly ten, now... Pippa...I want you to meet and like Pippa."
>
> He was not shocked and horrified, as he might have been, had she told him this astounding fact an hour ago. Now, in the warm glow of their love, he felt only tenderness, and kinship, and a strange, anticipatory excitement at the prospect of look upon a child that had emerged from her body. It brought her even closer to him. (*Suburb, 176*)

Lady In A Tower

Elaine Frith is that Lady. She had for five years been preparing herself for the wealthy male who will in time carry her away from the Avenue into a life of self-satisfied ease. Until now, she has suffered under her mother's sick attitude towards sexuality and the Sunday forced-marching of the family to the Methodist chapel that signified the death her husband and children have endured. Almost seventeen now, Elaine is "taller and stronger than Esther, or Sydney, besides being, in her own smouldering way, a good deal more ruthless than either of them."

> Elaine had travelled a long way since that far-off day when she had rescued *The Art of Marriage* from the cistern loft. It might be said that the study of the little volume had changed her life, for since then she had perfected a complicated network of defensive deceit around her, and the smoke-screen that she added to her defences would have done credit to a depraved bishop, bent on leading a worldly life whilst remaining a spiritual example to his flock. (*Suburb, 184–85*)

When she was not studying the theory of enslaving men through the power of sexual attraction, hiding the volumes which taught her under the cover of, for instance, Gregg's *Shortened Course of Double-Entry Book-Keeping*, Elaine was practicing in front of her mirror what the books preached. Her reflection revealed that "kiss-curls suited her." She turned this way and that, to assess "her firm breasts, her flat stomach, her long, straight legs, and small feet, the steep smoothness of the curves above her hips," along with "the roundness of her behind, and the way it emphasized her surprisingly small waist."

Standing there, turning this way and that, glancing over her shoulder, posing hand on hip, and studying the reflections of her hundred and one expressions, from the demure to the sultry, from the arch to the downright provocative, she looked like a young, pagan priestess performing some mystic, solitary ceremony. She had the serenity and confidence of a priestess. She did not envy the Avenue flappers their freedom, for she was aware that, in contradiction to the stridency of the decade, men did not really want flat-chested, comradely women, but the kind of woman she would be when her moment arrived. The books had taught her that the art of love was that of sustaining mystery, of promising so much and giving so little, until the time came when one could stupefy with generosity, and enslave the man who would pluck her from the tower, and install her in a mansion or palace, where she could be done with subterfuge, and spend the livelong day radiating beauty, reigning over a whole troop of lesser men, each of whom would consider it a high privilege to die for her.

This was the traditional destiny of all beautiful women. This was her dream and her plan. (*Suburb*, 186–87)

One cannot make oneself into a hall-of-fame quarterback or a Tiger-Woods-league golfer without study and practice, and Elaine is committed to reaching that kind of distinction in her own field. Having the right stuff, how can she miss?

It is time for Elaine to take the field and explore in the social world, for which she has been preparing herself, the effectiveness of her sexual magnetism upon an available male who will cooperate with her in that experiment. Esme Frazier lives across the street from her and Elaine has him in mind. Having selected and purchased "a dance-frock of deep crimson velvet, knee-length, and cut closely to her mature figure," Elaine is ready. Entering the hall she can see Ted Hartnell "sweating it out on the dais, leaping from drum to drum, flinging himself at the cymbals" and so forth (191). And there too was Esme, who "noticed the dress" and wondered "whether it was indeed the girl he had passed so often in the Avenue," the one who "always kept her eyes on the pavement" (193). It was, and he shall be used tonight to put her powers to the test. They dance, they talk, and as they walk home through the soft snow Elaine "fell into step with him, her gloved hand through his arm." She shows him her father's greenhouse, takes him inside, asks whether he wants a kiss, delivers a mighty one and sends him on his way. Then comes the post-game assessment: "If she too was ecstatic it was not on account of him but because of her own triumph." She knows the credit goes mostly to herself, "and to Elinor Glyn, with a few crumbs for the author of *Eve's World*. He was madly in love with her!" (203).

Carver Roundabout I

The spring of 1930 was memorable for the Carvers because of a reshuffling in the house, for when Berni and Boxer moved out the bedrooms were reassigned and those still living at home were less crowded. Jim now spent his time preparing political speeches, because only temporary work was available as the depression came nearer. He could see little future for himself or his country the way things were heading, despite the Socialist victory the previous summer, and it "galled him" that the Labour Party had done so little. Pondering these problems on his way back home one evening, Jim was involved in an event which "changed the course of his life" (206–07). He heard a crash of glass, the big car shot around the corner at high speed, missed him by inches, and stopped against the base of a streetlight. He saw the pile of stolen furs on the back seat, and before Jim saw the police car in pursuit, he jumped onto the running board and "drove his fist hard into the boy's ear." He attempted to slink away but was stopped by the police sergeant who said "You mustn't go, sir," they will need him as a witness.

Carver felt ashamed at the trial because the youth had wasted his adolescence in a State orphanage, had never had the opportunity to become productive, and yet was sent to prison for seven years. "He saw the boy as a symptom of the whole rotten system of exploitation, and dividends, and gold standard, and endless hair splitting over conference tables" (210). As Jim took his way to the street he met Jacob Sokolski, who owned the stolen furs, a Russian Jew whose family had been far more badly treated by the "bloody polis" than the English ever were. The two men liked each other immediately, and the next week Jim went to work for Jacob the next week, performing whatever menial tasks were needed (211–12).

Archie Carver remembered Spring 1930 because that was when he began his expansion, for his dream had changed over the years. "A Good Time as he had understood it when he was twenty-one" no longer occupied his waking thoughts, for "the Chain" was now all-important to him. When he started forging that chain, he was determined not to have "managers as master links" because, without having any stake in the business, given time they would be "certain to go sour, and become dishonest, disillusioned or slack." Archie knew too shop assistants "shied away from responsibility," and given it against their will, "they became sullen, or sick. Since he wished to avoid such problems, he made up his mind that by the age of thirty-five he would own a dozen "Pop-Ins," all within a five mile radius of his current store. And he would give each Pop-In two visits a day, the first to check stock and watch the service, the second to see the books to ensure that employees were not stealing him blind. Maria, his wife, was occupied with her three children. It never occurred to him that she and her father knew all about his mistresses, and had he known he would not have bothered to make an excuse (213–15).

Louise Carver remembered that time because "at the age of thirty, thin, flat-chested, and slightly stooping," she had her first mating season. Jack Strawbridge, a gardener employed by Stannard's nurseries, a man "as comfortable and as engaging as an old cart horse," came through the gap in the Carver's fence one morning "holding a forearm in a huge fist," bleeding badly from the four-inch gash made by his bill-hook. As Louise patched the wound, Jack quickly made up his mind and told her "I'm a widower." Their courtship was now under way. "If it rained they sat in the kitchen reading the evening paper," when the weather permitted they walked together, and when they married they would live just as placidly together as they had lived apart.

Far less content was Judith Carver, who found that she had lost Esme forever. Most Avenue people who lost a dream found another one, but Judy's was "an obsession." She knew that something was up with Esme. But it was not until she learned that he had bought "an enamel powder-compact" for Elaine, had it engraved and sent it to *Miss Elaine Firth* at the address written in Esme's familiar hand, that Judy was first stunned, and then despondent. After she sat down and began to reflect, "her rage against God began to abate, and with it came the first feeble glimmerings of objectivity" (224–27).

> It was then that she realized for the first time that perhaps she was being unfair to Esme, that she alone was able to assess the depths of her devotion, and that in all these years she had never once confessed her love, not even to Louise, or to one of her few school friends—certainly not to Esme himself. It was suddenly quite clear to her that he had never thought about her as a girl—had even perhaps found her vassalage a nuisance at times. (*Suburb*, 227)

She had gone into the rural area beyond the Avenue in order to lament her fortune, and while she ruminated she happened to look up, and "was astonished to see a big chestnut horse step sedately into the clearing, and lower its head over a few blades of grass that sprouted behind the seat" she sat on (228). The horse belongs to Miss Somerton, the middle-aged woman who owns the nearby riding stables and who gives riding lessons. The women soon strike up a friendship and Judy enters into a new life working for her new friend, who realizes immediately that the young woman has a marvellous talent for working with horses as well as guiding the girls who come to Somerton's for riding lessons. By the end of her first year spent doing real work, she had recovered.

> Judy began to see Esme as he really was, a rather self-conscious young man, with freshly slicked hair, and a dreamy expression, who pottered about the Avenue, waiting and waiting, in the hope of catching a momentary glimpse of Elaine coming or going about Number Seventeen, and looking, Judy thought, faintly ridiculous into the bargain. Sometimes, when she watched him objectively from the bedroom window, she was even a little sorry for him. The important thing was, she was no longer sorry for herself. (*Suburb*, 234–35)

Changes At Number Four

Edith Clegg no longer worked at the Grenada, since accompanists were redundant after the arrival of the talkies. Mr. Billings liked Edith and would have kept her as house-manager at a pianist's salary, but "the long columns of figures worried her, the atmosphere of bustle and stress overwhelmed her" and, more important, she could never watch a whole movie, which had become the real reason she enjoyed being a pianist during the silent era. The night she left the Granada, she went to see Jim Carver seeking advice, and he recommended that Edith take another lodger to recover the lost income. "How about your porch room?" he asked. "Couldn't you let that, and board someone at twenty-five shillings a week?" Edith thought not, but in principle she liked the idea, and since there had been a slump in piano students as more families "were installing wire-less sets," that is what she did (235-38).

The new lodger was Jean McInroy, a late teen-age Scots girl, so very pretty that Edith feared Teddy would fall in love with her. But Jean's "strange reluctance to speak" and her "hesitant manner" helped keep that from happening. She was quiet because of a severely cleft palate, such that when she attempted to speak, the words she formed "emerged from her pretty mouth mangled beyond recognition" (238-39). On the other hand, Jean was a talented artist who designed and drew product advertisements for magazines. She came to the Avenue with the dream of creating "a perfect man," the opportunity being provided by her employment at "Dyke and Dobson's, the advertising agency" (241), where she was held in "high esteem" by Mr. Keith, the staff manager. Miss McInroy's perfect man was occasionally seen in all of the women's magazines in various poses: pipe in mouth, surprise package under his raincoat, pruning the roses, shaving his chin, laying a stair carpet. "She was happier than most people in the Avenue, for not only could she put her dreams on paper, but was paid for dreaming them" (241-43).

Ted Hartnell did not fall in love with Miss McInroy because he was already in that condition, and his love was "reciprocated wholeheartedly" by Margy, the singer who sold cheap recordings of current songs at the Woolworth's, loved dance-music as much as Ted did, and was delighted when Ted praised her work to her Woolworth's boss. One morning she mentioned that she'd "love to do a cabaret number with your band, Ted," and Al Swinger agreed to that.

> If Ted Hartnell had needed a pushover he would have received it that first night, watching her from behind the drums, and tapping out the rhythm with his unemployed left foot. Her two numbers earned generous applause, and from then on she became a feature of the band. (*Suburb*, 243-47)

In the Spring of 1931 Ted was introduced to her family, and with marriage in the offing because she perceived it there, Margy told him "I'm going to see that you get somewhere." She intended to create a band of his own, something Ted did not aspire to, but which Margy was determined to bring into existence (248).

Esme

The crisis at the Frists' house had come and gone, "and Elaine departed, in the wake of her father." She had decided to "anticipate his rescue, and effect her solitary escape from the tower," which is how Esme had seen her—a captive princess, who, "hard won," was "suitably grateful" (248–49). But Elaine saw their relationship very differently. Each minute she spent with Esme was "a secret blow at Esther," payback for those long years of "seclusion and prohibition." Elaine made her admirer writhe upon an "emotional switchback," but the experience "did a good deal to mature him" (250–51). Esme wants to worship her, while Elaine expects to be needed violently, past reason hunted, not contemplated "like a statue or something" (259). She moves to Llandudno to be a "hotel receptionist," but he is not to accompany her to the station because "I want to do this on my own" (261). Elaine briefly returns to Esther's house before leaving, but only after making Esme promise to sit in his upstairs porch-room looking across the Avenue, a position from which he sees Elaine provocatively flash her erotic body towards him from an unreachable distance, as if to say "This is what you have spurned!" Suddenly "seized with a fit of violent shivering," the innocent voyeur "felt defiled" by her obscene gesture (262–63).

Jim Hears Rumblings

Carver has been worrying about the state of his society so long and so intensely that he has become a cultural seer, for he intuitively comprehends the events already unfolding in the public world, events to which others are blind. His children think him indifferent and would not have approached him for advice, while Jim had concluded that they "had no views at all, beyond a bland acceptance of life as something to be lived day by day" (264). "Like all men with strong political convictions," Jim Carver was "concerned with the mass, rather than the individuals who make up the mass" (266). It is this slant on reality which makes him the cultural historian of the Avenue, who can foresee what has not yet come to pass with the clarity of that prophet who is not honored in his own community. He does not preach to the many, but ruminates, and shares his fears with the few people capable of taking him seriously, like Jacob Sokolski.

Jim knows "no one party" could solve the unemployment problem. "Three million unemployed, he argued, meant big trouble for someone, and they had already seen how damaging failure to tackle the problem could be for the Government in power!" Therefore, "if an earthquake was to follow the landslide, it was far better that Tories should be sitting in Westminster." In the event the explosion would be heard very soon, and Jim was "himself rather more involved in it" than he wanted to be, and his employer, Jacob Sokolski, was in "even deeper trouble" (271). Carver relates to the fur dealer the newspaper story of the four despondent men who chipped in to buy an old car, sat in it, "and drove it slap over a cliff!"

> "It didn't happen in Russia, Mr. Sokolski, it happened in Bristol the other day!"
> The old man sat thinking for a moment, his hands clasped together over his huge, round belly. Suddenly he got up.

"It is enough," he said, "I do more dan give you time off, my friend, I come wid you! Let us go, hey?"

Jim was taken by surprise. "You'll come...but you don't believe in us, you've always said..."

"I begin to believe in der Zocialists ven dey spit so hard," said Sokolski. "Besides, it will be interesting to watch how you Pritish make der Revolutions!"

Jim grinned. "You're going to be disappointed. We don't believe in revolutions, over here. Even those chaps in the car didn't, Mr. Sokolski." He was touched, nevertheless, and added: "Are you *sure* you want to come?" (*Suburb*, 272)

The two companions attended the mass protest in the park, milling about in the crowd some of whom carried "*We Claim The Right to Work*" placards. Speakers harangued the crowd, while the number of police along Park Lane multiplied until a mounted police Inspector near Jim attempted to direct the demonstration.

"Not this way," he shouted; "down there—keep moving down there."

"They're heading them off," exclaimed Jim incredulously. "The bloody fools, they'll have a riot on their hands if they head them off!"

The solid wedges of spectators immediately behind suddenly surged forward, presumably in the hope of getting a better view of what was going on, and Jim had barely time to grab Sokolski's coat sleeve before the pair of them were projected into the road. Simultaneously the police cordon broke.

At the same moment, the halted ranks behind the Welsh banners broke formation, and pushed forward in a solid wedge, shouting and cat-calling. Police from the shattered cordon began to rally to the mounted group, fumbling for their batons as they ran. (*Suburb*, 275)

Jim regained consciousness on the jailhouse floor, his hair matted with congealed blood where he had been struck, hearing nearby one of the miners, the one who had unhorsed the Inspector, congratulate Sokolski for his valiant action in the battle just over. The miner opined that there'll be questions in Parliament about what happened. But Sokolski, whose cultural experience was far other than the miner's, asked "Vy you not pull bloddy Parliament down, and throw it in de bloddy river, brick by brick," his viewpoint standing in emphatic contrast against Carver's, who knows the temper of the English better than does his friend. The Avenue's cultural historian is contemplating current events from the stand-point half-way between the uninformed indifference of his own children and the militant anger of a foreigner, who remembers the "squalid Lithuanian village, the snow-covered landscape churned into slush by the Cossacks' horses, as yet another pogrom swept down on the half-starved community, and men were dragged screaming from their timber dwellings in the light of pine torches and burning barns, [with] his mother standing in the open doorway, screeching defiance, and himself and his brothers running swiftly across the snow towards the birch forests." Jim never forgot Sokolski's "gesture" when the miners were released from custody: he gave "each man the money for his railway fare to Wales," after paying the fine for whatever charge the police had brought against them (280-81).

> In his recounting of the incident, Delderfield moves forward from that event upon English soil to the far worse events which, once again, Jim perceives with a seer's eye. From his habit of reading and reflecting upon what he had read, he perceived the outlines of the coming war which the Treaty of Versailles made unavoidable. He realized that "something was happening across the Channel that made the wranglings between the cartels and the unions ridiculous, as fatuous as the arguments of wayfarers lost in a wood, disputing the ownership of a broken compass."
>
> The French Socialists were aware of it, and were striving to form a popular front against the strident bullies on the far side of the Maginot Line, but the French were old and wise, and knew that these same bullies would stop at nothing, not even firing their own Chancellory to win the support of reaction all over the world. Jim knew this too and recognized, in the strutting Jew-baiters of Berlin, the men who had the insufferable arrogance to assure *him* that they had been unbeaten in the autumn of 1918—*unbeaten*, when Jim, and his gaunt trench veterans, had herded them back over the Rhine, and had kept their children alive for months with sly gifts of Chocolate, and tinned milk.
>
> This was where the real trouble was going to come from if the League, and the bemused politicians over here, were content to see Germany flout the treaty, and build up an army, in the vain hope that their legions would turn east, and leave the west to vegetate until the time came to make a new treaty of their own devising. (*Suburb*, 283-84)

Sokolski explains to Jim that the English lack the sense of reality which his own people had been born with. "In dis country you have not suffered enough. Dat is something dat can be put right, eh? Dat is someding de flying machines vill teach you ven der moment is come!" (293-84).

The *Abdication And Usurpation* chapter of *The Dreaming Suburb* is focused upon the Frith family, Edgar and Elaine's *abdication* from the unspeakable tyranny of Esther, the wife and mother, and the *usurpation* by Sydney of her repressive dominance. Esther had spent her early life in a mansion in which no living creatures were about "apart from the crazy old woman" her aunt, the "stone-deaf cook-general" and the forty-three cats the aunt maintained. Her parents having died in India when she was a child, the single genuinely formative influence available to Esther was provided by the "hideous furniture and massive, ancestral portraits," which were only a shade less useless than the senile aunt. The furniture taught Esther that things inside a house should not move about, because stasis provides a kind of security. Capturing Edgar had been an accident, something Esther had instinctively grabbed hold of as the mansion was being sold out from under her. But the death-in-life she experienced there had by this time been transported into her brain, and Esther no doubt believed that marching the family about, or better yet making them sit *still*, was her life's mission.

Readers of the novel are not inclined to feel sorry for Esther, any more than the crowd who gather to view the horrendous automobile accident care about the twisted auto, their sympathies being focused on the mangled and bleeding victims; analogously, Esther's husband and children are the victims. The advantage her two children had over Esther in their formative period is that they saw models more active than furniture, one of them the negative example of how not to live, the other a small person, but admirable in his own way. Edgar could be described as a silent spirit of life who survived in the greenhouse adjoining the graveyard that was Number Seventeen. He stayed sane by living among other living things, i.e. plants that responded to his care by occasionally bursting into color, a transfiguration that his wife was incapable of imitating. Had the Avenue people known more about them, they would have understood that the Friths were not only the "strangest" family in the suburb, but "certainly the unhappiest" (97–100).

Within a week of his abdication from the Avenue house Edgar had begun to "develop a new personality," as he set out to prove to Frances that he was not the useless wretch Esther had almost persuaded him he was. The earliest signs of a recovery were that "he lost his timidity and reserve, and with it the slight stutter that he had exhibited when dealing with the tougher type of customer." No longer the bland Edgar, "he sang out his bids in a loud, clear voice, and went on bidding, right up to his limit, his steadiness giving other dealers the impression that he was a man not to be trifled with." He bought Frances flowers, "held back little pieces of antique jewellery" he knew she would like, and lavished upon her the pent-up affection that Esther had no desire for. Edgar brought his gifts to Frances "like a pagan worshipper expressing gratitude for a rich harvest." Her daughter Pippa, an observant child, noted that whenever Edgar was explaining anything to her, "her mother listened and smiled, her feet on the humpty, her book lowered to her lap, and the child came to the conclusion that she smiled because Edgar's patience with questions was one more proof that he was hopelessly in love with her" (196–97).

Elaine took a job as the receptionist at The Falconer and remained for nearly two years after she "left the flat over the antique shop at Llandudno in order to make way for Pippa" (297). An illusionist who called himself "The Great Eùgene" swept into the hotel one day "with a swish of his crimson-lined cloak," an imperious rascal, aging now though still making a living, still impressing young women until they had smoked him out. "It was just possible" Elaine had thought, that this mountebank, "carefully handled," might compensate for two almost wasted years as a receptionist, years that "promised much" but had thus far given "little" (297, 300). Eùgene had been formulating plans of his own, plans in which Elaine would have been "disturbed to learn" her part. Clearly, there is to be a contest between these two, but Eùgene had "nobody to warn him" that despite the fifty-seven names of earlier women in his diary "he had yet to encounter anyone as cold-blooded as Elaine Frith" (301–03). While he offered excellent practice, Elaine had been contemptuous of his unimpressive performance as a suitor. "My dear, you're such a waste, stuck in that little glass box downstairs," he told her one day, which disappointed the hotel clerk.

> She had expected him to be much more original. This speech, she thought, might have been lifted from one of the first batch of paper-backed reprints that she had once hidden under the floor of her bedroom, at Number Seventeen. He did not even look like a lover, pleading his cause, but more like a family doctor, prescribing a convalescent holiday. (*Suburb*, 307)

And yet when the occasion beckons, "without the slightest sign of haste or embarrassment," Elaine "began to unbutton her high-necked blouse" (310). If one prospective solution to the problem of attracting an adequately wealthy admirer falls flat, she can still enjoy a temporary windfall before moving ahead in her ruthless way.

As a youth Sydney Frith had been clever, especially in mathematics, but "there was something about the promptness with which he answered questions, and the meticulous neatness of his written work, that disturbed his teachers, and made them cautious in their dealings with him." That he was seldom in trouble with figures of authority did not persuade teachers that he had "a law-abiding disposition," for they suspected that he had "yet to be caught out." In time he became head boy at the school, and his tattling on the others eventually came to be seen "as evidence of zeal in an overseer." The seedy staff of teachers in the school he attended, without quite knowing why, "delegated more and more authority to him," and in his final year Sydney's "one regret was that he was not allowed to beat smaller boys and had to remain content with getting them beaten" (166–67). That was Sydney's character as it revealed itself early on.

In the Spring of 1934, Sydney Frith joined the British Union of Fascists, not because of political conviction but in imitation of "Boydie" Thompson, "a bizarre character, of the type that later found its extreme expression in a small band of stalwarts who did the washing-up for Propaganda Minister Goebbels and lived on to regret their bedevilment" (284). Boydie thought "the rabble had been getting badly out of hand since the General Strike and the Depression of 1931," and were "now demanding work with menaces." If not put in their place they "might use democratic machinery to vote in yet another Labour Government and slap on a capital levy" (285). Yet what Sydney admired was not the political stance but rather Boydie's *style*, everything from a public-school background and the sports car he drove to weekends hob-nobbing with "other young executives," to the girls he went out with and his curious but entrancing pronunciations of English words—"so that *match* became *metch*, and *back* became *beck*—which Sydney did his utmost to imitate, along with the forty-five degree angle at which Boydie tucked his newspaper "under the right arm" (286).

He enjoyed playing political dress-up, Sydney did, and admired in his mirror the black shirt he wore, even though his physique corresponded quite badly with riding breeches and jackboots. Further, he did not "welcome hecklers, for street scuffles were beneath his dignity." Push eventually came to shove while Boydie was delivering a speech, and to Sydney's surprise he was attacked. He "hardly had time to unfold his arms and raise them to shield his face" before a youth of about his own age twisted his head underneath his arm, holding it "in a pitiless grip, whilst he punched and punched with his free fist."

> Finally, the methodically punching youth surrendered his claims, and Sydney was dragged, feet foremost, across the uneven ground, his nose streaming blood, his bruised mouth still wide open in an uninterrupted scream" (*Suburb*, 188–89).

After that experience Sydney burned the black shirt, but he wrapped his breeches and boots in brown paper and put them away in the drawer of his sister's empty wardrobe, "in case he should need them again in the future." He listened to rumblings from the Continent still, yet decided to "ignore them" in practice. This is the Sydney who, his mother having collapsed following the flight of Edgar and Elaine, intends to usurp the power which currently stands vacant in Number Seventeen.

Progress For Two

Given Delderfield's presentational design of deploying several dozen characters to represent the attitudes of the English people as they change over the three decades between the Great War's end and the beginning of World War II, he must keep the pot stirred so that none of his characters drop out of the soup. Thus, for example, the *Abdication And Usurpation* section renews our focus on the Frist family before it glances off to another character cluster. This is particularly the case because Delderfield needs the others as a moving backdrop against which readers must focus on Jim Carver, the chief spokesman for the three decades being represented. The reader's attention must be riveted upon that trench veteran's journey from pacifist to war-supporter if it is to strike home with the impact that the author intends. Another of Jim's meditative interludes being near at hand, the backdrop characters need be updated before the focus shifts onto Carver's ruminations in Manor Woods. *Progress For Two* is one such preparatory updating featuring other characters.

Progress For Two is chiefly focused upon Ted Hartnell and Margie, the ambitious young woman who takes him in hand and touts his talent better than Ted left to himself could ever have done. But first, Delderfield gives his readers a potpourri of other characters and their interrelationships. Thus, while Elaine was being fitted for the hussar costume she will wear as Eùgene's assistant, Sydney was bringing his typist girl-friend home to meet his mother, while Miss Clegg taxied "in chirrupy high spirits" to Teddy's wedding. It was the spring when Esme began the three-year "Odyssey" that Silverton had recommended years earlier, prompted into action by Sydney's bad news that Elaine "had now passed out of his life forever." Judith moved to Devonshire to spend all her time at the riding stables, Louise came even closer to marrying her admirer, and "Jim Carver took to ruminating in Manor Woods." These events, remarks Delderfield, "might appear to be unrelated" to one another, but Teddy's wedding had bestirred "the placid Louise" to getting a move on her own, and Louise's decision "decided Judy to accept" Miss Somerton's invitation, while Sydney's habit of tattling bad news prompted Esme to begin his Grand Tour.

When Ted and Margy returned from their honeymoon, they began work on setting up "a dance orchestra with a style, and a *sound* of its own, more ambitious, and more original than Al Swingers' 'Rhythmateers.'" For Margy had decided, and she is now "sole custodian of Ted's future." But as it happens, Margy will not be wholly successful in managing her husband's actions, for when war comes and Ted discovers from the Jewish musician that Hitler has been gassing Jews, the Hartnell Override kicks in. She cannot rule him beyond that moment. But for the time being she has her way. She advertises "auditions [for] instrumentalists specializing in dance-music. New Orchestra" (314). This alerts Al that something is going on that he doesn't like, and he appears at the audition determined to hold onto his drummer. Margy faces him like a prizefighter going for the knockout.

> "Everyone's got to get a first chance from somewhere," she snapped, "and Ted would have been a drummer no matter what! Your finding him was just your good luck, not his!"
>
> "Oh, I dunno, Margy..." protested Ted miserably. "Al and me..."
>
> "Shut up, Ted," said Margy, very firmly.
>
> Al tried a flank attack.
>
> "I never could stick seeing a man run by his missus," he said, an unlit cigarette wobbling slackly on his lower lip, "and I must say you seem to have handed over your trousers even quicker than most honeymooners, pal!"
>
> It was the last exchange of conversation that was to pass between them, and it was terminated by a slap from Margy that brought a vivid flush to Al's pale cheeks, and sent him staggering back against the piano.
>
> Margy then followed him up, ignoring Ted's yelp of protest.
>
> "Don't, Margy...don't do that to Al!"
>
> "You talk cheap and you *are* cheap," she shouted at the band leader. "I've always thought so, right from the first day I sang for you, and now Ted's going to have a real band, not a half-baked imitation of a Yank set-up like yours! You get out of here! We've paid for our rehearsal rooms and that's something you never did until you were County Courted!"
>
> "Ted, old boy," he drawled, "I'm real sorry for you, brother! You seem to have hitched yourself to a first-class bitch!"
>
> He turned, intending to drift out through the wide door, and for a couple of yards he moved at his accustomed pace, half-roll, half-slouch. But as he crossed the threshold his exit was suddenly accelerated, not by Margy, but by Ted, who suddenly shot past the piano, and planted his toe squarely, and with terrible force, into the seat of Al's dirty flannels.
>
> It was the first time either of them had seen Al move fast. He seemed to fly horizontally out through the door, and half-way along the entrance passage, slithering to

a stop, face down, at the feet of a spare, bespectacled young man, who was on the way in, a violin case tucked under his arm. He was on his feet again in a flash, and before Ted could lay hands on him he was gone, with the violinist still poised on the doorstep, his eyebrows raised in an expression of quizzical interest.

"Was he *that* bad?" he asked Ted, and then, hearing Margy's peal of laughter, "I do hope I make a rather better impression!" (*Suburb*, 316-17)

Carver Roundabout II

While it is diversified by the narrative of Berni and Boxer's employment as stunt-drivers speeding "round the sides" of the Wall of Death motorcycle pit as "the Suicide Twins," Louise and Jack Strawbridge's wedding, and the death of "Old Piretta" that autumn—is intellectually focused on Jim Carver's ruminations in Manor Woods. Carver's thought recapitulates the gradual reversal of English public opinion that Delderfield documents, as we noted earlier, in his essay "The Left and the Right of It." *Carver Roundabout II* begins with Jim's reflections, before it glances off to competing areas of interest, which belong to the background of the core action, the trench veteran's thoughts, which are as follows:

Jim's conscience was giving him a great deal of trouble nowadays, so much in fact that it was upsetting his entire conception of Brotherly Love and International Socialism. For seventeen years now Jim had been a passionately convinced pacifist, a very militant pacifist it is true, but still a pacifist, that is, one who had pledged himself never again to fight for King, Country, and Empire and one who was opposed, to the point of bloody revolution, to rearmament and the traffic in weapons of war. His feelings regarding these matters had once been the burning convictions of a convert, not in any way subject to the fluctuations of the international scene. He had seen the boy on the bank at Mons and had therefore seen the light. War was a capitalists' racket. War was a profiteers' ruse. War was fought by the masses, who were the inevitable losers thereby. Therefore war was wrong. All wars were wrong.

But were they? What happened in cases like those of Manchuria and Abyssinia? What must a democrat do when Democracy itself was challenged, when the machinery for the outlawing of war was seen to be outmoded and useless? What did a man do when faced by the kind of challenge already looming up from Germany, where thousands of pacifists, as earnest as himself, were being torn from their beds, thrust into camps, and left to rot and starve, or to die under the bullets of uniformed thugs? What happened in one's own Avenue, when a young fool like Sydney Frith, the boy opposite, donned a black shirt and topboots, and promised to start the same sort of thing over here? In other words, where did one draw the line between doctrinaire pacifism and downright cowardice? (*Suburb*, 319-20)

Long walks in the winding paths around the derelict manor helped him comprehend the problem. More than fifty nations had "signed their willingness to accept Jim's ideas about war," but Mussolini, the Japanese War-lords and Hitler were treating the League of Nations as if it were a foolish old aunt. Would its "loyal signatories be obliged to go to war to stop a war, kill Italians in order to save Abyssinians?"

(320). Carver had howled against war for sixteen years, yet here was Jim's candidate Baldwin, "pledging support for the League, yet asking for a mandate to rearm, trotting out all the familiar cliches about capitalist arms barons, but coupling them with a noisy demand to sit on Mussolini!" No wonder he ruminated in the solitude of Manor Woods.

By the following spring things were even worse, for the Spanish Civil War, coupled with Non-Intervention, gave Carver "the gravest doubts" about the peace pretenses of street-corner orators.

> Here was an entire people struggling against a feudalism that had held them in thrall for centuries, and here were madmen like Hitler and Mussolini pouring in men and material to beat them to their knees. Standing aside, like two elderly parsons who were the unwilling spectators of a murder, were his own country and Republican France, both terrified of becoming involved, and doing nothing except to direct a few none too emphatic protests at the criminals. (*Suburb*, 321)

Nothing here was clear-cut, like the black-and-white issues of the 'twenties.

Because we are now familiar with the Avenue residents, and because the next half-dozen chapters are continuations of actions already well under way, we can move more rapidly through *Edith And The House Of Windsor*, *Esme's Odyssey*, *Jim Closes The Door*, *Archie Under An Umbrella*, *Elaine Comes In Out Of The Rain* and *Esme And The Promised Land*. The single exception is that Edith's chapter is not a continuance, but a stand-alone action—although it does continue to explore her determination to defend the people she admires or those in need of her assistance.

Edith and the House of Windsor

Edith's *House Of Windsor* performance occurs because of her high regard for the royal family. At the Jubilee of the King, as the Prince of Wales appeared, no one gave him "a louder cheer" than Edith when he rode by "and smiled at her from under his enormous bearskin" (336–37). Soon after that the King died and there was the "awful business of the Abdication," when people seemed to "forget everything the poor boy had done for the Empire." Even worse, Mrs. Rolfe, "a cross-grained woman who had recently moved into Number Eight," set up as a "censor of royal morals" and harangued the other customers in Carter's bookshop. "All I can say is Good Riddance" she proclaimed, which Edith did not agree with, expressing a contrary sentiment. Hearing that, the Rolfe woman pounced: "Well, I must say that's a fine thing, coming from someone *I* always thought of as *respectable*, not to say a little behind the times, if you don't mind me being so frank, Miss Clegg!" This new player in the Avenue being determined to make a cat fight of it, Edith lost what was left of her self-control.

> Half-turning, she swung her shopping bag with her free hand, and brought it down with all her force on Mrs. Rolfe's head, sending the pro-Abdicationist staggering back against

a revolving frame of picture-postcards, and this, in turn, overthrew a balanced pyramid of books built upon Carter's counter. Frame, cards, books, and Mrs. Rolfe crashed through the open counter-flap on to the floor. Edith waited no longer. Appalled by what she had done she fled into the Lower Road, but Mrs. Rolfe's cries pursued her: "I'll sue you!. Mark me words, I'll sue you!" And then there was something about "witnesses."

Nothing came of it except that within weeks of the incident the aggrieved woman "packed up and moved out, much to the relief" of her closest neighbors (340-41).

When his step-father Harold Godbeer reflects that Esme is still hanging around the house at age twenty, showing no evidence of doing anything in particular with his life, he recalls Headmaster Silverton's advice that Esme should find an artistic profession of some sort, and advises him to see Longjohn about it. Esme leaves some of his manuscripts for his former teacher to examine and when they meet to discuss them he says "They're kind of flat, aren't they, sir?" His mentor asks why that is, and Esme says "Because I was bored with them, sir." The older man's advice is to travel, not abroad, but through England, observing things, and writing about what he sees.

> Tell us what the Industrial Revolution has made of the people whose grandfathers drifted into the Northern and Midland towns from the farms and cottage looms. Distil for us some of the traditional humor of the Cockney, and the Lancashire people...That's the sort of shot in the arm that English fiction needs today, and I think you're a person who could do it. (Suburb, 346-48)

Esme's Odyssey

Esme's Odyssey takes him on a three-year journey where he sees many things, covering as wide a territory as Longjohn advised, and he even worked for a newspaper for a while. But all the time "he had been cheating" his advisor, since everything he tried to write about had led him "back to the Avenue, and this thread led only to Elaine" (353). Arguing with himself did no good. Elaine was all he cared about, and all roads led back to that long-lived infatuation.

Jim Closes The Door

Jim Closes The Door advances our cultural historian to Spring of 1937, "when the Spanish agony was at its height, and Munich was still more than a year away." The former socialist-pacifist resigned himself to World War II. Yet he refused to accompany Sokolski on his escape to Canada, the fur dealer having renewed his offer after Munich. It was that travesty which irrevocably decided Jim to stay.

> Munich filled him with shame. He had never considered that the British lacked courage, and the spectacle of the nation's hysterical joy at Chamberlain's return, waving an umbrella and a piece of paper, made him sick with dismay. He found it almost impossible to believe that any sane person could regard such a document as an infallible talisman against aerial bombardment. (Suburb, 358).

He had no patience with the socialist colleague who thought it "nonsense" to assume there would be a war. Amazed at such blindness, Jim shouted back, "The German Socialists, you bloody fool, where do you imagine they are? Do you think *anyone* has any say in what goes on over there, since that maniac and his gang took over?" (359).

Archie Under An Umbrella

The chapter title "*Archie Under An Umbrella*" refers to the Prime Minister's shielding him. Munich caused "serious reflection" that September, and in his own way Jim's oldest son was "grateful for the shelter" of that absurd talisman brandished so happily. Archie had the foresight to acquire stock "against the day when it was impossible to replenish" (361). He decided to buy and buy more, until his every odd corner was filled to bursting with "reserves." Even more critical to his success was the fact that he "consistently robbed his own tills," the better to deprive the Revenue people of "two or three thousand a year." But his success called for "split-second timing," and the exclusion of any nosy-parkers who might get wise to his deceptions. Archie had a hollowed-out cavern under the store's flooring where, in handy steel drums, he concealed his money in fire-proof boxes. While ignorant of the cavern, Gloria Hazelwood, who had "graduated from counter-hand to concubine," understood what Archie was doing. She decided to teach him a lesson. One day she bid him a cheerful adieu with 100 pounds of his money in her purse and wadded-up toilet paper in his wallet pretending to be the currency he did not yet know was gone. Archie was philosophical about the robbery.

> He was a man who was well accustomed to weighing profits against losses, and it seemed to him that this was a cheap enough price to pay for an invaluable lesson. And it was not all loss either, not when one took into account Gloria's company over several weekends (*Suburb*, 364–68).

Elaine Comes In Out Of The Rain

In *Elaine Comes In Out Of The Rain*, the Avenue's on-the-make damsel realizes, in the autumn of 1938, that her best hope of achieving the life of wealth and ease she has promised herself is to snap up her infatuated admirer, Esme Frazier. For two years she had associated with The Great Eùgene, quite enough to become "thoroughly bored", and for him to "wish he had never been born" (369). Benny Boy was her next victim, another instance of Elaine's pernicious effects upon men. "It was not that she was particularly foolish with money, but just that she seemed to disorganize them in some way, and prevented their earning the kind of money they were earning before they met her." After Eùgene and Benny Boy, Elaine "joined up with a circus," having by this time acquired experience "within the world of variety" and having "an even wider experience in the art of handling men" (371).

The circus she then joined, a "small, seedy outfit," was owned by the jovial little man whom everyone called Tom Tappertitt. Elaine soon met Tom's wife, "a loud, motherly woman, with a tread like that of a placid hippopotamus, and an overall gentleness of spirit." She it was who kept the show together, and sorted out the problems of the "various troupes" in the circus. One day as Elaine was loading the target rifles with tufted darts, Sydney appeared, surprised to find her that curiously employed. Elaine insults him, and Sydney retorts that she was crazy to "throw over" Esme, who "makes six hundred a year," as he has heard, and "came into money too!" Esme's "worth quite a bit now, they say." How much, she wondered. "That was what was important, how much?" (375–76).

For the time being she was stuck working in a circus. But all too soon it came to pass, the evening after she and Tom had "installed themselves" under a fictitious name in "a blameless little hotel" twelve miles from the circus, "at the unlikely hour of two in the morning," that the door of their room flew open and the lights were switched on; they revealed "to the tousled Elaine and her still sleeping partner the reality of a professional strong woman in the role of the outraged wife." The terror which gripped them was well founded. Mrs. T. "tucked Elaine under her massive arm as though she was a runaway puppy," tossed her husband "casually into a shallow closet" for punishment later on, "tore down Elaine's new pajama trousers, and commenced to administer a spanking that could be heard very clearly in the lobby downstairs" since the slapper had huge hands that covered "quite an area," and were used professionally for "tying knots in iron bars" (379–80). It was this episode that propelled the chastened Elaine on the road back to the Avenue to examine the reliability of Sydney's information. Journeying south, she reviewed her situation. Her life on stage and circus would never supply the husband who could "provide the terrace, the drinks, the hammock, and the hovering courtiers" which she had promised herself (383). But she remembered having read in a Sunday paper that "the way to make a million was to find something people wanted, and then corner the supply of that product. She had what men wanted" (384), and all she needed to do was "display it in the right market."

Esme And The Promised Land

An epigraph that accurately characterizes *Esme And The Promised Land* could be excerpted from a stanza in Spenser's *Faerie Queene*. That passage narrates the Fraudulent Woman misrepresenting herself to the Trusting Knight who believes her every word. Here is that epigraph, the generic pattern which Elaine adopts to disguise her intentions:

"In this sad plight, friendless, unfortunate,
Now miserable I Fidessa dwell,
Craving of you in pitty of my state,
To do none ill, if please ye not do well."
He in great passion all this while did dwell,
More busying his quicke eyes her face to view,

Than his dull eares, to heare what she did tell;
(I, ii., lines 226–232)

Elaine's letter to Esme announcing her return to the Avenue is a masterpiece of deceptive rhetoric. She concludes it "As ever, Elaine," though Esme is too smitten to remember that Elaine's *ever* had been awful. She wants to meet him under the Tate Gallery's picture "The Death of Chatterton," that is, Wordsworth's "marvellous boy who perished in his pride," having committed suicide. How exquisite the irony of their meeting beneath the portrait of a dead poet who did it to himself— as Esme will *do it to himself* again. He proposes marriage, she accepts, they marry, and for days afterward Esme "walked about in a trance." She had "turned her back on the circus to look for a base" and has secured one. Elaine was not in love with Esme, "but his adoration pleased her, and gave her confidence in the future" (405). They honeymooned in Paris, where Elaine was the first one to leave the bed after their initial night there.

> She wondered, still looking down on him, what he would think about it all this morning, and whether his recollections would be sufficiently clear to realize that he had had the benefit of her not inconsiderable experience. (*Suburb*, 408)

Two of the novel's final three chapters offer a rapid roundup towards closure and to move that along I amalgamate *Carver Roundabout II*, **and** *Heroics Strictly Rationed*. **But** *A Last Look At The Avenue* **deserves closer attention, for it is the thematic hinge which connects** *The Dreaming Suburb* **to** *The Avenue Goes To War*. **Thus, after summary observations regarding Archie, Judy, Elaine and others we will conclude with Frances and Pippa's conversation about dreams, and the thematically indispensable exchange between Jim Carver and Harold Godbeer. The curtain rises, and the action begins.**

In Christmas Week of 1939, Europe was at war again, not the war that many Avenue residents could remember from 1914 "with its terrifying casualty lists," nor the war they expected, with no casualty lists or air raids. There were fewer children about, and some young families had gone off in groups to "the remoter provinces," but for the most part the Avenue appeared to be unchanged. "The French were snug in their Maginot Line, and everyone in the Avenue had been told it was quite impregnable" (412). Archie was very busy altering his chain with the future in mind, replacing every man younger than himself with "a woman over forty." And he was snapping up fourteen-year-old boys who showed promise, interviewing their parents to ensure that they were content to have their boy employed by so thoughtful a man as Archie Carver. "He was now stripped for action, with fourteen branches, each staffed by employees too old, or too young, to be called up, and with sufficient stock to garrison a small town for a long siege" (416).

Jim Carver regarded Hitler and his thugs as "dangerous lunatics" capable of destroying Western Civilization. But what most frightened him was "the apathy of the Avenue as a whole." How, he wondered, could sane people "with access to the same sources of information as himself," hunch their shoulders against the storm and return to their gardens and lawn-mowers on weekends? (417-18). Standing in a queue one day in a long line of young men being turned away by the Sergeant behind a window marked *"Drivers Urgently Wanted"*, he heard one young fellow remark "You know what they say, we lose every battle but the last." Maybe that was it, Jim thought.

> Perhaps almost a thousand years of victory over all Continental armies had bred in the British a confidence that had become swollen to arrogance. Maybe Hitler was rely-ing on that. [But] he was sure that there was nothing basically wrong with the coun-try. Those boys were keen enough; their fathers and uncles had once stood shoulder to shoulder with him in flooded ditches all the way from Switzerland to the sea, and had fought like lions, year after year. What they needed was direction and inspiration from the top, but would they get it from Chamberlain and his gang? (*Suburb*, 419-20)

About this time, Judy married Tim Ascham, a delightful young man she met while working horses at the stables. Tim was destined to die when the troop-ship headed for Egypt was torpedoed. Miss Somerton had been right in advising Judith that the cure for love-sickness over Esme was hard work and openness to the future (422-26). Two other Carvers, Berni and Boxer, had been in the service since 1938, having sped down from the Midlands where they tested motorcycles for the manufacturer, and were already in France "towing brand-new Bofors guns and shouting 'Allez a la bloody trot-whah' to smiling citizens, whose plodding prog-ress caused them to apply brakes" (426-27). Ted and Margy Hartnell quarrelled for the first time because Ted, who learned about Hitler's ovens from the German accordianist, lost interest in music and hungered to enter combat, which Margy, determined that she would keep him at home, counteracted by attempting to get pregnant. The idea came to her since Elaine Frazier's baby's diapers were regularly drying on the clothesline at Number Forty-Three.

Having excluded children from her future, Elaine had been astonished when the doctor told her she was pregnant, a condition which made her very, very unhappy (432-33). As she walked the roadside at dusk alongside "a thin stream of traffic," when she turned to cross over to the Avenue side, headlights flashed, brakes screeched, and Elaine lept back, turned her ankle, and fell sideways into the gutter. The driver of the car, Archie Carver, stopped, helped her up, and helped her pick up her "powder-compact, keys, lipstick and coins." While this was trans-piring, Elaine found that a pleasant picture was forming in her mind.

> Away at the back of her mind a familiar picture was forming, and as he helped her into the car the picture began to merge into a series of pictures. She was on her terrace again, in the gently swinging hammock, with the courtiers standing round, and in the background, smiling complacently, was the Great Provider. (*Suburb*, 435)

Elaine's baby was a girl that Eunice wanted to name Guy after her heroically dead husband, but it was Harold's choice, "Barbara," which prevailed. For all the talk about birth pangs being compensated by "wave after wave of joy, love, and fulfilment," Elaine's experience was nothing like that. The delivery had been uncomfortable but not so bad as "the abcessed tooth she had had in Edinburgh," while she toured with Eùgene. The large basket of assorted fruits from Archie, and his note *"May I pop in and see you one day next week?"* are welcome. Archie may pop in, no doubt about it. Meanwhile, her brother Sydney was already an officer, having signed on as "a volunteer clerk," a position which he chose with the purpose of saving himself from violence. He picked up the "new slang" used by Spitfire and Hurricane pilots, but he had no desire to join them, "having learned his lesson in heroics long ago." Eager flying types "could have their Spits, and their Hurrys, by the hangar-full, for he was happy enough with his loose-leaf ledgers" (439–40).

Edgar Frith got the letter-card on the Monday after war was declared, which gave him severe indigestion. He feared that the war would "paralyse" the antique trade, for people lost interest in luxuries in wartime. Frances told him not to worry, but he did. Pippa had just come into the business to help her mother look after the shop, allowing Edgar "time to go further afield to auctions and private sales" (441). Would Edgar like to go back and see Sydney? He thought that a bad idea, for he wouldn't want to see his father, and the sentiment was mutual. "You see, Francie, I never really liked him, not even when he was a little chap. I always felt he was watching me, but in a nasty way, if you know what I mean" (442). Frances kissed Edgar and went into the kitchen, where Pippa was making coffee. Pippa, a very minor character it would appear, is the novel's *seer*, who sees with the wisdom of great age although barely past girlhood; she understands with unclouded clairvoyance what things are at stake, and how they will turn out. As *The Dreaming Suburb* approaches its conclusion, Pippa's voice, or rather her wisdom, echoes across the distant Avenue from her home in the north of England.

The reason war is terrible, Pippa tells her mother, is not "a *personal* thing. It's more the feeling of nothing mattering any more." Frances is not sure she understands.

> The girl said: "All the people you talk to are most afraid of air-raids, and gas, and things like that. I don't think those things are really important. What *is* important is that people have let it happen again, so soon after your war. That means that they always will let it happen, even after this is over and done with. You see, a war like this makes everything else useless, doesn't it? I mean, planning things, and looking forward to things."
>
> "What sort of things?" asked her mother, and it occurred to her that Pippa might have a secret or two after all.
>
> "The sort of things," said Pippa, "that you dream about, but without meaning to."

Frances discovered that she was crying and wondered if it was because Pippa had grown up and she hadn't noticed it. Covertly drying her eyes, she said "War or no war, there'll always be plenty to dream about."

Pippa shook her head slowly. "I don't think you understand what I'm trying to say, Mummy." She pointed down into the street below. "All those people...they've all got plans—coming here for the summer holiday was just one of them. But I don't really mean that sort of plan, I mean big plans, big for them anyway. They were all saving, or working, or falling in love, or studying for something; and now that thing's happened, and they might just as well have not made any plan, because at any moment now all the young ones will be given a railway ticket to go somewhere they've never wanted to go, and when they get there they'll be pushed into something that isn't part of their plan. Then all the old ones, like poor Edgar out there, won't count any more just because they *are* old, and when it's all over they really will be old, and they'll just go on living on things they remember before it happened. That's what's so awful about a thing like war—it stops people dreaming." (*The Dreaming Suburb*, 442-44)

The novel's concluding chapter, *A Last Look At The Avenue*, imitates the wide panoramic sweep of a movie camera documenting the states of mind of characters who "represent the greater part of Britain's population." Pippa had been only partly right, for in early Summer of 1940 the Avenue's dreams fell away, but "new ones began to germinate." That April, the rumblings of war were "not heard very clearly" in the suburb, though Jim heard them "more distinctly," for he was "a trained soldier" who read constantly (445).

By the end of May the word "Dunkirk" suggested to the Avenue folk the disappearance of Ted's ragtime music, along with Eunice's cloche hats and "the Charleston steps that Elaine tried to teach Esme." Dreams were going cheap, and one of the bargains was Jim's old dream of the Brotherhood of Man though he hardly noticed its passing, since in its place he already had a new vision, "the dream of a Militant Democracy, of the gathering of free men the world over for one frantic, pulverizing assault on the active forces of Fascism" (447).

Eunice Godbeer was sent to Torquay, the seaside resort in Devonshire, on May Day. She spent her days reading the same novels that had always delighted her, window shopping, talking to Barbara, and "brushing her long, golden hair" (449). Elaine's dream was still unchanged, except that she had added to the hammock and courtiers a private airplane and a sleek white yacht. She was "secretly delighted" to have the baby off her hands along with Esme, who had joined the R.A.F. Having the house to herself, "her appointments with Archie, and the handsome broad-shouldered Pole that neither Archie nor Esme had heard about," had become less complicated (449).

Archie's dream had undergone enriching modifications, for he was already "feeling his way into" real-estate and second-hand cars, and even nylons. In the meantime, there was Elaine to play with, his only genuine problem being the choice he faced: whether to seek more money, more power, or "a judicious combination of both" (450-51). Margy Hartnell put her dream in the deep-freeze because so many musicians has been "swept away by the Enemy Aliens Act," and Ted was beyond her reach, for Dunkirk had "coaxed his conscience" out of sleep (451).

At Number Four, Becky, reacting to the commotions she sensed, started
having her spells again, but so many years had gone by that Edith had forgotten
how to moderate them. Her lodger, Jean McInroy, was ecstatic to be helping First-
Officer Hargreaves conduct fire drills, while she fashioned him into "an Infantry
officer in the magazine article she was illustrating" (452-53). Hoping to be neighborly to the woman whose son had recently enlisted, Edith knocked at the Frist's
door, but nobody answered, though she knew Sydney's mother was in. Edith was
better received at the Carvers, where she called every day to ask about the twins,
who "had not come home" after that Dunkirk business. She wondered whether
in the end her house would be the only inhabited dwelling in the Avenue, and
the prospect so distressed her that as she went past the old Granada [now Odeon]
and read the advertisement for *Gone With The Wind*, she bought a ticket, watched
the movie, and fell in love again, deciding that "whenever things get unbearable
I'll slip down to the Odeon" (453-55).

When Judith received official word that Tim had gone down with the torpedoed troopship, rather than crying she went to the riding stables that Maud
Somerton was talking of selling, "saddled up Jason," the big chestnut, rode to the
spot "where she had first met Tim," and reflected upon their brief life together.
Tim had always been smiling and as she listened to the memory of his laughter,
Judy heard a message behind it "telling her to snap out of it for God's sake, and
to mount Jason and gallop off up the sunken lane, and into the future." It was
unreasonable for her to think she *had* no future. A week later she was back at the
Avenue and in a month "joined the W.A.A.F. as a trainee plotter," where she distinguished herself for her work (455-57).

Esme was in an R.A.F. Training Station in the south most of that summer, where a slight defect in his vision led to rejection for an air-crew, but he was
compensated by the secretarial work they gave him. The invasion of Poland had
caught him off guard, but when at last he saw things as they were, he did his best
to make amends. On the strength of his fast typing and competence with short-
hand, Esme "was spared the long period of deferment that attended most enlist-
ments in these days" (457-58). He was relieved when Eunice "offered to look after
the baby in Devon," and he snapped up the offer. During the twenty months of
Esme's marriage to Elaine, she continued to be the inscrutable woman she had
always been, "despite that brief glimpse he had had of her as the tender, submis-
sive, dutiful creature during the interval between their reunion under 'The Death
of Chatterton' and their return from the Paris honeymoon." They never fought,
but neither was there "any real accord between them" and Esme could do nothing
to change that. Of all the Avenue dreamers, he was probably the one person who
"was conscious of putting his dreams into cold storage," because that dream "was
fundamentally unchanged" (457-60).

Jim and Harold Join Forces

Toward the end of June, Jim had an interesting talk with Harold Godbeer.
They had never been intimate friends, for differences of temperament and political viewpoint kept them wary of one another. But under the stress of imminent conflict in Europe, that was about to change.

> "What do you make of it all, Godbeer?" Jim began. "Pretty frightening, isn't it?"
> Harold said nothing for a moment, but sucked his pipe, while he endeavoured to adjust himself to Jim's unexpected cordiality.
> "Well, I'm not as worried as I *was*, old man," he said at length. "No, I'm not nearly as worried as I was." (*Suburb*, 463)

If Pippa is the intuitive seer of the Avenue, Godbeer is second only to her, his expertise being based not upon pure intuition, but a shrewd comprehension of the evidence which reading and reflection had prepared him for.

> Jim was impressed by the man's quiet, forceful confidence. It wasn't the brand of confidence he had encountered in pubs and committee rooms recently, rehashes of hastily written leader-articles, or echoes of the bombast of bewildered politicians. It was a confidence that had obviously grown up inside the man while he was living *here*, in this Avenue, among millions of people almost exactly like him, it was a distillation of centuries of security and national triumph, with its roots deep down in Trafalgar and Waterloo, and the assault on the Hindenburg Line. It drew its strength from the dry bones of men like Palmerston, and Gladstone, and Sir Edward Grey, and its inspiration from the Chartist movement, and the Education Act, and Lloyd George's campaign against the House of Lords. It was born and belonged here, along the small, neatly-kept front gardens of the terrace, with their rough-cast fronts, little gatepost pillars, and looped chains, that seemed at this moment of history to make each little block of brick and slate a fortified castle, manned by a garrison who would count it a privilege to die where they stood, with or without some reserve ammunition in the back bedroom.
> Looking at Harold's pale, narrow face, in the soft glow of the pipe-bowl, Jim's doubts and fears of the last few weeks fell away from him. He felt immensely braced and refreshed by the contact, and intensely curious to hear more.
> "Go on, Godbeer," he said earnestly, "tell me *why* you think that, please—it's important to me...I don't mind admitting, I've been in a fog up to now!"
> Harold smiled into the gathering dusk, vaguely flattered by his neighbor's invitation.
> "Well now, I don't pretend to be a strategist, old man," he went on, "but I've always though of myself as a man of average intelligence, and I like to think about what I read, and what I see. Now here are those two boys of yours, I watched them grow up, and it always fascinated me to note how they always did everything together. Well, you see how it paid off in the end? Someone turned them loose over there, weaponless, as far as I can see, and with every card stacked against them. Just turned 'em loose, with the entire countryside in chaos, and what did they do? They just set out for home, using their heads, I imagine, and absolutely refusing to panic. But what struck me about it all when I talked to them earlier this evening was that they did it *together*, the same as they've always done everything together, and it seems to me—this is a bit far-fetched,

no doubt—that this is what we've all got to do from now on. We've got to stop nagging at one another, and face up to things as *a people* again, the way we did last time, and I don't doubt every time before that! Once we do that no one can beat us. We'll get hurt all right, and it wouldn't surprise me if a lot of us didn't live to see the end of it, but plenty will, enough to put paid to that mob of scoundrels. The point is, if we once *do* this, if we once show the rest of the world that we're not going to stand for the sort of thing that's been going on long enough over there, then we'll be a sort of front-line of our own, and everyone else in the world who thinks like us will come bustling up to lend a hand. When that happens it can't last very long, can it, old chap? Nobody's going to convince me that there aren't a damned sight more decent people about then there are bullies and perverts, who get a kick out of stamping on other people's corns. Does that seem sense to you, Carver?"

Jim took a deep breath, inhaling the scent of baking grass, that blew in from the meadow on the light breeze. He felt better, and more at peace with himself, than at any time since Munich.

"It makes a dam' sight more sense than anything I've read in the papers since the last Armistice, Godbeer," he said emphatically, "and if my guess is right, and all the people round here think even roughly as you do, then I'd say you're on a good wicket, old chap, and that that little bastard is in for the biggest surprise of his life!" (*Suburb*, 464–65)

Part II: *The Avenue Goes to War 1940–1947*

In terms of structure, *The Dreaming Suburb* could be described as a number of loosely-related subplots none of which is doggedly pursued, all of which have been broken into pieces resembling tesserae, which are being configured into a mosaic representing the British population from the time of Jim's return from the trenches of WWI, to Dunkirk. Delderfield tells us, "I have never been the kind of author who looks for his material in terms of plot or persons. With me it is the canvas on which I am going to paint that is the essential piece of apparatus" (*Amusement*, 16). On the other hand, however, the Bayeux Tapestry, essentially a very long strip of "background," exists in order to picture horses and soldiers crossing the Channel in boats to defeat King Harold, making English women sufficiently happy with the result to assemble a remarkable memorial of that event. Using another analogue, while the background of Brueghel's *Fall of Icarus* certainly presents a shepherd and a plowman at their work and a goods-laden ship sailing where it needs to get to, it also contains two winged figures in the sky above them, one of whom has just lost his wings. And these point to a completed plot sequence which antedates Icarus's unhappy demise, and which is more important than subsidiary figures in the picture Breughel designed and painted.

Having acquainted readers with the dramatis personae in *The Dreaming Suburb*, it is high time for this writer to cut to the chase, bring in the clowns, allow the players to get to the *action* that has been so thoroughly prepared for. Delderfield does that in *The Avenue Goes to War*. And while we could continue the nickle-and-dime progress of the first volume past Dunkirk, it makes vastly more sense to identify the small number of important plot lines which are explored in the second volume and concentrate upon them, turning our attention away from the minor characters. In my reading of *The Avenue Goes to War* there are five plots which merit our close attention. In the order of their relative importance they are 1) Jim and Harold, 2) Archie, 3) Elaine, 4) Esme and Judy, 5) Berni, Pippa, and Boxer. Why have I selected these? Having become friends near the end of *The Dreaming Suburb*, Jim and Harold, given their differing temperaments, are something akin to Masters of Ceremonies who oversee the action unfolding before them, agreeing and disagreeing with one another in ways useful to the novel's purpose. Second, Archie Carver is a "larger" figure than virtually any other character in the novel, and his contrarian activities ought to be followed out to their conclusions, rather than sourly passed over because he is a selfish wretch. Third, Elaine, like Archie in having deliberately set out upon a course of action that is antisocial in its essence, indeed predatory, is nevertheless too *interesting* a character to ignore; what will her conduct lead to? Fourth, the Esme and Judy action is a unified whole story, more detailed and absorbing than any other plot sequence in the novel, except for Archie and Elaine. Fifth, the Berni, Pippa and Boxer plot is the only other problem/resolution sequence which merits our careful attention. My presentational strategy is to bring each of the five plots forward to mid-novel, one at a time, setting earlier plots to marking time until the fifth is brought up alongside the others, in order that the several story lines not lose their interrelationships. Then, I will proceed as before, in single file that is, to the novel's end.

In his essay "Anatomy of a Saga," Delderfield tells us that "undisciplined characters are the most rewarding," and these would include Archie and Elaine, even though they are meticulously disciplined in their own contra-social action. They both engage in conduct which *Worm's Eye View*, so well-received by wartime audiences, hilariously excoriates. In "Anatomy of a Comedy" *Worm's Eye's* playwright explains that his satire "was not aimed specifically at landladies," but commented more widely upon the "very large section" of the British public "that stood aside between 1939 and 1945, and let things take their course, somehow managing to enjoy a tolerably comfortable war" (*Amusement*, 285–87; 277–78). The parasite, anyone who receives some advantage without giving anything useful or proper in return, is welcome in comedy because his expulsion strengthens the society by endorsing its better values, like Falstaff's repudiation in *Henry V*.

In *"Anatomy of a Saga"* Delderfield says further that in *The Avenue Story* and *A Horseman Riding By*, discussion of which will conclude this book, he had "set out to tell a straightforward story of a group of undistinguished British people—the only kind of people I know." This revelation speaks to the crucial matter of his credentials for writing cultural history, i.e., direct personal knowledge of the material he offers in fictional form. But he continues by saying he was thwarted in his straightforward expectations.

> Very few of the characters developed in the way I had hoped and intended, but I came to understand that the least of them were more specifically aware of their potentialities than I, so that the story that emerged at least possessed the merit of credibility. (*Amusement*, 285-87).

That is, Delderfield discovered that he really did not know very well "the only kind of people" that he "really knew." This is the sort of thing one discovers about characters who do not really know themselves until a crisis—war, for example, or their reaction to disappointment—demonstrates their essential being. In a cultural historical novel this is exactly what we hope to see happening. Will the English people as a whole stay strong under stress, until Hitler is finally taken down when the civilized countries at last get up off their knees and join the struggle alongside England? Will Archie and Elaine pull themselves together after their disappointments, straighten up and fly right? The play's the thing which will prove their mettle.

The Jim and Harold Plot

The friendship between the two men was settled by Jim's agreeing to move into Harold's otherwise empty house and keep him company. The occasion for that event was the German bomb which fell close enough to them to "scatter rubble far over the potato rows of Jack Strawbridge's dig-for-victory patch behind the first houses on the Avenue's even side." Godbeer's electric light went out, "the glass in Eunice's photograph frame cracked under his thumb," and the moment the blast wave had passed, Jim and the other rescue crew workers jumped aboard their crash tender and hurried to the disaster scene. Jim noticed that an arm protruded from the debris, and pulled at the debris until the body of an elderly woman came into view. Because he could do nothing for her, he continued through the house and found a live woman and two live children, saved by "the 'under-the-stairs' theory," while Grandma pottered about at the blackout curtain until it was curtains for her (29-31). When Jim came off-duty at early dawn, he heard his neighbor Godbeer calling him over for a cup of tea. Harold "kept tapping at the cracked frame of his wife's photograph," as if he had long been doing so. He asks apologetically, but Jim brushes off Harold's awkwardness about asking.

> "You needn't apologize for being a bit edgy. Another split second on that Jerry's bomb-release and it would have been curtains for this end of the Avenue!"
>
> Harold began to talk, rushing his sentences, but holding his glance down on Eunice's picture.
>
> "I thought it was superstition at first Carver...you know...at times like this we're all inclined to get little whims and fancies! I was frightened all right, but I felt I could cope with it, until this...this picture cracked in my hand. Then it seemed to me that, it was a...well, a kind of omen. I thought 'I'll never see my Eunice again...I'll be dead

before Christmas! Or she will, or we both will!' No, no, let me finish old man..."—as Jim lifted his hand,—"then I decided that it wasn't really an omen at all, but that I was telling myself it was, and using it as an excuse to run, to get the hell out of it, by the next train!" (*War*, 34-5)

Jim observes that nothing holds Harold in the Avenue, while he himself, being "a full-time A.R.P. worker", has to stay. Carver was puzzled by Godbeer's line of reasoning, until Harold confessed that "I want to stick it as long as people like you stay. You see...I believe in this war, and I don't want other people to fight it for me! If there's nothing else I can do, at least I can hang on, and not let them chase me out of my home."

> Jim looked at him with affection. Here was the staying power of the British, revealed in the person of a pigeon-chested little city clerk, hanging on to his terraced home in the suburb, while all hell broke loose round him, hanging on and staying put, simply because he was vaguely aware that, by doing so, he was identifying himself with the clear-cut issues of right and wrong, and with the one basic principle of democracy, that everybody understood—the right to let people and nations muddle along in their own way, without any pressure from outside. (*War*, 35)

When Godbeer invites him to stay Jim reflects that "there's more room in here, and obviously the poor chap is near the end of his tether," and smiling, holds out his hand. "It's a deal!" (36).

It's a good deal for both men. The small and timid Godbeer needs Jim's compensatory strength, his low-boiling-point irascibility. Conversely, Jim's hot temper, worsened by years of fighting for his life in trench combat, could profit from an emotional governor like Godbeer to maintain uniform speed regardless of changes of load which activate his impulse to strike out, to smash the fur-stealing boy in the face before noticing that the police are only seconds away from making the arrest. Moreover, the two men are now sixty-year-olds, and brawling is not an attractive quality in grandfathers. We can see these two neighbors engaged in forging the bond of friendship between them when Jim learns that his son Archie has been whoring with Elaine Frith.

The events leading to the scene we will examine are as follows. Having been abandoned by his wife Elaine, Esme is divorcing her, their baby Barbara having been placed in the care of Grandma Eunice, not-so-safely out of harm's way in Devon. A small notice of the divorce appears in the local newspaper among many such notices the war has brought on, and Harold had quietly hoped that somebody in Jim's family would break that news to him before it got into the paper. Yet nobody did. After all, who goes *looking* for trouble? Unfortunately, Jim's co-worker Hopner, making conversation, asks "is that your boy who's mixed up in the divorce?" No, that's Godbeer's step-son Esme, not my boy Archie. But the blabber-mouth continues to spill the beans by informing Jim that his grocer son has been fooling around with Godbeer's daughter-in-law Elaine. "Marvellous what some women'll do nowadays for a tin of pineapple chunks, isn't it?", Hopner quips. Puzzled, Jim asks "What's my boy, Archie got to do with it?", and Hopner hands him "a folded copy of *The News of the World.* Jim hadn't known, but *Harold* certainly knew, yet he said nothing (142–43). Some friend!

> Harold was brushing his clothes, preparatory to hurrying off for the 8.40., when Jim strode into the narrow hall, slamming the front-door behind him, and whipping the paper from his pocket. He flourished it angrily under Harold's nose.
>
> "Did you know about this, Harold?"
>
> Harold blinked, then nervously cleared his throat.
>
> "Well yes...actually I did...I've known about it from the start."
>
> "Why didn't you tell me? Why did you hint that the chap was a stranger?"
>
> "I don't know—I suppose because I knew it would upset you!"
>
> "You knew I was bound to find out sooner or later?"
>
> "Not necessarily, and anyway, it wasn't really my business to tell you, Jim."
>
> Jim recognised a note of pleading in Harold's voice.
>
> "No, I don't suppose it was," he said grudgingly, "but all the same, I'd much rather have known. Does everybody else in the Avenue know?"
>
> "Everybody who is interested," admitted Harold. Then quickly: "But who is interested in that sort of thing nowadays?"
>
> "*I* am," said Jim, quietly, suddenly peeling off his jacket and unbuckling the broad leather belt that he always wore in addition to braces.
>
> "What...what are you going to do, Jim?" enquired Harold, forgetting that he had a bare ten minutes to get to Woodside in time to catch the 8.40.
>
> "I'm going round to belt some decency into that bloody son of mine," said Jim shortly.
>
> Harold acted instinctively. He reached out and grabbed the buckle of the belt, holding on to it tightly.
>
> "You aren't going to do any such thing," he declared. "That won't help anybody, and it'll only get you into trouble. Besides, Archie's bigger than you, and a good deal younger, so you wouldn't be capable of doing it anyway."
>
> "I'll have a bloody good try," roared Jim, tugging hard at the belt, and jerking Harold halfway across the hall. "Let go of that buckle, damn you!"
>
> "No," squeaked Harold, "I won't! I'm not going to let you make such a fool of yourself, Jim!"
>
> "You've just said it was none of your business! Let go, blast you!"
>
> "No, I won't, and it *is* my business. I think you're behaving stupidly, and I'm going to stop you if I can! You've been a good friend to me and...."
>
> He was unable to complete the sentence, for Jim's fist struck him on his long, thin nose, and he crashed back against the hallstand, losing his balance, and sliding to the floor.
>
> The hall-stand ricochetted from the wall, and fell forward on his shoulders, bouncing off, striking the bannister, and finally coming to rest as a barrier between the two men. The belt remained swinging in Jim's hand.
>
> For a few seconds neither of them moved. Then Jim peered over the hall-stand and regarded Harold with dismay. With his spectacles suspended from one ear Harold

was groping for his handkerchief. Blood from his nose gushed over his white shirt-front, and dripped down his jacket on to the polished linoleum. The sight of the blood restored Jim's self-control.

"I say...I'm sorry Harold...I lost my temper...I didn't mean to hit you like that! Here, take this handkerchief! You're bleeding all over the blasted hall!"

Without a word Harold reached up for the handkerchief, as Jim lifted the hall-stand, replacing it against the wall, and began gathering up an assortment of walking-sticks and unbrellas that had rattled from its racks.

Harold rose slowly to his feet, dabbing his nose and breathing heavily through his mouth.

"I think I'd better go into the scullery," he said. "I've missed the 8.40 now and just look at me? Just *look* at my coat!"

Jim followed him into the scullery, and turned on the cold tap. For a few moments Harold dripped into the sink; then Jim said:

"You'd better lie on the floor and give it a chance to clot."

Harold obediently lay on the floor, and Jim bent over him, gently sponging chin and coat with a dish rag. When the bleeding had stopped Harold sat up and Jim, without another word, put on the kettle for tea.

As soon as it boiled they sat down facing one another. Harold smiled.

"Well, I stopped you, didn't I?"

Jim made no reply.

"You do see that you'd have made a fearful idiot of yourself, don't you, old man?"

"Yes," said Jim gruffly, "I see that, but it doesn't make me feel any better, I can tell you that!"

"Look here, old chap, I'd like to talk frankly if I may. May I?"

Jim grunted and Harold accepted the grunt as an affirmative.

"Well, it's like this, Jim! Here's a marriage that's gone on the rocks because of a war. At least, that's what we tell ourselves. We say it only happened because a husband went to the Forces, and a civilian moved in and took his place. But the fact of the matter is that it isn't the real reason at all. This was one of the marriages that would have gone on the rocks, anyway!"

"How can you assume that?" asked Jim.

"Because I know the girl, and I know the family! Hang it man, I acted for Elaine's father, years ago and she's a bad egg, Jim, bad right through! I've known that for some time, not from the beginning I grant you, because I don't mind admitting that at first she fooled me as much as she fooled Esme, but the fact remains that she's no good, and never will be. If it hadn't been your Archie, then it would have been someone else!"

"Is that supposed to make me proud of being Archie's father," growled Jim. "However, go on, since you seem determined to make light of it all."

"I am not," said Harold, in his best courtroom voice, "making light of it! I am simply attempting—and at considerable personal risk so far as I can see—to prevent you from washing a second lot of dirty linen in public before the first lot's dry! Go ahead! Make a newspaper story of this by assaulting your son! That way you'll expand the two lines in that paper to a front-page story for the whole country to read about!"

"Ah," said Jim, slowly, "you've got something there, Harold. I admit I hadn't looked at it like that. But by God, I'd like to tell Archie what I think of him, sitting there piling up money, and then shutting his shop and climbing into bed with your boy's wife!"

"Well," said Harold, beginning to feel more sure of himself, and pressing his advantage, "there's nothing whatever to prevent you from telling Archie what you think of him, but do it in private, with the edge of your tongue, and not in public with the buckle-end of what looks to me like a road-mender's belt!"

"I've always known Archie was a wrong 'un," said Jim gloomily, ignoring Harold's feeble joke, "he took a wrong turn somewhere, 'way back, when he was a boy, and he's left it too late to straighten himself out! I suppose that's the price a man pays for four years away in the trenches, when his kids are growing up, and he should be around keeping an eye on them! It'll be the same with half the kids today, you see if it isn't! The women too, they need the business end of a strap, some of 'em! It makes a man sick, when we're supposed to be fighting a war for national survival!"

"The war hasn't all that to do with it, Jim," said Harold. "I saw plenty of this sort of thing before the war. If people are born without a sense of responsibility they'll make a hash of marriage, war or no war. As for Esme, I can't help thinking that the boy is well rid of her, and I think he knows it. That's why he talked himself out of a safe job, and volunteered for air-gunner."

Jim set down his cup. "He's done that? Young Esme, put in for air-crew?"

"Didn't your girl, Judy tell you? She's still at the same camp isn't she?"

"No, she didn't tell me," said Jim, thoughtfully, "but I think I see what you mean about Esme. That's a direct result of his mother being killed, and then his wife letting him down?"

Harold shook his head. It was queer, he thought, how much better he was beginning to understand people, and people's notions lately. It was as though, through all these years, his blind devotion to Eunice had stood between him and everybody around him. Six months ago he too would have concluded that Esme's determination to volunteer for air-crew was a mere defiant gesture, something prompted by grief and bitterness, but now he knew that this was not so, that it was simply a part of Esme's growing up and therefore inevitable.

"No, Jim, this is nothing to do with heroics," he said. "Esme tried for air-crew right at the beginning, but they turned him down on account of a slight defect in his vision. They're not so fussy now it seems. I remember thinking that he was relieved at the time, and settled gladly enough for an office job, but now he's beginning to see things as they really are, and that makes him want to play a more active part in this business. You see, Esme's a romantic, and until quite recently he's been content to see life as he wanted to see it, and as he'd always seen it, right from the time he was just a little chap. He always seemed to be shying away from life as it was, and creating a world for himself to live in. You remember how he was always dressing up, and pretending to be someone out of a book?"

Jim remembered. "My girl, Judy was a bit like that," he said. "It's a pity they didn't marry each other, and go right on living in a dream! God knows, there's enough of the so-called practical people about. We could all do with a bit more chivalry and make-believe. When I think of that son of mine...."

Harold, anxious to keep the discussion in the abstract, hastily interrupted.

"You have to let people like Archie and Elaine go their own way for as long as they're able, Jim. They've got it coming to them, believe me! It's the decent people that are going to win out in the end and if I didn't believe that I'd cease to believe in everything!"

"'As ye sow, so ye shall reap'. Do you really believe in that any more, Harold, do you *really* believe in payment deferred?"

"Yes, I do," said Harold, emphatically, "Because it's being proved all round us! Look at the way this country pulled up its socks when it had to, last year, and look at the way the people round here weathered the blitz, and held on until things began to look a bit brighter! They aren't Archies and Elaines, Jim, they're the majority, and that's what's important! If the majority has guts and decency what does it matter if a few here and there don't pull their weight? What does anyone gain by turning aside to knock sense and decency into them? If it isn't there to begin with it's a waste of time trying to put it there! Now do you see what I'm getting at, Jim?"

Jim Carver traced a pattern in a tea-stain on the American cloth table-covering before him. He was silent for a while, extinguishing the final flickers of anger against a son who had shamed and humiliated him. As the last embers of his resentment died he felt once more the surge of affection and admiration for the peaky-faced little clerk who reasoned with him so earnestly, and with such sincerity, and his mind returned to the previous occasion when this same man had revitalised him by falling back on the philosophy of the suburbs, a 'get-on-with-the-job-and-stop-whining' outlook that epitomised every scrap of faith Jim had ever had in the common man.

"You're a good chap, Harold," he said, at length, "a real good chap, and you talk more common sense than anyone I know!" (*War*, 142–49)

While this lengthy quotation earns the space it consumes by so richly characterizing the relationship between these two men, it does more. It contexts three of the remaining four plots which deserve attention, foreshadowing the essence of the Archie, the Elaine, and the Esme and Judy story lines.

The Archie Plot

Jim's son the grocery man, "forty now and acquiring a paunch," worked long hours. His chain of small pop-in stores and their turnover had become "ends in themselves," demanding the close attention that governed the noiseless tenor of his days. After spending Saturday nights with Elaine, who accommodated him "at the agreed price," he would very early on Sundays slip into the store behind his house to take up the floorboards that concealed the "specially hollowed-out cavity" he had excavated, when he had "declared war against the Inland Revenue." This was where his buried treasure lay, those money-filled steel oil drums serving as his Holy of Holies (4–7). Whenever Archie reverted to the same topic that preoccupied him constantly, Elaine knew that to soothe him "she would have to switch his mind right away from incendiaries and food stocks," by pouring him a whiskey and soda, and letting drop her "pink nightdress" (65). Archie worked very hard but it would not be accurate to describe him as a happy man.

"The difference between Elaine and Archie," we learn from the narrator, "was that Elaine was an uncomplicated soul and Archie was not," although at one time he had been. That was before Archie began "thinking a great deal about his elder boy and had begun to relate his own efforts in the sphere of business to the boy's future, as his partner and successor" (68). The problem was that Tony "looked and behaved exactly like the typical public schoolboy of the school classics," for Archie had made the grievous mistake of sending him to one. The class's leader, Tony Carver was "clean, fearless, honest, truthful, loyal and terribly, terribly dull," so Archie was worried when the headmaster's letter suggested that they should discuss "Tony's future." The boy had clearly been more candid with the school-master than with his parents, for he has decided to spend his life in the military. This could never please Archie, but since stubbornness was the one trait that Tony inherited, there is nothing his father can do to move his mind. "Father and son had their talk, and it was a sterile one from Archie's point of view." He drove away "in sullen anger" because the boy had "flatly declined" to consider any alteration in the plans he made "without consulting" his parents (70-75). Archie wondered,

> for the first time, whether he had made a mistake in sending the boy to a place like Hearthover. Wouldn't it have been wiser to have put him to work in the shop, at four-teen, and teach him that the only protection against the buffets life had in store for you was a credit balance at the bank and a secret cash reserve? If he had done this, would Tony still have wanted to go out in search of a military funeral?...It was as though, Archie reflected, the contestants were not really divided into Fascists, and Democrats, Germans and British, but simply into two races of individuals, those who believed anything and everything they heard on the radio, or saw in print, and the others, who had learned long ago that each man's duty was to himself and that all else was claptrap. (*War*, 77-78).

By the autumn of 1941, Archie's mind was "obsessed" by a whole string of problems. His son Anthony had abused him for making money "out of the present emergency," and it had galled him to be "sneered at by a young man whose cricket boots had been bought" with the profits of an enterprise he condemned. The other children were equally disappointing. James, the fourteen-year-old, had no mathematical skill and spent his time looking for birds and small animals in the hedgerows and woods. Even worse, Maria had taught their youngest child, Juanita, to "distrust and dislike men," and therefore she was indifferent to her father. But Maria's real body-blow, her eventual revenge for her husband's long and contemptuous neglect, would be more direct and crushing than turning his children against him.

> She warmed herself with the reflection that Juanita's indifference to him, and his dis-appointment in both the boys, was only the beginning of her revenge, and that one day she would strike him where it really hurt, in his cashbox. She was in no hurry, however, for her real revenge on him could wait; in the meantime, she could amuse herself by frustrating him in other little ways, in the matter of witholding a divorce if he asked for one. (*War*, 155-58)

Archie was at this time worried by the rapid rate at which his pre-war stocks were being depleted. In order to obtain goods he "did business with some very shady people." And this, along with "the constant pressure" of accountants in matters of purchase tax, income tax, surtax, Schedule A, and "other demands of his purse and ingenuity" was mentally wearying. At times he envied Esme Frazier, "cruising about the night sky in a four-engined bomber." For at least they had "known enemies to contend with," flack and the Germans' fighter pilots, "whereas he, hedged about with batteries of forms," could at any time "be betrayed by someone he had been compelled to trust" in order to keep his shelves well stocked (158–59). Archie's situation and conduct makes him the potential target for a well-conducted sting operation.

As for his personal life, if he were to marry Elaine, which he sometimes thought of doing, he knew that he would be taking on "an expensive luxury," but at least she shared "his outlook" and would be companionable. Disappointingly, when he had sounded Elaine on this subject Archie had been "surprised, and slightly mortified," by her evasiveness. She had put him off, saying "You can come here whenever you like, and that's all you really want, isn't it?" Archie is not so sure, for sometimes when he visited her and she "sat hugging her knees and smiling tolerantly from the bed," he felt that he required "more than a soft, white, practiced body, that he needed if not a wife and helpmeet, than at any rate a friend," someone who could be relied upon to "console him without a thought as to whether it was worth it or not" (159–60).

When Archie had "declared war" on the Inland Revenue, it was only a matter of time until the Inland Revenue began to reciprocate in kind. The earliest sign that the agency had him in their sights came when "two plainclothes men," "lean, casual, softly-spoken men" came to interview him one evening. They asked Archie many questions during their two-hour interview, questions which taxed his "iron nerve, and his astonishing memory for figures." At last they went away, "presumably satisfied, and profuse in their thanks" for his time and cooperation. Archie's head "boiled with possibilities," particularly the source of "two cases of whisky and one case of gin" that he had acquired a month ago from a gentleman "by the name of 'Swift'". He had had doubts about Mr. Swift but had bought the merchandise anyway.

> Archie had had his doubts about Mr. Swift at the time. He now recollected his mental appraisal of him, on the occasion of their first meeting. It was 'Swift by name and Swift by nature', but his doubts had not prevented him from making certain arrangements with the gentleman and at the time these arrangements had appeared to be wholly satisfactory ones, and had resulted in Archie being enabled to supply certain of his privileged customers with a limited supply of good cheer.
>
> Now that the lean, raincoated gentlemen had called, however, and shown such a solicitous interest in his dealings with Mr. Swift, he was not at all sure that the acquaintanceship had been so satisfactory after all. He sat deep in thought for more than half an hour after the detectives had left, and then, after a couple of 'phone calls, he made

his decision. If they called once they would call again and next time they might have a search warrant.

It cost Archie a very big effort to destroy, in cold blood, the equivalent of a hundred pounds' capital gain, and for a few moments he toyed with the idea of concealing Mr. Swift's cases of spirit on the premises and not of destroying them utterly.

The moment soon passed, however, and he made up his mind to cut his losses. He put on his heavy overcoat and gumboots and stumped downstairs into the store, where he foraged about among cartons and crates until he unearthed three half-empty cases. He loaded them into the back of his car, covered them with sacks and then stuffed some cardboard cartons on top of the sacking, until the whole space at the back of the car was filled. Then he unlocked his yard gates and drove out into the Avenue, turning right into Shirley Rise and making for the hills, beyond the Old Mill. (*War*, 160-61)

The trip was uneventful except that a policeman stopped him for driving with his rear window blocked, a violation which Archie rectified by rearranging the sacking over the cases. It seemed to him that the coast was finally clear. But the old story is proceeding, and is already fairly well along towards its conclusion. From agents of the Fisc who pursue absconding tax defaulters through the sewers of provincial towns in Auden's "Fall of Rome," to the men who bring about Al Capone's conviction for tax fraud in "The Untouchables," and to Robert Redford's brief Q. and A.—"Who are these guys? They're good!"—when the outlaws cannot elude their intrepid trackers in "Butch Cassidy and the Sundance Kid." When Archie has thrown those three cases of liquor into the pond he experiences "a feeling of achievement" since "those nosy sods in raincoats" will find "nothing incriminating on his premises!" But while he is squelching his way towards the road, he hears the "polite voice" addressing him out of a patch of darkness: "Shall we resume our little chat now, Mr. Carver?" (163).

Archie managed to talk his way out of the whisky and gin situation. Part of the credit went to Mr. Swift, who looked like "a current cartoonist's caricature of the black marketeer," and lost his temper in cross-examination. When Archie's turn came, the prosecution argued that "a man who has purchased two cases of spirits in good faith does not normally throw them into a pond on a dark night" just after talking with detectives. Archie had apologized for having acted like "a hysterical fool," but he had been overworked, and he played the "slow-witted, bewildered" man, sincerely sorry if he had done wrong. In the end, the jury gave him the benefit of the doubt but sentenced Mr. Swift, "who had a record," to two years of prison. However, Archie did not get off scott free.

Something had happened to him when those two lean men had loomed out of the dusk in the muddy lane down by the pond and he was now like a man trying to stem a torrent assailing a crumbling dyke. As soon as he had planted his feet and braced himself to hold out the water at one point it poured through at another, until at last he began to lose heart and seek relief in the bottle. (*War*, 197-201)

Had Elaine been nearby he might have relaxed occasionally, but she was entertaining another man down in Cornwall, and when he solaced himself "in the arms of a shopgirl" that he had seduced, the girl's brother assaulted him in front of one of his shops. The Inland Revenue representatives began to "call on him," but being in no condition to endure their challenge, he passed them on to his "tame accountant," who settled for a whopping sum of money "rather than face court proceedings that might have been fatal to both of them."

Pulling himself together, Archie reasoned that nobody had "got anything on him" for under-the-counter wholesaling and he still had "three large oil-drums full of capital!" With this in reserve, and the war "still in full swing," he could begin again in a different field, "property perhaps, or government contracts of one kind or another." His heart warmed by the bright prospects opening before him, Archie moved the crates covering "the trapdoor to the tiny vault," the excavation "waist-deep and brick-lined." But when he jumped down into the recess, his foot "glanced against the nearest drum," and the hollow clang he heard already told the story his mind was unwilling to believe. Not only one, but all three drums were empty. Beyond any doubt, Maria had plucked poor robin bare. She had "chosen this way to get even," from which it followed that she hated him "with the vehemence that he reserved for the Inland Revenue," or the men who "caught him red-handed at the pond!". Jumping into his car, he tore off towards Somerset to "get his money back if he had to beat Maria to a pulp"; but he had a few drinks to steady his nerves along the way, and he drove too fast in the rain, hunched over the wheel, "his knuckles white with the intensity of his grip," and thus he hardly saw "the little cloud of cyclists" who suddenly were there before him. Several cyclists were hurt and one died. When Archie regained consciousness and saw the policeman sitting beside his hospital bed, with "a pencil in his hand and an open notebook on his knee," he was "fascinated by the hostility in the man's eyes" (201-06).

The Elaine Plot

After they had fled from Esther's domestic tyranny during her convalescence in the hospital, Edgar found Elaine a "steady job as a hotel receptionist" in Wales, but she had not stayed there long. The dream she had formulated in early adolescence had "shaped her life for many years now," involving her in touring the country with The Great Eùgene, crossing England "as the mistress of a middle-aged variety agent," and next joining the circus, which brought her into contact with the reality agent, Mrs. Tappertit. Having then married Esme Frazier as a fall-back security measure, she threw him over, their daughter having been "taken off her hands" while Esme disappeared from the scene. Elaine remained unsettled because hers had not been "a static dream", but one that was "constantly expanding." If the war continued "who could tell what possibilities lay ahead," so long as she kept socking away her money. She was "only twenty-nine," and there was still plenty of time for her to realize her dream (7–9).

For Elaine, the present is unimportant except as the gateway to her golden future, while the past is the history of her disappointments. She is seldom philosophical about her life, but one exception to her refusal to look backward is a conversation she has with Edgar concerning the family she grew up in. The occasion is Esther and Sydney's being blasted to smithereens by the bomb which "no one in Number Seventeen heard approach."

> It whistled down like the others, but their ears [Esther, Sydney and his girl friend Cora] were still singing with the previous explosions.... It burst squarely on the small concrete slab, immediately behind the kitchen window, and the sole witness of the explosion saw Numbers Seventeen, Fifteen, and Thirteen bulge out, hover, and then rocket away almost brick by brick, into the meadow behind the Avenue.

Sydney's remains were not found at the blast site, for "the wave had sucked him clear of the wreckage, and out across the gardens, flinging him over the little greenhouse, where his father had once consoled himself with potted hyacinths, and tossing him into the brick-strewn meadow, fifty yards or more from the house." No one had thought of looking for him there (130–32).

Edgar came from Llandudno for the double funeral, and afterwards called on Elaine at Number Forty-Three, to scold her for not having attended the service. She was friendly, thinner than he recalled, her voice huskier, but "as frank, and as down-to-earth as ever," so that he wondered how two people as limited as Esther and himself could have produced "a handsome extrovert" like Elaine. Edgar felt "like a shy adolescent, trying to ingratiate himself with a pretty and sophisticated aunt."

> "We're all alone now, Elaine," he said, as he addressed himself to a vigorous stirring of tea. "Perhaps we ought to try and see a bit more of each other in the future?"
>
> "We've always been alone, Father," she told him, very condescendingly he thought, "for neither one of them were anything to us! Why do we have to pretend, just because they're dead?" (*War*, 135)

One can see why Delderfield occasionally uses words such as ruthless to describe Elaine, though others might prefer to call her candid, which is how ruthless people would rather express it. *The Elaine Plot* becomes richer if we listen to more of their dialog. Esther and Sydney have been killed. "Well, and so what? It might have been us, mightn't it?"

> "It might still be us, any time, and would it do *us* any good if the people round here thought more of us simply because we'd been killed in an air-raid?"
>
> He made a series of deprecating clicking noises with his tongue, but she ignored them. "Think back, to the time when we were all living together, in that awful house! Mother treated you like an elderly lodger, and me—she got a hell of a kick out of thrashing me every time I put a foot wrong. I don't say it was altogether her fault, I always thought there was something a bit queer about her, something that they put people

away for, if it gets too bad! You were perfectly right to leave her, and go off with a nice normal woman, like Frances. And me? I was perfectly right to leave, too, the minute I was old enough to fend for myself. Why should we spend any more of our lives than we need with a person like that, someone who finds pleasure in being miserable? And how does her being killed in an air-raid make her a good mother, or a good wife? Then there's Sydney...what was he, but a spiteful, sneaky, smarmy little devil, from the time he was old enough to spy on us? I can see him now, with his piggy little eyes, looking us over before he scampered off to Mother, to earn me a welt or two with the cane. Of the two of them I must say I preferred Mother, but I'm not shedding tears over either of them. I'm sorry they were killed, in the way a person is sorry about strangers killed in a rail accident, or something of that sort, but I don't feel sorry inside, and it's no use asking me to pretend that I do, for the benefit of the neighbors!"

He was silent for a moment, considering her explanation with the same deliberation he employed assessing the genuineness of a piece of china, or a set of Georgian spoons. Finally his honesty won through.

"I daresay you're right, Elaine," he said, with a sigh. "We all make an attempt to register conventional emotions at a time like this, but I suppose it's only because we're afraid people will think less of us if we don't." He changed the subject abruptly.

"Are you and Esme really breaking up?"

"It looks like it," she told him, again without a trace of concern in her voice, "we weren't really much good for each other. It was wrong of me to marry him, I suppose, but nobody could have convinced him of that at the time, could they?"

Edgar remembered an earnest young man, calling on him at Llandudno in the first year of his second marriage, and asking, pitifully he thought at the time, if he had received any news of Elaine. He remembered the same young man's shining eyes, when he had seen him and Elaine off as a honeymoon couple. Finally he recalled Esme's tired face not long ago, when he had brought the baby up to Llandudno, to be cared for by Frances, and her daughter, Pippa.

"No," he said, "it's no use pretending about that either, Elaine. I'm sorry about little Barbara, though. She's a lovely little kid, and no trouble at all. Frances and Pippa are spoiling her quite shamelessly, and she'll make us all suffer for it I daresay, but she's going to be very pretty, very pretty indeed! She reminds me of you, when you were her age."

"She won't be much like me," said Elaine, and for the first time he thought he detected a trace of wistfulness in her voice. "She's half Esme's, and she'll put on his rose-coloured spectacles the moment he offers them to her!"

"Are you going to...marry this other chap, the grocer over the road?" asked Edgar, tentatively.

"God knows," said Elaine, "we'll cross that bridge when we come to it! He hasn't asked me yet, though I've got a feeling that he will before long. He's coming over directly, would you like to meet him?"

"No...no...I...er...don't think that would be very wise," said Edgar, "not with the divorce pending...I mean...! Besides, meeting me would embarrass him, wouldn't it?"

Elaine laughed. "It might embarrass you, but it wouldn't embarrass Archie! However, suit yourself, and thanks for looking in, Daddy, I'll keep in touch."

He got up, gladly enough, and she handed him his bowler hat, and dark, woollen gloves. He followed her into the hall, hesitating a moment as she opened the front door.

"Well...good-bye Elaine...if you want to talk you can always ring...I'm in the shop now, most of the time," and he bobbed forward, kissing her lightly on her cheek and hurried out in the Avenue.

He turned right at the gate, averting his eyes as he passed the ragged gap where Number Seventeen had stood. What a mess they were making of everything! And what a mess most people made of their lives! Surely, at a time like this, the only sane thing to do was to snatch at every dandelion clock of happiness as it drifted by, to live by the hour, and let the rest of the world go hang!

He was grateful to be going back to Frances, Pippa, and the baby, and to be leaving the Avenue, with all its memories, behind him. They were not very pleasant memories and he would never come here again, not if he could avoid it. (*War*, 136–38)

Edith Clegg saw something one day at the Odeon, where she was now seeing movies and working, as "a kind of under-manageress and usherette-supervisor," that moves *The Elaine Plot* along. Jean McInroy having married her now-deaf fire-fighter hero and moved out, Edith spoke to Jim Carver, who suggested that two American officers would do very well as lodgers. She followed his advice, and one of those two was "little Lieutenant Ericssohn," a man she had seen snuggling close to Elaine in the Odeon. He was "spooning" with "that naughty wife who had been Miss Frith, and later the guilty party in the divorce of that nice, dreamy boy, Esme, whose poor, pretty mother had been killed at Torquay." Ericssohn had looked away, "rather shamefacedly" Edith thought, when she accidentally "flashed her torch on him." But it was no business of hers. And he "did not have a framed photograph of Mrs. Ericssohn on the table beside his bed," so perhaps he was a bachelor "entitled to all the spooning he could get" (233–41). Edith dismissed the incident from her mind, though we, being privy to more information than Edith has, easily see what is going on. Elaine has gone on the hunt.

Looking back in time to view Elaine in her more recent engagements, Esme gave her the house at Number Forty-Three, and she had accepted the gift with considerable relief; she had been homeless and so knew "what it was like to lack a base," which had been her "principal reason" for returning home and marrying Esme before the war. A base provided her "independence," which she "treasured" because she had "won it against very heavy odds inside Number Seventeen." The current project, "her Dutchman, Van Loon," will soon prove to be "yet another blind alley in the search of a Great Provider," and she was "getting a little exasperated with blind alleys" by this time. Perhaps the little American Lieutenant will do, but "viewed as a whole, her career as a professional adventuress was unremarkable" (242–45). "Hope springs eternal" however, so the poet says, and perhaps she will soon strike oil, find gold, put her money on a winning horse. She had been wasting her time with Van Loon because "now that America had entered the war," her Great Provider must be hanging like fruit on a tree, begging to be taken.

> Somewhere among the Americans there must be a man who would understand her
> yearning for terraces, sports cars, iced drinks, steam yachts and Mediterranean anchor-
> ages. If the cinema was to be taken seriously such men were common place in America,
> and what she had to offer in exchange was readily marketable among them judging by
> the whistles she heard when she happened to walk past a trainload of Americans on
> Crewe station the other afternoon. (*War*, 247)

Her Dutch disaster had taught Elaine the lesson that if her dream was to be
realized, "it would be fulfilled in a way that bolted the door against future disasters." After she got settled in her hammock, Elaine would not "dispute legal possession of the terrace on which it was slung" (249). So when she had finished her
Dutchman by whirling his clarinet on high, and bringing it "crashing down on
the back of his neck" (251), she caught the next train to London and, there being
neither bus nor taxi available at 6.30 a. m. to take her to the Avenue, Elaine was
panting along with her heavy case past the gate of Number Four, Edith's house,
when the American officer wearing rimless spectacles ran after her, calling out "in
the rich drawl of the Deep South" his offer to assist this damsel in distress. She
stopped and smiled, "and thereby bestowed upon Lieutenant Ericssohn the fatal
glance, demure, yet vaguely promising, that she had once practiced before a wardrobe mirror not fifty yards from where they now stood" (252). Is Ericssohn now a
goner? Or have they begun a *mano a mano* whose outcome cannot as yet be foreseen?

The Esme and Judy Plot

One sunny morning in Torquay, Eunice Godbeer was shopping with her granddaughter Barbara, "Baba's large pram" serving as a carry-all into which her adoring
caretaker could "dump all the heavier purchases." Eunice looked up when she heard
the droning but did not recognize these aircraft as "German hit-and-run-raiders."
When the projectile struck her she felt no pain, but "just a small and final spurt
of irritation." When Harold was informed of his wife's death, he relayed the news
to Esme, and his C. O. assigned his secretary, Miss Redvers, "well trained and
resourceful," to deal with it. She accompanied Esme back to the Avenue where he
was surprised to find that Elaine was away from their home in the middle of the
night. He did not know that she was in Blackpool with Archie. Her troubled husband telephoned his father-in-law in Llandudno to see whether Elaine is there, but
Edgar has no idea where she might be.

> Esme said goodnight to Edgar, took a final look around the bedroom, where Elaine's
> perfume still hovered, and then recrossed the road to Number Twenty.
>   "She's not there, he told Jim, shortly, "I can't imagine where she is."
>   Jim could imagine, but he said nothing. After all, Elaine's wartime reputation was
> only an Avenue rumor, originating, as far as he could discover, from that fatuous ass
> Grubb, the A.R.P. warden.

> "You get some sleep," said Jim, "try, anyway! You've got a rotten time ahead of you. Would you care to stay here?" Esme declined, returning thoughtfully to Number Forty Three. (*War*, 84–90)

Elaine returns while Esme is still in the house enduring deep anxiety. She had left town, for "they said Blackpool was the only place to go for a break" from the stresses of war. The phone rings, Elaine hastens to pick it up first, but "a split second ahead of her" Esme answers it and hears Archie's voice. Elaine "knew that she was adrift again," and that "this odd but convenient marriage would dissolve." Yet the fault was Esme's. People like him "never learned the kind of things she could teach them because they did not want to learn them" (97–100). Esme silently confesses that he *had* wanted to be hoodwinked. There was nothing to gain by further self-deception, "and in a way he welcomed the crisis." He does not believe that Elaine has committed adultery, for "duplicity of that kind was alien to" people of the Avenue, yet he could not deny her adultery for long, and that Archie was her paramour "exascerbated his hurt," because it was "a betrayal among neighbors" (103).

What can he do with Barbara in this situation? There seemed no alternative to taking the baby back to camp with him and letting the R.A.F. deal with the problem. This was a wise decision, for the English military had rushed to the aid of thousands of servicemen whose domestic situation had to be remedied. Esme knew this was true, since he had seen it at first hand.

> He had been struck by the size and scope of the machinery set up to deal with this by-product of war. His own Commanding Officer, a Squadron Leader, was a bluff, middle-aged ex-seaman, who, after years in aircraft carriers, had strayed into the R.A.F. as a regular, in time to catch the floodtide of wartime promotion. Esme had watched him deal with a variety of delicate, personal problems and had been greatly impressed by his common sense and gruff kindness. He was typical, Esme learned, of all regular officers, a type that he had been prepared to dislike and distrust (105–06).

"Collie," Esme's C.O., was at his desk signing documents when Esme arrived back at base.

> "Have you got a baby there, L.A.C.?" he grunted, but without, Esme thought, a note of surprise.
> "Yes, sir, my daughter, sir," said Esme, half coming to attention, but relaxing as the Squadron Leader waved his hand.
> "H'm! What happened? Blitzed?"
> "No, sir," said Esme, "not exactly." (*War*, 109)

In the military Esme had "acquired that sense of *belonging* that the uniform seemed to give all who wore it." He was "a permanent member of one huge, sprawling, joke-cracking, grousing family" (118), and they came to his aid every way they could. Collie having prepared the way, Esme was next driven to the W.A.A.F. orderly room for the royal treatment that boisterous, competent young women know how

to provide, as Delderfield's essay "The Vivandieres" exemplifies from his own experience (*Overture*, 158–65). Esme entered their domain to hear Judy's voice, startled
and delighted, greet him and little Barbara. What could he say? "Hullo, Judy? So
you're the new sergeant the 'good type' who's 'buttoned up'?" Indeed she is. And
after the child has been washed, fed and deluged with presents, the happy Waffery
send them on their way, Barbara sitting on Judy's lap as they drive off in something
like a military parade. The lorry driver "slipped into neutral," then "winked down
at the corporal" and "jerked his head to the nearside of the cabin" in a way that sig-
naled the opportunity that was opening before them. "The corporal took the hint."

> "Preseennnnnnt *hi!*" he shouted, and the men about him, quickly catching on, shuffled
> into line, and smartly presented arms.
>
> "You see," said Judy, to the smiling but embarrassed Esme, "she's practically a V.I.P.
> around camp." (*War*, 120–21)

Though nobody planned it that way, we can recognize in this celebration of
Esme and Judy driving off together with the child in the woman's lap the unsched-
uled rehearsal, the anticipation of Judy's dream as an eight-year-old and for a dozen
years thereafter of being married to Esme and bearing their children—until Elaine
snapped him up with her red dress and mirror-practiced sexual antics. Judy's focus
was upon Esme and their children, Elaine's eyes were glued upon her mirror, and
nothing crucial had changed since then. In the chapter "Judy Full Circle" one follows the logistics of these two young adults, separated for a time by chance and
circumstance, returning to Manor Woods and picking up again where they had
left off years ago. Little Barbara goes to live with Pippa, Edgar and Frances, whom
she reduces "to the status of capering slaves" (164). Having completed his operational training course and come to know "the cold and loneliness of a rear-gunner's
turret" (165), Esme begins a fourteen day leave. As the train carried him towards
the Avenue, Esme reflected that Judy would like his radio-man, Snowball, for,
he recalled, "Judy had been interested in the same things as himself, right from
the days when they played King Arthur in the woods, and flung, oh, how many
Excaliburs, into the Manor Lake?" (167). Judy "wangled" a pass and arrived back
at Number Twenty late the same night as did Esme, who, she knows, is now "sleeping in the back room" of Number Twenty-Two, just next door to her.

 When they walk together on the following morning, they cross the meadow
and take the path to the Manor, having no particular destination but gravitating to
that place. Judy wanted to say "outside you've grown a little, but inside you haven't
changed a bit!", yet shyness stopped her. They had come to the crumbling wall
separating the trees from the ruined kitchen garden of the Manor, the "very spot,
she recalled, where she had overtaken him that first summer morning" when she
introduced herself and eagerly became his trusted helper. Foreseeing the likelihood
that he will soon be blown apart in his rear gunner's turret, Esme says "If I get the
chop, I'd like to go out remembering this place as it was, always." Why, she asks

him, and they have entered into the essential revelatory conversation that returns the two of them to the *together* condition of their childhood, which they both carry within them as unfinished business, a business to which they now return.

His frown of concentration relaxed and he smiled at her.

"Do you remember that day soon after we met, when we came here and you thought I ought to be called "David" because he was your favorite Biblical character? Remember how I played up to you because I wanted to show I was just as good as David with a sling?"

"It was the *first* day we met," she reminded him. "You made a sling out of your handkerchief and the stone went in the wrong direction, over your shoulder!"

"That's it, and I liked you for not commenting on it," he admitted, and as he remembered this fleeting thought, now nearly a quarter-century sped, he realised what it was about Judy that had made her such a pleasant companion in those days. It was the warm and generous understanding she showed of all he found romantic, and her subtle and stimulating appreciation of his ascendancy, as male and showman of the world of dreams.

For a moment, as he contemplated the long line of her jaw, and the curling lashes of her brown eyes, the years fell away, and he saw her again as she had stood before him as a child, so eager to serve and so dazzled by his majesty, the squire, the shieldbearer, the small but perfectly adequate audience for his essays in to the story-book world of plate-armour, and hell-raked galleons. He said, almost without hearing himself:

"How did we come to drift apart, Judy?"

She said nothing, turning quickly away to climb the wall, for the tears had welled up again. They jumped, she first, into the wilderness of the kitchen garden and she pushed on ahead of him, taking advantage of the screen of the old boathouse to whip a handkerchief from her service-issue shoulder-bag and dab her eyes.

"Dear God," she muttered to herself, "what the hell *is* the matter with me this morning? Why am I so damned weepy! It can't be Tim, for Tim never came here with me, and it can't be Esme, either, for I must be over Esme, after twelve years!"

He seemed aware of her embarrassment, for he dawdled over by the gazebo, the same octagonal structure in which they had played Sleeping Beauty on that first morning, and she had waited for him, terrified by the brooding stillness of the Manor, while he disappeared into the reeds in order to emerge as wonder-working Prince.

He had kissed her that morning, and had never kissed her again, not unless one counted kissing at Avenue parties, or hand-kissing when she was Guinevere and he was Lancelot about to set out on a quest.

That was very strange, she thought. Hundreds and hundreds of hours spent together, as they grew from childhood to adolescence, yet never a kiss, never a single step outside the world of make-believe and along the road that she once believed would lead to Shirley Church, and the semi-detached on the Wickham Estate.

She dabbed her eyes again and moved along under the sagging wall of the boathouse. (*War*, 171–72)

We are well enough acquainted with Judy and Elaine to compare them with respect to their engagements with others, and more importantly in their attitude towards temporality, human existence within time. Esther ruled the house Elaine grew up in through suppression and punishment, while Elaine aspires to rule through personal magnetism, the come-hither skills which attract men by promising what they all always want. But curiously enough, when we examine Elaine's ever-expanding dream, it turns out to be a purely static scene, a set piece. The hammock does not swing, the yachts never sail, the courtiers smile like the sun, but never *do* more than smile, while the Great Provider simply provides. The original model of the dream lives of both Esther and Elaine existed in the dotty old aunt's mansion: the furniture and the portraits, standing attendance without moving, without a future. But in bold contrast against this death-in-life, Francis Bacon says that the man who has a wife and children has given "hostages to fortune"; that strumpet can now have her will of him. Judy is willing to take that chance. She wants Esme but Elaine takes him. She marries Tim, then his troop ship is torpedoed and he dies. These thing hurt her, but Judy is strong enough to take the hit when it comes and go forward. Esme, too, that pitiful dreamer, learns how to suffer the "slings and arrows" that Hamlet brooded over and come back fighting. Elaine could learn to do that as well, but the propensity to substitute her personal security for unpredictable relationship makes it more difficult, whereas Judy is better able to prevail because she understands that relationship with others is the key to prevailing. Here is a brief illustration of the difference between them: there were to be no children in Elaine's marriage with Esme, but Judy instinctively grabs up little Barbara, sets her on her lap, and smiles her way forward. I suppose that this makes Delderfield a novelist that academics cannot find relevant, but they are not a last court of appeal. Not while Samuel Johnson's "common reader" is alive and kicking.

We return to Judy and her friend in Manor Woods renewing their former relationship. Nothing else mattered to Judy, the heart-aches of girlhood, Tim's death, "nothing else in the world was of the smallest importance; just Esme."

> They remained there a long time, saying little, for there was little that needed to be said. The wonder of their discovery, and the relief it brought to each of them, precluded discussion of plans and the certainty of separation within days. For the moment they were obsessed by the magnitude of the discovery, and by its inevitability, so clear to each of them now. It was like an absurdly simple solution to a mystery that had baffled them all their lives.
>
> Presently, Esme said:
>
> "Let's stay here a while, Judy. Let's light a fire!"
>
> Even his voice seemed to her to have softened. He was no longer issuing an order, as in the past—go here, do this, that's how I want it, that's how it should be done! His kisses had elevated her to equal rank and her shield-bearing days were over. Whatever they did now they would do side by side and it was clear that he too was aware of this readjustment in their relationship, for he awaited her nod and when she gave it he at once set about collecting twigs and cones, while she dived into her shoulder bag for old letters and scraps of paper....

> She had not known that it was possible to be so happy and serene as this, for her dream had never carried her this far, never to the point of physical contact, of letting her hand slide along his temples and feeling the weight of his head on her thighs.
>
> Her yearning for him swept over her in huge, measured waves, so that sometimes she felt she would drown under them. She cupped his face in her hands and kissed his mouth, gently and constantly and as her lips touched his she read gratitude in his eyes and knew that the majesty had gone from him and that from this point in their lives his need of her was the greater. (*War*, 176-77)

Judy and Esme decide to marry as soon as they can, but the "Change of Plans" chapter illustrates the difficulties that two people in the military can having getting on with their lives. In the spring of that year, "unpredictable" events kept them apart, and in late summer they were still unmarried and "widely separated" (273). Esme's operational tour was cut short and he was "packed off on a conversion course to Lancasters" in Scotland. He was then "posted to a Lancaster squadron," but came down with "shingles in his head," and by the time he recovered, Judy had been sent to St. Eval for "a plotter's course" which delayed any meeting for six weeks more. Yet aside from being unable to marry Judy, Esme felt at peace. Isolated in his gun turret "as the huge machine lumbered across the empty skies," he found himself able to divide his attention into two halves, one of which kept "a sharp lookout for night-fighters," while the other half was delighted by

> the huge and exhilarating emptiness of the sky, the fantastic cloud formations floodlit by slivers of moonshine, the soaring passage of distant tracer. There were the occasional jocular exchanges over the intercom and above all the sense of "belonging" that they brought with them, the sense of adventure, in matchless company, into infinite space.

Of the thirty operational flights Esme was now embarked on, eight passed without his seeing an enemy fighter or "more than a spattering of flak." When not in the air, he wrote long, affectionate letters to Judy, the kind he never could write to Elaine because of the "depressing inadequacy" of her letters to him. Judy, on the other hand, was a kindred spirit, "someone who shared his memories of sunlit days in the plough-land beyond the Manor Wood" (274-76).

In mid-September, Judy wired Esme to say that a change in her duty schedule allowed them to get married "almost at once" at Maud Somerton's home in Devon, if he could make it there quickly. She goes ahead of him and is reunited with her old companion, who is delighted to see her again, and drives her to "the decrepit Georgian manor-farm" which she has used as a headquarters since moving her riding-school into the west. When Judy told her of the problems Esme and she had encountered, Maud had exclaimed "What you need is a thundering good gallop," and Judy is in luck because half a dozen locals will be going "cubbing at 6 o'clock tomorrow." Not only that, but Maud has "borrowed back" Jason, Judy's favorite horse. "'Let's make it a cracking day, Jason,' she whispered, patting the sleek neck, 'because Esme's coming today, and tomorrow's my wedding day.'" The big stallion "threw his head about," and they're off on a fast, furious gallop as "the pack scrambled through hedges, overran the scent, found a new line, and finally poured across the stubble towards the sea" (280–81). In the excitement of the foxhunt, Judy "forgot Esme, the war, the convoys, and the bombing offensive, leaning far over Jason's mane and nursing him through the gaps with a sure, steady touch and never a thought to the kind of ground she was likely to jump down upon beyond."

> Thus she never saw or suspected the taut strand of pig-wire stretched a yard from the hedge, on the far side of the fifth bank.

She flew over the horse's head and down, "face foremost, on to a harrow" at the field's edge, and "glissaded across the field" with a muddy face and a broken collar-bone (281–82).

The bone having been set, Judy lies in a hospital bed when Esme arrives, and the two discuss the accident "in the ironic idiom which they used in the camps over the last two years." But then they grow serious and discuss the future, their future, in Devon. Judy tells him that the Avenue had been to her "like a piece of Devon that had strayed, and lost itself while playing near London." Esme confesses his intention of being a farmer, "because I've got the capital" to buy farmland and Harold has promised to advise him about "the right way to go about it." Judy is delighted, for she wants their children to live "in an unspoiled countryside, where nobody carried umbrellas or caught regular trains." It is hard not to be impressed by the *specificity* of Judy's and Esme's plan for the future compared with the shimmering vacuity of Elaine's dream of a Great Provider who satisfies her solipsistic yearnings. Two hearts which beat as one, Judy and Esme foresee a realistic future, ready to enjoy or endure together whatever their future holds.

Another unexpected change overtakes them immediately. On returning to his base, Esme is assigned to "a twin-force blitz on two widely-separated areas of the Ruhr" (287). He felt "the familiar bumping lift" when they soared aloft and joined a multitude of planes already filling the sky above. Finishing the bomb run, the Lancaster turned for home, and ten minutes later Esme heard "Hawley's thin voice, piping into the intercom from mid-upper turret: *Fighter, fighter! Corkscrew!*," followed by the "wild, senseless bucketing" of the Lancaster's evasive action, then Mac's voice, "terribly urgent," calling *"Jump...jump!"* as Esme groped his way to the hatch and bailed out, while the "shattered aircraft" disintegrated. He "did not think about landing, or of the men still in the aircraft, but only of the vast silence of the sky, and his strange, almost lunatic suspension in it" (290–92).

The Berni, Pippa and Boxer Plot

The first pair of Carver twins were known on the Avenue as the Inseparables, and the Unlikes, epithets that summed up their relationship until accidents of war separate them, and Bernard marries Pippa. Ever since the duckpond near-drowning, keeping his twin out of harm's way, protecting him, had been Bernard's Mission in life. For instance, when the vicious headmaster was about to whip Boxer unjustly, Bernie had snatched the cane from his upraised hand and catapulted it into Cawnpore Road before defending his brother verbally. After that the educational-cheating scheme had been cooked up by Berni and Esme, the scam Longjohn Silverton smoked out and stopped, in large part since it would have harmed Boxer, not helped him. As a young adult Berni continued his protective role, when as the "Suicide Twins" they had driven motorcycles for Sam Gulliver—whose daughter Jackie, "a pretty, impulsive, determined young woman," insisted that Boxer had proposed to her. She "roared up" to the rooming house and demanded that Berni give up Boxer, who "had not made an independent decision in twenty years, not since the day he had decided to test the ice on the pond in the Lane." Berni saw to it that Boxer had been sent off to the railway station.

> If anything was needed to strengthen him in his resolve to get Boxer out of this situation, Jackie Gulliver had provided it, here and now, for Boxer, he decided, would be better off at the bottom of the frozen pond than married to this spoiled, hysterical vixen.
> "You won't get him," he said at last and with great deliberation, "you won't ever get Boxer, not while I'm alive." (*Suburb*, 328)

Further, Berni tells her that "You won't have a baby, and if you did...*it wouldn't be Boxer's*." Upon hearing this the "rage ebbed out of" Jackie and her knees "began to tremble" (329).

 Then, several years later when Esme and Judy had come to an understanding but had not yet been able to wed, the news filtered down, from Louise, that Bernard had fallen in love with Pippa, and she loved him too. She had come to London to make camouflage nets. Jim tested the reliabiliy of Louise's information by observing the couple.

> He came to the conclusion that Louise was probably right, for Bernard, usually a phlegmatic young man, now seemed to be talking more than usual, and as he talked the girl listened, with her enormous brown eyes fixed upon him and her lips slightly parted, as though in breathless admiration.

Pippa had been living at Number Twenty for some weeks when Berni and Boxer came home on leave. Pippa watched the two "and after a brief observation she suddenly buttonholed Bernard in the back garden and said, without preamble, 'Is it like having a baby who won't grow up?'" The remark told Bernard that she "had understood his lifework at a glance." He had not talked of the relationship to anyone before now, "but after the incident of the grenade, at Vaagso" in which Boxer had appeared beyond doubt to have been killed, though he reappeared out from the rubble after some time, Bernard "did feel such a need." Pippa's remark blew up the dam and his anxieties came flooding out. "That's it! That's what it's like and that's what it's always been like, right down to the day he fell through the ice in the Lane" (194).

Berni did not let go of her hand while she counseled him: "Don't let anyone talk you into going to one of those psychiatrists they have in the army nowadays. There isn't anything wrong with you Bernard. It's just that you've had to go through twice as much as every other Commando!" (195). Pippa continues, and her practical advice not only calms him emotionally but points him toward the alteration of attitude he must make, for Boxer's sake and his own.

> "You've got to get used to letting him take his own chances, not only when you're fighting but at all other times, in camp and off duty. You've got to try and concentrate on looking after yourself for a bit and letting him learn to look after *himself.* If you don't you'll crack up and once that happens you'll be separated. Then he'll be on his own anyway. Do you see what I mean?" (*War*, 196)

He does see what Pippa means, and he hopes he can be strong enough to let Boxer decide things himself. Moreover, Pippa proposes marriage to Bernard, without a preamble but within a context, a clarifying explanation.

> "You see, you haven't really begun your own life yet but when you do you'll need someone to share it, because you've been so used to sharing that you wouldn't have any use for a life on your own.... When you remember that you'll come looking for me, and I'll be here, and we could be very happy together, because I love you and I'll always try and look after you the way you've looked after Boxer!"
>
> She had made up her mind to say more. She was going to be quite ruthless and tell him that he would find no release until Boxer was dead, but suddenly his head was against her breast and he was sobbing, so that there was no point in saying more and she could only hold him there, soothing him, as though he was a child who had been desperately frightened and had run to her for help and comfort.
>
> They remained still a long time but presently, when he was calmer, she inclined her head and softly kissed the short, fair hair on his neck. (*War*, 197)

An hour before Elaine had heard Lieutenant Ericssohn's call offering his assistance as she dragged her heavy case up Shirley Rise that August morning, Bernard and Boxer were nearing the end of the sea journey carrying them and their equipment for "blasting a passage through the wired gullies that led up towards the Hess battery west of Dieppe." They were going into combat again. "Suddenly the boat grated on sand" and the commandos "ran crouching into the blackness ahead." Boxer's face appeared out of the murk, and Bernard heard him shout:

> "Number One Gully's wired up! We're going to blast out Number Three—come on," and he shot off to the right, fumbling with equipment as he ran.
>
> Bernard sprinted in pursuit, overtaking an officer just as a series of ear-splitting explosions crashed out from the direction of the lighthouse.
>
> "Cannon-fire...! Thank God from the Spits! It'll cover the noise of our torps," gasped the officer. Then, without remembering at all how he came to be there, Bernard was kneeling at the foot of a wide cleft in the cliff-side, struggling with fuses as the first Bangalore torpedo blew a gap in the criss-cross of wire that was stretched tightly across the mouth of the gully.

> With the first detonation Bernard's confusion disappeared and with it went all his
> fears. The habit of military discipline, and month after month of specialized training,
> reasserted themselves and he became a fiendishly active automaton, linked to Boxer
> not because Boxer was his twin, but simply because he was his partner in this particu-
> lar enterprise. (*War*, 257-58)

When the signal came to get the hell out of there, Bernard started to "writhe back
from the blazing mass and seek what shelter he could find in the heavier undergrowth through which they had advanced." But Boxer was in no hurry to get back
and while "men were now doubling back toward the woods on each side of him,"
Boxer "remained upright against the tatters of the wire, deliberately firing into
the smoke wreaths in front of him." Bernard knew then that "this was what Pippa
must have meant, the stark reality of his double burden. 'You can't *do* this any
longer Bernard, nobody could...!' It was as though she was calling to him across
the quivering belt of woodland and urging him, at long last, to look out for himself, and leave Boxer to take his chance." The mortar shell which burst half way
between them crumpled Bernard "into a compact ball and hurled him forward
and upwards towards the trees" (259-60).

Boxer knew what immediate action he must take: he tore out his field-dressing
and used it partly as a bandage "and partly as a tourniquet on the calf-wound." But
Boxer never had developed the habit of independent thought, although he had
seen it modeled for him by his brother for decades now. As "dog-fights between
Spitfires and enemy fighters were filling the air with the drone of power-dives and
the harsh rattle of machine-gun fire," Boxer could see what had to be done, but
there seemed to be no way of doing it. Bernard would have to be carried somewhere, but where? From where he crouched in a ditch Boxer saw "blood welling
through the leg bandage, steadily, like the drip of a washerless tap," and the sight
"galvanized him into action." He picked up Berni and "headed due west along the
fringe of the wood," as good a direction as any, which might go "to Quiverville
beach" (261-63).

When he was found by the Frenchmen, three civilians "wearing revolvers and
Sten guns" who asked "Is this your invasion?," Boxer told them no, it was not the
big invasion but a reconnaisance "in force," thus they had best not tip their hand
by counter-attacking. Bernard is badly wounded, the French can neither conceal
nor help him, yet Boxer will not abandon him. The Frenchmen discuss the situation among themselves, then one of the group advises him:

> "If you wish to save his life and sacrifice your own chances of escape, there is only one
> course open to you, my friend. You must take him yourself to the Boche first-aid post
> beyond the crossroads but you must go there alone. It would be death for us to accom-
> pany you." (*War*, 267)

The French physician having re-tied the two tourniquets and "added a fresh bandage to the dressing on the shattered elbow," Boxer was ready to start walking

toward the German first-aid station. As he walked against the steady stream of Germans being lorried towards the battlefield, a staff car stopped, and directions were given to ambulance drivers which sent Bernard on his way towards medical attention.

> "They will dress your comrade's wounds," said the officer. "Then he will be sent to hospital, before going into honourable captivity, as yourself!" When Boxer hesitated, he added: "We are not barbarians!" (*War*, 271)

The Archie Plot, II

When we last saw Archie Carver he was in disgrace in fortune's and men's eyes, and that is where we find him now. He had managed by bluff and luck to avoid a jail sentence for tax evasion and for receiving and selling stolen goods. Now released from custody on his own recognizance, Archie awaits trial for manslaughter. The solicitors who represent him have sent a letter to his wife Maria, asking for help in preparing a defense, since Carver himself "seems reluctant to assist us in gathering material that might well prove helpful." Then, when Maria—who had stolen Archie's money and initiated his drunken pursuit of her—failed to answer the solicitors' letter, they wrote Jim, though "it was only with the utmost reluctance that we could persuade him we should get in touch with you." The law firm is looking for background material "to assist us in presenting the case to the best advantage," particularly because it is "a difficult case to defend," as there seems "very little that can be argued in our client's favour." In truth, his legal team have a defeatist attitude towards arguing even that little.

Maria being unwilling to assist Archie, his father is stubbornly inclined to do the same. Ever since that day when his son rose from the kitchen table, threw down some money, blew cigarette smoke through his nose and thereby expressed tacit opposition to his father, the two men have disdained one another, preferring sullen avoidance to angry horn-locking. Disapprobation has festered within them for twenty years. But at that moment another voice is heard, one which refuses to rest content with mutual hostility. That voice is Edith Clegg's.

In the chapter "Edith As Rod And Staff" the sixty year old spinster comes to the aid of the man she most respects, as he sulks over his porridge with the lawyers' letter open upon his kitchen table. He refuses comfort, but, says she, "If you're miserable it *is* my business," and "once bent upon comforting someone Edith was not easily repulsed." She has brought her troubles to Jim for years and comes now to return that favour. "Now sit down, eat your porridge, and tell me all about it, and it's not the slightest use trying to keep it to yourself because I won't go away until you have told me, so there!" Carver can look at her "in astonishment" but she will have her way. Misery shared is misery halved and Edith is about to perform that operation. Having read the letter, she tells him "You'll have to go, won't you?", Jim replies "give me one good reason" and she crushes his resistance with two: "He's in trouble and he's your boy" (328–32). Jim immediately saw Edith differently then he had seen her before. She typified "all the women of her generation, women who had successively challenged the casualty lists of the Somme, unemployment, the slump, and now German Fascism." They endured deprivations beyond number, yet they "retained both their dignity and courage, and often a sense of humor for good measure" (333). Seen in that cultural-historical light, as he is now seeing her, will Jim Carver keep his back up and refuse to go? No, he will do what she advises.

Edith suggests that they *both* go, because "It wouldn't seem so bad if you had someone to talk to all the way there and all the way back," which he sees is not her real reason but which he accepts as a kindly end-around. Softened by her charitable intervention, away they go, together. Edith had served an intervention-apprenticeship long before, when she defended poor Becky against the whole community, those Bad Samaritans who crossed the road and refused to help the brutalized victim whom they intended to lock in an asylum. The person who with her handbag whacked silly the loudmouth woman who was insulting the Prince of Wales is a twittering old spinster, but not a coward. Jim respects that, and he complies. *Now*, Archie is no longer alone. He has become a member of a society of three. Wherever two or three are gathered under Edith's wing, the world is a better place.

Edith and Jim travel to Wintlebury that evening. Jim makes an appointment to see the appropriate lawyer the next morning, and when they meet the barrister proves cheerfully negative about the case. They're putting in a guilty plea, for "we haven't a leg to stand on." The lawyer referring to the money Archie's wife had stolen, Jim, who had had no inkling that there was a *reason* for his son's barreling along fast and drunk when he killed the pedestrian, becomes interested. "Well, surely you'll bring this up in court, won't you?", he wonders. But as Mr. Betts points out, it would not be prudent to advert to how Carver's son *acquired* the money. At that point, Edith, who had been sitting in the background quietly, so that the two men had "forgotten her presence," spoke up.

> "It seems to me," she said, with a note of decision in her voice that Jim did not recall as being in any way characteristic of the spinster of Number Four, "it seems to me that you ought to imply that he had a kind of *brainstorm!*"
>
> They all looked at her, Jim in astonishment, Mr. Sills with alarm, and Mr. Malcolm Betts with a lively interest.
>
> "Can you elaborate that a little, madam," he said, politely.
>
> "Certainly, said Edith, pulling her chair a little nearer the table. "Here's a young man who suddenly finds he had been deprived of a large sum of money. Surely you won't need to say *how* he got that money, or even where it was stolen from, will you?"
>
> "Well," said Mr. Betts grinning, "that shouldn't be necessary, unless of course he insists on going into the box."
>
> "Well," continued Edith, "he discovers this loss and it puts everything else out of his head! He rushes off, down to his wife in order to try and get it back, and all the

time the thought of that money is going over and over in his head, so much so that he's not even looking where he's going!"

"What about the brandy?" prompted Mr. Sills.

"You can't get around that," mumbled Jim.

"Well, no, you can't, not exactly," said Edith, "but anyone might take a drink under these circumstances. I've known this young man for twenty years, and I've been in and out of his shop almost every day during this time. I've never once seen him the worse for drink, and you could just say he took it to steady himself and wasn't used to it, couldn't you?"

Jim gasped, and Mr. Sills coughed, but Mr. Malcolm Betts gave Edith an unmistakable look of approval.

"That's a line that hasn't occurred to me, I must say," he exclaimed. "Why, bless my soul, Miss Clegg, you ought to devil for us, you've got a naturally tortuous mind!"

He turned back to Mr. Sills and Jim: "That's not a bad line at all," he said, "at all events, it's a good deal better than nothing! I'll tell you what, we won't question a single witness but simply put in a strong plea of mitigation on the lines she suggests! Colorful too, might even interest the jury! Never know! There's one thing, however, we ought to establish that he's always been known for strict sobriety."

He turned back to Edith. "Look here, madam, would you go into the box as a friend and neighbor of twenty years' standing, and tell the court what you've just told me about never seeing him the worse for drink?"

"Why, of course I would," said Edith, promptly. "I was rather hoping that you might ask me to give evidence of character!"

"Wouldn't it be better if I went in the box," protested Jim, who was beginning to feel out of his depth.

"Not on your life!" rejoined the barrister, "Relatives' testimonies don't amount to a row of pins! Besides, she *looks* so right!"

"Well, it isn't a great deal, Mr. Carver, but it's about the best we can do," Mr. Sills told Him. "It might influence the sentence, don't you think Mr. Betts?"

"It might, indeed," agreed Betts, glancing across at Edith, with respect. It was not often, he reflected, that old souls who looked as drab and dowdy as this one came forward with any intelligent suggestions. Almost always they fell back on tears and juries were so indifferent to tears. (*War*, 336-37)

When the sentence of eighteen months in prison came down, Jim was able to feel a little sympathy for his son. In 1931, he had spent one day in gaol himself, after he had been involved in the Hunger March demonstration, but he was locked up with "a score of Welsh miners" who were conscious of martyrdom. There would be no alleviating "uplift" for Archie, imprisoned for a year and a half for the "criminal folly" that caused the death of a total stranger. Would he feel better had Archie been acquitted, Jim asked himself, but decided "that he would not." When the usher came by to ask whether he would like to see the defendant "for a few minutes," Edith "looked hesitantly at Jim" and wondered if he would "sooner see him alone?" One way or another he is *going* to see Archie, and by this time the father is willing to see him, though he'd much sooner Edith accompanied him.

When Archie began by saying "I'm very glad to have a chance of saying 'thank you' Miss Clegg," Jim "sensed at once that his embarrassment was the less because Edith was there" (340-41). Jim asks Archie "You heard about poor old Berni and Boxer?" both of whom are presumed dead. Yes, Archie had heard and he's sorry, "they were good kids". Anything innocuous or indirect is good for a start; mutuality in the acceptance of their mutual loss is healing. "It was damned decent of you to come down, Dad, and I appreciate it much more than you think!," Archie tells him. "It was more than Maria could bring herself to do!" His wife and his father had equally legitimate reasons for resenting his behaviour, but Jim Carver has proven to be the bigger person, the more forgiving one. Now that they are speaking to one another, Archie is emboldened to share his suppressed anguish over his son Tony who was killed in action, something "I haven't told anyone else."

> "Tony...he's dead. He was killed at Tobruk, about a month ago. He got the M.C. you know, he did damn well out there. In a way I'm glad he finished up like that...I wouldn't have liked him to hear about this lark. It would have upset him pretty much, I imagine.
>
> Jim could think of no comment to make. Tony was his eldest grandchild and secretly he had been very proud of him, although his long estrangement from Archie had meant that he had never had more than an occasional glimpse of the boy. He knew that Tony had been commissioned, and was serving abroad, but he had never seen him in uniform. Now he would never get to know him and for a moment the bitterness of this realization checked his natural sympathy for Archie.
>
> He saw Edith reach out and touch Archie's sleeve. The movement did not go unnoticed by the policeman at the door, who half turned into the room. (*War*, 343)
>
> "I'm afraid the time's up," said the officer.

Archie had not informed Tony's school of his performance as a soldier and asks his father, "Will you write them a line for me?" Of course he will, and Jim "suddenly shot out his hand in Archie's direction," saying "After this we'll...we'll try and manage to see a bit more of one another, son?" Well, so it's "Dad" and "son" after that many years. On their way home Edith remarks to Jim "You're friends now, you're much closer than you've ever been, so in a way it's been worth it, don't you think?" (342-44). What exactly was the "*it*" that was "worth it"? That is not altogether clear. All that matters is that in the relations between father and son, their losses are restored and sorrows end.

The New Years festivity on the last day of 1942 inside Archie's prison was limited to a Laurel and Hardy film along with an extra half-hour of free association. The pre-trial events involving Edith and Jim had been social exchanges, but New Years in gaol consisted of Archie's reflections as he ruminates about the bearing of his previous life upon his present condition of mind. When how one's time is spent has been decided in advance by others, the unexpected cannot happen, and "one's sense of values changed." It alters so utterly that "one's entire outlook became warped." Archie's word "warped" could be altered to "restructured" or "reconceived". Moreover, the intensely personal viewpoint in which he had been isolated for decades has slackened, since he now uses the generic reflexive pronoun "one," distancing himself from himself, from his *old* self. What had been important to him becomes trivial. Income tax once controlled his thoughts, but now one cigarette stub is more valuable to him "than all the money in the Inland Revenue" (403-04). Archie is becoming a philosopher, not in Descartes' or Kant's style but in the sense that he is intellectually detached, more thoughtful than during his many years as a money rat.

Women had not "dominated" his attention nor encroached on the time he formerly devoted to "business matters," but now "his mind was obsessed with women, and with one woman particularly." It astonished Archie how he could remember "the smallest particular of his association with Elaine Frazier and the capaciousness of his memory regarding her." How she stood before the mirror before getting into bed, for example. "Without him knowing it his mind must have formed a minutely accurate picture of her pose,"

> with both hands resting lightly on the glass-topped dressing-table, her body and one foot thrust forward, inclining one buttock towards him in what now seemed a provocative posture. He remembered her clear, white skin, her frank, laughing sensuality, and the sense of repose that she brought to him after a day spent wrestling with travellers, coupons, and stock returns.
>
> He yearned for her as he had never yearned for any human being; beside her the contents of all the tills in London seemed less than a heap of packing-case shavings. (*War*, 404)

This is a huge change in Archie, a geologic upheaval in his imagination, which pictures, evaluates and assigns relative importance to objects of desire. Prison is altering Archie in fundamental ways, and he is reflecting upon that change, conceding its importance, and trying to determine what that refocusing of imagination means. If Elaine is different, not in herself but in his perception of her, what else has been transvalued?

> In the long silences that followed lock-up he was able to go back over his life phase by phase, and re-examine all his decisions, not only those decisions regarding the management of his businesses, but those affecting his relationships with all kinds of people. He learned a great deal from these inquests and one of the first things he learned was the value of privacy. The kind of privacy that only a sentence of imprisonment can provide. (*War*, 405-06)

Privacy? What can he mean? The key word in the passage is "relationships," and privacy is linked to relationships—but relationships have not mattered to Archie heretofore. That is the pivotal value which is being revalued in silent thought.

He remembers the Old Year's Night dance he and Elaine attended two years before, the last night of 1940. Archie had been with her, and afterwards they were parked on "a high windy ridge, where they could look down on a blacked-

out London, silent under a brilliant moon and a sitting target for the Luftwaffe."
Elaine had said to him on that occasion:

> "Have you ever been in love with anyone, Archie? Have you ever *wanted* to love anyone?"
> Archie explains that love is "an appetite," and appetites exist simply to be satis-
> fied, "so don't ever try and sell me anything different."
> She had laughed at that and asked for a cigarette but presently she said:
> "About love, Archie! An awful lot of people have believed in it for a long time. We
> couldn't be wrong I suppose?"
> "Not a chance, Elaine, not a chance." (*War*, 407)

That was then, but this is now, when Archie finds himself revisiting that past scene.
Until now, in prison, Elaine had mattered to him neither more nor less than Rita
Ramage, or Gloria, who had stolen 100 pounds from his wallet and in place of the
cash stuffed toilet paper—a witty reflection upon Archie's crappy values, a witticism
he missed, which is too bad because it was such a definitive *gotcha!*. Now, though,
Archie realizes that Elaine had begun "to represent freedom in the abstract, and
everything one associated with what went on outside the walls." He decided that
he would write her asking that she "come and visit him."

> He thought it unlikely that she would respond to the first invitation, but at least it was
> worth trying, for either way it would help him. If she ignored his letter, then his resent-
> ment might enable him to put her out of mind along with all the others, but if she
> replied, if she actually came, then it must mean that he was as firmly rooted in her con-
> sciousness as she was in his and that surely gave him something to hope for? (*War*, 408)

The terminal question-mark is the best thing about Archie's prison reflection. If
Archie and Elaine have both allowed relationship to become more important than
their habitual "mirror-mirror-on-the-wall" self-absorption, that being the big question, a life together based on that mutuality could be in their future.

A final question, one that is pertinent to a study of Delderfield's work as cultural history: if Archie Carver spends the four hours between lock-down and midnight when he habitually goes to sleep meditating upon his performance in life,
how does he use the remainder of his time? In a prison, "only the privileged would
work a normal span of hours," while the others must make time pass any way they
can. Archie found "the constant struggle to find tasks" to occupy his mind and
hand "the most punishing feature of his sentence." He was lucky, however:

> The prison staff soon came to recognize his organizing ability, and made him a store-
> keeper, where his detailed knowledge of everyday commodities proved invaluable and
> he was able to set about reorganising the antiquated issue and withdrawal system of
> stores. This not only helped him to occupy his mind but it also recommended him to the
> elderly officer in charge of the department. Soon he was recognised as a model prisoner,
> bent on giving no trouble and gaining the maximum remission of sentence. (*War*, 406)

If a heavily-used system is "antiquated" in one gaol, the chances are that stocking, issuing and restocking food will be badly managed in other gaols too. But the likelihood is that when the superior system has been adopted in one gaol, the penal administration as a whole will in time adopt the improvements. Archie Carver is no patriot, but he may have helped ensure a more economical use of public funds.

The Elaine Plot, II. Ever since the age of thirteen, Lieutenant Woolston Ericssohn had been "the slave of a dream as demanding" as the one Elaine had served for so long. He dreamed of a lost civilization he was destined to revitalize, "the civilization of the Old and Martyred South." He had conceived that passion "as a teenager in local libraries rich in the legends" about the Confederacy, and Elaine attracted him, being "dark and winsome, just like the girls who had sewn sashes and embroidered banners for the heroes of Shiloh." She was the kind of woman, he told himself, "who would always remain dependent upon him," which was the role that Elaine would play to secure him as her Great Provider. There was "a quiet desperation" about Elaine's "stalking" of Ericssohn, since she was "now over thirty," and while this might be her last chance, "it also looked like being her best chance, and she was nervous about making a mistake" (346–51). Now the important thing to know about this near-sighted little fellow, apart from his self-delusion, is that in Elaine's words he's not a man but "half a pansy turned forty!" (372). His kisses fall on her cheeks, but not on her lips. Yet although her sexual attraction cannot arouse him, Woolston *does* care about the appearances, her reputation, and the purity of any southern belle he would think of taking home to the U.S.A.

Because Ericssohn is lodging in Edith's home and would learn about her past there, or from Avenue gossip about her divorce, Elaine decided that it would be better to "get her story comfortably planted before someone else whispered in his ear." She was right to do so, since "Woolston had no difficulty in seeing her as the long-suffering victim of a sadistic husband". Esme was vicious. "What did he lam you with, honey?" Woolston asks. "'A dog-whip,' said Elaine, without hesitation" (352). Her reputation being protected by this pre-emptive strike, she must now move forward on Woolston directly by playing upon his conception of what is expected of him should his own unworthy conduct jeopardize this woman's reputation. Helped by an accomplice, Elaine manages that by first luring him into her house with the pretence that she has a phonograph record of banjo songs of the deep south that he will enjoy hearing, next getting the sleeping pills into him after he has reclined upon the bed, then removing his shoes, unbuttoning him, and snugging the telephone close against his ear. Next, Elaine signals her accomplice to call the house, the hour being 3 A.M. The phone rings and rings, but the sleeping pills hold Woolston in thrall. At last he comes groggily awake, instinctively picks up the receiver, and speaks into it. Someone on the other end answers: "Who's

that? Who is it? Is that a man? Do you hear me? *Is that a man?*" Alas and woe is me
it was Aunt Dolly, at this ungodly hour. Elaine lays it on thick.

> "You...you *spoke* to her, Woolston! Oh, but you shouldn't have—you shouldn't have!
> What *will* she think. Whatever *can* she think? Oh Woolston...!" and she climbed off
> the bed, slumped into the armchair and buried her face in her hands.
>   He was beside her in an instant, a wincing, quivering figure of shame and con-
> trition. (*War*, 360)

The southern gentleman proposes marriage before we need to turn the page.
Elaine has won.

> It was a moment of supreme personal triumph, the climax of a campaign that reached
> back to the first day she had come to terms with her destiny, the day that she had
> decided that there was only one worthwhile goal for her, security in the embrace of a
> man who was "loaded"! (*War*, 361)

Elaine introduces Ericssohn to "Daddy" because meeting the relatives is important to any well-bred girl. Edgar is scandalized by her deceit, but Elaine explains
to him that ever since reading *The Art of Marriage* she had known that men are
ruled by sex, it's "just the way they're made" (374). Edgar counters by telling her
that his relationship with Frances has taught him that marriage can be wonderful, but Elaine isn't looking for a happy marriage, she wants a Great Provider, and
deception is essential for getting one. Much to her surprise, however, there is a
brand of conduct which strikes her as abhorrent and reprehensible. And when
Ericssohn approves of such conduct, Elaine realizes that the price of marrying
him might be too high.

America has come into the war now, American soldiers are no rarity in England
and some of them are blacks. One of these has formed a liason with a poor-white
English girl who is pregnant by him. The lovers had been "crossing the meadow
from the wood" when they were attacked by "a party of white Americans, half a
dozen or so, and all apparently drunk." This was the night of the "wolf hunt" as
those who killed the black soldier put it. When the girl's screams "rang out," Elaine,
sensing their urgency, told Ericssohn "you'd better go out there, it sounds as if
someone's in trouble" (465). Elaine hurried to the kitchen "just as a tousled girl in
her late 'teens rushed in" sobbing. Elaine asks her what's going on out there, and
as she finishes her story, "renewed uproar" broke out from the meadow, and the
man she had agreed to marry, his "expression hardened," commanded her "You get
that broad outer here, honey! It's just a wolf hunt, and that nigger had it coming
to him, I guess" (466). Elaine renews her plea that he do something, since "you're
an officer and you've got to stop them!" He goes to the meadow to see what is happening and comes back wearing a smile, for the black soldier has been killed; and
she *will not* phone the police, since the matter has already been dealt with. Elaine

"looked him up and down and there was contempt in the glance" (467). Alone once again after Ericssohn leaves, Elaine reflects on this pivotal incident.

> What was it to him, or to those other men, that the girl Rawlinson liked to walk out with a coloured soldier? What would it be like in America, where this kind of thing was presumably commonplace? *Wolf hunt! He had it coming to him. He was uppity, so beat him, kill him!*
>
> Suddenly, with an odd sense of relief, she began to think of Archie, and Archie's letter.
>
> She wondered why he should suddenly come into her mind, at a moment like this, when she was feeling upset, confused and frightened. Could it be because, of all the men in whose arms she had lain, Archie alone seemed strong, sane, and predictable?
>
> She found his letter, reading it again in the light of the bedside lamp. She knew then that she would go and see him, as soon as it could be arranged, for there was no one else who could advise her about Woolston...She had never needed advice before, but she needed it now, and Archie was the only person qualified to give the kind of advice she sought. (*War*, 469)

When she got to the gaol, Archie was in the visitor's room awaiting her, and "when she smiled at him through the wire mesh, his eyes lit up with pleasure." They're glad to see one another, and while nothing momentous passes between them, they take fresh impressions of one another. Archie's prison experience has obviously "blunted the cutting edge of his aggressive egotism," but without making him bitter. When he asks about Woolston and Elaine describes him as "I don't know...he's...he's so *slow*...Sometimes I think he's...well...almost...you know..." he gives her the word she cannot say: "A queer?" "Well, a bit of one," she says, and at Archie's boisterous laughter "the red-faced officer looked up sharply," while "the tiny woman sitting beside Elaine glanced at Archie reproachfully, as though he was mocking the solemnity of the place" (470-71). The visiting time was up soon after that, yet the visit had "done a good deal to steady her." As Elaine retrieved her belongings "at the brick shed" and waited with a group of other visitors for the light to turn green before crossing the road she muses to herself: "I never dreamed that he had that much guts," then "contemplates the word 'guts' in the abstract." There are several kinds, but, she asks herself, "could Woolston lay claim to any one of these?" If he found his world in ruins, would he have grinned as Archie did "when she faced him across that awful wire netting?" (473-74).

The Archie and Elaine Plot, III

Until now, there has not been an "Archie and Elaine" plot because neither one had been sufficiently free of obsessions to be capable of genuine relationship—something that Elaine had wistfully wondered about that New Years Night when, parked high above a moonlit London, they discussed the concept of love. Yet from the first, they have been moving towards relationship, which becomes a possibility for them in early middle age, hence the *III* in "Archie and Elaine, III." What kept them apart? Archie's obsessive desire to acquire money and Elaine's determination to secure a Great Provider. *Dreams*, along with the plans they valued thinking that plans could turn dreams into realities. Enjoyment of one another's bodies in sexual congress was never a genuine relationship but instead the thrashing liquidity of ships passing in the night, bent upon reaching their different ports. That has changed. Imprisonment for manslaughter, the hours Archie spends reviewing his earlier conduct, recognition of his superb talents by the prison staff, Tony's death, Edith and Jim's support in his trial—all of these helped release Archie from his bondage to isolation within himself. Nor has Elaine's crooked pilgrimage been unfruitful, making it clear that the road she is going down is not the road which she truly wants to travel, though she long thinks she does. The impact of her mother's bad example, Esther's selfish disregard for the good of others, has marked Elaine deeply. Yet her rejection of that example does not liberate her; it only sets Elaine singing Esther's song in a sexualized key, while she continues her tacitly contemptuous disregard of her sexual partners' human value. That the Great Eùgene, Tom Tappertit, the Dutch sailor, his neck bashed with his own clarinet, enjoyed copulating with Elaine is one thing, her indifferent use of them as commodities, as instruments for her personal gain, is another thing altogether. Her "Great Provider" dream has barred Elaine from interpersonal affection, wherein the good of the other is the freedom and fulfilment of the self. "The Other?" God! I'm starting to sound like a French philosopher, which I guess is better than a German philosopher but not much. It is difficult to settle the proportion of iniquity between them.

In prison Archie had been reading as well as thinking, practical volumes including *Everyman His Own Lawyer*, and *Gutteridge's Ownership of Property* to prepare himself for his post-gaol financial recovery. He "would get into the property market" by way of an intermediate effort, perhaps "something to do with cars." He was "immensely braced" by Elaine's visit, but disappointed that she neither visited a second time nor answered either of the letters he had sent her in the past two months. He would have taken a letter as "a gesture of comradeship" for old times' sake, no more.

> There was after all, a limit to a man's self-sufficiency, and Archie had now reached the age when he needed at least one confidant to combat his increasing fear of loneliness (485).

Maria had never been a confidante, Toni Piretta and Antony Carver were dead, while James and Juanita probably wouldn't have known him on sight. He and his father were "disposed to be friendly, but the gulf between them" still persisted, bridgeable by "handshaking and family gossip" (485–86). He is quite alone, not by choice but by circumstances brought about through his own prior conduct.

He had been released from gaol at 7:50, and it was now a little past eight A.M. Archie was waiting for the train, which was not due to leave town "until 9 forty-five," when he shaded his eyes against the morning sun and saw a parked sedan. His heart "glowed with pleasure" to see that the woman in the driver's seat was Elaine. In a moment he was sitting beside her, "with affection and admiration" for her because she looked wonderful in her "freshly-permed hair" and "expensive-looking Italian shoes" (483–87). Elaine has dressed for him, and Archie appreciates that gesture. He asks whether they might breakfast somewhere, because he had been too "keyed up" to eat the prison food. Elaine, too, has missed breakfast, "but in my case it wasn't excitement, it was getting up so damned early!" He is, he tells her, "pleased to see you."

> "Thank you, Archie," she said, so demurely that he laughed again and the sound of his own laughter lifted his spirits to such a peak that he had to resist the impulse to sing. She settled down to drive, snuggling down in the seat like a Persian cat he thought, glancing sideways at her. (*War*, 487).

At that point dialogue is displaced by the narrator's backgrounding summary of Elaine's cogitations in the time since we last looked in upon her conduct. Why had she come to meet Archie this morning? She had been driven to it by "a fresh wave of doubt in respect of the wisdom of marriage to Lieutenant Ericssohn." She had reconciled herself to his being "a pitiful substitute for any of the men in her past," and while he claimed to be thirty-nine she estimated his age to be "somewhere around forty-five," and sometimes he behaved "as if he were already a grandfather." Further, her inability to arouse him sexually made her "conscious of her own age in a way that she had never been aware of it prior to her engagement" to him. Over and over Elaine had reminded herself that she had sought "The Great Provider, not The Great Lover." On the other hand, if he didn't want her physically, "so much the better. For what woman in her senses wants to be pawed by Woolston?" She had made a plan and everything was going according to that plan.

> The real trouble lay in the fact that plan and instincts were now sadly at variance. For the time being the plan had lulled her instincts, and, as time went on, she came to understand that her mounting uncertainty was merely the manifestation of their reawakening. (*War*, 488–89)

The inescapable reality was that Elaine was a sensual woman who needed "a healthy, normal man, like Archie Carver," and it was on this issue that she "first quarrelled with Esme, resenting her elevation to the role of a beautiful but remote lady-in-the-tower." Ericssohn did not measure up to her needs, which would have mattered less except that "in addition to being pompous and pettifogging, he was also jealous and dictatorial." And there was something else: he was an American, and she was a girl raised in the Avenue. Those people from across the Atlantic "resembled children," having the same "impulsive generosity, and the same sudden streaks of cruelty, and the same brutal intolerance for those who did not conform" (489-90).

Then two bombshells dropped. Woolston's C. O. decided to use her wedding to Ericssohn "to further Anglo-American relations in the area," and the news came that Woolston was being "posted back home" almost immediately. Well, Elaine would have to consult "Daddy" about the new circumstances, but instead she rented the sedan and drove to the prison in the West, telling herself "Maybe I *will* go through with it in the end," but right now "I must see Archie" (491-92).

They had breakfast in a hostelry near Salisbury, and Elaine noticed, while drinking their second cup of coffee, that Archie "had hardly spoken during the meal. 'You've hardly looked at me' she said, and 'You haven't even kissed me, either,'" she said banteringly. But he responds badly to Elaine's light humor. "He looked up and she was amazed to see that his face was troubled and that her banter was actually hurting him." Archie doesn't want to joke around; he wants to sit quietly while she talks about her Yank; but Elaine *cannot* talk about that man, since he doesn't matter.

> "No, because Woolston isn't important today and you are, Archie."
> He considered this for a moment. Finally he said, but without looking at her:
> "No one's ever done a thing like this for me! Come to think of it, no one's ever shown me much decency or consideration. People have been all kinds of things to me, Elaine, nasty, patronizing, servile...you know...but always with their eye on the ball! No one's ever made the kind of effort you've made by coming down today, by getting this car and going to the trouble to look like you do! I won't ever forget that, Elaine, not even if we never saw one another again after today! That's something I'll always remember and I suppose it makes a man feel that there must be some better way of showing his appreciation than by the usual way!"
> She was touched by his words, more moved by them than she had been moved by anything anyone had ever said to her in the past. She was also amazed with herself for feeling so drawn towards him, so strongly that she dare not let him see it. She stood up, turning her back on him, and pretending to search for something in her bag.
> "Get the bill and let's go, Archie." (*War*, 493-94)

She suggests that they drive to Bournemouth and get a hotel room there, but Archie objects. "The last thing I want to do right now is put a spoke in your wheel. You'll be getting married to that Yank and..."

> "I'm not going to marry the Yank! It's over now, Archie!"
> "You mean you've broken it off...to come here like this?"
> "No, but I mean to break it off...I don't want to go through with it, so for God's sake don't try to talk me back into it!"
> He was quiet for a moment. When he spoke it seemed to her that he was choosing his words as carefully as a man chooses his steps down a steep, dangerous path.

Archie tells her how he intends to use the "two thousand saved from the wreck" to rebuild himself financially, tells her that he's forty-two now and it won't be easy, that he's never proposed to anyone before, Piretta having "fixed my marriage with Maria," that Maria will not divorce him, and with that Archie ends his brief informational speech.

"Well, that's how it is, so there's not much in it for you, is there? I will say this though. If you meant what you said just now, if you've really thought about it and that's why you're here, then I'll do everything I can to make a go of it. If I didn't succeed, and we came a mucker, then you'd be absolutely free to pack it in, and I'd never hold it against you, never in this world, Is that sort of proposition any good to you, Elaine?"

She closed her eyes and threw back her head, so that her neck was pressed hard against the threadbare cretonne of the seat-cover. He noticed then that her hands were trembling so violently that she lost her grip on her handbag and it slid from her lap onto the floor.

He required a powerful effort to prevent himself from twisting round and taking her in his arms, but he made the effort, knowing that, at this moment of time, a frenzied embrace would only have exascerbated their problem.

"You've got to have time to think about it, Elaine?"

She twisted round and faced him. "I don't *need* any more time," she shouted. It's the only kind of proposition that interests me!"

She seized his hand and pressed it hard against her breasts and with a wonder too deep and bewildering for words he saw that she was crying. The sight of her tears calmed him more than anything else could have done.

He freed his hand and ran the palm gently round the smooth contours of her chin. Then he kissed her very lightly on the forehead.

"Okay, then! We'll make it, Elaine, and even if we don't, we'll have a hell of a good time trying! Here...." He bent and retrieved her handbag, and tilted the driving mirror in her direction. "Get busy on your face before we hit Bournemouth! We can make it in twenty minutes if this vintage model holds out!" (*War*, 495–96)

The Esme and Judy Plot, II

The second half of their story consists of three phases: having safely parachuted from "R-for-Ronnie" as it disintegrated, Esme is concealed by the French underground and prepared for a secret mission to England; learning that her fiance's Lancaster did not return from its bombing run, Judy endures the anxiety and sorrow felt by so many English people at the time; Esme having gotten safely back to England, he and Judy buy the derelict farm in Devon that they had fallen in love with and begin making it a home, for themselves, little Barbara, and the new baby. The Archie and Elaine plot was rather small potatoes with respect to cultural history, but Esme and Judy in their representative function are in the thick of Britain's wartime experience.

"The Ju.88 came at them on the port bow about twenty minutes after they had made their bomb run and turned for home" (290). When he first applied for air-crew service Esme had been rejected because of "a slight defect" in one eye, but when the R.A.F. could not afford to be fussy about perfect eyes in its crews, he was accepted. Esme blames himself for the shootdown. He had betrayed men who trusted him, because his "tail-gunner's failure to spot the first enemy fighter," which had "allowed the first Ju.88 to rake the port engine before he fired a defensive burst," was "a powerful factor" in the Lancaster's destruction (298). He was in good company in being shot out of the sky by this distinguished Nazi airplane, since Ju.88s had brought down people more distinguished than this young airman from the Avenue. The London-born actor Leslie Howard who starred in "Gone With the Wind" was lost on commercial flight KLF 777 from Portugal to Britain when the aircraft was shot down by a squadron of Junker 88 fighters in 1943. Edith Clegg, an aficionado of film personalities who deeply mourned Rudolph Valentino's passing, would have read about Howard's death in her local newspaper. Some thought that Howard had been on a covert mission to prevent Spain from entering the war on the side of Germany and Italy—fascist dictator Franco having "formed an alliance" with Hitler which had "based Luftwaffe warplanes" on Spanish soil (ASK. COM). Cultural history, yes, *The Avenue Goes to War* contains much of it—large items, small ones, all of them historically accurate.

Now cultural history is not facts and dates but the thoughts and emotions of representative groups of people, like the French readers who clamored for those novels which anticipated the execution of the king and his replacement by the fraternal band of brothers who did not rule by royal command, but out of mutual affection. Esme Frazier, hiding himself and his parachute in the "kind of barn, piled high with root crops" somewhere in France, is both an isolated individual and the representative of thousands of soldiers who reflect upon their lives in moments of personal danger. He hears two men talking together indistinctly in the barn. Finally one of them, "without glancing towards the stack of mangolds where Esme lay," said aloud, in excellent English, "Remain where you are! We will come back for you when the first search is finished! Two of your friends are dead and three are already captured" (296). They are members of the French resistance, who immediately thereafter leave, giving Esme plenty of time hidden in the mangolds to reflect upon his life. Archie did it in prison, Esme does so in a barn, but the self-reflective purpose is the same in either case, self-understanding being the aim of that exercise.

> It seemed to him, lying in half-light at the back of a French barn, that so far he had achieved very little in his life, but that this was unimportant, now, for his achievements were on the point of commencing. Perhaps this was his big chance to achieve something. Perhaps this was something he might do well, escape across hundreds of miles of enemy territory, and get home to Judy and the Avenue. Perhaps, indeed, this was the big adventure that he had been seeking ever since he played in Manor Wood, and cast himself in an endless succession of heroic roles, many of them akin to the role he was now playing? He freely admitted to himself that all he had set out to do had not amounted to anything very much. He had dreamed his boyhood away, and then spent the next ten years in haphazard attempts to justify himself to himself, first as a lover, than as a writer, then as a romantic tramp, then as a husband, and finally as an airman, but so far he had made little impression on anyone. (*War*, 297-98)

If he could get home in one piece, "instead of going tamely behind barbed wire" for the remainder of the war, he would have "something to present to Judy to prove to her that he really was something of the man she had believed him to be all those years they had lived side by side in the Avenue." He would try anyway, and try "desperately" (298).

Near dark, the Agent returned and summoned Esme from "his nest in the roots," concealed him in a farm cart under a load of kale and moved him to a farmhouse where a young man sat at a table writing. "This is Claude! He will talk with you," said the Agent, but the man at the table showed "a disconcerting reluctance to break off his work and greet his visitor" (299). Ignoring the visitor and disconcerting him is part of Claude's strategy as an interviewer: he must place the interrogee at a disadvantage, generate discomfort in him, test him in various ways, not least with respect to his courage and coolness under stress. For his part, Esme has been trained to provide no information beyond his name, rank and serial number: "Frazier, Sergeant, Number 926565." Claude will have to squeeze him hard to determine what kind of an Englishman they have in hand, and he knows how to do that, firmly and fast.

"Please! I must insist."

Esme quailed under the Frenchman's eye and manner.

"Scratton Wold, in Lincolnshire," he growled.

The man wrote something in a notebook and then leaned back against the wall, shooting his long, thin legs beneath the table.

"When you are at home, where do you live?"

Esme shrugged. In for a penny, in for a pound, he thought, and this fellow's eye was almost hypnotic.

"Near Croyden, in Surrey."

"The man nodded: "*How* near?"

"An outer suburb of Croydon, actually, but you wouldn't know it!"

The man's thin mouth twitched but it was more of a grimace than a smile.

"You would be very surprised what I know my friend," he said, unpleasantly. Describe to me where you live, describe it exactly or I cannot help you!"

Esme gave it up. He was dominated by the man and his irritation gave place to dismay.

"It's an Avenue, called 'Manor Park Avenue.' I live at Number Twenty-Two. It's a turning off Shirley Rise, that branches off the Millbank Lower Road."

"And where does this 'Lower Road' lead?"

"To London."

"Via?"

"I beg your pardon?"

"To London, through what suburbs?"

The man now sounded like a testy schoolmaster, engaged in establishing the inadequacy of a small boy's excuses. (*War*, 300-301)

Satisfied by Esme's answers, which the closest coaching by Nazis agents could not have provided in such detail, Claude "shed his malignant personality like a shirt, and suddenly revealed himself as friend, confidant and neighbor," for he had resided in that suburb of London "until 1939," while he studied in "the London School of Chiropody" (302). Before long, Claude turned on the radio, tuned to the nine o'clock news bulletin of the B.B.C. and they heard, after a list of familiar items, this pertinent report:...Last night heavy forces of Bomber Command raided Hanover and Bremen, inflicting considerable damage on tractor works and chemical installations in one city, while other heavy forces destroyed port installations at the coastal target. There was strong opposition from enemy flak and night fighter formations; fourteen of our aircraft failed to return...."

When Claude provides cognac and they drink "To the Avenue, to your home, and your friends, Sergeant!", Esme remembers that Judy will have heard that bulletin, "and she'll ring the squadron, poor kid." Says Claude, "She will face some weeks of wretchedness, my friend, but in the end we shall return you intact to her! Let us drink to that, before we conduct you to safer quarters" (303).

Judy, recovering from her broken collar-bone in Maud's house, gets a phone call meant for her personally; thus she "hoisted herself out of bed" and went downstairs, hoping it might be Esme. But it was the orderly-room corporal of the squadron, who hopes she will relay the bad news to Esme's next of kin, Harold Godbeer, thus softening the blow before official notice arrives. "The orderly-room staff sometimes strayed outside the limit of official procedure in this matter, and the more intelligent officers encouraged them." The corporal phones Judy because he had once met her, and "because, well, because you're one of us I guess." On the train journey going to London, Judy "took stock" of Esme's chances, going about it "rather like a castaway, turning out his pockets after struggling ashore from the wreck" (312-14). She had little confidence in either her luck or Esme's, and, shifting her position slightly "to ease her aching shoulder," she reflected on the state of the English spirit at this moment in the war when cumulative fatigue is crushing everyone.

> It was, she reflected, no longer a crusade but simply a dull, dreary habit. People no longer talked of Hitler and Himmler as sadistic monsters but simply as bores, responsible for bull, blackouts, cheerless journeys in uncomfortable trains like this, shortages, sweet rationing, the price of cigarettes and the cost of trunk calls that were poor substitutes for lovers' meetings!
>
> Even inside the R.A.F. and the W.A.A.F. the old Battle of Britain spirit had disappeared. In 1940, everyone had been a volunteer, and the time-honoured rejoinder to a moan about service life had been: 'Shouldn't have joined!' There was no sense in that remark now, not with the steady intakes of thousands of sullen National Service recruits, yet all the time Esme was a prisoner for any length of time it might even be too late for them to have children!

She thought, objectively, of the child they might have had, for her child, Esme's child, had always played a prominent part in the dream, and now it seemed more important than anything else. (*War*, 316)

When she arrives in London, Judy telephones Harold at his office and asks for a meeting. "No, Mr. Godbeer, Esme isn't with me, I'm on my own. It's...It's really *about* Esme...I'd like to have a...well, a sort of chat about things." Godbeer, not a stupid man, can quite easily guess what Judy wishes to talk about, yet she hopes that he might "jump to the conclusion that she needed advice or sympathy." In any event, she "could not bring herself to blurt the truth over the telephone" (317). When they meet over coffee, Judy puts the best face she can upon the awful news, "stressing the number of operational crews" that have been saved this way or that. "Esme as a prisoner would be a Luftwaffe pigeon, and they don't get badly treated, not even when they're captured over the target. There's still a bit of chivalry left about the air war!" (319).

Having done what she can to ease the blow for Harold, Judy avoided Manor Woods; she sought instead "a tiny island of trees that still stood in the ploughed field, beyond the church," giving herself in spirit to the beeches and larch "still wearing green," where convulvulus and campion were "still growing" (321). Helped by a memory-laden landscape, Judy could, in her mind's eye, more easily see Esme "as the earnest, excitable little boy" rushing about "urging her to hurry and take cover before the cavalry pickets detected them" (321). With her back against a beech tree and "her hands limp on her lap" she prayed: "*Give me something to hope for, give old Harold something to hope for.*" As a breeze dislodged a few leaves from the branches above, Judy "shivered and got to her feet," retracing her way back to the Avenue (322).

Meanwhile, Esme spent most of his time "cooped up in attic bedrooms," passing "lonely hours until his journey into the south-west could be arranged." From Claude and his deputies, Esme had learned something of "the expanding network of the French underground movement," passwords, and forged papers, secret conclaves, and "all the trappings one had associated in pre-war days with light fiction." Esme had experienced the difficulty of moving about in France, "where German troops were stationed in every small town, and Vichy agents, informers and collaborators" were working inside every Government department. But knowing all this did not "check his impatience" to return to England, where he could walk about freely without "the nagging fear of sudden arrest, and the betrayal of friends." Although he admired the Resistance people, he could not believe that risking their lives for a few downed airmen was worth it. During one of these pessimistic moods, Esme discussed the subject with Claude, the Group Leader.

"You are regarding it too closely, or perhaps not closely enough, my friend," Claude had told him. "We do not do this so much for you as for ourselves! It is not as important to us that you should get home but that we should risk our lives trying to outwit

the Boche! You see, my friend, we Frenchmen helped to murder Western civilization,
1940. Yes, my friend, we did it by sloth and by cynicism. (*War*, 424-26)

It seemed "monstrous" to Esme that this man should feel "so humiliated" by
France's collapse and disputed its accuracy: "You couldn't control your crooked
politicians, any more than we could galvanize our wishful-thinking bunch into positive action, in 1938." We kept telling ourselves, Esme continues, that, except for
Jim Carver, "who saw what was happening," the rest of the Avenue and the country as a whole "backed Chamberlain and his piece of paper" (426-27).

> "That may be so," replied Claude, "but when it did happen you preferred to die rather
> than give up. Each of you, the highest and the lowest! That is something of which you
> should always be proud, my friend!"
>
> Esme wondered whether this was an exaggeration on the part of the Frenchman
> and decided that perhaps, after all, it was not. He had seen the suburb under non-stop
> bombardment and had sensed the spirit of defiance in people like Edith Clegg, and
> little Miss Baker across the road. Supposing England, or any other country, had been
> isolated and pounded in this ruthless manner? Suppose its fighting men had been
> thrown back on a defenceless base, and its food supplies menaced by U-boat blockage.
> Would that country have continued to resist or would it, like France, have glumly sued
> for peace and accepted German domination?
>
> He decided at once that this was one of those silly 'if' questions that had no real
> answer.... 'If there had been tanks at the Battle of Hastings'. 'If Napoleon had actually
> landed the Grande Armée on the shores of Kent....' Who could tell? One could only
> judge these matters by what did occur, not by what might have occurred.
>
> He made up his mind, however, to spare the Frenchman's pride and said: "We
> were saved by the Ditch, Claude and without it we'd have been no tougher than you
> people! Apart from that, I can't see a cagey old Devonshire farmer risking his neck to
> get a French aviator back into the fight, as you're doing right now!"
>
> "You are kind but not quite honest," smiled Claude, and the topic was dropped.
> (*War*, 427)

Two months after his first interview with Claude in the farmhouse, Esme had
a surprise visit by Snowball, the West Indian radioman on their bomber, who is
leaving France "disguised as a French Colonial N.C.O." For Snowball it is easy says
Claude, but "for you there is something important to be done first." The Germans
are building something near Calais, where the Channel crossing is the shortest. So
far there have been "large-scale diggings, tunnellings, and the laying of wide-gauge
railway tracks," preparations for some kind of "long-range weapon" to be aimed
at London, "rockets perhaps, or something like rockets." Thousands of Russian
slave labourers are at work on the project, and the British military needs to know
about it. Esme is to be the courier who takes drawings of the facility to England,
as soon as the sketches are completed. "If you were caught with them you would
of course, be treated as a spy!" The choice must be his, and the downed tail-gunner is willing (428-30).

A few days later, Esme was moved into a watchmaker's house near Paris, and from there he will cross the Channel "by Anson aircraft," the drawings being secured by adhesive tape to the inside of his thigh. Anticipating opposition, Claude hands Esme a loaded Sten gun to use should they be challenged, which they are, and in the middle of the night. At the sound of a car braking in the street, Esme rose from his mattress and heard "the terrifying crash of splintering woodwork," followed by a "confused uproar from the landing below!" Things happened so quickly that "blind instinct" governed. When the uniformed man "brandishing a revolver" appeared in the rectangle of light and "something whipped sharply at his right arm," Esme could hear Claude's voice shouting what he took to be "a command to fight his way downstairs." The instant that the man on the stair fired, "Esme's finger closed on the trigger, and he fired a full burst," running then down the stairs into "the pool of light, where Claude was standing astride the bodies of two men in black uniforms." Quickly he and Claude were through the kitchen into the yard, where "as they emerged someone came pounding over the cobbles and Claude suddenly stopped, faced about, and called over his shoulder to Esme. 'The lorry is at the end of the lane...Martin...get to him!'" and Claude goes down, covering the courier's escape. Somebody reached out and pulled Esme into the cab, and "the lorry shot away" cornering "at breakneck speed, heading for the open country," where he boarded the Anson that flew him back to England (433-37).

The final section of the Esme and Judy story—they marry and settle in Devon, Judy gives birth to their son Arthur—is best deferred until after we return to the Jim and Harold plot, which clamors for our present attention.

The Jim and Harold Plot, II

The chapter "Open House" celebrates "that brief period" in the summer of 1943 "when the war that had already lasted as long as its predecessor was almost forgotten" by the Avenue's inhabitants. During that week most of them became for a few days "a closer-knit community" than ever before (438). The occasion for it was the double wedding of two Avenue soldiers, "Private Bernard Carver, repatriated after more than eight months in German hospitals," and Flight Sergeant Esme Frazier, who was "due to be decorated for exceptional devotion to duty," alerting us that the adhesive tape held and the Anson made it across the Channel with the drawings. While the occasion had been supplied by the weddings the day's high point was "a lively little ceremony" Harold and Jim put together, "the symbolic demolition of the highboard fence that had separated" the verandas and gardens of Numbers Twenty and Twenty-Two for more than thirty years (439).

For years the fence had been "a token boundary," since Judy and Esme were little, when "there had been a swinging plank, held in place by a single nail," and after Jim moved in with Harold next door the plank had been "chopped up for firewood," although each side of what remained was annually given a coat of creosote by Jack Strawbridge and Harold. Looking ahead toward hosting nearly a hundred people in one backyard, especially when the younger twins Fetch and Carry intended to "jive with" their American soldier friends, it was clear that crowding would be a problem.

> Harold said: "It's a pity we can't have it in two gardens, old man!"
>
> "Well, and why can't we? asked Jim, suddenly.
>
> "There's the fence!"
>
> "Then to hell with the fence!" retorted Jim.
>
> They sat smiling at one another for a few seconds, both instantly appreciating the enormous significance of the proposal.
>
> For years now, it seemed, they had been ducking to and fro through the narrow gap between the two main supports of the fence, but the idea of removing the barrier altogether had never occurred to either of them. It did now and it appealed to them immensely, for each felt that in some way the removal of the fence would cement a friendship forged in the fires of war and ensure that this friendship survived the war. Never again, now that Esme and Judy were marrying, would Numbers Twenty and Twenty-Two be two houses, indeed, if one thought about it they had ceased to be two dwellings on the day that Harold had made his first tentative suggestion that Jim should move in and keep him company until Eunice returned from Torquay.
>
> Now Eunice would never return, and Harold supposed, rather glumly, that once Hitler had crossed into the shades in pursuit of Kaiser Wilhelm and everyone had made a victory bonfire of their blackouts, Jim would return to his own home, Esme would make a home of his own somewhere, and he, Harold, would be left in lonely isolation at Number Twenty-Two. No wonder that the idea of pulling down the fence struck him as a very happy one indeed. (*War*, 440–41)

Jim's reasons for taking the fence down were different from Harold's but similar in spirit for "he too thought the idea of destroying the fence a very sensible one." They got to the practicalities immediately.

> "We could do it right away," he told Harold, "it's rotten right through at the far end and only needs a pushover!"
>
> "No," said Harold, his brown eyes sparkling behind his thick-lensed spectacles, "let's make a kind of ceremony of it! Let's do it tomorrow, in front of everyone!"
>
> Jim at once saw what he was getting at and approved. It matched his own feelings about the Avenue since Churchill had taken charge of the war. The levelling of the fence would be symbolic of the unity of the British, of the sinking of party differences and social distinctions, and of the Avenue's implacable determination to scorch German fascism from the face of the earth!
>
> "Very well," he agreed, "we'll do it before the toasts, and we'll make a proper old issue of it!"
>
> And so they did, watched by a large and enthusiastic audience, for by the time they had returned home with the second bridal couple, the house and garden of number Twenty was teeming with guests, and Pippa, with Bernard standing shyly beside her, had as much as she could do to keep the party from beginning prematurely, and

was glad to step aside in favour of Judy, who, as a sergeant-instructor in the W.A.A.F. and an ex-marshal of Pony Clubs, was much more at home with exuberance en masse.

The symbolic levelling of the fence, with Jim swinging a 14-lb. sledge hammer at the verandah end, and Harold (assisted by an uplifted Mr. Baskerville) at the nursery end, was a spectacular opening to a party that, from its outset, proved the most joyful and uninhibited in the Avenue's history.

Not even on Armistice Day, 1918, or subsequently, when almost every thorough-fare in the suburb celebrated its VE Day by a communal meal in the open street, did the Avenue let its hair so far down as it did upon this occasion. (*War*, 441–42)

Edgar Frith attended the open house, Pippa's marriage to Berni being the immediate reason for his attending, his most important wedding present being the money he set aside "to install Pippa, and her disabled husband [he had lost an arm], in a little garage on the Caernarvon Road." Bernard was an experienced motor mechanic and there should be money in garages once "petrol-rationing was abolished" (444). A secondary reason for Edgar's presence in the Carver's yard was to deliver Elaine's "best wishes" to Esme. But Frances speaks up, saying "Edgar hasn't told you everything," since Elaine "is here now, and she'd rather like to wish both Esme and Judy good luck!" When told, Esme looked surprised and turned to Judy, "who smiled and nodded," while her father, watching her closely, thought "She *would*. There's not a spark of malice in Judy" (445).

When the time comes for speeches Harold defers to Jim, who stood on a chair and "shouted for silence in his best open-air-rally voice." What he *didn't* say mattered most.

Ten years ago, Jim Carver would have improved the occasion by airing his views on the state of the world. Two years ago he might have introduced into the toast a few comments on the activities of Government contract profiteers, and the danger of bad faith with our ally, Soviet Russia, but since the day that he had mourned his twins, and seen one of them miracuously restored to him, he had gone a long way toward acquiring a political tolerance...It was enough for him to rejoice that Bernard had found a girl who would love and care for him, in spite of his grave disablement, that Judy had also found and claimed the man she loved, that poor old Boxer was out of the war, and safe behind German wire, where he would have to stay whether he liked it or not until the Third Reich was hammered to pieces and he could return home again. In light of all this he contented himself with a conventional little speech, wishing the two couples great happiness, and a safe passage to victory. (*War*, 446–47)

When Esme is asked to say a few words, he shares what is on his mind, making observations which are subtantive as well as uplifting.

"When I was in France not long ago I met a lot of people who reminded me very much of the kind of people here today. One of them actually knew this Avenue, he'd lodged just around the corner, in Cawnpore Road. He was killed, helping me to get back, and I mention him only because it seems to me that he was typical of all the people over there who haven't given up, any more than we gave up at the time of Dunkirk. In saying

'thank you' for all the good wishes we've had showered on us today, I'd like to propose a
toast to the people I've learned to believe in since all this uproar and muddle started. I'd
like you to drink to ordinary people in roads like this all over the world!" (*War*, 447–48)

Jim shouted "Hear, hear!" as loud as he could, and welcomed a fellow-crusader into
the family, a moody dreamer the war had converted into "a man with whom he
had affinity." It did not cross his mind, the narrator observes, that "his daughter
must have been far more discerning than he," since she already knew that Esme
had the right stuff many years ago when they played together as children.

A change in presentational structure is in order here, for we no longer have
five separable plot lines to follow. Archie and Elaine have completed their grow-
ing-up and drift out of the action, leaving the other three plot-lines. But what we
can now think of as Jim Carver's family consists of himself and Harold, Esme and
Judy, Berni and Pippa, and off behind "German wire" for now, Boxer. That being
the state of the Avenue, the simplifying convention of separable plot lines, having
served its purpose, should be abandoned. For when the English people, along with
those others who prefer freedom rather than gas ovens and buzz bombs have triumphed over Hitler, Churchill will make the announcement and the whole world's
Avenues will go mad for joy. The destruction of the fence making way for the "open
house" at Harold and Jim's place anticipates that coalescing of individuals into an
even bigger, noisier party in the offing. Therefore, a more-fluid treatment of the
Carver family's activities from here forward is in keeping with the spirit of sharing
which is already gathering to a greatness.

The open house celebration having concluded, we follow first Esme and Judy,
then Bernard and Pippa, into honeymoon days. There is still in Esme something
of the "Lone Hero" spirit who would rather engage in imagined heroics than mix
with others, but that is on the way out. We sense the new note of social integra-
tion when the narrator tells us "Esme had not really cared for the idea of a reception and Avenue garden party but on leaving hospital, with his wound healed [the
gunshot wound in the arm], he had realized that a get-together was important to
Jim and Harold and had therefore raised no objections when Judy sounded him
on the matter." Well, goodness! If Jim Carver can abandon the isolation of being
locked inside his own political opinions and join the crowd, who is Esme to draw
back? He is now a war hero, who will always recall "the terse congratulations" of
the Air Commodore who interviewed him in Whitehall the day he left hospital.
Claude's drawings were useful, for although "we knew a great deal" about the pilot-
less weapons the Germans were preparing, "this is the first real confirmation we've
had," the Commodore admits (449). He is not a make-believe hero now. Moreover,
Esme's perception of women has changed as well. It is true that ever since that
day at the Manor when he and Judy recognized that they had a future together he
"valued her warm companionship and the sense of repose that she brought him."

But not until this moment [of her visit in hospital] had he felt drawn to her physically as compellingly as he had once been drawn to Elaine. She was, he decided, not only sweet, loyal and utterly reliable, but exciting in a way that she had never seemed in the past...Judy had always played a part in his dreams, but it had been a walk-on part, the role of the shield-bearer. Now, without trumpets or drums, she had moved into the centre of the stage, and had suddenly become the woman he would continue to weave his dreams around, a woman, who, so unlike Elaine, would regard such inclusion as the highest compliment he could pay her. (*War*, 450)

Delderfield's attention to Berni's disabilities is yet another instance of the broad range of cultural-historical realities this novel deals with, i.e., the struggle of war-wounded veterans to regain self-confidence and re-integrate into society. For Pippa and Bernard, that struggle begins before their wedding and continues in the honeymoon. They had greater difficulty than did Esme and Judy "arriving at a readjustment," since "the roots of their association were nearer the surface and their future was more uncertain." Pippa could cope with his disability "if she avoided making an issue of it," but harder to repair was the damage inside him which "had little to do with his empty sleeve, or the limp that resulted from the severed muscles of his leg" (453). Sensing the crisis approaching, Pippa "made up her mind," and made her move by saying "It's Boxer, isn't it, Bernard?" Yes, of course it is and he doesn't want to talk about it. She needs to not pick at his private troubles.

She realized that if she was to achieve anything at all with him she must take the lead now—this instant. No amount of time would make any difference to him, not so long as he was left floundering about on his own with his thoughts pounding the treadmill of memory.

"You'll have to talk about it some time, Berni," she said firmly. "You might as well start now and tell me! If you only knew it I'm the person who can help, because I'm the only one who has ever thought of you and Boxer as two persons and not one!"

He looked closely at her then, holding her in his glance for nearly a minute. Finally, he said:

"That was the one time that I left him to cope on his own, the *one time*, Pip! He wouldn't come away when we began pulling back but just stood there, firing into the battery! It was so bloody silly when you think of it. He couldn't have been firing *at* anything, there was so much smoke! Then, when I copped it, it was him who found *me* and carried me about for hours...It's so damned funny that he should have done that, after me turning my back on him the way I did!"

"Why do you feel so bad about it," she asked quietly, "Why aren't you proud of him? You ought to be!"

He shook his head impatiently.

"I'm telling you, it was only a minute or so after I'd turned my back on him! Don't you see, Pip? I was fed up to the back teeth with him! I remembered everything you'd said to me, that I couldn't go on and on looking out for him the way I'd always done! Then he went and did a thing like that for me! I can't get that out of my head!"

She was silent a moment, considering. "You're looking at it all wrong, Bernard," she said at length. "Sit down and listen to me. You've got to start looking at it the way it really is, and you've got to begin right here and now."

She pushed him towards the deck chair that stood against the boundary fence and took a seat facing him on the low railing separating the tiny verandah from the garden.

"You being hit like that was the luckiest thing that ever happened to Boxer," she said. "It gave him the one chance he's ever had of being someone, of doing something on his own and out of his own head, instead of just something you told him to do! Now then—listen Berni—how do you know that it hasn't done him a tremendous amount of good? How can you tell whether he's the same person any more, now that he hasn't got you to do all his thinking for him? You just turn that over for a minute or two while I go in and make some tea."

When Pippa returns with the tea, after an absence intended to allow Bernard time to contemplate his situation freshly, he was silent for a while as he slowly stirred his cup, and when he had emptied it he said:

"Do you really want us to get married, Pip? Are you quite sure you aren't doing it because I'm like this now?"

"That's right," she said with a smile, "now begin worrying about that side of it! At least I can do something about that!"

She did too, for afterwards he was much easier to manage and she soon discovered that by far the best way of handling him was to bully him.

Louise would sometimes hear her teaching him to reload his safety razor with one hand and would smile and nod to herself, as Pippa's voice came from the bathroom—"Now then, you'll only drop it if you scoop it towards you, stupid! Press your thumb against the handle and wedge the razor against the back of the basin...Here, let me show you...like that!" (*War*, 456)

There will be more difficulties, more despairing collapses into tearful exasperation, but in time Berni will learn how to manage a wrench underneath the auto he is repairing with surprising adroitness, while cheerfully talking with Pippa.

The D-Day invasion of June, 1944, delighted Jim, who considered it "the moment for the all-out assault on the northern shores of the Continent" that would "hammer Hitler on three fronts" (497). Esme did not participate in the invasion, although he had "a very busy day" at the Free French Headquarters, "decoding short-wave messages" from places like Grenoble and Limoge. His C.O. warned him that when the bridgehead expanded he would need to fly to France in order to make "personal contact" with the Free Forces of the French interior (506). Judy was occupied in Devonshire "making a home" out of the wilderness, the "ramshackle two-story house" she and Esme fell in love with and purchased. It stood on a knoll "about fifty yards from the shallow River Otter," part of a derelict farm the newlyweds hope to make productive by raising chickens and pigs, "and maybe a cow for your own use" Maud suggests, supplementing their income by taking summer visitors—"or run a riding school" since Maud will soon retire. By D-Day some little progress had been made, but their commitment was absolute. That is where a pregnant Judy is now "pouring cans of weed-killer between the cracked paving stones of the forecourt" (509).

Meanwhile, back in London, Jim had been monitoring the effects of V.1 bombs that came skating through "Doodlebug Alley" from near Calais. Some of these strange things were brought down by the steel wires strung perpendicularly in the sky by the moored balloons in Kent, but many others got through. The Germans used their last offensive weapon with the intent of striking terror, knowing that the war already was lost. The V.1s were particularly successful since "you could see them coming," thus people were "presented with a choice of where to run" to escape a weapon that one never could tell would land "a mile, or a few yards away." These intruders came at the end of a five-year war when Londoners "had persuaded themselves that the worst was behind them" (517-20). One summer afternoon, Jim was diverted by a loud commotion he thought required his assistance, but proved to be a large group of pedestrians watching "a window-cleaner rescue a trapped pigeon" that got itself "wedged behind the wired-up window of a tall building." Frightened, the bird refused to contribute to its own rescue, repeatedly eluding the workman's hand. Its audience paid no attention to "the familiar honk-honk of an approaching V.1" hearing which Jim had expected the crowd to dive for cover. When the bomb exploded near the Strand, the crowd "hardly flinched," for just then the window-cleaner grabbed the pigeon by its legs "and frenzied cheering broke out on all sides" (521-22). The V.1 caused terrible damage where it struck, but Carver reasoned that London was big, and since the chance of being hit during a two hundred bomber raid was small, the chances of "dodging a single warhead without a human being to guide it, were pretty good" (519). Many of us remember watching Glenn Miller's orchestra playing right through the approach and explosion of a German Doodlebug in that 'forties movie, and the psychology behind the band's auditors staying put and listening to the cheerful music is identical to that of the fascinated crowd watching a pigeon flutter about behind the wire. Yes, the V.1 was dangerous, but not *interesting*.

On another day, however, the bomb came in from a wrong direction, its mechanism having perhaps been damaged by "an ack-ack splinter," blasting the Avenue "obliquely at Number Thirty-Eight, after skimming over the chimneys of the odd numbers, opposite."

> It demolished every house between Number Thirty-Eight and the corner shop, nineteen in all, besides shattering parts of the even numbers opposite, and sending a solid chunk of Mr. Saunder's yard wall right through the front of Number One. It killed twenty-one of the residents at that end of the crescent and it injured another eighteen.
>
> Jack Strawbridge and his wife, Louise, were killed outright, Jack as he crossed the threshold, with Harold at his heels, and Louise as she moved away from the gas-stove, carrying the teapot.

> Harold was lifted and flung outward, towards the nursery, where he landed amidst
> debris on the vegetable rows that Jack had quitted but a moment before. (*War*, 529-30)

"How badly is he hurt?" Jim asked of a stretcher-bearer. "Difficult to say," said the man, "deep cuts and compound-fracture of the right leg and other fractures in the left leg and left arm. Ribs caught it too...He was blown about twenty-five yards, clean over the fence!" (533)

Edith and Jim, who have decided to be married, visited Harold in hospital. She was now a new woman, for from the moment Jim Carver proposed marriage, "her natural hesitancy of speech and manner had evaporated like mist in sunshine." Edith now "bubbled and beamed" and "looked younger and more alert." Visiting Harold in hospital, "she looked smart and trim in a new, tailored two-piece, with hat, gloves, shoes and handbag to match" (563). He quickly noticed the change and teased her, gently.

> "My word, Miss Clegg, it looks to me as if you've been buying clothing coupons on the
> black market!"
> "Oh, but I have," replied Edith, unblushingly, "the woman at the place where I
> was lodged sold me eight of them for two pounds! Was that a fair price do you think?"
> "I'm afraid I wouldn't know," said Harold, chuckling. "I always made do on my
> issue! Will you two be seeing our Judy while you're in the West?"
> "It depends," Jim told him. "She's expecting her baby any time now and I've
> arranged to ring her from Exeter. We shall go up to North Devon first and try to see
> her on the way back. How are you coming along, Harold? You look mobile enough in
> that odd contraption."
> Harold's invalid testiness returned.
> "Oh, I can move around," he said glumly, "but I get so damned bored! Do you
> know how long I've been cooped up here now?"
> Jim did know, to the very day, but he quickly by-passed the subject and told Harold
> how Archie had made them a wedding present of Number Forty-Three and that they
> would continue to live in what was left of the Avenue. Harold whistled but Jim, who
> knew him very well by this time, noticed a look of sadness steal over his face.
> "Oh, well, I suppose I shall have to go back into digs," he said, dismally, "and I can't
> say I like the idea at all, but there's no sense in buying another house at my time of life."
> Edith decided that she did not like this line of talk at all.
> "Now just you stop that, Mr. Godbeer," she said, severely. "You've as many years
> ahead of you as we have and you know very well that if you want a little place to your-
> self you can always have part of our house. We should all get along very well together,
> I'm sure!"
> The idea appealed to Jim and he said so at once, but Harold shook his head. Despite
> the happy occasion, he seemed very cast down, thought Jim. (*War*, 563-64)

Multiply Harold's situation by the number of English people who were perma-nently crippled by the war, whether they were old or young, and one is looking at a not inconsiderable aspect of the cultural history of Hitler's war. Jim wants to know "Exactly *what* did the surgeon tell you?" He had said Harold could hope to "get up and down stairs" with the assistance of irons, and walk "a short distance at a time," but little more.

In welcome contrast, Pippa is now pregnant and she and Berni are happy. When they visited, Jim was "struck by the tremendous strength [Bernie] displayed with his over-worked left hand, and the dexterity he showed in bracing tools against his chest, and even using his teeth when he needed to shift his grip on a wrench or a length of chain." Bernard and Pippa share the work in the garage and kitchen, and would continue doing that until they can afford hired help, "or at least until her baby arrived in June." Pippa doesn't know how she'll "cope with it all when there's a baby to see to, but we'll manage somehow" (537).

For a change of pace and a lighter mood than Harold's situation allows, we turn now to Esme's current efforts in France, and Delderfield's experience there when he was sent on a similar mission. Esme was feeling homesick, more so than in his "previous wanderings" after parachuting out of the doomed aircraft. At that time he had been "on the run" and had had "much to occupy his mind." But now France was "practically cleared of Germans" and the severest problems were broken bridges and the extreme scarcity of petrol.

> Officially he was supposed to be photographing bomb-damage, unofficially he was 'showing the flag' and collecting scraps of information about resistance groups. It was tiring work, entailing long journeys by road and air, and it did not seem to be serving a useful purpose now that the Germans were fighting on their own frontiers. (War, 549)

Esme's unpleasant situation is virtually identical with one that Delderfield lived through. But he transforms his own difficulties into a wonderful experience for readers of his essay "An Auster Odyssey" (For My Own Amusement, 342-60). Delderfield was not exactly sent on a wild goose chase, but he had to follow orders and do his utmost with a goofy idea "someone down on the Second Corridor came up with,"

> the eccentric idea that the bomb tonnage required to flatten Germany could be worked out (presumably to the last half-ounce) by a review and assessment of the damage to French and Belgian targets prior to the D-Day assault in June.
>
> The originator of this scheme, whoever he was, must have substituted clairvoyance for arithmetic. The object of the R.A.F. air onslaught on France, in the period between January and June, 1944, had two specific objects. The first and most important was to isolate the Normandy coastline. The secondary and subsequent object was to strike at the launching sites of the flying bombs and rockets. For years now the air attacks on German cities had been mounted with the object of reducing her war potential and there was absolutely no way, at that time, of assessing their effectiveness with any degree of accuracy. However, the Second Corridor wanted that set of facts and figures, and possibly my report on Le Havre encouraged Dudley Barker to name me as the man to collect them, not as a lone observer, with a single ground-to-ground photographer, but as C.O. of a small flight made up of three pilots flying Austers, a P.R. photographer

with experience of air-to-ground photography, a motion-picture cameraman, a driver and a fifteen-hundredweight van.

Briefing was sketchy. I was to command whilst the flight was on the ground and the senior pilot was in charge once we were in the air. I was given fifty-six major targets in France and Belgium and was told to visit them all, collect detailed information on the effectiveness of the bombing, secure corroborative film and pictures, and send back the data as I assembled it. My secondary instructions were to contact and interview people of the Resistance movement who had promoted the escapes of large numbers of R.A.F. personnel during the last four years, to look out for propaganda angles with an R.A.F. slant, and generally show the flag in all the places I visited where the British had not yet penetrated.

When I raised the vulgar question as to how I was to keep the team fed in areas remote from Allied bases they said, gaily, "Oh, you live on the country, old boy," and gave me an impressive-looking pass signed by Eisenhower and expressing his earnest wish that, as one of his investigators, I "would be given aid and comfort by all." I was very flattered to represent the Supremo in all the areas of by-passed territory, and I liked the phrase "live on the country." Somehow it smacked of a Napoleonic advance down the valley of the Danube in the year of Austerlitz and Trafalgar. I was less sanguine, however, about extracting aid and comfort from the civilians I had seen during my recent trip to LeHavre.

This was his task in all its complex splendor. But to make it work smoothly, Delderfield's competence as a speaker of the French language ought to have been better than it was.

It took a little time to evolve effective methods of gathering the material Air Ministry was seeking. Officers attached to Second Tactical Air Force gave us some useful, large-scale maps, and we began covering centers like Louvaine, Courtrai and Malines whilst based on Brussels. In areas like this the main bombing attacks had been concentrated on the railway stations and goods yards and the wrecked station was usually the first port of call. I spoke French indifferently, my principal trouble (apart from tenses) being a strong and apparently guttural accent that led me, on two occasions, to be mistaken for a Luftwaffe officer on the run. Our uniforms were not dissimilar, and an old lady, watching a friendly railway official take me firmly by the arm, cackled with glee and said something that embarrassed my guide. Pressed to interpret he said, with a smile, "She said, 'I see you've captured another of the swine. Are you going to shoot him?'" Something similar occurred at a country hamlet much further south. Seeing me step from van to farmyard two venturesome farmworkers leaped down from the loft aperture, shouting abuse and brandishing pitchforks, and this despite Dudley Barker's revolver that had never been fired in anger. On that occasion I discovered that I could speak French fluently, and once I had identified myself we all three shared the joke over a glass of Pernod. (*Amusement*, 342–46)

In a different essay, Delderfield is not jocular when he recalls reading Marbot's *Memoirs* during the mission. "With Marbot's book in my pocket I traveled over some of the same roads as those along which he had ridden in the company of men like Ney, Lannes and Masséna." Marbot was "a kind of patron saint for me when

I crossed France and Belgium in the final stages of World War II, and I thought of him when De Gaulle walked down the Champs Elysees, surrounded by cheering Parisians...And how proud he would have been of that section of the French nation that had kept its courage and will to resist during the German occupation" (*Amusement*, 274-75).

Delderfield's comment that Marbot was a "patron saint" accompanying him through France ought to alert us that he sees the past as "present-within" the present, since in all psychological essentials people change little from one era to the next. We can observe that as *The Avenue Goes to War* winds down, Delderfield opens its action towards the future by anticipating the day when Judy and Esme's newborn child Arthur's great-great-grandchildren will look back upon the Twentieth Century's conflicts with the indifference we feel towards Napolean's wars. In that sense the novel does not dribble away but presses onward, since in "The Bulldozers," the book's last chapter, the bomb-ravaged Avenue is already being prepared for the newer suburbs that ex-soldiers and their wives will live in. On quasi-military command, the "mechanical grabs" started to "bite into the mound opposite Number Twenty and Twenty-Two, driving a broad furrow down the old cart-track that crossed the meadow to the wood," (613), that is, Manor Woods, where the crumbling mansion is patiently disintegrating in the path of bulldozers soon to obliterate any sign of the architectural grandeur that once graced "the days of the Prince Regent and Beau Brummel" (*Suburb*, 18). After many dull days indoors in March 1947, "the people comprising the Avenue rump came out to watch the men and machines at their work" (*War*, 614). They watch the future in the making out of the rubble of World War II.

Already looking towards "The Bulldozers," the next-to-next-to-last chapter "The Coming of Arthur" dramatizes the contributions, even this early on, of the Avenue's coming generation. "It is not often," says the narrator, "that a man attends his own wedding in the morning and is also present at the birth of his own grandson before midnight of the same day, but such a privilege was Jim Carver's, on January 22nd, 1945" (556). Can a novelist be more explicit in drawing attention to the continuity of history? Carver has earned his central role as the monitoring participant in the great events of his time, but is about to step aside as Judy's child is born in Devonshire. Yet as it happens, there are no adults handy at the critical moment to call in the doctor to attend the birth. That privilege is given to little Barbara, now a lively and intelligent five-year-old. She knows horses well enough to saddle-up and gallop away like Black Beauty in the story to get the doctor. "Listen Baba," says Judy as labor pains produce the twisted grimace through which she talks, "this is important," which Barbara need not be told. "I want you to saddle up old Gramp and ride down to Mrs. Southcott. Tell her Mummy's baby's coming...", and Judy heard the delighted little girl's feet "flying across the cobbled yard to the stables" (570-71). When Grandpa Jim and Grandma Edith arrive, the elated child chanted "The baby's here, the baby's here, and it was me and Gramp who fetched everybody from the pub" (573). Not to worry, the future is already in good hands. The astonished Jim *had* been concerned, though he need not have distressed himself, since as Judy says, "It's just like the Avenue. The people around are all that really count, Dad!" (576).

The chapter "King Boxer The First" comes late in the novel since this other twin, when cooped in a concentration camp, found his inventiveness limited to practical jokes by which he discombobulated the Third Reich. Boxer will need to break free to demonstrate his independence, which Pippa foreknew he was capable of. He does not share the view of his fellow prisoner "The Coldstreamer" that "the only smart thing to do now is to stick close to the krauts who know us, and who look upon us as their insurance!" He is having none of that malarkey. Instead, Boxer breaks out and goes off on his own to "seek out whatever new adventures fate had in store for him" (580–81). Almost immediately, Boxer discovers "an unopened crate of pilchards," more than a hundred tins, two of which he eats before going to sleep. When he wakes at first light he hears "dragging footsteps" in the dead leaves by the roadside made by a young woman searching for food. "He knew at once that hunger alone prevented her from diving into the woods like a startled hare" (582). This is scanty evidence, but Boxer already senses that she is a kindred spirit who like himself weighs danger against opportunity.

Boxer quickly becomes the center of a group of hungry people who congregate around him, some of them trustworthy, others not.

> For some reason that he could not explain Boxer trusted the woman more than he trusted the Belgian. He was getting very good at sign-language by this time and soon made her understand that she was to stay with the crate while he and the old man were away from the clearing. The Belgian began to argue but Boxer cut him short. "You bloody will do as I say and don't chew the cud, gran'pa! (*War*, 586)

One decision at a time, Berni's twin creates a functioning society out of chaos by delegating authority and policing the unreliable. "Without quite knowing how it came about Boxer now assumed full leadership of the group," which grew when other strays, needing security and leadership, joined them in the clearing. During this time the young woman who had first joined Boxer continues to increase in his regard. A Russian named Olga, she instinctively sets about cleaning the communal mess tin and spoon "with handfuls of leaves."

> Watching her Boxer relaxed, thinking her action typical of her entire sex. Louise, his sister, would have done just that, even under these conditions. Here was artillery grumbling all round them, the sky vibrating with bombers, and twenty-two women and children trying to sleep in home-made huts on a supper of tinned pilchards, yet Olga still practiced the trade of housewife! He wondered how old she was and how she came to be here. (*War*, 589)

When he is home in England again, Boxer will find a way to trace her where-abouts, since he likes her style. Olga is purposeful and considerate in everything she does, as, for instance, when there are two of them but only one blanket. She indicates that Boxer should lie down first "and when he did so she lay beside him and threw the edge of the blanket over his shoulders, jerking it towards her so that they were pressed together in its fold" (589). Heat retention, a very sound principle in the out-of-doors, very wise.

Boxer remained in the clearing for fourteen days, and this period was "the final stage in the true discovery of himself as an individual."

> Ever since that August day almost three years ago, when he had been faced with the ter-rible necessity of making a whole series of decisions regarding the disposal of Bernard, Boxer had been moving steadily towards the achievement of independence. (*War*, 590)

Eventually his temporary society must disperse and go their various ways. When Boxer says good-bye to Olga "she caught and kissed his hand but he hastily with-drew it when he saw the jeep driver's knowing grin."

> "Looks like you bin frattin' in them woods, Limey," he said.
> "It wasn't like that, chum," insisted Boxer, as the jeep sped across the bridge, "believe it or not, it wasn't that way at all."
> He pondered a moment, then added: "Queer that! Don't ask me why it wasn't, but it wasn't." (*War*, 596)

Pippa had been the only person to realize that, given the opportunity, Boxer could become an independent actor. As a clairvoyant who *knows* things, she knew that when both twins were presumed dead, they were still alive, and she assured their grieving father that they were. But Pippa knows more than that. She had told Berni "you haven't really begun your own life yet but when you do you'll need some-one to share it with, because you've been so used to sharing that you wouldn't have any use for a life on your own" (*War*, 197). She was right, and the same is true of Berni's twin. When they are separated into independent persons, and Boxer has *his* "own life," he, too, will need someone to share it with, and Olga, who instinctively shared the blanket with him, has already chosen for both of them. It's not unlike the Lord God in *Genesis* saying "it is not good that man should be alone," he needs "an help meet." Adam recognizes her as "bone of my bones, flesh of my flesh" (2:18, 2:23). Or as Boxer un-clairvoyantly puts it, it wasn't funny stuff that happened out in the woods: "Don't ask me why it wasn't that way, but it wasn't" (596).

After the excitement of Churchill's electrifying words "This is *your* victory" quiets down, Jim reflects in his own habitual manner that "peace held no prom-ise of working out in a single, straightforward way," for reaction was already set-ting in, the Socialists beginning to call Churchill "the champion of Big Business and the war-profiteers." There would be an election soon, and mud-slinging would resume, the Right entrenching themselves "against the Unions," the Left demanding "nationalization and vast multiplication of Government controls." Where would the money come from for large-scale changes? "From America in the form of loans?" Would these "shackle" the British to American capital and tie England forever "to Washington's coat-tails" in foreign policy? (607–08). Skeptical and inclined to see problems as always, Carver helps conclude the novel by gazing toward the future, and he is no longer mired in the slough of his earlier anxieties. He knows that since it is "not possible to learn about people from books and pamphlets," it isn't possible "to learn how to govern from these sources."

> To understand, and evaluate democracy, one had to live in a place like this, and live here for a very long time! One had to see all the penny-plain democrats at their weddings and funerals; one had to watch how they behaved under fire, but most of all one had to understand and sympathize with their dreams...That was what living in this Avenue had taught him, and by God, it was something worth learning! If the politicians Left, Right and Centre learned as much in the decade ahead then they could all hope to profit by the past, and shape some kind of future for children waiting to be born! (*War*, 629-30)

· 3 ·

THE DEVONSHIRE TRILOGY

Delderfield's Devonshire trilogy, *A Horseman Riding By*, dramatizes events in England from 1900 until the middle 1960s, the time span consumed by *Long Summer's Day*, *Post of Honour* and *The Green Gauntlet*. Once again he fictionalizes a locale he was well acquainted with, "locale" being taken expansively to include the British Empire from its heyday into its decline, as well as the 1300 acre estate purchased by Paul Craddock, the trilogy protagonist. Wounded in the Boer War and returned to England virtually at death's door, he recovers from the Mauser bullet in his knee and engages vigorously in England's life from then until he dies sixty-some years later. Since the trilogy is a jam-packed story of many associates during Craddock's long lifetime, it will be helpful to begin with an abbreviated cast of characters for *Long Summer's Day*. In that novel, the repatriated Army casualty, finding to his surprise that he has the financial means to do so, purchases and becomes the squire of a badly neglected Devonshire estate, into which he will invest both money and sweat equity improving the lives and productivity of the farmers and artizans whose squire he becomes.

Cast of Characters

Chief Characters

> *Paul Craddock*, the new squire of Shallowford Estate.
> *Grace Lovell*, his mis-matched first wife.
> *Claire Derwent*, his beloved second wife.

Support Characters (information sources and evaluation partners)

> *Franz Zorndorff*, Paul's farsighted financier.
> *John Rudd*, the estate's agent, retained by Paul.
> *James Grenfell*, Liberal politician, Paul's friend.

Special-Case Characters

> *Ikey Palfrey*, Paul's "adopted" son, whose lineage and experiences make him
> culturally amphibious.
> *Simon Craddock*, Paul's son by his first wife, who after long political mat-
> uration becomes his father's spiritual successor, though not the
> estate's owner.

Other Characters

> The resident farmers and artisans of Shallowford and their children along
> with Paul's six children by his second wife.

Part I: *Long Summer's Day*

The novel opens with Franz Zorndorff, a Hungarian Jew who in England has
made a fortune in the scrap-metal trade, arriving at the Hospital for Convalescent
Officers where young Craddock lies dying from medical neglect. Presently serving
on the Board of Volunteer Hospitals in the London area, he announces himself
with "a banker's draft for five hundred guineas, earmarked for this institution,"
the same amount "to be paid over the day my late partner's son is removed from
the dangerously ill list." With that, he lays down an envelope alongside his visitors
card and tells the hospital's matron that the wounded officer *will* be granted a private room and the services of the finest specialist physician money can buy. Thus,
in a twinkling the arrogant little bastard who came in without showing deference
to the Hospital's Rulers is quickly treated like visiting royalty.

Cutting away from Zorndorff, we turn to Paul Craddock in his private hospital
room, lying with "one leg suspended from a pulley" as he "conjures fantasies from
the stains etched into" the ceiling's plaster. While pain and drugs battle within

him, Paul struggles to reconcile the contrast between "lines of infantry and squadrons of cavalry" locked in static conflict overhead, while alternately, he endures the pain of "pressing his left cheek to the pillow to bring his right eye in line with the french windows opposite and staring out at the prospect beyond the terrace" of what had been a luxurious private home. Through the windows he saw clouds "drifting over the elms," "occasionally a farm wagon crawling along the hillside track," now and then a cow.

> Gradually he began to relate the two vistas, the one fraught with anxiety and stress, the other bringing him joy and tranquillity, so that as the days passed, and the hillside view slowly began to assume mastery over the armies above, he knew that he would live, drawing more reassurance from the contrast than from anything the surgeon said or the soothing remarks made by the plump nurse who brought him drinks. And with the growing belief in his survival the battle on the ceiling lost its horrid significance, and the vision of serenity framed in woods resolved itself into a kind of Promised Land where he, Lieutenant Paul Craddock, whom they had given up for dead, roamed in the splendour of his youth. (*Summer's Day*, 8-9)

As his mind is released from its life/death struggle, Paul reflects that he had not taken pleasure in "harassing" the wretched Veldt farmers, "and it was not long before doubts obscured his vision of Imperial infallibility." He knew that in this very hospital there were many junior officers now "cursing the impulse that had involved them in a war for which many serving soldiers now felt a slight disgust, causing them to ask themselves if, after all, the pro-Boer Lloyd George and his following had not been justified in condemning the adventure from the outset" (11). Paul has abandoned patriotic fervor for the more responsible mindset of the informed citizen obliged to weigh the merits against the demerits of Imperial action.

Craddock is now sufficiently healthy to have his first conversation with the Zorndorff delighted by his "excellent progress" in hospital. He has come to tell the ex-sergeant how much money will be his as heir of his father's fortune, a whopping sum because "the coarse metal trade prospers in wartime" particularly because of "the blunders the generals made over there," not to mention future prospects now that "the Kaiser has obliged the trade by entering the naval race" (14). This is food for thought, and Paul feeds upon the contrast between the ceiling vision of endless military conflict and the green countryside that signifies peace and productive labor.

> He had never had thoughts like this before and it occurred to him that pain, and the prolonged flirtation with death, had matured him in a way that had been leap-frogged by the other convalescents, many of whom had had more shattering experiences in the field. Some the war had left cynical and a few, among them the permanently maimed, bitter but all the regular officers seemed to have emerged from the war with their prejudices intact and talked of little else but sport, women, and the military lessons learned from the campaigns. They continued, Paul thought, to regard England as a jumping-

off ground for an eternal summer holiday in the sun among lesser breeds, looking to
them and the Empire for protection and economic stability, but had little or no sense
of kinship with the sun-drenched field beyond the terrace, or the chawbacons seen toil-
ing there taking advantage of the Coronation weather [Queen Victoria having recently
died] to cut and stack the long grass. (*Summer's Day*, 16)

When able to leave his room, Paul sits on the terrace reading during the long
afternoons. He keeps to himself, and two weeks after Zorndorff's visit comes upon
a two-page advertisement in the *Illustrated London News* that "gave him at least a
glimmering of an idea concerning his future." It advertised the coming sale of a
Westcountry estate owned by the Lovell family, hard hit "by Boer marksmanship,"
for the two brothers who stood to inherit the estate had been killed. When Paul
goes to London to watch from Zorndorff's box Edward VII's coronation [post-
poned for 19 months], the scrap dealer and the farm fancier have a conversation
that is unimpeded by the cancelled royal celebration. Zorndorff invites Paul on
a tour of the scrapyard before deciding to reject it in favor of buying a run-down
estate. Paul sees what the yard can tell him, but his most interesting yard experience was the explosive reaction of the quick-witted urchin who saved a carter
from being crushed to death by a frightened cart-horse; the boy "moved at fantas-
tic speed" as he sprang onto the horse's back, tore off his jacket and "flung it over
the animal's head, holding it there as his body was flung backwards and forwards
by the violent heaving" (26), until the horse finally settled down. This boy is Ikey
Palfrey, "one of Sophie Carrilovic's brood," as Zorndorff reveals. "She's a Croat,
one of the many who got word of me and migrated for pickings" (28). Ikey might
be, indeed is, the son of a Cockney wife-beater and a Hungarian Croat mother,
but his personal credentials are impeccable. After he has purchased Shallowford,
Paul will summon the lad to Devonshire to work for him, and Ikey will be dropped
into an entirely different environment, one wherein people speak a language he
cannot understand but soon masters, and where he absorbs cultural assumptions
that will enrich his individual human capital as he marinates in that new world.
Meanwhile, Paul reflects upon the contrast between Cockney London and "the
woods and hedgerows of the farmland on the Kent-Surry border, where he had
spent his childhood and boyhood" (16).

> Down here, he reflected, the children of the poor fought for coppers, risking their
> lives handling half-blind horses and counting the acquisition of an extra sixpence a
> triumph. He thought again of all the men who had died in South Africa to maintain
> the momentum of the machine that opportunists like Franz Zorndorff thought of as
> a modern highly-industrialized state. Well, at least the volunteers in South Africa had
> spent their final moments breathing fresh air, and under a sun that was not blotted
> out by sulphurous smoke and floating smuts—surely to God there was a compromise
> between the England of yesterday, and the grinding, impersonal money-machine that
> England had become in the last few decades? Surely somewhere, somehow, the indus-

trial skills of the Watts and Stephensons and Faradays could be applied to a land that could still grow good corn and breed the best cattle in Europe?" (*Summer's Day*, 29)

These were Paul's thoughts as he decided, with a finality Zorndorff recognized ["You possess a quiet obstinacy wedded to a somewhat shattering directness of manner" (21)], that he would have nothing to do with the scrap-metal business. Nevertheless, scrap-metal profits, or Paul's share in them as heir of his father's estate, would fund the purchase of Shallowford and its day-to-day expenses, until Shallowford could show a profit.

When Paul arrives at Shallowford, he is greeted by its manager, John Rudd, who expects to be dismissed by any new owner. When Rudd does not hide his dislike of the family, Craddock remarks "Then the Lovells were bad people to work for?", and substantive conversation between them has begun.

"They were but I don't hate them for that," Rudd said, "any more than do the rest of the people around here, folk dependent upon them for one reason or another." He seemed to rise slightly in his stirrups and survey the whole sweep of the moor as far as the sea. "This has been a bad place to be," he said quietly, "rotten bad for three generations if you had no means to escape from it! It need not have been but it was, for they made it so, one and all! It took me years to make up my mind about that, that it was them and not the place itself. However, that doesn't explain my touchiness does it?", and unexpectedly he smiled again and kicked his heels, so that the cob began to walk on down the slope and the well-mannered grey [Paul's mount] followed.

"I don't see that you are under the slightest obligation to explain things to me at this stage," Paul said.

"Oh come, Mr. Craddock," said Rudd, good-humouredly now, "suppose I left it there? You would only get to wondering and wondering and be driven to find out one way or another. Anyone would, especially a lad your age, who could never imagine it happening to him."

Ah yes, "a lad your age," wet behind the ears, Rudd thinks. He does not know Paul has faced death and pulled through "only by a miracle", that he had got used to "hearing [his] chances chewed over by doctors and nurses," an experience which has taught him "a thing or two." Rudd looks at him frankly, "and for the first time there was tolerance in his eyes. 'Exactly what did it teach you that was new, Mr. Craddock?'"

"Patience, I suppose, and gratitude for being alive. Also respect for people who seemed to go to a great deal of trouble to improve one's chances—those kinds of things." (*Summer's Day*, 36-7)

Taking stock, one sees that their survey of the estate has not yet begun, yet the pair are already becoming intimately acquainted with one another. The beginnings of friendship are quickly setting roots, based upon their mutual regard for courage, patience, honesty, and openness to compassion. Not a bad beginning.

As their first meeting ends, the two agree that Paul will stay the night in Rudd's lodge, the Estate House being in bad repair, and they will see the farms and the tenants who work the land in the morning. Being at leisure to poke about, Craddock experiences two memorable encounters, one with the sorely-decayed house, the other with Grace Lovell. As he gazed at the old place, which was "really two houses, of widely separated periods," Paul has a waking vision. As he "stood looking up at it for several minutes,"

> watching the west windows turn ruby in the sun, the silent building began to stir with life, so that he saw it as an ageing and once beautiful woman, awaiting the return of sons who had marched away centuries since and been swallowed up in a forgotten war. There was patience here, patience and a kind of desperate dignity, as though all hope of their return had never been abandoned, and that one day all the windows would glow with candles. Craddock tried to relate this dignity and repose with the little Rudd had told him of the family who had lived here for a century or more but he found this very difficult, for somehow the house did not strike him as morose, merely forsaken and resigned. Yet about the middle section of it, the oldest, Elizabethan block, vitality lingered, the older tenants still seeming to exert more influence than the Lovells and this conviction was so real that Craddock would not have been surprised if, as he watched, lights had flickered in that part of the house leaving each wing dark and lifeless (44).

He climbed the stone steps and let himself inside, looked about at the furnishings and various portraits Paul guessed featured the Lovells from 1806 onwards, all with "the same bleakness of eye and stiff formality of dress" he had seen in the magazine advertisement. While standing there, Paul was surprised to hear the sound of a footfall on a wooden floor, "the sound of someone walking in one of the rooms in the west wing" of a house that should have been unoccupied. He walked into what had been a nursery, with toys strewn on the floor, and then he saw her, and stared, "and she stared back, an instinctive defiance stemming from anger rather than alarm."

> She was, Craddock decided on the spot, the most exciting woman he had ever seen. Not in illustrated books, nor in the course of his visits to picture galleries or in his dreams, did he recall having seen anyone who made such an immediate impact upon his senses (45).

They exchange a certain amount of what it would hardly seem accurate to call conversation, because the woman is wholly consumed by what reaches beyond arrogance to a disdainfully haughty expression of outrage. When this exasperated state passes off the woman apologizes: "I'm sorry I startled you. I should have asked Rudd for the key. I only came here to look at some furniture," and she is gone, leaving behind "a slightly eerie silence he thought, as though she had been a ghost and he had imagined the encounter" (47). That night, Paul describes the intruder "and her curiously aggressive reception" to Rudd, who identifies her as Grace Lovell, "a family hanger-on of a kind." More to the point, Rudd, who knows what he is talking about, advises Paul that if he has been "smitten" by her he had best "forget" that, because "she's tarred with the same old brush, an indiscipline that can show itself in obstinacy, bloody mindedness, or a sort of madness. There's congenital rottenness in the family somewhere along the line" (49). But it is too late to warn Paul, who *has* been "smitten" by her, even though the first phrase which came to his mind upon seeing her face-to-face was "instinctive defiance." This is the default setting of Grace Lovell's character, as will become clear to Craddock through the instructive experience of having married her.

The next morning Craddock and Rudd tour the estate, seeing the tenants and being seen by them. As they ride home, Paul confesses himself surprised and intrigued by the place, which has proved utterly unlike anything he had imagined from having read the magazine advertisement. When Rudd asks him to be more specific, Craddock offers his best evaluation of what he has seen and reveals something of his attitude towards what he has seen, its human possibilities.

> "I think it's a private world, populated by a few hundred castaways from a wreck about a century ago! On your own admission its commercial prospects are very thin but frankly I'm not much concerned about that. I should expect to put money into any property I took and it boils down to this in the end; what kind of person are these farmers and their families looking for as a landlord, or 'squire' if you like? What would be his responsibility to them? Or theirs to him?" (*Summer's Day*, 74)

No attitude towards the estate could be more different from that of the Lovells who took money out but invested nothing in the population. If Craddock buys the estate, those who farm the land will experience a period of cultural shock, their initial response to his initiatives being that their squire is not in his right mind. What precedent have they for intuiting the truth, which is that he intends to create among them a community of neighbors and friends?

By summer of 1902, Paul had come to know his tenants well enough to sort them into three groups, those like the Derwents who were relieved to find themselves in promising hands, the feckless Tamer Potter who grumbled that the new squire expected genuine agricultural productivity from him, and the neutrals. Although the banker's draft had secured the estate for him, Paul realized that the "conquest of the community" would be more difficult. Fortunately, he finds Claire Derwent, the vivacious, companionable nineteen-year-old who frequently rides the estate with him, very helpful in giving "plenty of frank advice," such as her observation about the women of the valley. They want to be considered the equals of the men, which is pure fiction, yet a useful one since "the women are flattered and their menfolk regard your approach as proof that they have married wives of good sense" (104). It was that observation which persuaded Paul that Claire is very sensible along with being generous with her time in showing him the dells, slopes and short cuts of the estate, even introducing him to the elegant dwelling of Lord Gilroy, the neighboring squire they visited—Gilroy stiffly polite, Claire at ease

pouring the tea they sipped from "thin Rockingham china." Paul likes her and is
deeply grateful for her help. But while she was a pretty woman, "she did not stir
him in the way that Grace Lovell had when they had met on that first occasion
in the nursery" (108). Paul does not confide in Claire or in anyone else about his
infatuation with the Lovell woman.

Having made a wonderful impression, Claire arrives at the house one day "on
foot", her horse having gone lame, looking as "fresh as a spring daffodil" after
walking four miles in the sultry afternoon to help Paul arrange the new furniture,
which unfortunately will not be delivered until the next afternoon. But he assuages
her disappointment by suggesting that they "take a picnic lunch to Shallowford
woods" today, then "receive the vans" tomorrow. Paul takes the initiative now to
ease Claire's disappointment; thus he will blame himself for the close-body contact
between them that surprises them both as they thrash about in the grass. Which
is almost what occurs, except that Claire at the last moment pulls up short, extri-
cating the two of them from the inevitability which she herself engineered. Out
in the woods, Paul likes the contrast between the dull riding gear he had seen her
wearing heretofore, and the lovely feminine impression she makes in her bright and
trim picnic costume. On request, Paul rolls up his trouser leg to show her where
the bullet had shattered his knee. Closeness allowing it, he kisses her mouth; to
this, she "offered neither protest nor encouragement but continued to smile, saying,
with the utmost self-possession, 'Well, what now, Wicked Squire?'" (110–11). Yet
when push moves towards shove, Claire breaks free from his embrace, rearranges
her rumpled clothing and refuses to accept his apology because she had intended
it all. "Don't apologize! Just listen to me, so that we have a chance of starting again,
of starting differently!" (114). She had set out to do what is *done* in Shallowford:
"the girl baits a trap in the grass and the man walks into it" and that's how marriages come about here. However, the downside for them is that "You would have
resented me for the rest of your life, whereas now—well, at least we can go on
being civil to one another!" Claire has turned the sexual seduction into a human
encounter, one that given the enabling circumstances could go somewhere. "Let's
get the things and go home" (115) she says, having the last word—"home" being
the merest wisp of a prophetic insight.

Looking back on that sorry situation four weeks later, Claire realizes that she
had made "three tactical mistakes in as many minutes. She had been far too forward, far too backward and ultimately, far too honest." She needed a new approach,
and the plan she adopted "had the hall-mark of first-class strategy in any kind of
warfare," being simple and direct, and allowing for a "dignified retreat" should it
go badly. She would write Paul "advising him to give a combined coronation sup-
per-dance and house-warming for the estate tenantry and their dependants" which
he would surely take as "a piece of friendly, patriotic advice." If Paul liked the idea,
he would write for "further advice," and if he did not "good manners alone would

compel a reply" (122). When he adopts her suggestion, he finds in Claire Derwent "an enthusiastic chairwoman" who throws herself into their project, and under her "driving force" Paul saw the event "mushroom from a local soiree...into the most important social event in the history of the Valley" (141). Claire is in all respects the celebration's mover and shaker, and her last, best inspiration is to end the party with a stirring fireworks display! It was a memorable conclusion, but disastrous for Claire, who had thrown the spotlight on the flaw in her scheme—Paul's infatuation over Grace.

> Hancock discharged another shower of green and crimson balls, and the glare lit up the paddock like a search-light, so that everyone there might have been standing under strong lamplight, and this was the biggest betrayal of all, for it showed both Claire and her father the face of Paul Craddock, who was looking down on Grace Lovell, standing close beside him. In that moment father and daughter conceded complete and utter defeat. (*Summer's Day*, 166–67)

That night Claire disappears "abruptly and completely," and was "likely to be away for some time." Her strategy had succeeded according to her plan, yet she was compelled to make a "dignified retreat" seeing that the field was lost.

One of Craddock's early initiatives on behalf of his tenants is to make Sam Potter, the most energetic member of a family of slackers, the estate's woodsman, and to get him and his wife Joanie housed in their own cottage. Some time later on, the ecstatic Sam hails him with news that their first child has just been born. "Will 'ee...will 'ee go up, an' taake a look at 'er, Squire? 'Er's the prettiest maid in the Valley!" (189). They want to name her after him, but Paul says *Pauline* would be better, since she's a girl, and that suits Sam. As he rides home after a drink with the new father, Craddock reflects upon his aims in Shallowford. Those reflections, in the context of less sensitive practices in the British Empire across the world, are crucial for the novel as cultural historical narrative.

> What was his true purpose in the Valley? What was he trying to do with and for the scattered families, enclosed by the sea, the railway line, and Gilroy's boundary in the west? Had he elected himself judge, jury and custodian of their lives over the next half-century? Or was his role rather that of referee? Or, again, was he simply a landlord, with the power to pull on the rein or bestow occasional bonuses?
>   Did ownership of the soil that sustained these people give him the right to plot their destinies? And if not, then who would? Perhaps his true responsibility was confined to his pocket and even to Zorndorff's, so long as he kept the scrapyard revenue in reserve; or perhaps, by coddling them too much, he would sap their initiative. Was his a conception of Imperialism in miniature? Did the investors in Britain's overseas possessions think along these lines, when they poured in their capital, hogged all the lucrative posts, and talked of the white man's burden over their whiskies and sodas in jungle clearings and delta warehouses? How much imperial outlay and effort was inspired by benevolence and how much by the profit motive, or the sweets of personal power? Surely there was a parallel here, for had he not enjoyed the power he wielded

within the Shallowford boundaries? And might it not, as he grew older and more cynical, corrupt him? The Lovells, presumably, had been corrupted by it, for what had any
one of them been prepared to contribute to the Valley? A harvest supper once a year
and an undertaking to do outside repairs on half-derelict property but only so long as
local forelocks were stretched. (*Summer's Day*, 192-93)

His mind explored these questions but soon, in the spell of the creeping dusk, lost
its way, so that he put aside those questions until later. Riding into the yard, Paul
was told that Mr. James Grenfell, from Paxtonbury, had called on him and left his
card, but would call again to pay his respects to the new master of Shallowford.

To prepare for his discussion with Grenfell, Craddock sorted through old
newspapers until he "ran him down in the caption of a picture" showing a slightly
built man wearing "a very earnest expression that gave his face a slightly fanatical look." James ["Jimmy"] Grenfell, he learned, was the Liberal candidate for the
Paxtonbury area that included Paul's estate as well as Gilroy's. Craddock was happy
that he could anticipate their conversation, because he was "far too undecided
as yet to commit himself" (193-94). Actually though, Paul's attitude towards his
estate and its tenants already tipped the balance in Grenfell's favor. The stage is
prepared for a dogfight between Liberal and Conservative candidates over which
party shall drag Craddock's carcass into their camp. Landowners like Gilroy assume
that, since he's a landowner, Paul's vote is secure, for all landowners defend their
existing privileges, like those the Lovells so long enjoyed. Inevitably, there will be
a shootout at the Shallowford Corral.

Jimmy Grenfell proves to be a considerate man anxious not to impose upon
his host, about whom he has heard quite a lot through his "intelligence service."
He has come not to solicit, but because he is curious. When Paul invites him to
stay for lunch, Grenfell, with "genuine humility," says "I oughtn't take advantage
of you. They said you were a friendly chap but I didn't expect this civility." But
Paul insists that he stay, despite Grenfell's worry that he might harm his host's
relations "with certain influential people around here" who would be irritated
by his lunching with the enemy. Paul is uncommitted, he admits, but "what the
devil has that to do with inviting a casual visitor to have a bite to eat and a glass
of sherry?" (196-97). Jimmy shows interest in his experiences in South Africa, and
Paul tells his visitor "something of the reaction among rank and file volunteers
concerning the herding of Boer families into camps that had been sited without
regard to water supplies or sanitary facilities"—not exactly history, but *cultural* history. Grenfell correctly presumes that Mrs. Handcock who serves them lunch is
"an enemy camp-follower," as she is, violently committed to political positions she
does not understand. That's the "real trouble in places like this," he says. Tories
"bundle them off" to vote and they "put a cross for the man who pays the fare" to
get them to the polls and back.

"I wonder what the Chartists would think about it all, or going further back, men like Hampden, and old John Ball? Sometimes I'd like to call a party truce for five years—the life of a Pariament, say—so that both parties could drive home the fact the the most important single gain of the British people over the centuries was the Reform Bill and the Redistribution Act that followed it" (*Summer's Day*, 197-98)

Finding Grenfell's remarks very interesting, Paul asks "How would you personally go about it?," and these two men are already launched upon a friendship based in one another's accuracy of observation and concern for things other than personal enrichment.

Lord Gilroy and Mr. Raymond Cribb arrive virtually on Grenfell's heels. These sudden visitors are well aware that the Liberal candidate has just gone and, as Cribb says, "it doesn't do to let these things go unchallenged, Craddock."

Paul's first reaction to this challenge was astonishment. It seemed to him impossible that two men of their years could be so sure of themselves on another's hearthrug. Then, in the wake of his astonishment, resentment rose in his throat and irritation changed to anger when Gilroy, without even looking at him, said in his thin, rustling voice, "They tell me that little rat of a Radical has been courting you, Craddock! Won't do, you know! Best show the rascal the door straight away! Don't stand on politeness with scum of that kind! Give 'em an inch and they take an ell!"

Amazement at the man's insufferable arrogance held Paul's anger in check for a moment and he said, vaguely, "Rascal? Ruffian?...I can only suppose you must be referring to Mr. James Grenfell. He's just been here. He looks in almost every week when he's over this way," and Gilroy said, with a glare, "The devil he does! Then it's true then?" but without the least indication that he was aware of Paul's resentment.

"Yes he does," Paul said, sullenly, "and I'm bound to say that I find him not only extremely civil but exceptionally good company! Moreover, I can't help feeling that he wouldn't speak of either of you gentlemen as you have spoken of him!" (240-41).

Persistent as leeches, these two visitors continue their attempt to persuade Paul through their scurrilous disregard for common decency.

"You're open to reason, I take it? You haven't actually promised Grenfell political support in the constituency?"

Paul said, deliberately, "No, Mr. Cribb, I haven't. As a matter of fact he's never asked for it."

"He wouldn't," said Cribb savagely, "that's his way! Now listen to me, young man...", but Paul, plunging both hands in his breeches pockets, said, "No, Mr. Cribb, *you* listen to *me*! Before I came down here I never gave a thought to politics, except to wonder sometimes, when I saw what was happening to the Boers, how our treatment of them could be justified but I've learned a good deal about politics this morning, and I don't like what I've learned! You say this isn't the way to canvass votes and by God, you're right! I can't imagine a more hamfisted way of going about it! Grenfell, as I said, hasn't canvassed me in several visits here but neither has he treated me like a stupid child or a recently liberated serf! I'm not clear in my own mind what the Conservative Unionist Party stand for, or even what the Liberal Party stand for but you've made me eager to find out! I can see that your party lacks two things—-tact and good manners, neither of which have been in evidence since you walked in that door!"

He moved above the fireplace to pull the bellrope but Gilroy cheated him by stamping out of the room before he could ring. Cribb remained, however, and seemed to be bouncing with rage, so that Paul, again seizing the advantage, said, "I'm sorry it had to happen like this, Cribb. I don't think you or I would have lost our tempers if you had come alone. But what else would you expect a man to do when complete strangers walk into his house and quarrel with his choice of friends?" 242-3

Unknown to Paul, Grace Lovell has been eavesdropping [she habitually does that] but now stands forth and introjects herself into the conversation: "I'm sorry to interrupt you, but I just couldn't let you go without knowing I approve of every word my fiancee said, Mr. Cribb!" It's news to Paul that he's her fiancee, but he has just *assumed* that dignity by expressing sentiments which, to her mind, make Craddock a political radical, qualifying him as a potential husband. Then, to Paul, Grace continues:

> "I thought of you as someone pleasant, kind, and well-meaning but I didn't know you were a rebel and I certainly didn't give you credit for that much nerve! I loathe people like Gilroy and Cribb, and everything they stand for, but until ten minutes ago I assumed you were only a watered-down version of them! Well, you aren't, quite obviously you aren't, and it makes a big difference! I'm not in love with you and it wouldn't be honest of me to pretend I was but we've got more in common than either of us imagined and that's a better basis for marriage than story-book slush!" (245)

Being smitten, Paul savors every word; yet there is no hope whatever that he could fashion a satisfactory marriage with that stance-driven woman, who completely misunderstands him at the very instant when she recreates Paul Craddock in her own image. It is an act of creation, but not an instance of truthful comprehension of reality. John Rudd's word for it was madness, which on his testimony runs in the family. Paul's phrase, the first time he laid eyes on Grace Lovell, had been "instinctive defiance." And *that* is what she sees and loves as Paul defies Cribb, her own image and likeness.

Given her family background, it is not surprising that Grace has difficulties finding her place in the world. She is a young woman seeking a vocation, looking for her place in the world despite the forces ranked against her. Her mother drowned herself in a reservoir in India rather than suffer her husband's bad treatment any longer, which is not a good start for Grace. Her step-mother wants to get Grace into a suitable marriage, the Devonshire boondocks being an adequately remote location to place her. Early experiences with men, touched upon ever-so-lightly by Delderfield, were not of a nature to inspire confidence in that sorry gender. But she marries Paul Craddock and they spend the honeymoon in Paris, where he is surprised to discover that Grace is a cultured woman, one who for instance could "identify many of Napoleon's marshals from busts that seemed identical as they looked down from niches in the Old Palais Royale." Grace seemed to be enjoying guiding him "as though he had been an adolescent son instead of a husband," while Paul "trailed dutifully behind her" (256). Their days and nights passed amicably, "but one day she gave him a brief inkling of what seemed to him contempt for the dominion of men." She took him, guidebook in hand, to the house on the left bank where Charlotte Corday stayed the night she "came to Paris to kill Marat." To his joking remark that she must have been "a cold-blooded little devil," Grace snapped

> "Cold-blooded? No, she wasn't that! Fearless and resolute if you like, but not cold-blooded. The cold-blooded stayed home and talked of achieving something. She went out and did it, while all the men of her party were content to posture on the rostrum!" and as she said this he thought for a moment of [step-mother] Celia's warning concerning Grace's flirtation with the suffragists and wondered if she identified Charlotte Corday with the Pankhursts [the most militant group] (258–59).

There is enough evidence of such potential friction between their two value systems for us to conjecture not that they would disagree but that ultimately they would be travelling roads so divergent that the marriage would collapse, even though Grace was a successful hostess, practical enough to fashion a marvellous rose garden with a sunken fish-pond to beautify Shallowford House. But her domestic sense did not annul her militant determination to set the world right.

It's one thing for Paul to see the wisdom of falling silent when for example Grace berates him about his "cold-blooded" comment regarding Charlotte Corday, and for Grace to restrain herself in like manner rather than pick fights with Paul, but there are times when husband and wife simply hunker down and insist upon their divergent points of view, a process that often arrives at some prudential middle way. That is not always possible though, and with Grace it's not likely. The Smut Potter poaching affair is the outstanding example of an irreconcilable difference between them. Here is the situation: Smut Potter, a remarkably good poacher, has a Paxtonbury customer for the buck he intends to kill on Gilroy's estate; Gilroy's head gamekeeper, outwitted by Smut so often that he has "come close to being sacked" by Gilroy, is ready for Smut's attempt, along with two friends who also desire to beat the crap out of Smut before turning him over to the law for prosecution; things go awry and the gamekeeper gets his face bashed in, Smut goes into hiding in his secure cave in Shallowford Woods, until Ikey, who is inadvertently tipped off by Hazel Potter bringing him food, informs Craddock. The Gilroy gamekeepers entourage, loaded for bear, come seeking frontier justice at Shallowford, but Paul tells them "I'll see you all off our land and for your own sakes as much as Potter's! This isn't Czarist Russia and we aren't living in the Middle Ages!" Paul's point of view, that the law should be applied and settle the matter, runs afoul of Grace's perception that the law is corrupted, preempted by landowners, and landowner judges, who twist it to their own advantage, Gilroy's desire at the moment being to punish Craddock for insulting him and for voting against what one might call the Landowner's Value System.

That is what in fact happens: Paul expects judges to judge the case fairly and set a reasonable sentence; Grace knows that will not happen. It's not that she's right and Paul is wrong in estimating the outcome. It is rather that *he* is the estate's owner engaging in estate business, while *she* is interfering with the performance of his office. She lectures her husband that "They'd pull every string within reach to get [Smut] gaoled for half a lifetime and partly to teach you your place! If I did speak out of turn this morning it was in your interests as well as Potter's" (283–84). Grace can believe that, and Paul can concede that she thinks she acted properly. But she is *still* interfering in something she is not directly responsible for; *he* is. The underlying difficulty that cannot be ameliorated is Grace's *attitude*.

> Grace seemed only to respect him as long as he was waving a rebel banner under the noses of authority. She would, he felt sure, back him every inch of the way if he resolved himself into a kind of Sorrel Valley Robin Hood, contemptuous of even such social reforms as those advocated by progressives like Grenfell. She was really, he reflected, a kind of anarchist who welcomed turmoil but he had no wish to live like that. He favoured steady, ordered, constitutional progress, where tolerance and education for the underprivileged promised hope of justice and stability but she had no faith at all in this dream. Her sympathies were with people like the Pankhursts, still raising hell up and down the country and it was on this cleavage that their relationship, so fragile from the beginning, seemed likely to founder, for what was that she had said when he told her Smut Potter had agreed to give himself up? "I was badly wrong about you, Paul. You aren't a rebel at all and could never be! That scene with Gilroy and Cribb was just a flash in the pan. Perhaps you knew I was listening and hoped to make an impression!" He thought it a bitter thing to have said and realized now that she regretted it but they had been strangers to one another ever since, with Grace resisting all his attempts to put this stupid business into its correct perspective and stop her using it as a looking-glass held in front of his character. (*Summer's Day*, 295)

By the middle of *Long Summer's Day* the chief conflict has been solidly established. And when we think about the narrative as a cultural historical document, Grace Lovell's function is clear. She exemplifies the opposing political left wing which is symmetrical to the Tory right wing while Paul's convictions develop in the space between. The novel would be weaker were Grace not on hand to present her views and to endure hostility to them. Moreover, Grace is not simply a rebel but an intelligent, companionable woman when not presenting attitudes. She is interestingly complex and remarkably supportive of others when they need help. It is difficult to make Grace "this" or "that" because she eludes categories. She is not a chameleon, because inconstancy is not one of her characteristics, while complexity always is. As readers, we have to patiently experience the vacillation between Grace's deep-seated grievances against men, and the other side of her character, which is not wounded that way.

Now begins "The Grace Fugue," the fugue as an analogy, that is, a polyphonic composition based on several themes enunciated by several voices in turn—Grace herself, for example, Paul, and Grenfell. The fugue figure lends itself to the combining of scattered texts into a shapely thematic composite. At first, Grace, pregnant with Paul's son, had thought that having a baby would "compensate for" her exile in the Shallowford wilderness, but quite to the contrary she found it the "final proof of submission to men," the one consolation being that the child would inherit a world in which "ideas were likely to blow up in the noses of people like Gilroy" (297-98). The Craddock's child, Simon, was born during the night of the great storm when Martin Codsall, driven mad by Arabella's unending henpeckery and his own alcoholism, butchered her with a hay knife in the upstairs bedroom of Four Winds farm before hanging himself from a beam in the barn. Paul, reflecting upon the event after he has managed the situation and installed Eveleigh and his family at Four Winds, sees its deeper significance.

> Events seemed to be justifying the nagging suspicion that, in some way, Grace had revived the bad luck of the Valley simply by being who she was, a hangover of the Lovell tradition. There had been the quarrel with Gilroy, then the Smut Potter affair, and now this, all within a matter of a year. And there was more to come he wouldn't wonder (329-30).

Yet there is evidence to the contrary in Grace's fully supportive reception of Claire Derwent when she visits the Valley for the season's final hunt. Grace recognizes that Claire remains madly in love with Paul; she sees the warmly maternal instinct expressed in how Claire holds baby Simon; she points Claire in Paul's direction without seeming to be shedding a husband. Rather, Grace is hoping to enhance his life when she celebrates Claire's feminine beauty.

> "As soon as [Claire] sat down, holding her knees together and sitting half sideways as I handed her tea, she reminded me very vividly of someone and I couldn't think who but now I think I've got it! Wait a minute…".

Going to the bookcase, Grace locates the volume of artistic reproductions she is looking for and finds Rubens' portrait *Bathsheba receiving King David's letter*. "She would have children very easily, I'd swear to that" (338-39). This is the graciously generous side of Paul's present wife, who desires the best for a man who deserves a better helpmeet.

Now, a medley of three voices. First Grenfell, along with Paul, who "a little forlornly" wishes he would "openly espouse the cause of Women's Suffrage and bring Grace in."

> But he did not, holding to his theory that, while universal franchise was bound to come, it was an issue that would cost precious votes and to some extent Paul agreed with him for whenever Women's Suffrage was raised at a meeting the issue was invariably greeted with derision. (*Summer's Day*, 349)

Next, Grace's voice, answering Paul's complaint in her own distinctively abrasive manner.

> "Women's sufferage is very important to me but I concede that it isn't to you, or to your
> precious James Grenfell. There are plenty of fundamental issues but political parties
> dependent on a flow of wealth from one class or the other, aren't deeply concerned
> with them. Their impetus doesn't depend on a cause but on personal ambitions. That
> isn't true of you and it isn't true of Grenfell but it is true of all the other rabble rousers!
> Do we have to prolong this stupid quarrel, Paul?" (351)

Paul's voice sounds again now as he reflects on John's son, Roddy Rudd, the sailor
boy with the spiffy automobile. It had been

> the ease with which he had captured and held [Grace's] interest from the moment
> he came honking up the drive, that crystallised his resentment and it was not resent-
> ment against her for a single indiscretion but for their failure, after more than a year,
> to achieve harmony as individuals. She was his wife in bed and about the house and
> garden but beyond these narrow limits they shared nothing and while, for some men,
> this was enough to make a marriage work, for him it was not. She continued, in her
> secret way, to deride him and the Roddy incident, so trivial in itself, emphasized the
> cleavage. (Summer's Day, 365)

To complete this fugal testimony to their incompabitility, Paul had promised Grace
that when the opera Giselle which they had seen in Paris played in England he
would take her. Grace reports that "they are due in Bristol on Thursday for two
nights so I wrote for tickets. I think you badly need a change...". That is unaccept-
able to a Paul whose back is finally against the wall, such that he cannot honor his
earlier promise. He reflects that

> had the approach been made earlier, he would have surrendered but he was under no
> illusion as to what surrender would mean. It would be the final acceptance of a mea-
> sure of spiritual isolation down the years ahead and they were still young, and there
> were many years, too many to renounce all hopes of the full partnership on which he
> had set his heart (367).

Having made his decision, Paul tells her "Thursday is eve-of-poll and Friday is poll-
ing day." He cannot be absent, but she can go to Bristol. "You do what you think
best, Grace"(367). What she thinks best is to pack her belongings into their largest
wagon and board the next train to London for good, which she does.

Although the fugue proper ends here it is commented on by the Valley's full-
orchestra thoughts about events taking place in their midst.

> All that autumn and the winter that followed there was a conspiracy of sympathy in
> the Valley. Nobody could have said how it communicated itself to Paul, or how and
> where it originated but it was there, perhaps the first bittersweet fruits of his stay among
> them. It was this, more than anything, that encouraged him to stay. (Summer's Day, 374)

As for his own insight, Paul's reason told him "that this was monstrous and ridiculous, that it was the gesture of a hysterical woman not given to theatrical gestures"; yet he was certain she would not come back, "that threats and promises would leave her unmoved," which was "the sum total of the little she had taught him of herself" (374–75).

John Rudd spoke frankly. "I did what I could to warn you when this began, and I say this even though to come between a man and his wife is unforgiveable! She never did belong here, Paul, any more than the Lovells belonged!" Grace could "stand outside and see what you were trying to do down here," and admire him for the helping hand he gave people like Will Codsall by getting him established in his own farm at Periwinkle. But "people can admire an effort without wanting to take part in it." And Grenfell's advice gave even less comfort than Rudd's. The new Liberal member of Parliament told Paul that what happened had little to do with him personally.

> "Her preoccupation with the Women's Suffrage movement is a manifestation of what she feels about everything important to her, and I believe that goes for a good many of those gallant but misguided women! They want a *purpose*, Paul, like yours or mine and we have been denying them one ever since they lived in caves."

Is there nothing Paul can do about it, the abandoned spouse wonders. "Not at present," Grenfell replies after weighing soberly. If Grace tried and failed to achieve what she's after "would you take her back on her own terms—freedom of action to go where she wished and to do what she liked? To make her own friends so long as she was loyal to you in the conventional sense?"

> "No," he said after a moment's hesitation. "I don't think I would Jimmy. That isn't enough to stop a marriage like ours from going sour. At least, not the kind of marriage I need so long as I stay here. (*Summer's Day*, 374–78)

The up-side of this personal disaster was that as Paul continued riding about the Valley attending to the squire's responsibilities, he became conscious of his tenants' "mute concern." He contained "his sullenness and bitterness" and "perhaps it was this that won their respect."

> Slowly, and imperceptibly, he was able to translate their curiosity into warmth, so that he became aware of a kinship with them that had not existed in his most sanguine days before his marriage, when he had thought of himself as a well-meaning, bungling amateur and hoped that they would make generous allowances for his inexperience. Something was reaching out to him from all of them and he noted and welcomed it in all parts of the Valley…[the] subtle communication of their friendship would have gone unnoticed by anyone who had grown up among them but to Paul they were the first evidence that he was accepted, that his good intentions were recognized and that he was already regarded by them not as a brash young man with a bushel of fancy ideas but as the natural leader of the community. (*Summer's Day*, 379–80)

Now if the Lovells had represented the Old Style master-to- servant relation, i.e., the go-there-and-do-that paradigm, Craddock in the midst of his defeat and dejection sees that a New Style of squire/serf relationship has taken hold. He lost a wife to the new politics that are in the air, but he has won something that Grace had it not within her to give, something older, deeper, more durable. Craddock's tenants are not serfs, but his friends. And without overtly saying anything of the sort, they have told him that. Now if cultural history is not quite events but people's reactions to the changing realities wherein they live, ought not Paul Craddock's defeat by the-Grace-Lovell-that-was-and-still-is be considered authentic cultural history? Gilroy, the next door squire, remains immobilized in an 18th century pattern, but Paul's people have abandoned that archaic construct.

Those among Delderfield's characters who are important for the story are distinctively different from one another. In this, they stand in contrast to the backgrounders, like Gilroy's gamekeepers, who differ as much as cigarettes from the same pack, the exception being that poor fellow who is invested with individuality by having his face smashed by the stock of Smut's deer rifle. Character differentiation, to the contrary, is illustrated by the Potter family. Meg, the Gypsy who weaves baskets, brews potions and accurately tells fortunes, brings some money into the family, whereas Tamer, that huge tub of guts who spends his time drinking and giving orders, never lifts a hand to improve his acres. These two spouses are distinctive characters, while some of their daughters, those slutty young animals who take turns rushing into the same bushes to assuage their lusts with the same eager males, differ only in their names. But that is deliberate, for when Big Jem the circus giant comes to Shallowford and adopts them as co-wives, cutting his giant switch for vigorous application to their hinders when they stray from virtue, their sameness contributes something to the novel. And when time passes and life sobers them, even the Potter harlots settle down and become the individuals they had not been before.

Now of the many characters in the Craddock trilogy, one of the most interesting is Ikey Palfrey, the culturally amphibious Cockney boy Paul brings to the Valley, his tacit reason being the potential for personal development that he sees. Nobody can predict what Ikey could become, but he is capable of adjustment to rapidly changing circumstances and deftly imaginative in confronting them. He is young, and knows that when real danger appears on the estate he cannot himself deal with it. He must tell Paul, the man he loves and hungers to emulate. We learn by doing, but we can also learn by watching others, and Ikey, a *de facto* apprentice, watches Paul constantly. He learns not how to do *that*, for the "that" will be different the next time. Ikey learns to understand problems and [hardest of all because one must be born with the imaginative gift] intuit the essence of the likely solution. Sometimes problems cannot be solved, but only rendered less harmful, so as to reduce their fall-out. One such dangerous situation that Ikey knows himself unable to deal with erupts the night of the big storm, when out of the darkness Martin Codsell, thinking Ikey the devil, aims at that figment of his drunken imagination and squeezes off a shotgun blast. Ikey cannot see what Codsall has in mind, but the pellet-holes in his raincoat make it clear that he must tell the squire, and his own eagerness to learn keeps him close at Paul's heels as their horses splash across the dangerously inundated Codsall bridge near Four Winds farm. Two people are dead, but Harold Eveleigh and his wife will make the farm prosperous since Will Codsall has no interest in returning to his old home. That is a sort-of solution.

Older and more experienced, Paul is also an excellent teacher. Yet Ikey has the greater imaginative gift. Paul sees what needs to be done and does it, but Ikey sees what *could* be done. Ikey has the greater creative capacity, and he has the ingenuity required for arranging the *means* which bring what might be done into reality. The best example is his scrap-yard performance, in which there is no time lag between (1) realizing that the excited horse will crush the carter and (2) whipping off his jacket to "blind" and calm the frightened animal. It cannot be taught, this quickness of insight and response. Edison invented the light bulb by grasping the concept and finding the means; the discoverer of the benzene ring was stepping onto a trolly when he saw in his mind's eye a vision of couples dancing in a circle; Ikey can do that likewise. Paul is an intelligent man, but he could not have looked at the battlefield and conceived the tank—an armored enclosure that was mobile and capable of firing explosives at the enemy (*Post of Honour*, 160–61). Ikey could, and did, although early models were ineffective until trial-and-error experimentation revealed how the tank could become the mainstay of field warfare it is today.

When he comes to a certain age, Ikey would need to go to a school wherein he could learn things that Shallowford could not teach, wherein he would enter the mainstream of English life by his contact with boys whose backgrounds are different from his own. He will go to High Wood, where cultural deficiences would become educational opportunities which the school's teachers would never have suspected were available for him. High Wood presented problems, and Ikey would need to find solutions. Paul, foreseeing that "the English caste system and the snobberies it spawned" would raise barriers, offers this lineage: "I'm your stepbrother and official British guardian. The word 'guardian' always seems to impress the snobs somehow" (391). Beyond that, Ikey will be on his own. His "acute observation" made it "absurdly easy" for him to learn the proper angle at which to wear one's cap, and the degree of familiarity to show towards some masters and certain boys. Taken overall, his "triple background gave him an enormous advantage" over the other High Wood students (408–09).

However, school sports were a more difficult hurdle. He was ignorant of Rugby, couldn't swim or play cricket to any effect and his "short, rather clumsy legs" made him the last to finish the junior house sprint. What to do? Ikey knew he could never run fast, but he could learn to run *far* if he trained himself. When told that the following term, cross-country running would take precedence over every-thing except Rugby football, he had the potential solution to his problem. Back in Shallowford he began his running training at Coombe Bay, morning and evening, having "seven weeks to translate himself into a potential runner of marathons" and by himself discovered what none of the books had told him. Running the tideline was far more "punishing" than covering the same distance on "springy turf" and by training in sand "his calf muscles and wind" developed rapidly and gave him "the edge on boys who did not have the luck to live by the sea" (410). In fact, he became famous in High Wood's halls by the trophies he won all during his years there. Faced with difficulty, Ikey assessed the problem and set about to find the available solution. What he learned at High Wood was not geometry but his own potential as a problem-solver.

In Shallowford, he recognized that Squire Craddock was sorely missing the wife who had abandoned him and Ikey felt obliged to ameliorate the problem. He admired Grace and "refused to believe that she could have lost her wits in the manner of Farmer Codsall." Although he was certain he could help bring about a reconciliation, it was some time before he could "hit upon a plan" for effecting that (412). Part of his duties at High Wood brought Ikey into contact with political reports in the *Daily Mail*, where he "came to read a lengthy report dealing with suf-fragette activities in London," which "interested him far more than he thought it would." He learned what these women were doing and how badly they were treated, "always going to prison" and found there "more often than not."

> It came to him then precisely what he must do to restore happiness to the Squire. Somehow or other he must travel to London, find her, and bring her back with him, and although he realized that this might prove a very difficult undertaking he had faith in his lucky star, and more in his ability to tell such a harrowing story that she would have little choice but to accompany him home at once. (*Summer's Day*, 412–13)

Now as Ikey was preparing to make a getaway from High Wood to London, by fabricating white lies and fashioning a dummy body to be mistaken for himself fast asleep, the Headmaster called him in to hear the shocking news just received from a Mr. John Rudd: "There has been a shipwreck a few miles from your home and your guardian, along with a number of his tenants, was instrumental in saving several lives. The place has been turned into a hospital and everything is at sixes and sevens" and Rudd has asked that they keep Ikey at High Wood "for a day or so." Perfect! When Ikey gets to London, his harrowing tale will not be needed on account of the stunning rescue in Devonshire—no fabrication but the true story of heroic action by Craddock and his tenants.

It was indeed heroic action, begun by the unlikeliest inhabitant of Shallowford, Tamer Potter, who had gone down to "Potter's Cove," that inaccessible beach where the tides brought him treasures, once "a watertight box of Virginia tobacco," another day "a strongly-built dinghy which he had repaired and still used for inshore fishing" (418-19). The dinghy would be essential in saving the "poor devils" who were marooned on a rock offshore, their ship have gone down and time being short before the changing tide would silence the "overtones of voices raised in fear and punctuated by hoarse shouts" of panic. No hero by any measure, Tamer is about to become one now, as he shouts encouragement to the German castaways and forces his fat body up the rabbit run to the cliff-top to arouse the community for a lightening-quick rescue operation. Alerting Shallowford started with Violet Potter's arrival in Coombe Bay. It was carried by word of mouth across the Valley with "a speed and precision absent from the war games of professional generals working with trained soldiers,"

> and this was because, basically, it was a tribal exercise, performed by men who had been dependent upon one another's good will all their lives. The impulse to unite in a common cause was in their blood and bone and although, in fact, twentieth-century apparatus had been employed to summon Winmouth lifeboat and coastguard, the feat was achieved by the people of the Valley and was due not so much to the courage and ingenuity of a sixty-year-old gypsy farmer and his twenty-six-year-old landlord, or even to the men who controlled the boat [with a guide-rope] from the beach, but to the tribal instinct that had assembled them on an inaccessible stretch of shore in a little over one hour from the moment Tamer had galloped into the Dell with news that men were needed and time was short. (*Summer's Day*, 429-30)

In the two round-trips between the mist-hidden rock and the cliff-base, sixteen men saved half that number of stranded Germans, the bodies of two others drifting ashore the next day. In the action's final moments, "a spent breaker tore the rudder bar from Paul's hand and pitched him into the bows" where "he, Tamer and the two men amidships [were all] tangled as the stern lifted under the suck of another backwash. Then [Paul] was flung clear and an oar, shooting past like a javelin, struck him a shattering blow on the temple," after which "a tumult of water rolled him six feet under, towards the breaker line" (437). Ikey need not make up a story. Shallowford has delivered a smashing one.

From her seat on the speaker's platform, Grace notices Ikey working his way, "like a cautious private detective," edging forward to "touch his cap and grin" as though unsure of his welcome. "All right, Ikey! What do you want? Is Mr. Craddock with you?" She has not heard, so he hands her his crumpled copy of the *Daily News* and permits her to read the story without comment. Grace asks him sharply "How bad is he?" but he doesn't know. She will get him something to eat and he'll sleep at her lodgings while she takes steps to tell Shallowford where he is. "They'll be frantic and I expect the police are looking for you!" Grace is stronger than ever in her convictions and has renounced all men to the degree that "she envied the spinsters of the movement their virginity" and their "physical repugnance of men as men." Ikey makes his pitch to Grace, to which she replies "I can't ever come back, Ikey, and I don't think the Squire wants me back, unless I changed my whole life and I can't do that." She and Paul have different missions. "He wants the *old* kind of England and I want a very different one. When married people think as opposite as that they cease to get any pleasure out of one another's company."

Grace has a plan of her own, one that displaces Ikey's scheme, though [he] "would have to give his word of honour never to tell a soul, not even the Squire, that I had a hand in it." Had Craddock not married *her*, Grace reveals, "he would have almost certainly married Claire Derwent," who is "still very much in love with him," and she is "the one you ought to spirit back to Shallowford, not me." How, he asks, ready to support any plan that would help the Squire recover his health and contentment. However, she has done her part by moving Ikey into an intellectual open space where he could invent some better procedure, and when Grace spoke again "she was the pupil, he the instructor."

> "What new mischief are you planning now, Ikey?"
>
> "It would have to be done by a letter," he said slowly, "and the letter would have to be posted in Shallowford. I could write it here tho', and you could read it. Then I could post it as soon as I get home and it would have a local postmark on it and she [Claire, living near London] wouldn't suspect." He had clearly made up his mind on the essentials. "Could you lend me a sheet of paper and pen and ink, ma'am?"

Indeed she could, and Ikey writes the most brilliant letter in the trilogy, its most explosive passage being this: "I was in and out of his room before he began to come round from the whack on the head and he kept asking for you, not nowing it of course but calling out your name as if you were in the room." When Grace finishes reading that letter twice, she says "Either you'll end up in gaol like Smut Potter, or you'll be Prime Minister! I couldn't improve on that in a thousand years." (*Summer's Day*, 439-39)

It was not until she was alone in the room with him that Claire Derwent knew she was home for good. It was mid-April, and in the afternoons "the sunlight over the paddock was the colour of buttermilk." She stood at the big window "occasionally glancing at the man on the bed" who had still not regained consciousness. She had attended enough V.A.D [volunteer nurse] lectures to know Paul would be "feverish for a day or so" as he was now. Thinking back to his influence here since he arrived, Claire reflected that Craddock "was like a wedge that had first attached itself to the soil of the Valley by its own weight and every blow strengthened its bite," such that no one could dislodge it. Anyone could have told Grace, "a well-bred woman," that she could never have seconded Paul's "arch ideas", an arch's keystone being a wedge-shaped rock (457).

It occurred one day as Claire sat sideways to the bed with "an open book on her lap and the afternoon sun playing games with the tendrils that escaped her golden 'bun' and hung like tiny tongues of autumn bracken over her ears."

> It took him a moment or two to realise who she was for when he saw her sitting there, with her knees pressed together and her head bent low over the page, he at once asso-

ciated her with a picture he had seen somewhere and the effort of establishing the link tired him, so that he closed his eyes again and went about disentangling the fabric of dreams from reality. Then, when he opened his eyes again, he remembered. The woman sitting beside the bed, knees pressed together, smooth, rounded face half-turned to the window and a book on her lap, was Bathsheba, reading the message from King David, yet also—and this was puzzling—she was Claire Derwent, late of High Coombe farm. He studied her very carefully, or as carefully as his damnably awkward posture would permit, trying to remember whether she had been there during his few lucid intervals when he had exchanged a word or two with John Rudd before being pulled this way and that by a strange woman said to be a doctor and the daughter of the drunken old Irishman, O'Keefe. He could not recall seeing Claire in the room then and this disturbed him, for it suggested that he was still dreaming and that Claire Derwent, or Bathsheba, belonged to the world of fantasy. Then she looked up and saw that he was awake, and her eyes lit up as she smiled in a way that somehow reassured him. She said softly, "Hullo, Paul! More yourself?", and reached out to take his pulse. This again struck him as odd, for it seemed extremely improbable that there should be two lady doctors in the Valley.

"What are you doing here?" he asked, "and why the devil am I still trussed up like this?" but this time her smile was professional as she said calmly, "Which question would you like answered first, Paul?" (*Summer's Day*, 453–54)

Craddock's slow convalescence interrupted his habitual pattern, riding his 1300 acres to see how his tenants and their crops and livestock were getting on, dealing with the problems that arose. Yet he did not find that his lengthy period of enforced bed rest was time lost since it gave him leisure to indulge in woolgathering, allowing his thoughts to wander as they might, and Claire Derwent was the subject of his ruminations—what she had been, how she had changed and the nature of their relationship.

He was aware of her less as a nurse and a personable young woman with a glowing complexion and corn-coloured hair, than as an agent whose presence completed a cycle of years, beginning with the long weeks of drought when he had first ridden about the Valley in her company, and ending in another spell of unbroken sunshine that followed the mild spring and promised a record crop providing sufficient rain fell by the first week of July. Thus, in a sense, she was impersonal, not a woman at all but a spirit of the Valley unexpectedly restored to him and bringing the promise of better times.

He did not remember her as a tranquil person. Spirited and joyous perhaps, and always eager for laughter but certainly not a woman who could communicate repose. Yet she was so now and sometimes he wondered what experience outside the Valley had changed her, calming her without making her moody and withdrawn. Her stillness was now an essential part of her, like her watchful blue eyes and a head of hair that was sometimes gold, sometimes almost auburn and sometimes the bronze shade of the sea an hour or so before sunset. He would watch her for long minutes as she stood by the tall window, supposing him to be taking his afternoon nap although in fact he seldom did take it, but maintained the pretence of doing so for a fortnight or more in order that he could study her through half-closed eyes when she thought herself unobserved. He would lie still and wonder about her, comparing her in a thousand ways to Grace and pondering questions that never suggested themselves during their brief conversations in the evenings. Privately he thought it odd that she should sit here at all through the short nights, for once he became accustomed to the awkwardness of his posture caused by the splint and the plaster that itched so mercilessly, he felt he no longer needed a night nurse and wondered why the woman doctor John Rudd had introduced into the house insisted someone should watch him until splint and plaster were removed. He did not quarrel with the decision, however, because Clair's presence gave him something to think about and he much preferred her to a stranger. (*Summer's Day*, 479–80)

Eventually Paul is well enough for their first conversation and when he remarks that she has changed a great deal since she left Shallowford Claire observes that he has, too, "and not altogether for the better." He wants the particulars, and she, observing him coolly, wonders if he's "prepared to digest home truths." She decides that he is, and lets him have it when Paul says "finish what you were going to say. I'm still cock of the roost round here but nobody talks to me anymore, not even old John."

She sat down beside him, saying, "You're a natural optimist, Paul, but lately you've been hard at work converting yourself into a pessimist, just like my father! There isn't so much enthusiasm about that we can spare it, least of all in a place like this, while everyone in the big world outside is making money and mistaking it for progress! All right, you took a toss over Martin Codsall, and another over Smut Potter. Then your wife walked out on you and from what I hear you've been sulking ever since, or at least until the wreck. But things like that happen to everyone who lives anything but a fenced-in life. They shouldn't stop a man with your kind of enterprise, at least, not at your age! Perhaps you don't realize it but you've already made a name for yourself round here and not only because you fished seven people off that rock! Folk round here believe in you and believe in what you're trying to do, although some of them don't really understand it yet. My advice, for what it's worth, is that you should go right on doing it, not gloomily and doggedly, the way you have since Grace left but the way you began, with a sense of fun and adventure, do you understand?"

"Yes," he said slowly, "that's easy to understand Claire but by God I badly needed someone to spell it out for me!" (*Summer's Day*, 483)

Before long, Paul becomes irritated by Shallowford's conspiracy of silence regarding Grace. Valley silence was running "all his personal relationships into cul-de-sacs where the mere mention of her was regarded as unmannerly" and Claire shows signs of entering into the conspiracy with the others. Paul will not stand for it. Her presence and impact on him have "opened up an entirely new vista on his marriage," which had never been a "real fusion of interest and responsibilities," but a façade marked by "resignation on her part and hope deferred on his." This self-knowledge brought with it a sense of relief that he found "reassuring and uplifting." Riding with Claire when that breakthrough happens, Paul commands her, "get down, for I can't say what I've got to say to you jog-jogging along the beach," asking her

"If I get a divorce will you marry me? And if you do will you guarantee to stay put and not run off and open a teashop at our first difference of opinion?"

"You're insufferable!" she said, trying to dodge between the horses but he caught her round the waist, dropped the reins and kissed her on the lips. It was a claim advanced with such determination that it threw her weight against the bay, who shied seaward and made off at a smart trot with reins trailing over the sand.

"Well?" he said, without relaxing his hold, "what else do I have to do to convince you?"

"You might ride after Rusty and take me somewhere a little more private!" she suggested, "for if anyone sees us from the cliff path I shall be packed off to Tunbridge Wells again within an hour of getting home!"

"I'll catch him but wait here!" he said, and dashed off after the bay. She stood watching him circle and head the horse off, hands pressed to her tousled hair, a slow, half-rueful smile puckering the corners of her mouth. How was she to know that her thoughts were identical to his when she said to herself, "Well, if we had pushed that first encounter in the woods to its logical conclusion we should have saved everybody a great deal of time, trouble and expense!" (495-98)

They marry, and on their first wedding annniversary, April 30, 1908, the pregnant and barefoot Claire walks up to Priory Wood as she often does, "enjoying the sensation of the dew passing between her toes and savouring the smell of the long grass and the great clumps of late primroses and early bluebells that grew all the way up the slope." This was her favorite spot, high above "the great sprawling house" where Paul still lay asleep and she had leisure to "take out her life and prospects and examine them, as a craftsman might examine a half-finished piece of work." He had recovered his confidence and energy, and the Valley was "expanding under his thrust and initiative." She reflects that she "had become wholly his, as much as this wide, wooded Valley and everything growing on it, as much a part of him as his secret dreams" (518-19). He had given the estate record into her hands, and Claire took pains keeping it up-to-date, her personality being seen in everything she wrote: "Under her pen, it had become less of a record and more of a great gossipy diary." Back at the house, her husband still asleep, Claire was updating the estate record when her eye was caught by the bearskin hearthrug on which the child in her round, smooth belly had been conceived the night that too much of Martin Pitt's punch at Hallow'en had made them boisterous. She recalls Paul's remarking on that occasion that "Every time I touch you, look at you even, I feel about seventeen, and surely it must be good for a man to have that kind of wife within reach!" Recollecting that night, she flushes again with "the satisfied glow she had experienced at the time, so that she no longer had patience with the book and put off writing an entry about his purchase of the cart horses" (521-22). She went downstairs to make tea before waking Paul.

After the twins have been delivered on the second of September, Paul, grateful for the excuse to be alone, takes up the estate record [he likes reading it since every entry she makes shows her personality] and peruses her current entries, noting "how proudly and self-consciously" Claire had written of

> his trial scheme to set up a shuttle service of carts moving on a planned route through the Valley to dispose of produce from points as far apart as Smut's greenhouse [he had taken to growing flowers in prison and now grows them for sale] in the east and Eveleigh's dairy in the west. He saw that she had referred to the innovation by the name used for it in the Valley—"Squire's Wagon Train," an offshoot, he supposed, of the recent visit of the Buffalo Bill's Wild West Show to Paxtonbury, but although they made jokes about it it seemed to work satisfactorily and eliminate a great deal of duplicated labour [because] in the past each farmer had used his own transport to take milk, eggs, vegetables and plants to the railway...but now, with three light carts and their teams in constant commission, they were relieved of this chore and their individual output had soared as the latest figures proved. (*Summer's Day*, 535)

The most eccentric, off-the-wall, peculiar, and unique individual in the Valley is Hazel Potter, who since a child had marched to a remarkably different drummer. Many of the Shallowfordians considered her retarded or crazed, clearly out-of-touch with reality, but Ikey Palfrey could not share that opinion. His experience had persuaded him that Hazel is shrewd in her own way. When he was a youth, lost in the suddenly deepening snow in which he would soon be frozen to death, he was rescued by Hazel, who knew exactly where Ikey was and gave him directions for getting home. She lives in her "house" in Shallowford Woods, "Hazel's Cave" on the map of the estate. She had seen life in the Potter household, and had elected to live alone in the woods among the foxes, the voles and stoats who live more purposeful lives. They are recessively social creatures who conduct their business undisturbed, but hardly unobserved, since to Hazel they are fellow beings whose wisdom she appreciates and emulates.

> At the extreme north-west corner of the mere, beyond the maze of rhododendrons in which Ikey had lost himself in the snow, the ground rose steeply to a great outcrop of sandstone where the older trees fell away...giving place to a straggle of dwarf pines and Scots firs that had crept down from the evergreen belt of the Hermitage plateau. It was here that the Shallowford badgers had their sets and from her eyrie at the top of the slope Hazel Potter could watch them lumbering to and fro, like paunched merchants in the streets of a sleepy country town. This was the spot she preferred beyond all others. Nobody ever came here now that Smut had turned horticulturalist and it was here, under the overhang of a great, slapsided rock, that she had made her home...Its hearth was a triangle of flat stones and its south side was open to sun and wind but inside it was always dry and warm. (*Summer's Day*, 549)

She had been preferring this spot to any other place in the Valley since she was a girl, but puberty will at last find girls and transform them into young women. Hazel had long watched the animals' reproductive habits and knew something about sexuality but without a subscription to *Nature Girl's Guide* she approaches motherhood as best she can by admiring her own reflection, using "the burnished lid of one of her tins" in her makeshift kitchen as a mirror. She is pleased by what she sees and engages in this colloquy with herself: "Youm bootiful, Hazel! Bootiful, do 'ee yer, now? Youm the most bootiful of all, for youm smooth an' white an' goldy and you baint much fur about 'ee, neither." Hazel was "not in the least mad but simply primitive", and her self-appraisal "differed little from that of her sisters' or any other woman in the Valley, twisting and cheek-sucking before a bedroom mirror" (551). At seventeen, she had begun to feel the urge to mate, and upon one warm April day she saw and recognized "Boy," her friend and sometime visitor. "Her heart gave a great leap of pleasure, as she thought 'I'll show un the house, an' mebbe he'd stay on a bit to watch things.'"

Hazel has watched and absorbed the courting techniques of animals and seen "pride, caprice and ferocity but never humility on the part of the female," and on their model she approaches Ikey directly. "Woulden 'ee like to kiss me?" she asks him "with shattering directness," and Ikey does. But when he recollects the High Wood braggarts' reports of their exploits, he realizes that "this beautiful, half-wild creature" could within minutes "be reduced to the status of one of the simpering, broad-hipped blondes in Tovey Major's magazines," and he would not do that. Yet "it crossed his mind that they should make some kind of pledge, a promise that would ensure repetition of this unspoken declaration but he had no idea how to convert his feelings into words" (558). And how could he tell the Squire that he is in love with "the half-wit of the Valley?" It was impossible since it would imply a contemptuous disregard for everything Paul had done for him since his London scrap-yard days. Back in Shallowford to see Paul before he begins training towards a military career not with the cavalry but the Engineers, he sneaks off to meet Hazel again and they set about drinking Meg Potter's hedgerow wine, which Hazel has stolen from the family's farmhouse for the occasion. Ikey soon experiences "a great glow spreading under his navel and his ears were singing" as evening light filtered into the cave through the gorse with "the radiance of a celestial sunset." They had another half cup apiece. When he leaves for his Army training, Ikey had befuddledly impregnated Hazel with one of the more colorful characters in the trilogy, Rumble Patrick Palfrey. When he discovers that she has borne his child, he marries Hazel before going into battle and being blown apart by the booby-trapped German helmet he finds in the trench at the end of the Great War's hostilities. Ikey had been reaching for what struck him as the ideal souvenir to give the Squire on his return when the blast struck him.

As Long Summer's Day approaches its conclusion, again Delderfield focuses upon the cultural historical phenomenon that dominates the novel, women's suffrage, personalized in Grace Lovell the Craddock-that-was as Shallowfordians might have described her. She is demonstrating in London when not in gaol, and Craddock has recovered his enthusiasm in the Valley, where one morning he was delighted to welcome Jimmy Grenfell, who intends to back the sufragettes in the next election. When Paul "exclaimed in amazement" at this news, Grenfell explained his motive for coming.

> "I haven't told anyone this because I felt you should be the first to judge my motives. I suppose, knowing your first wife so well, I got in on the ground floor of the controversy but for a long time I wasn't convinced. There was so much else to be done and all of it uphill work. Then it became clear that the Cabinet was very divided on the subject and that many Liberal Members, as convinced as I am that women's suffrage is inevitable, are hoping to hold it at bay as long as possible and maybe pass it to the Tories as a hot potato! Well, some of the colours have faded for me since I graduated from soap-box to the House and discovered how fiendishly difficult the art of government really is but not so much as I can't distinguish black from white! What our people are doing to those women at the moment is a damned outrage! If the Tories did it we should make all the capital we could of their manhandling women in the streets and forcibly feeding them in gaol!" (*Summer's Day*, 565)

To Paul's rejoinder that he probably won't be of much help because his only basis for judging is "unpleasant memories and newspaper talk," and suspicion that "some of them enjoy martyrdom," Grenfell started unstrapping his briefcase and taking out photos proving that what the women suffered was indeed martyrdom. He showed photographs of women being so brutally abused by policemen that one's face grimaces with horror and disgust. "Take a look at this," says Grenfell, "It's one of several and not the worst by any means."

> "I haven't seen forcible feeding," said Grenfell, "but I've seen practically everything else! The police aren't so bad, it's the public who make me vomit!"

He then describes at length some of the things he has seen done to suffragettes in the public squares where statues of British heroes like Nelson tower above the land of freedom.

> "When I make my next public speech down here I'm pulling no punches! I'm not simply paying lip service to women votes, I'm going to attack what's happening inside gaol and out of it!"
>
> "How will that affect your poll?"
>
> "Very adversely, I should think." (565–68)

Grenfell is right, for January of 1910 saw "the most bitter electioneering in the history of the constituency," followed by the vote, which Jimmy lost by a narrow margin. However, he fought "a second election within twelve months" and won by a thousand-vote majority, "regaining lost ground after the announcement that a Women's Suffrage Bill was to be placed before Parliament" (570, 604). Now Claire, who in mid-July of 1910 gave birth to Mary, their first girl, was set upon going to London to buy "little girls' frocks and bonnets" and to watch the king's Coronation. Added to the fact that Grenfell had won the January 1911 election, "the new year opened in triumph." When they arrived in the capitol city the Craddocks booked a small hotel overlooking St. James' Park before strolling about among the crowds of sightseers, looking up at "huge, cardboard portraits of the King and Queen, wired against the tug of the breeze" (611). On the terrace at Westminster the next afternoon, Jimmy was optimistic about getting ahead with the Liberal agenda, but while Grenfell was talking Paul "saw a party of police dash by, whistles shrilling, in the direction of the railings fronting the House" (617). His Boer War service warned him that something is up, and he knows that this is exactly the right time and place for suffragettes to resist the police and suffer a beating the better to spread their message. Seeing what is coming, he knows they should get away fast, but Claire asks "*Why?* Why do we have to turn our backs on it? We backed you in two elections and I think we ought to see for ourselves!" The die is cast, the Rubicon crossed.

Parted from the others by the crowd action in which he was swallowed up, Paul saw the ugliness of the struggle "far more vividly than in James' photographs," and "stood aghast at the brutishness of the spectacle." Savaged women were screaming and an old Man brandishing a VOTES sign lost it when "a mounted policeman tore the banner from him" and

> began using it as a stave to clear the struggling pedestrians from the area about his horse. Then, almost under his feet, he saw a young woman in grey, crouched on hands and knees, hatless and with a mass of dark hair masking her face as she contracted herself to avoid being trampled.
>
> He recognized her as Grace even before a young, helmeted policeman seized her by the shoulders and half raised her and he grabbed the man just as someone laid hold of him from behind, so that all four of them, locked in a grotesque chain, lurched and cannoned into the group struggling around the remains of the banner. The din was hellish for by now the cordon had broken and the crowd, predominantly men, were pressing in from all sides so that the [police] van lifted on two wheels and would have overturned but for the plinth of the statue [of Richard I]. A certainty that, in a matter of moments, Grace would be crushed to death in the melee, gave him the impetus to shoulder the young policeman aside and break free of the restraining hand on his collar. His hat flew off and his collar burst loose but he steadied himself by shooting out his arms and bracing himself against the plinth so that, for a moment or two, he formed an arch over Grace who now lay flat on her face, the man who had been holding the banner crouching almost on top of her. At that moment mounted police moved forward three abreast, clearing a small space under the statue and an inspector, running round the plinth, shouted to Paul, "Get her on her feet, man!" and he shouted back, on impulse, "She's nothing to do with the damned riot! She's my wife, we've been in the House…!" and taking advantage of the momentary lull, tore out his wallet and flourished Grenfell's card under the inspector's nose. The man glanced at it and shouted, "Hold hard, there!" as if he had been in the hunting field and to Paul, "Work your way behind the statue! I'll get the van moving! If some of these fools are run over so much the worse for them!" (*Summer's Day*, 619-20)

As the police van carried Grace from the unruly crowd towards safety Paul saw her "open her eyes, then close them again, rather too swiftly." Grace is play-acting, "making the most of the situation." When the policeman has gone, Paul can rec- ognize "an element of glee in her expression" as she stood up and "began to tidy her hair." But he also observes that she was now "much thinner," her blouse was "ripped across," and her shirt "stained with patches of manure and road dust." He asks Grenfell "'Isn't there some other way?'", and he replies "'They've tried all the other ways'", after which the M.P. and the suffragette share "a look of understand- ing" which excluded Paul.

> "I'm half persuaded that people like Grace enjoy it in a way. Is that prejudice on my part, would you say?"
> "No, not entirely," James said, sipping his drink, "but even if they do I don't see why they should apologize for it. There's self-satisfaction in fighting that hard for something you believe in deeply and sincerely and they'll win, quite soon I believe." (Summer's Day, 621-23)

Delderfield continues lowering the novel's temperature from the high drama of the Parliament Square melee down to the cool dialogues of Paul and James, Grace and Claire, who lived in the Valley as contemporaries long before Paul came onto the scene—two women who admire one another. Claire notices that all of Grace's "curves" have disappeared from self-starvation "and along with them her indifferent, half-vacant air that had seemed at times close to boredom." She has changed, for "every movement she made whilst brushing and underpinning her hair were crisp and decisive, as though physical energy was something to be carefully husbanded." Only a day earlier, Claire had thought Grace sensual, "but she had changed her mind now and wondered if dedication to a political cause demanded the discipline of a nun entering an order" (623-24). Claire had been jealous she admits to Grace when they talk, "but that's done with, I'm not jealous now, any more than you are of me." But though she and Paul are happy, "he'll be very upset by what happened today." Grace replies that Paul is "far happier than I could have made him and believe me, I'm grateful to you too."

> "You were the means of soothing my conscience about him. All the same, I still think you should have fought for him in the first place."
> "But it wouldn't have worked that way," Claire retorted, although it secretly pleased her to have proof of the fact that she knew Paul so much better than this strange, eclec- tic creature, "and you haven't answered my question! I've got a reason for asking it!"

Claire's question, asked earlier on, was "are you happier now Grace?", which she answers here as best she can.

> "I made a bad mistake and so did he but I made mine deliberately, so it wasn't fair that he should help pay for it! Am I happier? I don't know, I never had much expectation of

happiness so it's difficult to judge. I'm doing what I want to do, I've found a purpose to justify myself so that's something." (*Summer's Day*, 624–25)

If we contemplate Grace's background, her mother's suicidal drowning in the reservoir in India to escape her husband's abuse, the sexual predation Delderfield deftly implies she suffered under the hands of the Lowell cousin she had grown up with, her mother-in-law's eager determination to dispose of the troublesome girl into any convenient marriage she is able to arrange, and Grace's guilt for marrying Paul when she clearly knew she should not, added onto the congenital madness Rudd believes infects all the Lovells, it is no surprise that she had little expectation of happiness. But there is even more at issue, for while this intelligent and reflective woman is fully dedicated to the cause of women's right to vote, there is also clear evidence that her self-immolation in that cause is the symbolic sacrifice through which she inchoately yearns to expiate, atone for, all the cumulative sins of all the Lovells, down to the very last obscene photograph of naked Shallowford girls taken by that pretty-good Lowell photographer who satisfied his old-guy's lust in that way, Grace herself having when a nymphet posed for him. What goes around comes around. The fathers have bitten the sour grape but the children's teeth are set on edge.

Part II: *Post of Honour*

The trilogy's second novel showcases events that occur in the Shallowford Valley and elsewhere during the three decades between the 1911 Coronation of King George V and the Dunkirk rescue operation. The "chief characters" list changes somewhat, Grace having dropped out and Zorndorff making only cameo appearances to announce an impending war or imminent financial collapse, that sort of thing. The chief characters of this volume are

> Paul Craddock
> Claire Craddock
> Ikey Palfrey
> Simon Craddock
> James Grenfell

A full-grown man, Ikey is powerfully drawn to Hazel Potter, and their mutual love is important for the revelation of his suppressed insecurity; she is more like Ikey's adjunct than herself a central character. As a professional Army man, Ikey's reading of the Great War is shrewd since he has developed into a field philosopher regarding that conflict. Simon, who is "approaching his eighth birthday" when the novel opens, will be almost forty when it ends; he and Paul converse regularly about his convictions and world affairs as he moves from youth to maturity. Grenfell, last on the chief characters list, is not now pivotal, his role being limited to occasional political observations astute enough to merit his inclusion in this honorable listing.

A good place to begin the discussion of *Post of Honour* is with the tale "How Simon Saved the Fox", or rather, with a brief discussion between Claire and Ikey a year earlier. "A difficult child to know," one who was "inclined to walk alone" (19), Simon would eventually need to be told about his parentage. But in good time, and Claire was "furiously angry" when Ikey told her that in answer to Simon's direct question, he had already explained the matter. Suppressing her feelings, she asked "crisply, 'He *came* to you? After hearing gossip from somebody else?'", but Ikey didn't know, for he hadn't asked Simon.

> "Wouldn't it have been wiser to have sent him to me or his father?"
>
> "I don't think so, Ma'am. If he had wanted that he would have gone to you or Squire instead of me."
>
> She bit her lip and at that moment she could cheerfully have boxed his ears but behind her resentment she could not help admiring his grasp of essentials. (*Honour*, 20)

Claire "found a way of telling Paul without making an issue of it," to which he had responded "Well, good for him! It was something I should have put off indefinitely." That might have ended the matter, except that one year later she "found herself in uneasy alliance with Ikey," an alliance that nearly engaged her in her "first serious quarrel" with Paul (21).

It happened during lunchtime on a late-September day. Paul came out of the woods "very put out about something" relating to Simon. As Master of the Farmers' Hunt, he had intended that Simon stay back from the covert, and "as soon as the fox in the thick undergrowth crossed the ride," he was to holler out and alert the hunters. But Simon neither held his position nor called out, the fox got away, and when Paul asked the boy about it he admitted that, yes, he had seen the fox but "had turned away rather than holler."

> "Why ever did he do that?" asked Claire much surprised, and Paul said that on the way home Simon had told him he did not want to go hunting again and that he thought hunting "wasn't really a gentleman's sport!"
>
> This was too much for Ikey who let out a loud guffaw and even Claire smiled but Paul, whose sense of humour was unpredictable, said, "What's funny about it? I felt a damned ass I can tell you! And as for him feeling squeamish about hunting we don't want the boy to develop into a milksop, do we?"
>
> "He'll not do that," Ikey said and with so much emphasis that Claire saw he no longer treated the incident as a joke. "If the kid really feels that way," he went on, "then jolly good luck to him! He's probably right anyway!"
>
> "Now what the devil am I to make of that?" demanded Paul angrily and Claire said they were both making too much of the matter, and that if he took Simon at his word, and left him behind the next time, the boy would probably be disappointed.

"I wouldn't bank on that," Ikey said, quietly, and when they both looked at him, added, "He's got a natural sympathy for the fox. He always has given me the impression he's signed on with the hunted!"

"Sometimes, Ikey," Paul said, gruffly, "I wish to God you would stop favouring us with undergraduate drivel when you're at home! It doesn't suit you and it damned well irritates me!"

It was the first time Claire had ever heard him address Ikey sharply and she suddenly was aware that the chasm between them went beyond Simon's quixotic sympathy for the hunted fox. She said, hastily, "All right, all right! Don't let's quarrel about it, it isn't that important."

"It might be," Ikey said, ignoring her cautionary glance, "if the Gov'nor is determined to warp Simon into being the kind of person he isn't, and never will be!"

"Well he isn't likely to do that," snapped Claire, feeling annoyed with both of them but she could not help noticing that Paul winced at Ikey's remark as he said, sharply, "Look here, Ikey, I happen to think young Simon made an exhibition of himself turning his back on the field the way he did! I daresay the incident seems trivial to both of you but to my mind it was a blatant piece of showing off! If he really felt that way he could easily have made some kind of excuse."

"What kind of excuse?" Ikey asked, and Paul replied, irritably, "Any kind! He could have pretended he wasn't looking, or that he had just taken a toss!"

"Yes," said Ikey, still quietly, "he could have done that and revealed himself as a liar and a coward when he's neither."

"Oh do let's get Simon down and forget it," said Claire but Paul said, "No, I'm damned if I will for I'll not have Ikey trying to teach me how to bring up my own son! I tell you the boy was showing off and nothing more!" whereupon Ikey growled, "That isn't true and you know it, Gov'nor! It's a damned pompous attitude and I'm hanged if I'll sit here and listen to it! The kid was perfectly justified in doing what he did and as his father you ought to sympathise with him instead of bullying him!" and he got up, nodded to Claire and strode towards the door.

He was stopped by Claire who shot out her arm as he passed and caught him by the wrist. She said, in a way that made them both feel slightly ashamed of themselves, "You can't walk out on this now, Ikey! And neither can you, Paul! You've both said too much for my peace of mind and it's quite wrong to begin an argument like this and then turn your backs on it!"

"I wasn't turning my back on it," Paul said, although he had in fact half risen. "All the same I can't see any sense in prolonging it and upsetting everybody. You'd better go, Ikey, and I hope you mind your manners better than this in the mess!"

"Stop it, Paul," Claire almost shouted, "just stop it and let me say something!"

They both looked at her then, Paul settling back in his chair, Ikey standing irresolutely by the door.

"Now then," she said, trying hard to get her voice under control, "this is something we must have out here and now if only because I happen to be concerned. Very much concerned!"

"I don't see how," Paul grumbled but in a more reasonable tone. "What are you driving at, Claire?"

Claire looked at Ikey, realising that he was very well aware what she was driving at and went on, "Ikey is implying that Simon is...well, is his mother all over again! That's what you meant, isn't it?"

"Yes, it is, Ma'am," he said, "and I'm sorry."

"You needn't be sorry but for heaven's sake do stop calling me 'Ma'am', as if I was someone who had usurped Queen Victoria!" she snapped and a ghost of a grin plucked at the corners of his mouth and then vanished as he saw thunder in Paul's glance.

"I've never heard such damned nonsense in my life," Paul said but Claire, turning on him, said that it wasn't nonsense and if he would have the patience to think about it he would see that it wasn't. Paul said, helplessly, "But hang it, woman, Grace hunted twice a week! She was one of the best riders to hounds in the country."

"It isn't simply a matter of hounds and foxes, Gov'nor," Ikey said, patiently, "it's an attitude to life, an inherited attitude maybe. That's what you meant, wasn't it—Claire?"

Colour came back into her cheeks and through the fog of the issue that had them snapping at one another she saw that, for the first time since they had sat around this table together, they were of a single generation, no longer a man, his wife and a boy but three adults, each equally involved. She said, more calmly, "Yes, Ikey, that was exactly what I meant, and because of it I entirely agree with you! It would be wrong of Paul to bully Simon into hunting against his will, or looking on him as a ninny because he wouldn't! I don't like saying this, Paul, but you can be very stupid about some things and you're being stupid now, because your pride as the local M.F.H. is involved."

Ikey looked at her admiringly and for a moment nobody spoke. Then, when Paul moved as though to get up, and they both made sure he was going to storm out of the room, the door opened and Simon came in, silently taking his place and helping himself to vegetables. Claire said, gently, "You really must come when I call, Simon, we've all been waiting for you," and the boy, looking slightly startled, said, "I'm sorry, Mother, I was changing," and began to eat with catlike deliberation.

It was the strangest meal they had ever sat through but any prospect of further discussion was averted by Ikey's tact for he talked to Simon about one thing and another and occasionally included both Paul and Claire in the conversation so that Claire, whose heart was still beating in uncertain rhythm, had cause to be grateful to him but wondered bleakly what Paul would say to her when they were alone.

After about twenty minutes Paul rose, saying, "Run along and give Chivers a hand rubbing down, Simon, he's on his own this afternoon," and the boy slipped off, glad to be out of it so cheaply.

"Well, I'm not exactly climbing down," Paul said, as soon as he had gone, "but there might be something in what you say. It's worth thinking over at all events because if it is so then it will need tackling one way or another! To have Simon go Grace's way wouldn't bring him much joy, would it? Or us either?" and with that he stumped out. Ikey said, "I'm sorry I let you in for that, Claire. If I had to open my big mouth I shouldn't have done it in your presence!"

"It's just as well you did," she told him, "for there's little enough you could have done on your own, Ikey. Paul is hard to drive but I do flatter myself I've learned how to lead him."

"Yes," he said, with a grin, "I'm quite sure you have!" and he thought, "Grace certainly knew her business when she urged me to write that letter, for Claire understands him better than any of us, yet he can manage her when he wouldn't have managed Grace in a thousand years!" (*Honour*, 22–25)

Here we have a model argument, one focused upon an important issue, one which had better be addressed early on because otherwise when Simon's voice deepens in adolescence the festering dispute will explode in their faces, so that Paul and Simon will find themselves as walled off from one another as Jim and Archie Carver. Ikey knows that Simon's having "signed on with" the fox is foundational, and Paul's angry "I will not have Ikey trying to teach me how to bring up my own son" overlooks the fact that Simon is Grace's son too. Actually, we have evidence that the Squire is not so much overlooking as *suppressing* that fact. Paul confesses he "should have put off indefinitely" telling Simon about Grace. Does he think to tip-toe around the sleeping bear? Does he believe that early intervention will save the boy from tragically turning into Grace redivivus?

Although Delderfield does not tell us, we suspect that as Grace's son Simon is lurking in the wings with very big ears, eavesdropping to find out things he needs to know for self-defensive purposes. He's front-and-center the subject of their dispute, and he's in-the-wings waiting for things to cool sufficiently for him to make his appearance after "dressing". What does Simon put onto his plate when he has entered the room to sit down and eat? Vegetables. He does not reach for a rasher of bacon or ham since he knows where meat comes from, and signing on with the hunted means that his dietary habits should be of-a-piece with his attitude towards fox-hunting.

Claire's role in the argument is to avoid it so far as that is possible ["if you left him behind the next time" he would be disappointed and change his conduct]. But when it clearly cannot be avoided, she becomes the pivot, the hinge upon which the male irreconcilables can be turned away from pointless rage, Paul quieted down until she is able to help him assimilate Ikey's key fact which the boy's father needs to shut up long enough to hear. Paul's "You'd better go, Ikey" slams up against Claire's "Stop it, Paul," taking the starch out of both the men, since Ikey is no longer a boy. Finding the coast clear enough for his own entrance, Simon enters the room and spoons vegetables onto his plate, after which the four of them spend twenty minutes together at the table—signifying that they're not angry with one another or with the boy, as Paul chews upon the home truth which he cannot any longer suppress, returning to a normal paternal role by giving Simon a stable-task which frees him to leave and, almost ceremonially, ends the exchange.

As Ikey is leaving after the Simon discussion, Claire suddenly asks whether he is "depressed" about having to go to India. No, he is "relieved" but does not indicate why, and sensing that he needs a sympathetic ear, she offers to listen if ever he wants to talk. Her offer strikes through his show of self-confidence to the extent that he "bent and brushed her cheek with his lips" as he leaves. Afterwards, she thought of him as "a youth as confused and uncertain as any of them" despite his "show of self-containment" (25).

> Claire was learning about him. The shifts of his life had taught him how to deceive most people, to cod them into believing that he had all the self-confidence necessary to make a place for himself wherever he went, but he had stopped deceiving himself long ago, soon after finding himself in a straitjacket tighter than any he had worn at High Wood or Shallowford. Yet he still might have worn it comfortably had it not been for Hazel Potter who stood squarely between past and future and was always there, clutching her rags and freedom no matter how many new friends he made, how many cadet sprees he embarked upon, how enthusiastically he threw himself into the business of learning to be a gunner. (*Honour*, 25-6)

Hazel made "everything he did seem profitless," as if "she alone was the one substantial force in his world" and every other consideration meant nothing. He was still "tormented by the demands of loyalty to the Squire," who with the best motives had "turned him loose in this desert," but Hazel it was "who triumphed." As soon as he could after coming back on leave, Ikey "slipped off into the woods to find her and here, so long as they were alone, he was happy again, his tensions miraculously eased". They did not return to being lovers on his first leave, "but when he came home again in the spring the temptation to slam that door and go to Heaven or hell with a flower in his mouth was too strong for him; and having once recrossed into her world" Ikey had "no regrets" (25-6). Maybe it was the flower in his mouth when Ikey again went in unto Hazel that did it, but it was that coupling which produced Rumble Patrick Palfrey.

Keith Horsey, the too-scholarly youth whose stay at High Wood was made easier by Ikey, who defended him against bullies, was wooing Rachel Eveleigh "at such a pedestrian pace" that she worried "how to bring him to boil" (32). As they were walking together one day near Hazel's Cave, they heard the "low, choked cry" coming from the gorse thicket near their path which told them "Someone is hurt in there!" It was Hazel, struggling alone to free herself of the baby. Taking charge, Rachel says "I'll have to stay and help but you must go for the lady doctor fast." They've gotten past Keith's cry "there's a bbbaby coming", and assistance is on the way. When the crisis is past, Keith walks Rachel home. She giggles reflecting that it took "Hazel Potter's bastard child, born in a cave in Shallowford Woods" to convert him [Keith] from a possibility into a certainty" (33-9).

Dr. Maureen scoured the Valley in search of the father but to no avail. But Keith made "a practical suggestion". If Hazel could find a reasonable place to live, his father, the rector, would pay her "a small weekly sum out of parish funds for cleaning the church". Dr. Maureen found Hazel a place to live; that "half-ruined cottage near the old mill" on the river road could be repaired, and Paul saw to that. Best of all, "motherhood had sobered" Hazel somewhat, and though she was still the same "half-wild creature," she did not wander so far, and took good care of Patrick (40-1).

Time passes, and late in November a week before Keith and Rachel marry, Ikey reappears "after an absence of more than two years" and already assigned to France "in a matter of days" (79). Keith does what he must. He remembers that he heard Hazel cry "Where's The Boy?" as the baby was being born. Keith informs Ikey that she "had a child" eighteen months ago "and I've always believed it was yours!" Ikey says "If Hazel had a child it would be mine, Keith. Whose child do they think it is?" They don't bother about it any more, and "she wouldn't say." Sergeant Palfrey, who has three days "clear" before going to France, asks "Would your father marry us if I got a special license?" He would.

What awed Ikey most of all when he saw Hazel through the window of her new home was not the child's likeness to himself "but the domesticity etched on her and the room" as though having a child "had changed her" as nothing else had been able to, "drawing out her wild blood" and replacing it with "the blood of a cottager's wife."

> He thought, "It's like looking into the cottage of the Three Bears and I wouldn't won-
> der if she was pretending to be a bear." And suddenly a rush of tenderness choked him
> and he felt his eyes pricking and for a moment was a child again himself but one shut
> out of the simple delights of childhood looking in upon security and certainty he had
> never enjoyed. (*Honour*, 83)

He knocks, Hazel answers, and the small family enjoy their evening together before he goes to France. Talking to Meg Potter later on, Ikey conjectures that when the war is over people would have seen the folly of "money-grubbing" and "flag-waving" and would return to "agriculture, the family unit and simple basic things." Meg nodded in agreement, sensing "a spirit attuned to the rhythm of the seasons" in him. Having read his palm, she knew he would die soon "and was glad that he had spawned a son in whose veins ran the oldest blood in the Valley," for her ancestors "had hunted about here before the first church was built" (86-7).

This book's title, *R. F. Delderfield's Novels as Cultural History*, describes the narrative marriage between stories about ordinary people and historical events as they were experienced by those people when they occurred—the pattern established by Erckmann-Chatrien in their *History of a Conscript of 1813*. But while that *History* is entirely focused upon the final stage of the Napoleonic wars, the people of the Shallowford Valley are engaged in any number of things, war being the interrupter rather than the norm. That being so, and since everything cannot be said at once, after focusing closely upon Ikey's engagements and personal sorrows, we here take leave of individuals' lives and focus on a variety of characters' attitudes towards the impending Great War. That is done most economically by gathering and massing extended passages together into a rolling symposium on the question of whether World War I is possible. Could it happen? There is a range of opinions on that question.

The War Symposium begins with a conversation between Paul, Grenfell, and Professor Scholtzer, a German living in Shallowford and well liked by the locals until war-provoked frenzy sets them to attack his home one night. Scholtzer's view differs from his English friends' since he understands how Germans *feel* about their situation, and he knows that wars begin not because people want them to but because guns "have a vay of going off by themselves."

> James Grenfell was down in early June and Paul invited him to dine with Professor Scholtzer with whom he was now on cordial terms. James liked the old German on sight and it was over their port that night that Paul took part in his first discussion on the dangers inherent in the rivalry Germany, France, Russia and Great Britain had been practising for more than a decade. He was mildly surprised when the Professor put forward a theory that, without justifying the Kaiser's antics in the diplomatic field, at least shed a little light on them for he declared that, rightly or wrongly, fear of encircle-ment was very real to many Germans, even intelligent Germans. The Junkers, he told them in his expansive but guttural English, were anxious to come to some agreement with Great Britain and their fear of France and Russia was not merely a ruse to compel politicians into granting more and more money for military purposes. They saw Russia as a steam-roller driven by barbarians and France as an irresponsible nationalist mob determined to avenge the defeat of 1870. "I am not excusing them, my friends," he went on earnestly, when James Grenfell pointed out that sooner or later Germany would be obliged to restore the provinces of Alsace-Lorraine, "I try to make you look at Europe through German eyes. Only if you British do that can we stop this Gadarene rush to destruction." James said, with a smile, "Oh, I don't question your thesis, Professor, but surely it is generally accepted that war, even on the scale of 1870, is an impossibility? Threats and border incidents yes—we'll always have those, but civilized nations, grind-ing one another to pieces? That's a very different matter, if only on account of cost!"
>
> "Guns," said the Professor sadly, "have a vay of going off by themselves and vonce they bang there are always plenty of people to profit from refilling cartridge pouches! That has been my reading of history; it remains my greatest fear! Not a vor started by the Emperors or by the politicians or even the Junkers but those who profit by conflict!"
>
> Neither Paul nor James took the Professor's warnings very seriously, James because he was too deeply imbued by Westminster's views that no power could afford to fight a modern war, Paul because he found it difficult to believe that anyone, even a crass idiot like the Kaiser, would, when it came to the touch, challenge the British Empire. He did not say this; it would have seemed to him a breach of good manners but he mentioned it to James after the Professor had gone home and they were smoking their last cigars in the library. (*Honour*, 52–3)

When Scholtzer had gone, James and Paul reflected upon his views. Grenfell thought that even if war began "we should stay clear of it," for "the pacifist group in the Cabinet would resign in a body and we should lose the backing of the Labour Party," forcing an election. Then too, there's "the Ulster question" and the abuse still visited upon the suffragettes, and such domestic problems make it impossible for England to enter a war.

Franz Zorndorff is the next Symposium member to voice his view. The suffragettes in Holloway prison will soon be released on condition that they support the war effort, for "the balloon goes up!" very soon he tells Craddock. "Don't even wait for the morning papers. Germany, France and Austria have mobilized" and "we shall be in by Tuesday at the latest." Paul objects that Grenfell assures him that England cannot go to war, but Franz, in his inimitable way, replies "My dear boy, the politicians are the clowns who provide the curtain raiser, an entirely different cast act the play!" What will be the outcome? Paul asks. "A very long war... Kitchener's view is three years, although everybody is laughing at him right now. Personally I think he's an optimist." His advice to Craddock is to "put every acre you've got under plow" before your farmhands are given rifles and sent off to die. Paul's subsequent reflections, "sweat pouring from under his arms and striking cold in the draught from the big door" as he hangs up the telephone, is an exemplification of *cultural* history, how people react to public events wherein they are circumstantially caught up.

> There was a waning moon low in the sky over the Home Farm meadows and the night was so still that the whisper of the avenue chestnuts reached him across the paddock. He thought, grimly, "All over Europe men are shuffling along in the dark with their packs and weapons, and I daresay, by now, every main road in Germany is noisy with the rattle of waggons. Almost everyone here and there thinks of war as I thought of it, during the voyage to Table Bay fifteen years ago, but it didn't take me long to discover that war is a boring, bloody muddle, punctuated by moments of fear and disgust!" And suddenly his memory turned on a peepshow that he would have thought forgotten, of smoke rising from a burned-out Boer farm, of sunbonneted women and snivelling children standing behind the wire of a waterless concentration camp, of a private of the King's Royal Rifles with a Mauser bullet in his belly calling on his mates to put another through his head. "It was bad enough then," he said half-aloud, "but that was a piffling affair by today's standards! I don't suppose a hundred thousand ever met on one field and now there are millions, and fighting will occur in densely-populated areas! Who the hell is to blame for misery on that scale? The Kaiser? The Tsar? Those tricky French politicians or the starchy British ones, like Asquith, Grey and that Jack-in-the-Box Lloyd George?" He moved along the terrace to Grace's sunken garden and when the perfume of roses she had planted reached him he thought of her again, and how pitiful The Glorious Cause looked measured against a European war. What, precisely, had the cynical old rascal Franz meant when he implied there were men behind the politicians and generals pulling the strings? Did he mean merchants like himself, who made a profit on war as his father had done years before? Or rabble-rousers, high and low, obsessed by the cult of nationalism who used their influence to convert happy-go-lucky chaps like Smut Potter and Horace Handcock into blood-thirsty patriots? And how did he himself view the prospect of war against the Kaiser's Germany? He had never considered it a serious possibility, not really, in spite of all the years of

newspaper talk and even now found it difficult to whip up rage or resentment against the Germans. (*Honour*, 64)

What was Paul to believe? Whose opinions were most likely to be reliable? "I'd sooner take Uncle Franz's word than Grenfell's on an issue like this," he told Claire the next morning. "If there are people around prepared to pay that much money for a five-year lease on a scrapyard they must have a good idea what's likely to happen! Those kind of people, Uncle Franz's kind, don't make mistakes that cost money, not their money!" (65).

The war began in August, 1914, and by early November the Shallowford gulls, who "knew the features of the Valley better than any earthbound creature," must have been aware of "changes that had taken place there in the last few weeks": the sudden Army Camp which "covered the moor" near Periwinkle Farm, where the gulls always found food; and the attack on Scholtzer's home, caused by "the strange madness that had seized people since newspapers had begun calling Germans 'Huns' and printing stories of crucified Belgian babies that no man in his senses could believe" (66–8). Scholtzer gratefully receives Paul's consolation over the incident, but "It will soon be happening all over Europe." As for the Squire's suggestion that he move into Home Farm, the German replies "It is kind that you should ask me to your house but it would not be wise, I think, to go," since people "would remember it against you" (70).

Rudd weighs in on the subject when Paul asks "How do you see this war, John?" As the crusade that most people think? Or as "an appalling, stupid waste, without a shred of glory about it?" John has lived sixty years in Britain, and "a man ought to learn something about his own people in more than half a century."

"What did you learn that makes you so cocksure, John? For you are cocksure, aren't you?"

"About the outcome? Yes, I am. We'll win all right though I don't know that it will do us much good in the end. I suppose I've seemed to you to take the war in my stride because I've been anticipating it so long and there isn't much point in arguing the rights and wrongs of an inevitability. The line-up started round about the time you settled here and if it hadn't been poor little Belgium this year, it would have been poor old Turkey next year, or hands off India the year after that! Now it's here the only thing left is to hold on and the British do that much better than most of them!"

"It looks to me as if it's all that's left to us," Paul said, "so what makes you confident about us getting anything better than stalemate or a compromise peace?"

"Ah no," John said quickly, "you can rule that out! A nation that achieves all this one has in a century has to have special qualities and I don't say that in the spirit of somebody paid to write for the popular press, it's just a feeling, down here," and he tapped his paunch with his pipe-stem.

"Then all I can say is I wish to God I had it," Paul said emphatically. "It seems to me we rushed into the business without a thought as to what was at stake and these people here, the Walt Pascoes and the Smut Potters, are amateurs. We all know what happens when an amateur takes on a professional!"

"They'll stay amateurs for a bit," John said, "but that's what I'm driving at. When they get desperate enough they'll knock hell out of everybody. Go up to that camp and watch those cotton-spinners at bayonet practice."

"Not me," Paul told him, "I've no stomach for the business and I still think we were damned stupid to get drawn into it."

"Well," John said, "I can understand that, knowing you. For too long now you've been giving your attention to what happens in you own backyard but when you realise that backyard is at stake you'll outdo the rest of them! That'll be when your Puritan streak shows. Puritans only show fight when they've convinced themselves their way of life is threatened. After that there isn't many who can stand up to them for long." He got up and knocked out his pipe. "Will you tell Maureen not to wait supper? I think I'll take a turn along the river road." (*Honour*, 94–5)

The difference between John Rudd's view regarding the Great War and Harold Godbeer's sober estimate of how World War II would turn out is "not spacious," as Mark Twain would have put it. Their confidence about long-term outcomes despite short-term disasters is Delderfield's narrative expression of a cultural reality which is palpable, if one understands how to put one's finger on it, as Rudd and Godbeer both do.

The last member of our cultural historical Symposium, Ikey Palfrey, spent the month of April, 1915, in an area of France "where the Germans held one half of the rubble and the British held the lower, disadvantageous half." Palfrey spent his time either "aloft in a captive balloon" spotting targets for the artillery, or "checking map references with divisional infantry officers in and about the grotesque ruin where the two lines of trenches ran as close as fifty yards".

He cheerfully accepted the risk of being shot down from his balloon or sniped on his way to and from the front-line if he could spend whole days out of reach of the sahibs further back. By the time spring had come round he had developed a theory about the war that, to a degree, blunted its impact upon his sensibilities. All his life, or so it seemed to him, he had stood exactly half-way between the possessors and the possessed, between people who jingled the bell when the fire burned low and those who came trotting up to replenish it. He had been acutely conscious of this personal neutrality during his schooldays and whilst engaging in his clandestine association with Hazel, and although it would seem that, by marrying Hazel Potter, he had crossed from one social sphere to the other this was not really so. As long as the war continued or as long as he was actively engaged in it he still retained a foot in each camp. It was this time-truce that helped to clarify and then buttress his sense of detachment so that he came to see the war as a kind of surgical operation that civilization was performing upon itself, an agonising but extremely interesting attempt to demolish class-barriers that had been building in Western Europe since the early days of feudalism, a gigantic and masochistic combined assault by masters and men upon the bonds they had forged for each other over twelve centuries of pride, bigotry and licensed greed. Unlike the majority of his comrades-in-arms he could not view it as an exercise in national rivalry or even, as the more sophisticated were beginning to regard it, as a cynical struggle for world markets that would last, perhaps another few months, or at worst another year.

He saw it for what it was, the explosion of a magazine of myths and the trappings of myths such as flags and tribal cultures and although its barbarity horrified him, and he could pity the little people trapped in the cogs, he could also accept the slaughter as inevitable during a vast shift in the pattern of life on the planet. It was his sincere belief in this that enabled him to shorten the recoil of his emotional reaction to scenes that he would have thought himself incapable of witnessing without disgust and perhaps a protest that would have led, sooner or later, to direct conflict with brother officers.

His letters to Hazel encouraged the growth of his detachment. He enclosed one, at least once a week, in his cheerful, factual letters to Paul, who now paid Hazel a weekly visit for the express purpose of reading Ikey's letter to her. To Hazel herself Ikey said little about the war but confined himself to irrelevant minutiae, a patch of clover growing beside the trench; the fatness and multiplicity of rats and their dexterity in dodging revolver shots; the wandering flight of a chalkhill blue butterfly braving shellfire over the brickstacks; and sometimes even a comic quote from the gunners' letters he censored. He did not know whether Paul, in reading his letters aloud, ever attempted to convert his words into the brogue that he himself had always used when talking to her but he deeply appreciated Paul's kindness in fulfilling his promise to keep an eye on wife and child and was touched when Paul enclosed a letter allegedly dictated by Hazel, describing his small son's attempt to wade the Sorrel that had ended in a drenching. (*Honour*, 112-13)

A year later in April, 1916, when Ikey returns to the Valley on leave, he and the Squire discuss the war, Paul initiating the conversation by contrasting the attitudes of soldiers in the field and those of Shallowford's "hearthrug patriots."

"What strikes me as odd," Paul said, "is that you chaps aren't anything like so emphatic about the war as the people at home. You don't foam at the mouth about the Germans and I get the impression you half admire people like Keith Horsey [a conscientious objector]. Is that cussedness on your part or is it general among men on active service?"

"General I'd say, at least below the rank of colonel but I don't see why it should surprise you. Fritz lives under the same hellish conditions as we do and you can't help admiring his guts. Most of the chaps feel more akin to him than to the people at home and I daresay he feels the same way. You can't live a week out there and go on believing all the bloody nonsense people write and talk back here, not unless you happen to be on the staff that is!"

"But if things are as bad as that," Paul said, "isn't there a chance of it petering out of its own accord?"

"Not a snowball in hell's chance, Gov," Ikey told him cheerfully, "but if you ask me why I couldn't give you a short answer. It has to do with self-respect, regimental pride, the habit of discipline and even the warrior cult thousands of years old but more than any of those things it's probably reluctance to let other chaps down. I suppose that sounds facetious but it isn't, it's just that we're all so closely involved with each other and, in a way, with Fritz. I don't think things are like that on the other fronts, or at sea, but out there, in that great sprawling mud-bath where, to show the top of your head is certain death, a man ceases to have anything in common with ordinary civilised people. They've stopped believing in the war, or in the way it is regarded in

London or Berlin, but they'll go on sticking it until one side breaks. Do you find that impossible to understand?"

"Not entirely," Paul said thoughtfully and he did understand in a way, in fact he went to bed thinking he had learned more about the war from Ikey than from any other source over the last eighteen months. (*Honour*, 174)

By early spring 1915, the Valley people were scattered as they had not been since 1685 when the Duke of Monmouth "came recruiting and some of the Sorrel men volunteered" for a war which for most of them "ended on the field of Sedgmoor or in transportation to the sugar plantations of Barbados" (99). Their dispersal was distressing, for Paul saw his tenants "as a family," his own, and he "shared the mounting desperation" of women such as Elinor Codsall and Marian Eveleigh over the lives of their men. The Army Camp was not an improvement of the land, and although Paul had temporarily "saved the old timber of the estate" from being cut down for pit props, he feared "fresh ultimatums" from officials whose one concern was present need. But Craddock is learning to measure time with an eye to the future, to continuity, enduring presence. The woman sleeping beside him as he lay awake worrying was "a living symbol" of the land, "her breasts were its contours, and in her thighs lived its abundancy," which Paul thought is not "fanciful". For "there were Derwents hereabouts when the first Tudor arrived" if they could be traced. He himself was playing at being "stud-horse and caretaker," since it would not be truly Craddock land "until her children, and her children's children, take on where I leave off" (129-30).

Paul's conception of the Valley's tenants, or rather their lives as families, including long-dead relatives who have been working the land for centuries, echoes the sedate line in Gray's *Elegy*, "Along the cool, sequestered vale of life/ They kept the noiseless tenor of their way" (75-6). Paul's emotional apprehension of the Devonshire land itself is of an aboriginal being, similar to the heath in Hardy's *Return of the Native*, or the primeval forest in Faulkner's *The Bear*, which was not owned by anyone, never belonged to the Chickasaw chief Ikkemotubbe to sell "to Grandfather or any man" when "a wilderness of wild beasts" before it was cleared by men who thought they bought it. Shallowford has its own existence, being something alive from which people take what they need, returning upon their deaths whatever they borrowed. The Valley's cemeteries seem rather an act of homage to the land than anything specifically religious. One finds in Delderfield's fiction, especially in his two *Diana* novels, something of an implicit nature non-worship, an allegiance to the land, a recognition of indebtedness thereto. Witness Craddock's non-negotiable preference for a death faced calmly, alone, high above the estate he cared for so tirelessly—that favored place for looking with his clearsighted eye on life and death, a horseman passing by.

John Rudd's prediction is that once Paul realizes that the war is threatening his own backyard, his Puritan streak will kick in and he will be ready to fight.

Craddock was the one man uninfected by "the virus of war-fever, devoting his energies exclusively to buttressing the Valley against the pressures exerted upon it" (131) from outside, but when the casualties began to mount Paul began to change his stance. John's son, Roddy, who had written home *"We are looking for Von Spee; when we find him we shall go to the bottom,"* (133), has gone down as he predicted. Walt Pascoe has died in Gallipoli; his comrade Dandy Timberlake, though badly wounded, survived and married Walt's widow, Pansy Potter-that-was (134, 144-6). Scholtzer's son Gottfried, no "ravisher of Belgian women," had been "whisked into the Kaiser's Army whilst on holiday, and been killed in Champagne" (134). Poor Will Codsall, who signed up early on without any idea what he was getting into, was tried and shot for desertion. In his final days on the front, the shell-shocked farmer fled the noise and slaughter while two figures shouted at him—his father with "a rope around his neck," and his mother Arabella, who was "headless." Shot by his own people, Codsall was listed as "killed in action" (135-38). Big Jem Pollock, who husbanded two of the Potter girls and would have serviced Hazel if they had sent her to the Dell when her baby was born, died while holding up the entrance of a collapsing British tunnel—one riveted with steel rails which held for a matter of about fifty seconds, which would not have happened if Jem had not "instinctively reached up and braced himself against a key crossbar," the act which permitted five English soldiers to escape. This heroic deed did not earn him the Military Medal since "none of the witnesses had been officers" (138). Henry Pitts, standing near the Army Camp on the moor, was so mesmerized by "the crispness and precision" of the soldiers' marching to commands "At the halt, by the left, form close company of pla-*toon!* (140), that he enlisted. He served bravely, and survived the war. The Squire attempted to dissuade him but Henry and his wife's views were decisive. "Paul argued that food-growing was just as important as killing Germans and that Henry, as a professional farmer, would almost certainly be rejected by the authorities. Henry countered by saying that his eldest boy was already big enough to take his place and Gloria, outraged by the Squire's attempt to snatch the halo of patriotism from the Hermitage [their home], said she would never hold up her head if theirs was the only farm in the Valley that failed to contribute a man to the forces of the Crown." (*Honour*, 141)

While the "chawbacons" were being killed or wounded in distressing numbers, Ikey Palfrey, an officer rather than a footsoldier, and a good evaluator of situations, as we have seen, had concluded that two changes were essential before the Western Front could move forward. First, "all British ex-cavalry officers bent over maps at H.Q. would have to be put out of harm's way, preferably by a bullet through the head." Second, a new General Staff was needed, of officers who could "devise a means of penetrating the German trench system and covering the advance of infantry men across open ground traversed by enemy machine guns" (160). Ikey is as inventive as anyone in the British Army and he goes forward on his own. He began to study the battle around him "in a tactical sense,"

> reasoning that before the fortified ground on either side could be taken and held something far more imaginative than a preliminary bombardment was needed to fortify the attacker during the initial stage of a breakthrough. His mind began to toy with smoke-screens, low-level aerial machine-gunning and even bullet-proof vests but he rejected all three as too clumsy, too revolutionary and to ineffectual. Then, on the third day, he had the germ of an idea and it excited him; what was surely needed out here, what would have to be found before substantial progress could be made, was some kind of war chariot mounted with quick-firing guns, something impervious to all but a direct hit from a mortar or long-range shell, a machine, moreover, that could crush wire and circumnavigate all but the smallest shell-holes, a moving fort behind which the hardy infantry could advance without being scythed down by traversing machine-guns and rifle fire. That night, back in his dug-out, he took pencil and paper and began to sketch but he was less than half-satisfied with the drawing he produced, thinking that it resembled a memory copy of one of the sketches of military engines made by Leonardo da Vinci that he remembered seeing in a magazine in the mess at Quetta. He persisted, however and at last evolved something that seemed to him to be at least partially practical, a kind of squat armoured car, with broad, steel-plated wheels looking a little like an armadillo. He was so absorbed that he got behind with his real work and it was not until the candle burned low that he put the sketch-pad in his valise, marked his maps and finally rolled on to his wire-netting bed to sleep. Outside the guns went on grumbling, not violently but persistently, somewhere to the south and before he slept Ikey thought the distant cannonade sounded exactly like autumn thunder in the Sorrel Valley. (*Honour*, 161)

While Ikey was thus employed, Grace Lovell was working as an ambulance driver "not forty miles" from where he sat sketching war-chariots. Grace was now "more familiar with the extremes of pain and human desolation" than soldiers on the front line. She had been in France for nearly a year after transferring out of the London hospital where she had first tried to do her part. Ever since 1904, she had been "hounded, hunted, man-handled, forcibly fed and hectored by men," and after being reduced to skin and bones thought the war "a fitting punishment for a world of men who had been callous, sadistic and mulish in response to a demand for basic human rights." Veteran suffragettes had assured her that after the war "every woman in Britain would have the franchise".

> She did not know whether she believed them but after a spell as a V.A.D. in a London hospital it did not seem to matter much for the keen edge of her fanaticism was blunted by a factor removed from the purely physical suffering she witnessed in the wards. This was a creeping doubt as to whether women in authority were any more reasonable, or even as efficient as men. She had the bad luck to come within the orbit of a fat-rumped martinet whose only qualification for her position as Commandant was newly-acquired wealth and Grace soon had good reason to despise this type of woman as wholeheartedly as she despised Cabinet Ministers. The titled Commandant administered the hos-

pital like an eighteenth-century school, treating her volunteer nurses much as the more ignorant of the wardresses had treated prisoners in Holloway. Grace came to suspect that, again like some of the wardresses, the Commandant was not only a bully and a snob but also a Lesbian for she made favourites of all the doll-faced little nurses from aristocratic houses and was hostile to any member of her staff who had been a suffragette. After two or three months of back-breaking toil and humiliation Grace knew that she would have to choose between resigning or changing her hospital, and since almost every reception-centre for the wounded was in charge of middle-aged women enjoying the exercise of despotism she managed, by pulling various strings, to transfer to the transport section of the Department and was sent to France in time to evacuate some of the casualties of the battle of Veuve Chapelle, in April.

It was here, driving between clearing-station and base, that her re-orientation really began, for during her ten years in and out of gaol she had forgotten that men also possess the capacity to suffer. (*Honour*, 162–63)

Eager to do something to help the wounded returning to England, Claire transformed the Estate's big house into a convalescent hospital for fifty to sixty men who wouldn't arrive "until they were on the road to recovery," an idea she got from seeing the Dandy Timberlake who had returned from Gallipoli. After wounds have begun healing, "they're still suffering from shock and nervous exhaustion," and "fresh air and sea-bathing from May to October" would do them a world of good. As for Paul, he was summoned for initial training in November, 1916, and assigned to service in the Transportation Corps (187–80). After some months in France, he knew the terrain as well as he knew the Sorrel Valley. To Craddock, the devastated landscape "had a kind of bloated emptiness, like the mottled remains of a half-eaten crab stranded above the Coombe Bay tide-line and everything that crossed it was contaminated by its foulness, its utter and stupid uselessness." But that was before he recognized something else. He had tried hard to create a community in the Valley "but without getting anywhere near the ideal of comradeship and interdependence of this array of clerks, labourers, factory workers and schoolboy officers, in their faded, mud-stained tunics and puttees." This sense of discovery, and "his absorption into the fellowship" around him, converted Paul's pessimism about the war into optimism. "For it seemed to him that, if this almost holy relationship between Englishman and Englishman survived the war," no obstacle he would meet in the future could "defeat or discourage him" (213–14). And it was out here that he and Grace encountered one another again.

He was struck by the "bitterness" of Grace's voice and the terrible exhaustion it expressed. What are you doing here? he wonders, to which she replies "When I discovered women handle authority even more despotically than men I got a transfer!" (219). When Paul shows her photographs of his family, he notices that Grace "studied the one of Simon intently but unemotionally." She asks "Is he troublesome, like his mother?" No, he's not troublesome, but he is "far more introspective" than the twins and "more sensitive to reproof than Mary". Other than that, "He has your passion for facts and your wonderful memory. He's very good at history and writes a very good essay, I'm told" (223). And what does she do when she's on leave here in France? Grace "looked at him steadily" and replied. "'Saluting men who are about to die,' she said. 'Youngsters mostly, some of them young enough to need a little mothering,'" which she provides by feeding and deflowering them before they go to their deaths in the mud-fields (224). Six days later Paul was waiting for her to come so that they could have dinner together again, but her ambulance "did not show up," for "a lone-flying Gotha" had attacked her convoy and "there had been a few casualties," Grace being one of them. Paul reflected upon her life, an unlucky one in every respect.

> She had been unlucky the whole of her life, with a father who goaded her mother into drowning herself, a wretched and rootless adolescence, a failed marriage, years of prison and persecution for a principle, and finally a foreign bomb out of the sky. And yet, as he made his way back to his lorry, he remembered to be glad that they had met again and, to a great extent, buried the past, and also that he was here to salute her as a great war comrade rather than a woman whom he had held in his arms. (*Honour*, 227-28)

When Claire learns that Paul is coming home for a nine day leave in October, she begins turning Crabpot Willie's Shanty, a tumbledown shack near the water's edge on the way to Whinmouth, into a love nest where, unseen by the rest of the family, the two of them would spend the first four days of his leave, and her design proved a huge success. Paul's *next* four days were spent in seclusion and rest "up at the house," but his last day he "devoted to Simon who had gone to High Wood," a "sadly disorganized" place staffed by "an asthmatic temporary headmaster, invalided trench veterans and Grade III civilians" (246). Simon was always a private person who "rebuffed" most people—Ikey and to some extent Claire, being the exceptions. Simon told him the family's cook had "said you were there when [his mother] was killed, sir." Yes. "You can call me 'Gov'nor' if you like," as Ikey had done, and the boy grinned, more at ease now. Yes, he had been there when she was killed, Paul answers.

At Simon's request, Paul tells him about his mother as best he can without providing the boy with "material for morbid reflection." He says "She got a bee in her bonnet about votes for women and in the end" that became more important than "me or the estate."

> "Were you against votes for women?"
> "No, I wasn't, and neither was our M.P. Jimmy Grenfell, who also admired her but the odd thing is I've come to believe your mother left me because, in a funny sort of way, she thought it was unfair to me to stay." He looked sideways at the boy. "Do you find that hopeless to understand?"
> "No," said Simon, "I believe I can see what you mean, Gov'nor."
> "Then try and tell me," Paul said, gratefully, and Simon went on, "She must have thought you ought to be married to someone keen on the Valley."

"That's exactly it!" said Paul, excited by the boy's perception, "she told me I ought to have married a farmer's daughter in the first place but what I'd really like to get home to you is that just because we got divorced she wasn't a mother to be ashamed of but rather the opposite. She didn't run off with anyone else, she just had to give herself to politics and she was prepared to go to prison for her belief which is a damned sight more than most politicians are!" (*Honour*, 248)

The other thing Simon is bothered by and wants his father's opinion about is the war. Paul temporizes, concerned that the boy might "express himself too freely on the subject in case Simon quoted him in an unguarded moment," but "the boy was not to be fobbed off with this and again reminded Paul of Grace when one of her principles was challenged."

"But you must know whether you think it right or wrong."

"Well then, it's wrong," Paul said, reluctantly, "it's the biggest crime against humanity that's every happened but I daresay some good will come out of it, at least, that's what most of us out there like to think, the Germans as well as the English."

"If everybody fighting thinks that why isn't it stopped," Simon persisted, with his mother's maddening logic.

"Because, for the moment, neither side is ready to give in. The men in the trenches would be very happy to call it a day but the war isn't directed by them..." (*Honour*, 249)

As Paul returned to Home Farm, he thought "how small a part environment played in promoting character," and how clear it was that Simon was his mother's son, since "what's in the blood stays there" (250).

The sequence of battlefield events which began on the night of March 20th, 1918, ended in a serious injury that nearly terminated Paul's life. He was leading a convoy of ammunition lorries to a battery near the Defence Zone in front of St. Quentin when at 3 a.m. "all hell broke loose." The German's "big push" began, they having transferred "a sufficient number of troops from the Russian front" (268–69). The Germans drove all before them with surprising new tactics and astonishing firepower, and Paul remembered that day clearly, though his experience of "the next few weeks" he could recollect only as "a grey, misted-over" interval of "stress, fear and constant movement." When the northern offensive against the Germans held, Paul was assigned to an unravaged landscape where he and other exhausted survivors "were just in time for" the enemy's May offensive on Chemin des Dames, where Ludendorff's stormtroopers smashed through "a broad front, penetrating to the Marne" (273). Early on May 29th "the tide finally engulfed him, blotting out past and present for a period of fifty-nine days" during which he lay in a coma, badly wounded.

It came without pain, without even realization. Just a soundless explosion like the red-gold wink of distant shell fire at night and then an eternity of dreams, some troubled, like the recurring dream of his fever in hospital sixteen years before, some tranquil, like the memory of long summer afternoons in the Valley, with Claire coming down the goyle to Crabpot Willie's shack wearing an old-fashioned sun bonnet and waving as she approached yet never seeming to reach his side. (*Honour*, 274)

He had been about his field work when he saw and tried to help the wounded man lying there.

> The Frenchman rolled his eyes upward as Paul knelt beside him. His shoulder had been laid open by shrapnel that was scything down from a battery behind the hill and as Paul raised him, grunting under his weight, another splinter whanged through the poilu's helmet, scattering his brains and ricocheting into Paul's temple. They fell together…and it was a German stretcher-party that found Paul still breathing at dawn the next day [and took him to the Soissons infirmary where] a Leipzig specialist skilfully removed another half-ounce splinter from a shallow wound forward of the left ear and told the grinning orderlies that the Englishman evidently possessed an even thicker skull than his commander-in-chief, Sir Douglas Haig, and thus stood a chance of recovery. (*Honour*, 275)

It was only when Paul was being invalided by way of Paris to England that a British doctor told him he "probably owed his life to two factors, one French and one German." The shell-splinters had already "spent most of their force" on the Frenchman's head, but without "Quirnheim's skill in replacing a section of bone with a silver plate the largest of them would have caused death" (276).

When Craddock returns to Shallowford, Dr. Maureen and her husband discuss the Squire's impact on the Valley. She asks "Where does Paul Craddock's archaic dream fit into the switchback pattern," wherein new arrivals replaced the one-third of Europe that died in the Black Death, and yet ten years later "this country alone was exporting enough wool to mine gold for a thousand families like the Gilroys and the Lovells." Maureen continues: "In an age dominated by machines when the best brains in Europe seem to have lost their way", how did Paul manage to succeed? "Was it simply obstinacy, vanity?" John thought for a long time before he answered the question he had often asked himself.

> "He was the only one who neither looked on land as property or as a way of life that carried an insurance against hunger. To him it was the flesh and bones of humanity, the only true essential and whatever success he had here was the result of that plus a natural talent for administration inherited from money-grubbing ancestry on some other side of the family! And that isn't the whole of it either! There was something else that held him in—two things, and kept him from overreaching himself and getting the backing of men he couldn't afford to lose."

What was that? his wife asks, and Rudd replies: "He never once put money before human dignity" (278-79).

Smut Potter—who had been first a poacher, after that a horticulturalist, and finally a combination part sniper, part picker-up-of-unconsidered-trifles to enrich the lives of the officers to whom he presented his boodle—had been crippled by a machine-gun bullet "three hours before the cease-fire." Like most soldiers on the front lines, Smut fought without personal rancour, looking upon the war as a kind of "gigantic poaching expedition," the German soldiers as "homicidal but impersonal gamekeepers." As he recovered during his long stay in hospital, Smut's reflections gently turned to thoughts of Madame Viriot, the baker's widow whom he marries and brings to Shallowford to open a bakery, his role being to drive the old delivery van that "she herself had assembled from a number of derelict vehicles rusting on the dump behind Nun's Bay camp" (283–85).

Henry Pitts, "the Valley immortal," was as bewildered as his comrades the morning of November 11th by "the abrupt cessation of gunfire" but on Henry alone "the occasion made a deep and lasting impression." Ignoring the warnings of more wary soldiers, Henry "clawed his way over the parapet rising to his full height" and stood there, "the only thing above ground in all that vast, dreary landscape." And then the Germans began taking heart, standing up, lumbering in Henry's direction, which astonished the Devonshire farmer.

> Somehow it never occurred to him that the men he had been fighting all this time were identical, men who in better times plodded about tending pigs, herding cows, ploughing up land and banking swedes for winter cattle feed...The encounter in no-man's-land undermined his entire philosophy of war and now, looking back, it seemed to him a very stupid, profitless business and he wanted nothing so much as to be done with it and go home. (*Honour*, 286–89)

The cheerfulness that had unwaveringly supported his fellow soldiers until that moment, deserted him, "and in its place was impatient pessisism."

Craddock was discharged from the convalescent centre in Wales soon after the armistice and recovered so quickly it surprised everyone. He had a new daughter, conceived in the love nest Claire had made for them the previous autumn. Was the war worth it, Claire wonders. Yes, Paul replies, *if* everybody "throws bombast and national prejudice on the ash heap." However, it cannot happen again. "Nobody will ever stand for it again in any case and that goes for Fritz as well as us." On June 1st, 1919, his fortieth birthday, Paul rode over the estate, reflecting that though "Sydney Codsall types" wanted to ruin the landscape "with gimcrack bungalows, most of them in cahoots with faceless allies on local and county councils" (294–95), he himself was "nicely placed" to stop them. Franz had reported the "staggering" profits the scrap-yard had yielded, which made Craddock a war profiteer in spite of himself, and Paul ploughed those monies into "a special Trust Fund earmarked exclusively for estate development" (294–96).

A decade later on the afternoon of September 1st, 1929, "the eve of the twins" 21st birthday, Paul left the house to escape the bustle. The boys' mother and sisters created a "frenzied upheaval" as they prepared for their all-night birthday celebration dance (299). Paul rode up to French Wood, the small grove where he had planted "a tree for each man instead of carving their names on a lump of granite in the church yard." The individual trees expressed his sense that the land which had produced them ought not entirely to forget them. Paul preferred them to "pseudo-heroic statues of glaring infantrymen," which did nothing to bring to mind the eighteen local men who died in the Great War. French Wood was Craddock's way of "commemorating the Valley dead," which is correct, for commemorabilia are the artifacts that remain behind, enabling our recollection of the past—like Napoleon's "Waterloo coach in Madame Tussaud's", Lockhart's *Life of Napoleon* which Delderfield discovered in Appleby's bookstore (Casey, 159; *Own Amusement*, 273).

As Craddock meditates in French Wood he comes upon his eldest son Simon, who is doing much the same thing, and the two have a lengthy conversation on his activities since he left High Wood.

Paul had chosen each young tree with care—a mountain ash for Ikey; oaks for the older men like Tremlett, the huntsman and Tom Williams, the fisherman; an elm for Jem Pollock already as thick as the Dell giant's thigh and a small cluster of silver birches for the younger set, men like Tod Glover who had once flown low over this spot showing off his wind-riding skill like a buzzard. In the centre of the wood was a flowering cherry for Grace, killed hauling wounded back from Vimy and as he crossed the turf Paul was not much surprised to find his eldest son Simon sitting there, with a cherrywood pipe in his mouth contemplating the metal plaque which read: *"Grace Craddock, ambulance driver, killed April 1917,"* and underneath the only Scriptural quotation inscribed on a plaque— *"Greater love hath no man..."* Simon said, without looking round, "You should have done your bit of Bible thumping under old Tom Williams' tree, Gov'nor! He was a Methodist and would have thought it fitting." Then, with laughter in his eyes, "She never had much truck with organized religion, did she?"

"No," Paul said, aware that the boy was teasing him but not resenting it in any way, "she didn't! As a matter of fact she didn't have much truck with anything except Women's Rights and Compassion."

The boy looked at him in a way that Paul had learned to associate with his questing, mildly cynical nature, akin to his mother's but more tolerant and far less likely to give offence.

"It was a sentimental idea, this wood of the dead," he said, "but taken all round it does you credit, Gov'nor."

"Thank you," said Paul with a grin, for he suddenly remembered after all these years when and where he had invited Simon to call him "Gov'nor"—sitting on a fence near his school, during a hurried visit on Paul's leave from the Front in the autumn of 1917. He thought of reminding the boy and then decided not. Simon affected to despise the past and to regard everything that had happened up to the Labour Government's first term of office, in 1924, as a pitiable failure of all human achievement. He said, instead, "What made you come here, today of all days?"

"For the same reason as you; to get away from the racket! Anyway, I had some thinking to do. I've had a letter from Ned Stokes. He wants to know if I'd care to take over the literary editorship of *The Forum*. It's a new magazine his uncle is backing. Might have a future now that Labour is back again."

Paul was resigned to Simon's false starts and news that he was contemplating a journalistic career, after turning his back on teaching and forestry, had no power to irritate him. He said, tolerantly, "You're old enough to dispense with my advice, Si. I daresay you'd find it amusing for a time but those magazines don't last long as a rule, do they?"

"No," Si said seriously, "but what does?"

"Land," said Paul, not unexpectedly, and Simon smiled and shook his head as though he had long ago accepted the fact that, when it came to the estate, his father was slightly off his head and everybody in the Valley acknowledged as much.

"I suppose your mob will want to nationalise us," Paul said and without waiting for an answer, "Well, I daresay it'll come to that in the end but until it does I'm staying put! It will take more than your precious Ramsay Mac' to shift me."

Simon took his pipe from his mouth and ran his hand through his dark hair. It was a gesture that always reminded Paul vividly of his first wife, one of the many quirks she had passed on to the child she had abandoned for the Women's Suffrage Campaign, when he was no more than a few months old. He said, resignedly, "You might just as well go over to the Tories, Gov'nor. You're a Tory in everything but name you know." (*Honour*, 300–01)

Being occupied with preparations for the dance, Claire had fallen behind on the estate diary, and busy as this day was she found a moment to take up the book and write "*Today the twins celebrated their 21st...*" browsing then through what Paul had written since his return. There she found "a theme that was absent from her own recordings, a pattern of subdued anxiety running from page to page," entries such as the one in May, 1924, "Codsall is developing east of Nun's Bay, blast him..." and enigmatic entries such as "Quarry project through County Council." It was the first time she had noticed that Paul used the diary "as a safety valve" or that Codsall's actions around the estate's periphery were important to him. Curious, she went into the estate office where she found a map dated 1929, unrolled it, and what it showed confirmed her suspicion that her husband feared the gradual "encirclement" of Shallowford. Taking her concern to Paul, he admits that he is worrying. He does not hate Sydney Codsall,

"just what he stands for, what all Sydney Codsalls stand for. There are one or two operating in every area of the country. They stand up in public spouting about development and progress but what they really mean is exploitation and rural rape! They are the new *condottiere*, marching through England as the medieval mercinaries marched across France, taking everything out and putting nothing back...Somebody has to stand up to the bastards or the country won't be worth living in in a generation from now. (*Honour*, 303–09)

Simon was Master of Ceremonies at the big birthday bash for Andrew and Stevie but he was bored by his six-hour task and, soon after two a.m., Paul and Claire having departed for their shanty and the traditional "Tally-ho crocodile" having gotten under way to the "scream of three horns" that echoed across the estate, Simon wandered out on the terrace and down to the rose garden, where he watched "the harvest moon ride over the avenue chestnuts down by the ford" (313-14). Seeing a shadow and the glow of a cigarette in the darkness, he approached and found a woman, evidently not a guest. Furthermore, there was "something about her posture that suggested here was someone else impatient with noise and buffoonery." It was Rachel Horsey, the widow of Keith Horsey who had helped in the delivery of Hazel's child, and who died serving as a stretcher-bearer in the war. Rachel had come to collect her sister and brother, staying on "to help clean up". When he apologizes for her inadvertently being left off the guest list, she laughed in a way which embarrassed him. There's no reason why anyone here should remember her or Keith, she says. "I remember you both," he declared, still a little ruffled. "As a matter of fact I was thinking of Keith only this afternoon," which made her not only surprised but defensive. Why would anyone recall him? "For the same reason as they think occasionally of all the other poor chaps who went west," Simon replies. If that very afternoon Simon had been borderline supercilious to Paul, he is getting some of that treatment from Rachel, which already sounds less than encouraging were they to get married, as they eventually do (314-15).

Neither one has any use for the festivities inside the house, but, Simon tells her, "Ikey would have *thought* the same as we do of that kind of horse play but it wouldn't have prevented him from joining in and outdoing the wildest of them" before going to bed "stone sober" to laugh himself to sleep. Ikey had written him "many letters, fifty-three actually," but he would never have shared them with those "boneheads, The Pair" because one doesn't share things like that, things important to you. When Rachel reached out and caught him by the hand Simon knew she was a kindred spirit, and he disburdens himself to the extent of asking "What's eating the bloody heart out of us? Why is it we can't *be* young and *act* young, like all the others up there." They talk for some time, and there were many things Simon wanted to ask her: "How secure was the recent Labour victory at the polls, how sincere was her avowed contempt for men of whatever political persuasion, and what remedies, if any, she prescribed for the anaemia of Western civilization but at that moment the music stopped and he heard Stephen bawling to him from the terrace" (317-19).

Now that Andy and Stevie have come of age, they intend to get on with the making of money, which is the reason why they invited Uncle Franz to visit the Valley. As Zorndorff has tea with Claire, the twins present their proposition to the Squire.

> "Uncle Franz has asked us to take over his Birmingham Branch," said Andy, rather too bluntly it would seem for his brother's liking for Stevie swung round in protest but was checked by a gesture on the part of Andy, confirming Paul's theory that although Stephen was the more dominant of the two Andy was the brains of the alliance. He said, trying to keep his voice level, "What the devil do you mean? *What* Birmingham branch? And branch of what, for God's sake?" (*Honour*, 321)

Have they already talked it over with both their mother and Simon? "No," admitted Stephen, "we thought of doing so but didn't. It didn't seem fair to involve her in case you blew your top" (322), which showed at least that they had accurately "measured Claire's loyalty." Paul wanted them to "follow on here," but even before he heard Zorndorff's footsteps he knew that "if he had a successor here it would have to be a grandson" though that was hardly likely (323). Franz points out that "those boys are as far away from us as we were from the French Revolution," for which Paul can blame the war if he wants but not the boys.

There being little point in arguing what was already a done deal, Paul asks Zorndorff's advice on another matter. "There are pretty clear signs of another slump setting in," Craddock acknowledges. "Is it likely to be easier or more difficult to ride out than the last one?" Franz answers that unambiguously: "We're heading directly into the worst economic blizzard of our lifetime." What, Paul asks him, is causing the anxiety? "The American Stock-market. You don't still cherish the fiction we're still the financial hub of the world, do you? We're in for a bad time, the whole lot of us." When Zorndorff left in his Daimler, the family "looked like a group of anxious children whose ball has just sailed over an alien fence and were calculating the risks of retrieving it" (323–27).

A characteristic of cultural history in any country is its lack of homogeneity, war being the exception because the whole population faces a single mortal threat together. But war aside, the citizens' attitudes vary depending upon their physical location, mode of employment and other such variables. Zorndorff used the word "blizzard" to describe the Great Depression that was issued in by the stock-market crash. But, says Delderfield,

> the depression that resulted in three million unemployed in Britain, and had most of its cities and great areas of the countryside sick and gasping by 1931, did not visit the Valley as a blizzard, or anything like a blizzard. Instead it crept in from the north and east like a malign, leisurely blight, touching first one family then another, plucking at a farm here, a man there, leaving any number of small, scabrous wounds that were slow to heal and seemed at first unrelated to one another or to hurts such as those caused, say, by the war (328).

The generalizing historian might pass over these unaffected pockets, the less-disrupted areas, in order not to lose the impact of the larger picture by niggling at the edges. But the cultural historian could afford to paint a more complex picture in order not to lose the "shading" which makes for greater precision. Craddock, with a finger on the Valley's pulse, knew in minute detail the condition of the estate in that economic slump but *depression* is too coarse a measure to characterize what Paul observes.

> No single man's care and capital could nourish the Valley, no matter how single-minded and dedicated that man might be. It needed a dozen or more and they were getting fewer as time went on. Some were not being replaced as surely as Arthur Pitts at Hermitage

had been [by Henry] and Edward Derwent, his father-in-law at High Coombe but he had been lucky so far. Of the seven farms only Periwinkle and Four Winds were in rough water, the one because it had always been too small and inadequately staffed, the other because Eveleigh's eldest son had been killed in the war and none of the others seemed interested in carrying on. He stood there in the wet wind making a sort of accounting to the dead man in the lodge [John Rudd]. Prices were atrocious, more and more skilled men were drifting into the towns, hedging and ditching was in arrears because of labour shortage, reliefs and government subsidies were unrealistic, and older men like Henry Pitts and the failing Eveleigh were slow to take to new methods and develop new markets like those for sugar-beet, cereal wheat and peas for canning. If it were not for Paul's policy of keeping rents at a minimum figure, and feeding fresh capital into the estate by way of pedigree livestock, farm machines hired out at nominal rates and free gifts of chemical manure to those who would use it, the estate would have contracted long ago and land would have been sold off to keep what remained in good heart. (*Honour*, 332–33)

An estate teetering economically because of the complex set of factors that Paul has here articulated is not the victim of the general depression, except so far as it exascerbates the estate's intrinsic problems. No wonder that Paul, who was worried about "encirclement" before the depression set in, has even more reason to be concerned now. Shallowford is ripe for picking, i.e., "what the grim Woolf with privy paw/ Daily devours apace", as Milton elsewhere put it.

Of the three Valley weddings that took place during the winter of 1931–32, one occurred in the Registry Office in Manchester, the five-minute yoking wherein Simon married Rachel Eveleigh Horsey. Simon telephoned Paul reluctantly because while Rachel refused to invite her own parents, she insisted that the Squire have a chance to attend (338–39). In a separate letter Rachel explains to Craddock that he's not a rack-renter, and so doesn't "qualify as a landlord in my book", where truths are unambiguously inscribed. "That will do for a preamble," she continues, "now to the grist."

> "Honestly, Mr. Craddock, you've made a real mess of Simon and sometimes I feel it's almost too late to unravel him. I'm going to try, though…Simon has terrific potential—a receptive mind, good reasoning powers, good health, a first-class memory and so on, but what are these worth without *drive* and *purpose* and *direction*. (*Honour*, 344)

Paul should not worry; Rachel will make something of him in the end. For a moment the letter took his breath away "and then the chuckle that had been trying to escape for the last ten minutes emerged as a bellow." For several days he wondered whether to show Claire the letter and decided that he would, handing it over with the preamble "I think you'll enjoy it as much as I did." Claire read what Rachel wrote, "tried to stifle a giggle, then a series of giggles," and at last gave her opinion.

> "Oh dear," she said, laying it down, "poor Simon! All those capitals and underlinings. The Movement! Opposition! The W.E.A.!…See here—she's healthy, Valley-bred and thirty-four. She's been without a man twelve years and if she's an Eveleigh she's no

prude! Along comes Simon, young, good-looking but, what's more important, pliable! Why bless you, she needs him more than he needs her but because of the age gap she has to justify herself! So what does she do? Sets about convincing herself the marriage is near-platonic but you can take it from me that now she's got him she won't address herself exclusively to the task of healing sick society." (*Honour*, 346–48)

Rumble Patrick is not a major character in the novel but, like Hazel, an adjunct or a variation of Ikey, whom he resembles in certain key traits. At this point in time, Rumble has just been politely dismissed from High Wood with the suggestion that his disruptive pranks would do better in some "outpost of the Empire where his originality would have free play among the primitives" (351). Nothing is the matter with Rumble yet it was as though "shortly before his birth, he had been given the rare privilege of assembling his own psychological make-up" from elements found on "both sides of his family."

> He had a broad streak of urchin impudence, the legacy of Ikey's Thames-side forbears and fused with this was the cheerful contempt for authority that had been a characteristic of the Potter clan for generations. This was by no means all. Woven into his character were strands of Ikey's objectiveness, Mother Meg's pride, Old Tamer's cussedness and Smut's initiative, all subject, it would seem, to a belief that every day was April Fool's day. (*Homour*, 349)

As Samuel Johnson once remarked, a few strokes will lop a cedar "but who can elevate a shrub?" Applied to Rumble the quip acknowledges that however disruptive his irrepressible energy had been to High Wood faculty, the boy has a massive potential which boils and festers until the young man takes charge of his own capacities. Paul asks him, what will you do now? He'd like to "get out and about" for a few years, nothing boring like Simon's politics or the twins' business ambitions but "overseas," where he can pick up in Australia and Canada skills, knowledge, different viewpoints and that sort of thing. "So here it was again," Paul thought, "none of them had a particle of affection for the Valley," all of them saw him as an "anachronism, clinging to a way of life" that started withering "as long ago as the summer of 1914." But Paul could not have been more wrong, because the young man would leave the Valley for years then come back, to wed Craddock's daughter Mary, and prove himself the indigenous, authentic energy of the estate which is reinvigorated, even reborn in this apparently feckless young comedian. Before he leaves, Rumble talks with Mary, with whom he has had an "understanding" since the days when she watched him as a toddler. Who would suspect that Rumble has a deep and abiding affection for the Squire, one no less vigorous than Ikey's had been, and he intuits Paul's disappointment, which Mary is never, ever to "pass on, even to your mother or to Simon!" He virtually scolds Mary for insensitivity.

> "Don't you realize what a sickener it was for him? The twins going off like that, and Simon never having the remotest wish to carry on? It was part of his dream that at

least one of them would finish what he started. I imagine that's why he had a family in the first place!"

"Well, even if that were true," she said, and privately thought he was taking far too much for granted, "You could go to Agricultural College and take on the Home Farm in time."

"It wouldn't be the same," he said, shaking his head. "I'm not his son you see, just the byblow of a kid he fished out of the slums and the scattiest of the Potters. We respect one another and he's been more than a father to me. It would be a poor sort of return if I paid him back by horning in ahead of his children! Surely you can understand that, Mar?"

"No I can't!" she said, stubbornly. "For you've just said neither Simon, Steve nor Andy want to stay here and farm. The Valley has never meant a thing to any one of them!"

"They may come round to it, one or other of them, sooner or later", he said, "but they certainly wouldn't if I got my oar in first and staked a claim! Simon is too unselfish and the twins would just use me as an excuse. You must see that, Mar."

Rumble is Ikey's son, for his puckishness and apparent lack of seriousness is the surface appearance concealing what is indeed an immensely sensitive heart—Mary being the single Craddock who realizes that. Rumble Patrick is her man, and he will return to her and the Valley. And being assured of that, she can feel the stress of recent weeks easing, "like the slackening of a cable hitching her to a drag-load of despondency and deprivation" (365-67).

After three decades in the Valley, Paul realizes that "the seasons had their cycles and the years their rhythms." Moreover, the cycles and rhythms of the seasons and years in Shallowford are "a small graph within a larger one that was then caught up in the rhythm of the world outside." The cultural history narrated in the Shallowford trilogy is the counterpoint merging the Valley rhythms with those that activate "the world outside" (368). In the Valley, "just as the bumpy run of 1904 began at Four Winds" with the murder of Arabella and Martin's suicide, "so the 1931 run of bad luck began with an event that left Four Winds masterless and laid open the flank to the west" (369). The strong man at Four Winds, Norman Eveleigh, had his "second stroke" on January 3rd, which worried Paul deeply although it could not have come as a surprise. What did astonish everybody was that Hugh Derwent had surreptitiously sold High Coombe to Sydney Codsall. The ramifications of that foolishly deceitful action were far more serious since High Coombe had been the barrier to further inroads threatening from the east. With these two hammer-blows, Grenfell's visit brought the further bad news that he will die before long, and that the Tories, who will win the next election, are "putting up a local man," the "young speculator called Codsall." "Sydney Codsall? That young bastard?", Craddock wants to know. The same. And when Sydney has been elected he will be in an excellent position to influence decisions about zoning and to approve of forward-looking developments designed to bring new business into the area. The only bit of good news is that Jimmy will stay at Home Farm with them while he completes the book he's working on, taking Simon's old room for his study. It's roomy, and convenient because the retiring Parliament man can "come and go as he pleases by the garden stairs" (337-78).

When election day approached, Paul had "other things to think about" than Shallowford's affairs, because one and all had been "caught up" in the world outside. "The alarm bells of national bankruptcy were ringing in Fleet Street," and even in the Valley people knew there might be a general election *To Give the Government a Mandate for Economy*, in which the emphasis falls on what would be expected of the governed, rather than expected from the governors. A world depression is one thing, national bankruptcy another thing altogether; bankruptcy results from the inadequate policies of public officials, rather than from the tenuous state of the world economy—which at worst had generated the fiscal challenge that had been mismanaged by the elected officials who are responsible for the results. Paul's view of the matter is appropriately jaundiced.

> The men in charge muddled along, bickering one with the other and trying this and that expedient until the machine slithered to a halt. Then, like the feckless head of an improvident household, they announced that there would have to be a cut in house-keeping, sacrifices all round and no more pocket money for anyone. His cynical attitude towards politics, fostered by a decade of agricultural depression, had been deepened by the arrival of Jimmy Grenfell, with the benefit of thirty years' close-range experience of professional politicians. Sentence of death had put a cutting edge on Grenfell's sense of humour and he beguiled some of his sleepless hours in front of the library fire after Claire had gone to bed sketching for Paul a gallery of lively portraits of the shady, the earnest and the pompous with whom he had hobnobbed since he first entered "The Club", as he called it..."I daresay we shall stagger on for another decade or so, but as for finding the right answers, as we believed ourselves capable of doing in 1906, that's just a pipe-dream! The Holy Grail was lost long ago and it's not likely to turn up in Westminster." (*Honour*, 389)

Yet it was Grenfell's thinking that "reminded Paul of his own broadly-based faith in Democracy, a credo that, in his view, offered few fireworks but rather a steady promise of improvement for those dedicated to the ideal of personal liberty practised within a framework of disciplined free enterprise. It was very difficult for him to stand aside altogether and see a man [Codsall] who despised farmers as clod-hoppers seek to represent the Valley," and when Claire blurted, "as they were sitting before the library fire one night," without preamble, "*Do it, Paul. You won't win but do it anyway, as a gesture!*" Run against Sydney Codsall in the up-coming election. Why the sudden change of heart, he asks her. Claire replies "I think Hugh has something to do with it, Hugh and the man who bought him" (391). He runs, and he loses, but narrowly. When the votes are counted,

Sydney had won but by so small a margin that it was nothing to crow about and certainly not so when his massive organization was taken into account. To Paul it was better than a victory, for it meant justification without the horrid necessity of turning his back on the Valley and his relief was so great that he felt almost sorry for his opponent faced with the prospect of making good his electoral promises and discovering, as Grenfell had prophesied, that attendance at Westminster called for a great deal more stamina than the old-pals atmosphere of County and Urban politics in the provinces. Perhaps Sydney already realized this; his formal speech of thanks was delivered in a high, piping voice and interrupted by a volley of catcalls, organised, Paul suspected, by stalwarts like Henry and Smut. (*Honour*, 394)

In their last conversation before Grenfell died under the anaesthetic a day later, Paul thanks Jimmy for having alerted him to events outside the valley, which stopped him from "becoming dangerously parochial". Mary enjoys reading his *History of the English Chartists* in manuscript, finding it "one of the most absorbing books I've ever read." Why, Paul wonders, and his daughter makes the case for cultural history. Grenfell's study is about "The way people lived, the working people and the fight they had. You don't hear about that kind of thing in school history lessons, at least I never did, just kings, battles and treaties". What interests her is that Paul's own father and Grandpa Derwent "must have been alive" then, which makes the past palpable, animated, not-wholly-past. Because what she has just read makes her eager to know more, she asks "Why *did* you come here, Daddy?", a question Paul hadn't asked himself for decades. "Because of a dream I had when I was in hospital after the Boer war but it's far too complicated" to explain now. Another time, he will (434–36).

Claire was astonished and not pleased to find herself pregnant again. She was irritated and depressed, and when a son, John Craddock, was born she was indifferent to the infant. Mary had thought she'd "change" when the newborn arrived, but "she doesn't seem interested" (439–44). Paul makes a feeble joke about calling him "Tail-piece", but she doesn't find it funny. Claire has not lost interest in her life, however. Far from it, for her beautiful and talented sweet-sixteen *daughter* Claire has entered the "Dairy Queen" finals, the contest to select the most fetching young woman to represent the English dairy industry. All the family's women are in a tizzy as Claire beats her competition, then flies away to Holland, to test whether she can become queen of all Europe. When the airplane goes down in the English channel without survivors, her mother, re-living her youth vicariously through the lovely teenager's success, found no comfort. What could console the distraught parent in this circumstance? "A kind of emotional petrifaction checked her tears" since her only comfort was the "confirmation of the disaster." As Claire wonders whether to await Doctor Maureen in the hall,

she had another thought, retracing her steps upstairs, and going along to the nursery. The baby was awake, threshing away with his fat little fists, and as she stared down at him she found herself smiling. She thought, "I wonder why he always struck me as a plain child? He isn't plain, just—comical." She picked him up, carried him downstairs and out on to the terrace, holding him tightly and occasionally brushing his head with her lips." (*Honour*, 470)

The first mention that World War II is looming on the horizon occurs in the midst of the Dairy Queen frenzy, when Simon, in closer touch with European events than his father has leisure to be, points out that "the whole damned lot of us are living on borrowed time." Paul had not taken Hitler seriously, since "tin-pot ranters" such as the Fuehrer and Mussolini are "ninety-five percent blather." But as Simon reminds him, "the Kaiser blathered" as well. Politically, the boy had matured considerably since he had married Rachel.

Two weeks following the Dairy Queen contest disaster, Rumble Patrick surprised Shallowford by reappearing after returning from his travels. Mary came upon him when he was "absorbed in the task of estimating the floor-space" of a room in the small house at Periwinkle farm, which he would soon rebuild. Mary welcomed him by pointing out that "he was a pig to have given her such a shock," Rumble's defense being that his train had not stopped; "It slowed down and I couldn't see the sense of going on to Paxtonbury and hiring a taxi so I jumped for it. We're going to need all I've saved to put this place in order," and he's going to repair the house himself, for that's how they do it abroad. Paul asks, does Rumble intend to "specialize or follow a policy of mixed farming," the general practice in the Valley.

> "That depends entirely on available markets and the growth of Government subsidies," Rumble said. "The canning industry is bound to go on expanding and when it does it might pay to try fruit on the western side. In the meantime I shan't bother with beef or pigs, and if I follow Elinor [Codsall] in the matter of hens you won't catch mine outside of a deep litter! Free-range is old-hat and damned wasteful on farms as small as they are in this country. What do you want for Periwinkle as it stands, Gov? I shall have to make a start right away if I'm to be ready for spring sowing, and there's not so much as a fence in repair over there!"

Paul offers Periwinkle as a wedding present but Rumble does not accept handouts. "Where I've been we don't waste money on builders...we do things ourselves. All I want out of you is your price. And your daughter!" (476–77).

Zorndorff paid his final visit to the Valley shortly before he died at age ninety-three. He had fled Hungary seventy years earlier because his people, the Croats, were at that time a persecuted minority; having recently crossed Germany to visit Hungary, Franz has seen that the Jews are being savagely persecuted, elderly women and young children kept scrubbing the streets by "arrogant young thugs with dog-whips." He returned to England by sea rather than be in Germany again; he would not "even fly over it again." For one last time he gives Craddock expert advice: "Buy all the pedigree stock you can afford and the latest machinery," along with plenty of reserve fuel. In everything possible, "Make yourself as tight and self-contained as Noah," and *do not believe* the reports you will hear about "pacts and arms agreements." Franz having gone, Paul reflects that he sees little evidence that Zorndorff is predicting accurately.

> But then, as he looked up and saw the slender silhouette of French Wood on the skyline, he remembered he had sons and sons-in-law, the eldest thirty-one, the youngest still a boy, and he hurried on, saying, "Christ! Not again! Not after what we endured for four years at the hands of boneheads like Haig!" (*Honour*, 501-08)

Some decades earlier, "the ripples of the world beyond Paxtonbury" didn't touch "the lower reaches of the Sorrel", but that time has passed. It began changing quite abruptly between fall 1935 and the summer of 1936, and Paul was the first to take note that the Valley's previous "dissociation with the world outside" had vanished. Henry Pitts, who was as insular a farmer as the Valley had ever raised, hollered out from his new tractor "I zee that ole varmint be zettin' about 'em niggermen, Maister!," and Paul somehow understood that he was referring to Mussolini's attack on Abyssinia.

Rachel stopped by, and was persuaded to "stay for on a day or two", giving Paul the opportunity to discuss current events with her. Her husband being absent, he asks Rachel "Where is Simon right now?"

> "In Falmouth, unless he's already sailed."
> "Sailed where?"
> "For Spain, as a volunteer."
> "Good God!" Paul exclaimed, deeply shocked. "What the devil made him do a damned silly thing like that?"

Rachel would happily see Paul step in to prevent Simon from going, but there's little chance of that happening. The two of them engage in a prickly conversation rather than an argument, Rachel softening to the point of giving Paul this left-handed compliment: "You might be the odd one who goes the whole way while we short-cutters get lost in the woods." He found it "the most oblique endorsement of his policy that anyone ever stated to his face" (518-22).

Paul is able to locate Simon, but cannot dissuade him from leaving with the International Brigade. Grace's son's testimony is that despite their having lectured England for the past six years, "Capital is more firmly entrenched in Westminster" than ever, while in Germany and Italy at this moment "Anyone with enough guts to oppose racialism and rule-by-rubber-truncheon is shot out of hand or sent to rot behind barbed wire!" Has Paul thought about "the logical outcome of Fascism?" He has, but "insurance against that kind of thing happening here won't be bought by your death in a Spanish ditch!" And he thought "they're only a later edition of the young idiots" who went off to fight Kreuger. Yet "I wish Grace could see him now! He's so very like her in her suffragette days, with the same passionate belief in theory and the same compulsion to put theory to the touch!" (524-25).

Craddock had at first been bemused by the dust raised over the Prince of Wales' "morganatic marriage to Mrs. Simpson." But when Claire accuses him of having a wrong attitude on the subject, Paul gets hot under the collar and observes that everybody loved him when he travelled abroad advertising England, while now, "because he happens to fall for a mature, intelligent woman, everybody suddenly becomes a bloody Sunday School superintendent!" Paul bolted out of the house to his horse, taking out his rage in "a breakneck gallop across the dunes" where he was hailed by Dr. Maureen in her old Morris. Her news took his mind off the troubles of the King: "Hold on there! I've just heard a rumour that will set tongues wagging! Sydney Codsall is flat broke and resigning his seat. Have you heard anything to confirm it?" The story had large elements of truth. Tapscott, the builder, had indeed gone bankrupt but Sydney "had saved his bacon by withdrawing capital before the crash." Yes, it is true that he's resigning his Parliamentary seat, but that was due to "domestic rather than financial difficulties." A private detective had gathered the evidence which hit the newspapers, putting the Sorrel Valley on the front page for the first time since the German ship was wrecked at Tamer's Cove in 1906. One newspaper in particular gave the luridly graphic details by featuring

> a picture of Sydney's alleged mistress and horsefaced wife side by side, under the banner headline, "*M. P. flees Love-Nest by Fire Escape*" and below "*Nude Woman hits Photographer with Table Lamp.*"

With this scandal drawing attention away from the affair of Mrs. Simpson, the royal couple "departed for France almost unnoticed." Not long after, Paul wondered whether Tapscott "would be interested in an offer for what's left of High Coombe?" He would, and the estate recovered part of its earlier loss, its eastern flank becoming relatively secure against builders' encroachments.

> Tapscott was only too eager to sell and before the New Year was a fortnight old the rump of the old Derwent Farm had been repurchased, a parcel consisting of the original farmhouse, some ruinous buildings and about ninety-five acres between the tail-end of Tapscott's bungalows and the north-eastern tip of Shallowford Woods. Paul got it for a song—less than half the price paid to Hugh Derwent by Sydney five years before. (*Honour*, 530)

The most obvious characteristic of the *Avenue* novels is the *de*-centralizing of its characters, such that its two dozen actors go their separate ways so tenaciously that by the second volume, *The Avenue Goes to War*, I was obliged to manage my commentary in terms of drawing-together subplots. In contrast, the Devonshire trilogy is *centralized* upon the single figure of Paul Craddock, whose hospital vision of a war being fought upon the ceiling of his room is contrasted against the pleasant landscape he sees outside the window; the central character and the encompassing theme are fused together inextricably. One can find as wide a variety of characters in the Valley as in the *Avenue* novels, but in Shallowford a solitary character draws together the threads which lead away from him. Paul's reflective interiority is an assimilative force overseeing the action, in contrast to Jim Carver's ruminations, which are starkly personal except to the extent that Harold Godbeer joins him in the task of interpreting England's ramp-up to the Second World War.

It is critical to distinguish between action swirling around Paul, which we have been seeing of late—the Dairy Queen accident, Simon's articulation of youthful commitment to the defense of Spain, Rumble Patrick's bracing return to the Valley, Sydney Codsall's humiliation and the estate's recovery of an eastern-flank buffer—and Paul's reflective interiority, i.e., his intelligible melding of events (and of views-upon-events) within which he is immersed. This is particularly critical *here*, because as *Post of Honour* moves towards closure, what Delderfield has informed us about the cultural history of his time in his essays is dramatized by Craddock's reflections, sometimes complemented by Claire's.

One recalls what Delderfield says of England's painful final attempts to convince itself that Chamberlain's "piece of paper" guaranteed peace, and its subsequent recovery,

> when Churchill took Chamberlain's place and the epic of Dunkirk was followed by the Battle of Britain...People hoped and grinned, people didn't give a damn about standing alone and fighting it out on the beaches. (*Own Amusement*, 227)

As *Post of Honour* moves towards its completion the novelist backs up in time just a bit, to the moment when "the Munich crisis set everybody (including constitutional optimists like Claire, Henry Pitts and Smut Potter) by the ears."

> Their complacency [over Chamberlain's assurances] angered him, although he went out of his way not to show it...His fear now was not so much that there would be a war but that there would not, that he was laying up stock against a day when the Valley lost its identity in an almost bloodless absorption of Western Europe. For that, it would seem, was the alternative that most people preferred, including those he would have classed as rebels in the old society...Winter passed and spring followed and with spring came the pounce on Prague, and after that Mussolini's grab at Albania, and in the confused weeks that followed they began to drift back to him, bringing with them what he most needed, a feeling of unity of purpose and comradeship, that made him feel less a prophet of doom stalking the Valley and muttering of wrath to come. Henry Pitts was the first of the prodigals . . and Harold Codsall was the next...Then Smut, holding forth in the bar of The Raven one night, declar[ing] that "only Squire and his boy" had been right about what would follow Munich and word of this reached Paul the next day by Parson Horsey who confessed, sadly, that sooner or later.... (*Honour*, 540–41)

Claire has surprising news for Paul, "and perhaps you can make sense of it" because she cannot. Their daughters-in-law, Monica and Margie, think their husbands "have gone raving mad! They've joined the Air Force!" (541). That interests Paul since now he can discuss the situation with his wife, who is beginning to concede the likelihood of the impending war. Claire opens their conversation:

"You sound very cheerful about it," she said, and he replied that he was, in spite of all it might mean, for even a war was better than watching Europe taken over piecemeal and half the world enslaved without so much as a whimper on the part of the victims.

"You never used to think like that, Paul. You were always utterly opposed to war, even when everyone about here was war-crazy in 1914."

"It was quite different then," he said, "and it amazes me that everybody doesn't *see* it's different! I still think the last war was an act of madness of everybody's part––certainly continuing it after 1916 was––but there's simply no other way of containing that bunch of psychopaths. They haven't a damn thing in common with the Kaiser's bunch. Losing to Germany in '14 or '15 would have been bad but if we'd agreed to a patched-up peace after a year or so, it would have all been forgotten by now!" He leaned forward, earnestly, and she was impressed by the note of pleading in his voice. "Tell me, Claire, tell me honestly, do *you* think I'm a nervous old maid laying in all these stocks and building that fuel-storage tank? If you do then for God's sake say so and give me a chance to convince you!"

She said, quietly, "No, I think you know what you're doing, Paul. I think you always know what you're doing if it concerns the Valley."

"You've been in a minority of two then," he said, but with relief in his voice. "Only Smut's [French] wife, old Marie, encouraged me at the time. You didn't! Why didn't you?"

"Why didn't I what?"

"Back me up, tell me I was right. I would have appreciated it."

She said, levelly, "You show me any woman about here with sons who is ready to admit, even to herself, to the prospect of seeing them face what you faced last time, or the possibility of suffering what wives and mothers like me and Marian Eveleigh and Elinor Codsall suffered all the time you were out there. No Paul, you don't bring it into the open, you go on pretending it's a bad dream that will fade out as soon as it's light! That's what I've been doing ever since Simon went off to fight in Spain."

He pondered her confession, finding it not only human but logical. One was so apt to think of war as a man's business whereas, of course, it was not and involved everybody one way or another, not because the methods of waging war had changed with the introduction of bombers but because feather-distributing women [humiliating cowards who would not fight] of Gloria Pitts' type were rare. The majority, the Claires, the Marians and the Elinors of this world, seldom came forward to claim their fair share of the misery when their menfolk were lying out in mud under a barrage, or were home again, flaunting their medals and heroism. Usually, as in Claire's case, they kept their thoughts and misgivings to themselves, and tried to look interested when they had to listen to stories of blood and privation. This was the first time in twenty years he had ever given a thought to all she must have suffered during the period he had been in France. Was it any different in any other home in the Valley? He said, gently, "You should have told me that before, Claire, but I'm glad it popped out!" and suddenly she was on the rug beside him with her arms round his knees, as though interposing herself between him and the pointing finger of Kitchener in 1914. "You won't go again, Paul! You wouldn't? I couldn't face that time again, no matter what!" and he said, stroking her hair, "Good heavens, no, I shan't go! How could I at my age? Besides, if it does come there will be more than enough to do right here, I can tell you." She nodded, eagerly, and he thought it strange that his reassurance, which did not include immunity for Simon, Stevie, Andy or her two sons-in-law, Ian and Rumble, should bring her such immediate comfort. Then he remembered what Maureen had said, what he himself had always suspected. She didn't give a damn about her children now they were grown and dispersed. All her adult life her eggs had been in one basket. (*Honour*, 542-44)

Post of Honour's concluding chapter opens in the early hours of May 31ˢᵗ, 1940, the midst of the Dunkirk evacuation from May 16ᵗʰ to June 4ᵗʰ. Paul and his companions are guarding their beach as members of Churchill's L.D.V.s, or "Lame-Duck-Vagabonds as Henry designated the Local Defence Volunteers." They are enjoying the comradeship which that impossible task fostered. The "alchemy of Churchill" and "the whiff of Gestapo breath in our nostrils," Delderfield wrote as a cultural-historical essayist, raised everyone's spirits. "It was as though we had not survived a chain of frightful disasters, but had won a brilliant victory and in a way, I suppose, we had" (*Amusement*, 227). *Honour*'s final chapter does present some dramatic dialogue between various characters, but the chapter's weight devolves upon Paul's silent ruminations. He is the central character drawing together the threads leading away from him, as I described it earlier. His reflective interiority is an *assimilative* force overseeing the action, and what he sees in his mind's eye is the substance of the concluding chapter, except for enough interpersonal dialogue to maintain readers' interest in the Valley's people.

Riding past "the bizarre structure that was now known as 'The Fort,'" really "a café, idiotically disguised as a pillbox" of the kind wherein so many died at Passchendaele, Craddock reflected upon "the contradictions" of the English people.

> As he rode along the last stretch of beach Paul found himself pondering the curious contradictions of the British race, indolent to the point of national suicide in the face of so many stark warnings, and then, given a lead from Westminster, in such a hurry to make up for lost time that they became eager victims of ten thousand bureaucrats. Two months ago, apart from the tiresome (and to Paul, useless blackout), no one could have supposed the country committed to war. Today the entire countryside was in an uproar, with signposts torn down, the names removed from such tiny stations as Sorrel Halt, tank-traps showing their teeth all the way to Paxtonbury, sandbars covered by a *chevaux de frise* of tubular ironwork, and finally, this absurd little sea-front cafe disguised as a pillbox! And in a way everyone seemed to be enjoying themselves hugely, as though it was a vast relief to face the prospect of meeting heavy tanks and dive-bombers with a few rabbit-guns and petrol bombs made out of ginger-beer bottles. It was commendable, perhaps, this illogical upsurge of defiance, but it was also pitiful. A people who had survived the Somme and third Ypres should be waging total war with a better prospect of winning it. (*Honour*, 559-60)

Francis Willoughby was at the coastguard hut, his lookout post, where he was "sunning himself" alongside "'Bon-Bon', Smut's only child by his French wife, brewing tea on an open fire. The boy seemed glad of Paul's arrival as a break in the

monotony of the long watch," and a stretch of dialogue between them returns us
to the activities on the beach which arouse and justify Paul's interior reflections.

> The bird chorus was deafening and behind it, like the wash of a distant sea, he could
> hear the summer insect murmur, always audible about here whenever the temperature
> rose above the sixties. As he rode he looked about him sharply, noting the great banks
> of foxgloves that grew in the clearings and the last of the bluebell drifts under the
> trees. Suppose they were not playing soldiers? Suppose, on a morning like this, next
> week or the week after, German parachutists should crash into this cover and Panzers
> storm ashore to batter the Coombe Bay cob and thatch into rubble? He forced him-
> self to review the possibility. Where would they run and what would become of them?
> How and where could the enemy be stopped or even checked? There was no kind of
> precedent for such a calamity. Men of the Valley had gone out to fight in wars over the
> last thousand years but no fields and woods nearer than Normandy had been their
> battlegrounds, if one excepted the local brawls, like the Wars of the Roses, the Great
> Rebellion, and Monmouth's sorry venture in the west. There was, he supposed, some
> kind of parallel here. Getting on for three hundred years ago Jeffreys and Colonel Kirke
> had ridden into Paxtonbury, with their summary justice and hangman's ropes, but today
> a far worse threat hovered over every man, woman and child living hereabouts. The
> Bloody Assizes had been a very short-lived tyranny, whereas Hitler and his Nazis prom-
> ised to establish themselves for all time and boasted of a Reich that would last a thou-
> sand years! Nobody, not even the most optimistic in the Valley, had any illusions as to
> the kind of future that faced them if the Nazis did establish a permanent bridgehead.
> There would, no doubt, be murder and rape and pillage, on a scale that had not been
> practised in civilized countries since the Thirty Years War. And as he thought this and
> dropped down the last terrace to the mereside track, the heat went out of the sun and
> he shivered, finding the entire situation too terrible to contemplate. One would fight,
> he supposed, fight with shot-gun, Service revolver and pitchfork, with Molotov cock-
> tails and brickbats, but what would it avail in the end? Up in Westminster Churchill
> was breathing fire and slaughter and undoubtedly people had taken heart from his
> words, but who among them had heard Winston's ironic aside after making his famous
> fight-on-the-beaches oration? Paul had, having passed the time of day with the local
> M.P. when he went into Paxtonbury to buy ammunition a week since. The Member
> had been close to Churchill when he sat down and claimed to have heard him say, in
> that curious, slurred growl of his, 'I don't know what we'll fight with—bloody axes and
> pick-handles, I imagine!'" (*Honour*, 564–65)

Of the novel's five chief characters, two of them are dead, Ikey Palfrey and
James Grenfell, leaving Paul, Simon and Claire to conclude the novel. Paul having
had his say, we will focus briefly upon Simon, safely home from Dunkirk, and conclude with Claire's love song to her husband. Back from the beach and ready for
breakfast, Paul went into the hall to answer the phone. When he lifted the receiver
"his heart began to hammer and his eyes misted a little," and he said, breathlessly,

> "*Simon!* It's really you! You're…you're home and dry, lad?"
> "Not so dry!," Simon said, "but home okay! I'm ringing from near Folkestone. I
> got in during the night. Pretty well the last of 'em I'd say!"

"God, but I'm glad to hear from you!" Paul said, fumbling for a cigarette to steady himself. "What happened? How did you make it?"

"Too long a yarn to spin from a public call-box but the bare bones aren't so remarkable. I just walked into the bloody sea and swam for it!"

"You're joking!"

"No, I'm not!" He heard Simon smother a chuckle. "I could see 'em mopping up along the beaches, north of Calais, so as it was every man for himself I stripped off and struck out. I was damned lucky, mind, I not only found an empty oil-drum a mile or so out but I was sighted by a destroyer late in the afternoon. That's why I've been so long getting in; they only docked last night!"

"You're...you're quite fit!"

"Fit as a fiddle! They gave me lashings of Navy rum on board and I don't think I've sobered up yet. We're getting nine days survival leave. Tell Rachel I'll be down some time during the next forty-eight hours. Look, I can't stop, Gov, there's a queue outside...see you soon!" and the line went dead. (*Honour*, 567)

Finally, Claire, who gets and deserves the last word, since she has been "loading for" her husband for decades while he struggled to succeed in the Valley.

He might, she reflected, have been a very rich man and he was not, had never wanted to be, for all the money he had ever had had been poured into these acres and dribbled away without a sigh on his part, and he was not even rich in kind, for most of it had gone to those whose lives, in a sense, he had held in trust over the years. And yet, she decided, it was not his generosity that made him the acknowledged leader here but his terrible earnestness, his sense of purpose and dedication that only today was finding wider expression from one end of the country to the other. Realizing this, and identifying his steadfastness with the national mood in the face of final disaster, she decided something else about him that was both old and new. He had been right all the time, every moment of his working life, since he had first ridden into the Valley when she was a girl of nineteen. He had, as it were, selected a target that most men of his means and single-mindedness would have regarded as far too modest, but whereas the big-game hunters had missed he had scored a succession of bull's-eyes and was still scoring. It gave her a queer sense of pride to realise that, over most of the time, she had been loading for him. He had prescience but also a kind of innocence. The one had enabled him to evaluate soil and comradeship in excess of everything else that touched his life and the other had matured him as a human being and brother to whom everyone about here turned, in good times and bad, for advice, steadfastness and friendship. In a way he was the antithesis of the spirit of the century, of the dismal trends of laissez-faire, usury and triviality that had led, after all, to another global calamity and yet he had never lost a certain modesty that some mistook for naivety, forgetting that, under his seeming mildness was a core of proofed steel. Perhaps she was the only person in the world who was fully aware of this, having seen it tempered over the years but there were still plenty who thought of him as an anachronism, a reactionary, a benevolent autocrat or a genial soft touch but she knew otherwise. He was all these things on the surface but primarily he was a man of faith and a romantic, whose fibres were far tougher and more weatherproof than the fibres of professional adventurers and men in counting-houses, if only because, by now, they probed so deeply into Valley soil. There was enormous strength here, and abundant tenderness. There was virility, at sixty-one, that still retained the power to make her wilt and there was also self-assurance equal to all the stresses of peace and war, change and catastrophe. A woman who troubled herself to understand and appreciate this would always be safe with him; safe, satisfied and grateful for the hand she had been dealt.

She went to the window, remembering how she had stood on this same spot through the long afternoons watching him recover from his tremendous exertions after the wreck in the Cove. Thirty-three years with the same man, and she could still feel about him as she had felt the day he rode over that hill where the south-easterly tongue of the woods melted into the tip of the sloping meadow running down the near side of the Coombe. It was something to be thankful for. She went out, softly closing the door, leaving him to whatever dreams he had. They must have been rewarding. He was smiling slightly as he slept. (*Honour*, 572-73)

Part III: *The Green Gauntlet*

The Green Gauntlet extends the story which had seemed well-ended by *Post of Honour*. Claire's body represents the fertile Shallowford valley, a symbol of that sceptered isle of kings among whom her husband deserves to be numbered. Claire's love-song to Paul, which had concluded the second volume, celebrates what Shallowford's squire represents at a time when England is accepting the task of resisting the Gestapo and rallying the world, which his tenants along with the rest of England had been slow to embrace. His "sense of purpose and dedication that only today was finding wider expression from one end of the country to another" is, as Claire puts it, "the antithesis of the spirit of the century"—a selfish spirit which had led to "another global calamity" (*Honour*, 572-73). And yet, "the world that had tried so unavailingly to resolve itself into the older pattern" (*Honour*, 544) is not easily changed into something better, and *Gauntlet* dramatizes not simply the apparent defeat of the old pattern but the incipient dryrot of the subsequent societal direction, which is not so very different from that of its predecessor and is infected by the same "spirit."

The third novel of the trilogy begins in February of 1942, as a tired and angry Paul reflects upon the German hit-and-run raid that has killed another two tenants, while the "deadly game" being played throughout the world and the drift of events that it signifies continue to destroy "the pattern of order and progressive change" to which he has dedicated his life (*Gauntlet*, 21). *The Green Gauntlet* continues to explore from the 1940s into the mid-1960s that drift of events by which civilization is constantly being threatened, though it concludes with a celebration of its staying power, i.e., civilization's resilience in the face of its enemies. Whereas *Honour* ends with Claire's private ruminations upon her husband's efforts, *Gauntlet* concludes with a public event, Churchill's funeral, with its cortege mounting the steps towards the Cathedral's slowly-opening doors, through which world-leaders who have survived will enter. Churchill's funeral is "the finale of an epoch that no film producer" could adequately characterize.

> It was as though, in that moment of time, a century of human experience peculiar to these islands and to the people standing about him [i.e., Paul, watching the funeral], was being taken out of the stream of history and stored away with all the other experiences assembled in that place, the Great Fire, the Duke of Wellington, Trafalgar, the Jubilees, and the latest of them, the fire-blitz of 1941 when, on a rare visit to London, he had made his way here and seen the enormous bulk of St. Paul's standing almost alone amid acres of blackened rubble. His taxi-driver, equally impressed, had said, "Marvellous, ain't it? Bloody marvellous," and that, he thought, was as good an estimate as any. It was marvellous. Bloody marvellous! Every last aspect of it, all the way from a cavalry charge at Omdurman to St. Paul's. (Gauntlet, 493–94)

Churchill's funeral is history, the taxi driver's remark is *cultural* history, and that is the arena where Delderfield's characters play their parts, for unless the past be brought into mind, recollected and reanimated, it will slide out of human memory leaving us less human for having forgotten.

The trilogy's closing novel is structured differently from the earlier two, both of which consist of untitled chapters which follow, in chronological order, events which are essentially continuous. *Gauntlet* is different, because while its layout remains chronological, the text is broken into two titled sections, "The Beleaguered," which covers the two-year period from early 1942 to the Normandy landing in 1944 and consumes two-thirds of the novel's textual space, and "Conditional Surrender," the concluding third, which covers the twenty-year span from V.E. Day in 1945 to Paul's 86th birthday in the mid-1960s. The lack of symmetry between the two parts, both in time covered and in textual space consumed, is not accidental. To put it very briefly, "The Beleaguered" narrates accidents of war and its effects upon Valley people, while "Conditional Surrender" addresses Paul's betrayal by some members of his own family, while exploring the best deal that can be cut with the conditions of the time in a land still as much governed by the profit motive as it had been in Zorndorff's scrap metal yard.

The chief characters in *The Green Gauntlet* are Paul, Claire, Simon and Andy Craddock, with "honorable mention" going to young John, who while not a pivotal player will be essential for the continuity Paul hopes to achieve. John will carry forward what his parents have begun, but not as Shallowford's squire. Rumble Patrick, while not negligible in the action, drops back into a secondary role, smoothly effected by his being active in the Merchant Marine and for the most part absent from the Valley. "The Beleaguered" consists of thirteen relatively brief narratives, episodes similar to short stories in their stand-alone independence, although they share a loose thematic harmony which makes them comfortable in their adjacency. Some are serious, a few others provide comic relief in wartime. The important exception to stand-alone narrative independence is Claire's secret mission to fix an emergent family problem, which she accomplishes in episodes 7 through 10. Stevie's ambitious wife abandons him since he refuses to leave the R.A.F. for a cushy civilian job she has lined up for him, but Stevie is comforted by Andy's distraught wife Margie, who bears his child at the moment Andy proves not to have died in the fighter-plane crash that partially crippled him, while his twin brother Stevie dies landing his crippled Lancaster to save its wounded rear-gunner. Having assimilated the whole situation, Claire's challenge becomes how to tell Paul what has happened and explain how it has all been for the best. Her expertise in dealing with the complicated mess goes far towards making her one of *The Gauntlet's* chief characters.

Hit and run

Paul is 62 years old and unable to do anything helpful when Harold Eveleigh and Rachel Craddock, Simon's wife, are killed by two of the bombs the Germans' planes dropped on the Valley. Lacking anything purposeful, he visits "his favorite spot on the estate," French Wood, where he has a clear view of the whole Valley. The biggest change is the Army camp spread across Blackberry Moor, like "an enormous chicken farm" with rows and rows of identical huts. He reflects that, were the camp removed, foxhunting on the land would not be wise, for the site is "a labyrinth of hidden drains, slit trenches and coils of barbed wire," very bad for horses and their riders.

> The vast camp [was] a permanent reminder that freewill had blown away with the piece of paper that well-meaning ass Chamberlain had flourished after the Munich debacle. That was how it had seemed for a long time now and even the reckless mood of 1940 had departed, leaving a vacuum filled with glumness, boredom and worry. (*Gauntlet*, 24–5)

His family was scattered, there was no continuity, and that was what Paul had "striven for" during his forty years in Shallowford (26).

Craddocks at war

The emphasis in this narrative-and-dialogue segment is the next generation of Craddocks, i.e., Simon; Steve and his wife Monica; Steve and his brother's wife Margie; and (briefly) Andy. Of Paul's seven children, five are off-the-table one way or another. Whiz lives far away and is a stuffy prig whose occasional letters announce the birth of another grandchild so condescendingly that her parents smile reading her stiffly-formal sentences. Claire the Dairy Queen champion lies at the bottom of the English Channel. At eight years old, John is hardly a factor yet. While Mary is a lovely girl, she is modestly recessive and busy raising her own family. Steven is currently living, but will soon have been heroically killed-in-action.

Simon "disappeared into the murk of the Northcountry after a number of false starts in life," but he is the best of the lot and continues to develop as the decades pass and experiences enrich his understanding. At the moment, Simon thinks Paul and Claire are "pleasant anachronisms" with "no meaningful place in the structure of Western civilization" (34–5). When Rachel is killed by the hit-and-run bomb, he is not sorrowful. Marriage had made them "partners" in the quest for "progress, social justice, self-determination for minorities" and like abstractions. When Simon asks himself "Had there ever been any ecstacy?", the correct answer is "no". Then "on September 3rd, 1939," Rachel had "turned her face to the wall." She was killed at Periwinkle farm while washing eggs (38–9).

The Monica-and-Steve argument which ended in Monica's leaving him (42–50), and the Steve-and-Margy illicit affair (53–68), need not be examined in detail because a single block quotation summarizes the inter-relationships between these married couples—and does so more pungently and more economically than a tedious walk-through of the situation.

> Andy was bewitched by the droll little Welsh girl [Margie]. [Monica] got used to her, however, for Andy had seen to that and so, in a less direct way, had Stephen himself, for he had never underestimated the value of her cheerfulness that offset, to a great extent, Monica's starchiness and Andy's occasional sulks. Until now he had never thought of her as anything more than a woman who was pretty and companionable, and he realised that this was because, without actually giving offence, Monica had always contrived to downgrade her into the shop-girl class. (*Gauntlet*, 50).

As for Andy himself, the fighter pilot assigned to the African desert, home "belonged in the past." Home meant "contracts and bargaining" and "second-rate espionage waged from behind desks and over the telephone." But now, as he flew his fighter "into the sun," searching the vast desert wasteland for targets, all that could not satisfy him. He still hungered to find "outlets for his explosive energy and technical know-how" while still young enough to "profit by it" (71).

Garrison duty

By midsummer Paul had absorbed Rumble Patrick's "desertion from the Valley garrison." The house he rebuilt at Periwinkle having been bombed into blackened rubble, Rumble's thoughts turned to military service, which distressed Paul since his Valley allies were thinning out. Meanwhile, Smut Potter, seconded by "his avaricious French wife, Marie," were in league with Jumbo Bellchamber in the Dell, the clearing house for the local black market, which was an expression of the atmosphere of "let's-see-what-we-can-make-out-of-the-damned-war" in Shallowford, which did not augur well for "post-war trends". Yet here was Rumble putting the future at risk by trading "the continuity of a way of life" in exchange for a single soldier in the field (76–80). The two men, the tenant and his father-in-law, discuss that decision, Rumble explaining why the argument for military service trumps "staying". Rumble begins the discussion.

"There were only four of us who ever made a cult out of this place and two of those are dead. That leaves you and me."

"Isn't that an argument for staying?"

"No, it isn't," Rumble said, with an emphasis Paul never heard him use in the past, "because the Valley will tick over so long as you're alive and Claire and Mary are around to back you, but the *idea* of it—everything it has been, is, and will be—needs fighting for and by fighting I don't mean loading guns for other people to fire. I don't see this business as one war, I see it as three. One for stopping the bloody lunatic putting the clock back, one for preserving national independence, and the other—the one that's vital to you and me—a war to stop the local patterns changing so drastically that it won't be the same place any more, not even after we've beaten Jerry. Sure I could stay on as your lodger, and move back into Periwinkle the moment it had a new roof on it, but afterwards it wouldn't be the same, don't you see? It would belong to people like Simon and Andy and Stevie, all those Marines up on the hill, people who risked their lives defending it. Me? I should have pawned it for the duration and have it handed back to me as a gesture. It wouldn't work, Gov'nor, not for me, and not really for you if you're honest.

He was beaten and he knew it...this had nothing to do with Rumble's present decision...It's source was older and one deeply buried in his being, the boy's logic was the nag of a wound received half-a-lifetime ago, the bitterness of having sired four sons and seen three of them grow to manhood without giving a damn what happened to the stones and trees and red clay of this corner of the West where each of them had been born and raised. Alone among all the children who had lived in this house since Simon's birth, in January 1904, Rumble Patrick, son of a Thameside urchin and the postscript of Gypsy Meg Potter, both understood and cherished his mystical love of the Valley, and here he was putting into words what Paul himself could never have spoken. (*Gauntlet*, 84-5)

When he leaves home, having "signed for a Canadian ship as gunner's mate," Rumble asks a favor of Paul. Show Mary the secret place near the Badger Slope where Hazel Potter had given birth to him—an exhalation from the Valley's heart, an incarnation of the spirit that is indifferent to black market profit-seeking.

Birth of a legend

The first of the comic relief sections, begins as a terrifying situation which resolves itself into high comedy when Henry Pitts, Claire, and young John work together to defeat the threat posed by the daring escaped prisoner Otto von Shratt, a U-boat commander whose submarine had been sunk though he had survived. Shratt was "not only a dedicated Nazi, fed and nurtured on the theory and practice of Teutonic supremacy," but a man who realized that starving Britain to death was the best way to win the war. "No country could hope to replace an annual shipping loss of upwards of three million tons." If U-boat captains like himself attended to their duty, "Winston Churchill would be in the mood to agree to a truce in the West in order that Germany could eliminate Russia," after which the task of polishing off Britain and America would be simple. Shratt looks forward to commanding one of Germany's "most up-to-date U-boats" and having his picture in the papers (99–105). First though, he must return to the Fatherland.

But Shratt's intention was thwarted by the unlikeliest residents of the Shallowford Valley in a sequence of events constituting the plot of a comedy. "It had, in retrospect, an almost classic form in that its cast included not only a hero-clown, a heroine, and a cleanshaven Victorian villain, but a maltreated child plus any number of walk-on parts, most of them armed to the teeth." Those walk-ons were all the other farmers who were creeping systematically through the woods looking for the escapee, "holed up" nearby Hazel Potter's little house. Now Henry had turned aside from the hunt to fortify himself for the effort by sampling Sam's cider barrel, which required that he unhitch a gate, an operation that demanded briefly setting down his .22 rifle. But when he reached for the gun a minute later it was gone. Having acquired the rifle, an excellent intimidation tool, Shratt made towards the big house, imagining himself being driven the length of England by cowed civilians whom he could jettison in lonely stretches of country as he stayed ahead of the hounds. Moving fast, he got inside the house, ripping out the telephone, taking John hostage, and leaving in the Craddock's bull-nosed Morris, with John behind the wheel as Shratt rode shotgun. But his plan did not take into account the deer rifle that Claire had given Paul for his sixty-first birthday, a weapon which she knew how to load, and aim, and *fire* if her youngest son was in danger. John looked blank as his mother watched him out the window,

> but his expression must have deceived both Claire and Shratt for when the car was reversing, and the German's head was turned, he suddenly jerked himself upright and half-projected himself over the edge of the nearside door. The German reacted very quickly. Lifting his left hand from the wheel he struck the boy's cheek with his open palm and the sound of the impact, and the cry that followed it, reached Claire where she stood with her nose pressed to the pane. (*Gauntlet*, 115)

A "kind of demoniac pleasure" took hold of Claire as she remembered that deer rifle, loaded it with I-mean-business cartridges, and began peppering the car, jamming the rifle barrel through the window-glass and blowing out one of the tires—the Morris lurching, John scrambling out then and ducking to safety as the German "bobbed up from the offside of the car," he too unhurt, glaring at Henry as he reached into the debris for the rifle. But not quickly enough, for Henry, armed with the "massive, six-foot pitchfork, with curved wooden prongs" he had snatched up on his way towards the crime scene let fly with the impromptu weapon, "hurling it across the width of the drive with the full strength of his arm," heightened with indignation fired by Sam's cider barrel. "The prongs enclosed Shratt's neck just as he was gathering himself for a leap," knocking him head over heels into Maureen Rudd's delphiniums. Says Delderfield in his capacity as a military historian, von Shratt was "the first man brought down by a javelin hereabout for more than a thousand years" (121-22). The incident was memorialized by "some Shallowford jester with a sense of occasion but no particular regard for accuracy."

> Jerry came to Shallowford
> Us woulden let un pass
> Us stuck a wooden pitchfork
> Right up his arse.

Paul had lamented the loss of the tribal instinct in the Valley, but it clearly persists, and shows itself whenever the chips are down and communal action is required.

Tour of inspection

Tour of inspection transitions from John-the-Morris-driver to John-the-intellectual-omnivore. He is interested in everything, his eventual problem being to decide which of his many interests to select as his calling. The choice is crucial for the Valley's survival, because after he has become a TV professional John produces a documentary, using aerial footage of the Shallowford estate which reveals that it is shaped like a left-handed gauntlet—a TV documentary that throws down the gauntlet against the depredations of profit-hungry land developers. John's strongest talent is his assimilative capacity, his genius for understanding not only the details of butterfly wings but the implications of the Camp sentry's cap badge, which "dropped off his beret" and lay on the ground "shining like a silver star" just as the eyes-forward sentry was about to step on it, while the officers approached to warn John "You can't take pictures here!" John side-kicks the badge towards the soldier, who deftly snatches it up and puts it in place, the two of them quietly enjoying the joke together while military superiors suppose that they have had an appropriate boys-will-be-boys laugh on John: "Run along then, there's a war on" they say, to which the boy answers deferentially "Yes, sir." He left the moor "having crossed yet another profession off the list, for who, in his senses, would want to be at the mercy of little tin badges and superiors who indulged in Second Form jokes?"

> It was not even worth the glory of dying on a bloodstained cloak like General Wolfe and whispering "Thank God" when the aide-de-camp cried "They run, sir! They run!" (*Gauntlet*, 134)

Ration party

Ration party, the other comic section of the novel's first half, dramatizes Smut's foiling of Constable Voysey's efforts to arrest the pivotal members of the Valley's black market organization. Voysey knows that Smut Potter, his wife Marie, and Jumbo Bellchamber are "the big fish" of the operation, which reached across the estate "through farms and cottages, to the cold storage rooms of innumerable retailers extracting a steady profit from their regular peace-time customers." But for all his efforts, Voysey has landed only the occasional customer, the bigger pike being beyond his reach. The survivors of one war, Smut and Jumbo "saw nothing unpatriotic in making a modest profit out of another," emphasizing the service they were providing their neighbors through their cat-and-mouse contest with Voysey. They defended their own corruption, persuading themselves that supplying food to English families "surely stiffened their determination and might even encourage them to launch a Second Front" more quickly (142–43). While Voysey knows that they are laughing at *him*, the only man who recognizes the *damage* the black market does to the community is Paul. As in the last war, he reflects, once again fortunes were being amassed by men "who continued to think of themselves as patriots and by these standards the trickle of food that left the Valley by unauthorized routes was hardly worth a thought," though in fact they are "seedy rascals cashing in on the U-boat campaign" (145). While this illicit trading continues, the intellectual honesty of calling corruption by its right name, instead of cracking jokes to justify the practice, remains out of reach. The black market parodies the common good which it weakens by its insidious dryrot. In his heart Smut understands that, though Bellchamber is permanently blinded to moral truth by self-absorption.

Paul is sufficiently discouraged to accept what he is unable to change. "If I'm honest I suppose I don't give a damn what they do so long as they aren't caught red-handed and front-paged" (146), he tells himself, which they very nearly are. Voysey, lying in ambush to nab the rascals, is already savouring a "magisterial commendation when the case came to court." But Smut's "poacher's instinct", a "sixth sense inherent in all the Potters, whose ancestors had taken deer from Norman overlords hereabouts as far back as the twelfth century," saves their bacon. He tells Jumbo to stay with the truck while he reconnoiters to guarantee that their coast is clear: "If I whistle turn the van and we'll double back to Henry's", and in the nick of time the big fish disappear again (147–48). The three of them decide that the Christmas feast will be flushed out to sea, though Jumbo is horrified by the waste. Bellchamber is "a bliddy vorriner", Henry explains, and cannot understand what bad publicity would do to Craddock. Says Henry,

> "I don't give a tinker's curse wot folks say o' me but Squire's been on to us zame as he has you and Jumbo, and it doan zeem right somehow to mix him in with it. Takin' one thing with another I reckon we'd best cut our losses an dump it, [because] ever zince he came here as a townee he's stood by us. Smut'll vouch for that, Jumbo, if you need tellin' that is." (*Gauntlet*, 151)

Two days later, "soggy bundles" lay all along the tideline west of Sorrel outfall, and "word was passed around that there had been a U-boat sinking far out to sea". Craddock, hearing the rumor, "asked around but nobody could give him accurate information, not even his oldest friend, Henry Pitts." All Henry would say was, "Well, zeeing they'm geese an' chicken, Squire, tiz clear enough they came off a ship outalong but us didden 'ear no gunvire did us?" (153–54). Knowing Henry's "wry sense of humour," Paul kept his doubts to himself. Once again the Valley's communal spirit rises when it must.

Survival

Survival opens with the brief, idyllic domestic life that Steve and Margie share at the Welsh cottage she bought for them, *"Ty-Bach," "The Little House"* as Margie explains. When Stephen asks "Where did we go wrong?" Margaret replies "In telling ourselves that all that rushing around and money-making was fun. Happiness is stillness, and putting down roots and taking stock." While they stayed at Ty-Bach there was no urgency about their love-making nor any guilt. But when Steve phones the airbase on the chance that he may be recalled from leave, he is told that Andy is "missing," which sets him to wondering whether there ever was "such a grotesque obligation" as "telling a twin-brother's wife who was also a mistress that she was now a widow." They don't *know* that, but they need to find out, because "I'm having your child in less than seven months" (159–65). What is to be done? Margie will travel to Shallowford and tell Claire everything. Couldn't she telephone? No, for "I could tell Claire everything but not over the telephone" (167). Thus the couple separate, Stevie going back to base to fly his final mission as a Lancaster pilot, Margie to begin finding a place for herself in their extended family.

Andy has been brought from the crash-site to Tunis by Arabs, his left hand amputated above the wrist, his face repaired sufficiently to "not frighten kids in the street" (171–72). During his hospital convalescence, Andy became acquainted with Shawcrosse, "who boasted that he would find a way of making his artificial leg show a profit in Civvy Street and skim the cream from the post-war property boom as soon as he got back to his North London estate agency." In Shawcrosse, Andy finds a man after his own heart, whose "ruthlessness and ingenuity and singlemindedness would make him a hard man to beat." The population explosion and post-war expansion would make Shawcrosse a millionaire, and Andy, wanting to be a part of that expansion, offers to put his scrap-yard profits at the disposal of this rising-star, particularly since Shallowford will need some upgrading to satisfy the requirements of post-war England.

Long range salvo

Long range salvo narrates the exchange between Paul and Simon, home on a nine-day leave and seeming healthier than Paul remembered him looking in years. They saddle up and ride the estate together, Paul interpreting his sense of humour as representing "a growth of tolerance" in Simon. Paul answered his questions, observing that "this was the first time" any one of his sons "had shown even a passing interest in his life's work." Simon said with a chuckle,

> "Well, Gov'nor, we all used to snigger at you and your medieval villeins down here, but the laugh was on us after all. I'm taking you more seriously from now on."
>
> "Ah yes," Paul said, unable to resist a sly backhander. "I daresay you are, but you'll want all land nationalized after the war and chaps like me booted off to make room for civil servants!"

"No I won't," Simon said, unexpectedly, "I'm mellowing. We all wasted time and energy slanging one another through the 'twenties and 'thirties. In the end what happened? We had to form a Coalition and it worked a lot better than I hoped. The fact is, I suppose we ought to be grateful to that little bastard and his gang of psychopaths. At least he succeeded in uniting Left, Right and Centre. (*Gauntlet*, 183–84)

They talk easily of one thing and another, and when they finish their ride together what strikes Paul most of all is the form of address Simon used. The Valley will keep, he had said, "so long as you're around, Dad, and that's what is important to me". Not Gov'nor, that "semi-ironic term every one of them but Mary used," but the familiar term for father. Clearly, Paul muses to himself himself, "Something *has* happened to him" (186).

On the fourth day of his leave, Simon, having gone to the beach where Claire taught him to swim, encounters the Parson's niece, Evelyn Horsey, Evie, and asks her to marry him, but not at the moment because there isn't enough time. His second wife will prove very different from poor Rachel (186–200). This section is enlivened by the crash landing of a German bomber on the estate, one of whose crew managed to parachute to safety. Little comes of it except a stark reminder that there's still a war on and Devonshire remains well within range of the enemy.

A variety of sallies

A variety of sallies continues to address Claire's problem, introduced in *Long range salvo*, what to do about a daughter-in-law who is pregnant by the wrong Craddock twin. Margaret had stayed on at Shallowford for a few days after Andy had been reported "missing" and Claire "recoiled" from the "unsavoury problem," which she realized was no prank but "a desperately serious business," especially serious after Andy "turned up again," alive although wounded. She did not know her sons well. They had always seemed able to take care of themselves, but now she saw that "this was a fiction and that both had been engaged in a game of bluff of which the end-product was a scandal that would age Paul twenty years." Keeping it from him was essential, "but how could this be achieved after Andy got home and found a wife six months gone with his brother's child" (196).

Desperately needing an impartial counsellor, Claire invites Maureen Rudd to visit Shallowford and "stay on for a spell," which she does. They talk, Claire outlines the situation, and Maureen replies "Well, girl, there's only one role you can play in a farce like this," and that is to get the three of them "straightened out before it's too late." Easily said, but how could it be managed? Claire fills in the details of "how it all began," but for Maureen the crucial issue is "how it ends. She's got to tell Andy the full truth and leave it to him." The real problem, she tells Claire, is Stevie, who might back out of intending to marry Margie, but "if you put your skates on" there might still be time to "talk to him" at the airbase outside York, where he's stationed (219). Claire had wanted sound advice and now she has it. She's no coward and when the going get tough the tough gets going, the sooner the better.

From the train taking her to Stevie's airbase, Claire sees for the first time the "skeletal ruins" of suburbs out the window, and observes the "strain and boredom" in the faces of servicemen and women around her. It seemed to her that "every living person was sucked into the vortex" of a war now in its fifth year, all sharing in "its dangers and shortages and its stale, unprofitable atmosphere" (221-22). The loquacious W.A.A.F. who asks Claire about Steven tells her that "He'll have changed, I daresay. You can spot the difference right away. Bomber pilots are mostly—well, more serious if you know what I mean, and usually nicer." And they're mostly married, the W.A.A.F. says, as she very accurately describes Claire's son. Arrived at the airbase, she learns that Stevie has been killed giving the wounded tail-gunner a chance to survive. Delderfield narrates the Lancaster pilot's soliloquy as he nurses the doomed bomber in its final moments.

> With Pidgeon injured there could be no question of ditching. Neither was there any question of returning to base. They would have to fly as long as possible and then a bit longer, and when the nearest piece of coastline showed he could order the able-bodied to bale out. From then it would be every man for himself and for him and Pidgeon a miserable attempt to pancake. (*Gauntlet*, 229)

A kind of confrontation

A kind of confrontation begins when Claire telephones the airbase from a nearby pub. One of the surviving crew members tells her that "Crad stayed with the kite… the aircraft", and because he did the wounded man is "in pretty good shape" (233), but her son didn't make it. Claire's plan of talking candidly with Steve having been voided, she next visits Margie in the Welsh nursing home where she had just delivered her baby, relaying the sad report about Vanessa's father. She "watched Margaret take refuge in the Celtic awareness of losing every fight in the end, the fight against Anglo-Saxons beyond Offa's Dyke, against the mountains, the weather, the rock-sown soil of the hill farms, and the unremitting greed of industrialists" (241). The scope and richness of Delderfield's cultural historical grasp, reflected in casual observations of passengers on a train, the stolidity of a Welshwoman told that her baby's father is dead, is impressive. The two women then discuss, without rancour, what to do next. Claire will soon have to telephone Paul, who will be wondering why she hasn't called him back.

> "He'll find out then?" Margaret said, "about us and Vanessa? He's bound to, isn't he?"
> "Not until I think he can take it. I didn't come here without some kind of plan but it involves all of us, not just you and Andy and that baby of your." (*Gauntlet*, 243)

Paul heard stoically the news of Stevie's death during Bomber Command's non-stop offensive, yet on her return home Claire found that it was not fatalism or courage that had sustained him, but pride. His pride that Steven had died in "the only war I've ever heard about worth fighting", for the Great War had been not only "murder badly managed", but "unnecessary", while this war hinges on "a straight choice between civilization and barbarism." When Paul meditates in French Wood, thinking about not only the twins, but also Simon "swimming for it" at Dunkirk, and Rumble sailing off because "he felt he had to," Paul is hugely proud of them (247). After Paul had absorbed Stevie's death for about a week Claire considered him "ready to withstand another kind of shock," made necessary by Margie's phone call saying she intended to "arrive on Saturday," shortly before Andy was expected home from his hospital treatments. She begins her account as tactfully as she knows how, and for some minutes Paul listens without interrupting. But then it became too much for him and he shouted "They're like a lot of barnyard animals!", but Claire reminds him "You promised to listen. I did what I did because somebody had to try and it was way beyond your capacity." Then she continues, Paul becoming capable of grasping her "courage and coolheadedness," which blurs "the harsh outlines of the dilemma" she had faced and enables him to recognize that the sordid liason of one twin with the other's wife had "disgusted her as it disgusted him now, and yet she had managed to live with it," and even "made some kind of attempt to sort things out." He begins to see that Claire has dealt with an insoluble situation as expertly as he routinely does on the Estate. "Somehow she had found the nerve and resolution to hold onto her purpose in circumstances that would have sent most women reeling to the nearest source of comfort" (252). He's a tough nut to crack, but when the nut is tough the tough gets cracking.

Recognizing that Paul is finally *listening* instead of resisting, Claire "told him, then, everything she knew and much of what she had guessed." When she informs him that Margie "tried strangers [in bed, but] it only made things worse because there was no love in it," Paul explodes once again, but that emotion is only an aftershock. "You didn't go screaming round the Valley for someone to take my place of a night" while he had spent twenty months in France, he bellows. That's true, she replies, but she had two things to sustain her which Margie lacked. First, she had the whole estate on her hands and plenty of old friends to help her. Second, "You took the trouble to write me a lot of affectionate letters, letters which I still keep, and even re-read when I need a pick-me-up!" Andy's letters to his wife were like "a note left at the back door for the baker or a milkman" (253-54). Paul by this time has come all the way down from his initial exasperation, his return to calm being signalled by the question, is it "a boy or a girl?" It's a girl and a granddaughter, his granddaughter. Claire and Paul are now upon the cusp of getting prone alongside one another, their usual way of ending disagreements (255).

Nevertheless, although Paul has been brought into the information loop without having been emotionally damaged by his own indignation, the problem of Margie and the baby has not been solved. If Maureen Rudd's foresight is accurate, it remains for the erring wife, after telling Andy the full truth, to "leave it to him."

The reason this sorry episode belongs in *A Horseman Riding By* is precisely the reason why Elaine's liason with Archie Carver and its effect on Esme is included in *The Avenue Goes to War*; marital breakdown is one of the commonest cultural results of wartime stress, an amplification of what occurs in peacetime too. As cultural historian, Delderfield does well to examine the phenomenon, because it is as predictable as black market activities in compensation for the U-boat campaign's success is creating food shortages. Killing everybody who lives in England is not the only way of undermining the nation's morale.

Sallies by all concerned

Sallies by all concerned brings the war up to June, 1944, the Normandy invasion by the allies—the aramada of men and materiel that can be taken as the beginning of the end for "that little bastard" in Berlin. The D-Day landing was a sally in the strictly military sense, i.e., a sortie of troops from a beseiged place upon an enemy, but the word serves equally well in an analogous sense, namely, a flurry of resistance, a counter-thrust. For the Craddock family, June, 1944, was a moment for taking stock, summing up their situations, principally as it involved Andrew and Margaret, Simon, and Claire as she painfully compares the differences between her twin boys. Andy, feeding the Valley's crippled gull with the piece of bread proferred on his gloved hand, shares a sour reflection with his wife Margie in a domestic slice-of-life which brings readers up-to-date on how badly their marriage is going.

> "Well, at least the poor old bugger is still airborne," he said, and lounged off into the house to turn on the radio. Sounds of a news-bulletin reached Margaret as she stood by the pram, rocking it gently, but the words carried on the breeze were only intermittently heard and therefore made little sense. "...making good their landing...considerable opposition at scattered points...advancing on two sectors..." And then, one complete sentence: "So far only one vessel reported lost." She called, "How is it going, Andy? Is there anything fresh?" and Andy, appearing at the french window with a cigarette in his mouth, said, "They've all got ashore and seem to be in business."
>
> He stood there a minute and Margaret wondered uncertainly, if she should try and console him again. She knew the source and depth of his bitterness—an armada of aircraft, ships and men committed to the biggest enterprise of the war, and himself pottering about a garden with a woman, a child and an artificial hand. His depression had increased, she noticed, when the papers had begun to talk of the Second Front and all the American Rangers down on the shore had packed up and gone, taking their landing-craft with them. Then Andy came lounging out of the house, calling, "I'm going to have a yarn with Ken Shawcrosse. Give me a shout when Lunch is up." She thought, unhappily, "I'll probably have to give three shouts, and then Ken Shawcrosse will come lumbering back with you and expect me to feed him on our rations. And after that you'll both swill gin and French, and tonight you'll be sour-tempered until it's time for bed and might want to use me, as if I was something from the far end of a Sultan's harem." Then, as the baby gurgled, she drew her finger along the child's cheek.

"We'll stick it out, Vanessa," she said, "we'll stick it out until it improves. And everyone except me seems to think it will." (*Gauntlet*, 261)

As he leaves to see Shawcrosse, Andy's state of mind is not unlike that of Swift's metaphorical spider ["The Battle of the Books"], who "sallies forth" to do intellectual battle with the bee which has blundered into its web, the arachnid being determined to prove its own superiority by pointing to its production of flybane and cobweb, as compared with the bee's honey and wax, i.e., sweetness and light. Those Shallowford land deals the co-conspiritors contrive will be the poisonous equivalents of flybane and cobweb.

At that moment, Simon's glider had landed safely upon French soil, a winged-craft "gliding in from the north-west to crash within fifty yards of the bridges of the little river and the Caen canal." The first twenty minutes of the engagement with German soldiers was "the liveliest and, in some ways, the most rewarding of his career" (263). Simon compares his earliest military effort, sailing off to fight with the Spanish resistance, with his D-Day success.

In Spain, he had counted himself lucky to carry a 1914 Lebel rifle...The men beside him were amateurs, now as then. Tonight they were fresh-faced youngsters, keyed up to a terrific pitch and probably terrified by the hazards of their assignment and yet, like himself, fortified by the certainty of ultimate victory, and this was half-way to survival. In Spain it had not been that way at all. Always they were staring over their shoulders at defeat, a mob of peasants fighting Italian armour and German dive-bombers in a contest from which the Democracies had stood aside, calling their cowardice non-intervention. (*Gauntlet*, 263-64)

When Simon heard "the long, final swish of the glider and felt the grinding, bumping slither of its impact," his training took over and he and the men he commanded quickly completed their mission of securing the Orne bridge (263). In the years before this moment, Simon had been "sustained by" hatred of the enemy, an emotion moderated by marriage to Evie, and now "altogether spent." He felt no hatred for the German officer "spreadeagled on the bridge" because he knew that from there the allies would roll over "First War battlefields" and then over the Rhine, "but it would be a campaign, not a crusade." In the Normandy morning mists he could hear the toot of a hunting horn and "as in every war, the moaning of bagpipes" (265-66).

In Shallowford, meanwhile, Claire was reflecting that the stresses of war had brought about "dramatic changes" in the character of people around her. On Margie's testimony, Steven had "developed a new personality" after he switched from fighter-pilot to bomber-pilot, and Andy had "changed so dramatically" that even casual acquaintances noticed it.

He had gone to war a loud, cheerful extrovert and had returned, some three years later, a morose, truculent, glowering young man, quick to fly off the handle, silent and brooding when left alone. She didn't know what to make of him these days and neither, it seemed, did poor Margaret, who was having a very difficult time with him. (*Gauntlet*, 267)

Margie had her own take on the twins. Stevie "would never have gone back to scrap, or anything that meant keeping the kind of company we kept" then, people of Shawcrosse's type. Stevie might have gone into farming, while Andy remained "interested in money for its own sake". He is "forming a company with Shawcrosse, something to do with houses and land," but because Andy doesn't confide in her, she cannot be more specific than that.

Claire can only wait and see whether Andy and Margie's problems would "resolve themselves," but Simon, she senses, was doing much better, for she noticed "a subtle change" in him since the D-Day assault. His most recent letters—and it is significant that Simon confides in her, the woman who defended his conduct in that argument between Paul and Ikey three decades earlier, rather than in his father—Simon's most recent letter to Claire had expressed a "tolerance and maturity" which had been foreign to him earlier in life.

> I don't see this as a Left-versus-Right contest any more," he wrote, "but as a kind of Sanitary Squad exercise! I've always lived for politics, and they've always presented a straight choice for me, as they did for Rachel, but since I got back here I've had to shift my sights for a variety of reasons. The prisoners we took after the break-through to the Seine aren't the Germans I remember, those arrogant, indoctrinated bullies, who bombed Guernica and threw us out of France, in 1940. Mostly they reminded me of the kind of Jerry one met in Remarque's "All Quiet..." The French too are not all 'gallant resisters', who have been running around with secret codes and homemade explosives ever since Dunkirk. Many did, of course, but others just sat and waited, and there were some who made a packet of money out of the Occupation. It isn't a matter of politics any more, but expedience. There are plenty of cruel bastards on the Left, as well as the Right. I had to threaten to shoot two of them yesterday, after they had shaved a seventeen-year-old girl because somebody pointed her out as someone who had once slept with a German. I've seen a lot of that since June and it isn't the kind of Democracy I've been fighting for ever since Spain." (*Gauntlet*, 269–70)

Booby Trap and Outpost Incident

As the novel's initial portion advances towards its conclusion, narrative attention shifts away from Craddock problems to a broader view of Valley activities, in *Booby trap* and *Outpost incident*, featuring two minor characters who are spotlighted for the first time, Noah Williams and Prudence Honeyman. However, Paul is the booby, the dunce or slow-witted fellow in *Booby trap*, because he seriously misjudges Noah Williams, the Coombe Bay longshoreman whom he has always considered an unreliable layabout. Paul has developed a swelled head, which renders him vulnerable to "grievous misjudgments" about people, although with "wry humor" he would admit to these "when he had got over the shock" of finding himself fallible. This flaw came about gradually when not merely locals, but "authorities outside the Valley accepted his leadership" and delegated to him responsibilities perhaps too easily, even though Paul would have "resented them going elsewhere for help or advice" (277). Yes, his head has swelled over the years, though he will be taken down a peg during the local crisis which emerged in the winter of 1944-45.

Paul gets a call from the Marine Camp on the Moor that they've just received a message "from the naval sub-depot at Whinmouth" about "a possible danger from floating mines" (278). These are most likely World War I mines, which were hurriedly "laid outside the estuary early in the war," two dozen of them, all of them now recovered except for "two that slipped their cables in the last night's gale." Not to worry, however, for the Navy is "sending a cutter along" to retrieve the free-floating ones. When the sudden blast echoes up the Valley it becomes clear that one of the mines has damaged the jetty where the mock café is located which blind Alf Willis still uses as his switchboard position. Alf had been at his post when the mine blew up. What about the remaining mine? Where is it and who's dealing with it? Nobody, since the Navy cutter sent for that purpose has, as Noah explains, "gone aground in shallow water and they'll have to bide until the tide's run an hour." Paul sourly tells the feckless layabout "This is no time to be funny." But Noah understands the bay and its tides intimately from long experience, while the Navy has no clue. "They'm stuck I tell 'ee. You got to be right smart to catch that harbor at turn o' tide and they should ha' waited on for a spell." Noah had told them that before, "but they bliddy vorriners alwas knows best". Their rocket "soaring from the cutter and arching its way over the western slope of the Bluff" indicated that the disposal team was itself "appealing for help" (281). Reluctantly, Paul begins to take a certain interest in Noah's explanations of the current situation, but having long ago dismissed him as unreliable, he cannot bring himself to enlist the services of the one man best able to deal with the dangerous reality that Alf Willis is still in "that ole fort" and his chances of survival are poor. Very soon "the surviving mine would be alongside the jetty and projecting underwater beams, splintered by the first explosion, would probably touch it off before it reached the main structure" (285).

When that happens, bye-bye Alf, unless a rescue party can remove him from the ruined structure quickly. Thus the solution, if there be one, is to get Willis out of death's path while concurrently snagging the floating mine in order to hold it off from shore until the on-land operation saves the endangered blind man. Considering himself in charge of the situation, Paul begins giving Noah directives, but the Coombe Bay longshoreman, angered by being brusquely ignored when he knows better than anyone else what has to be done, blows his top and sets off with his son Jaffsie to capture the mine.

> "There's a long ladder in The Raven yard," began Paul, "you and me could…" but Noah, still glowering, made a sudden, emphatic gesture and growled. "Bugger the ladder! You and Smut can zee to that end of it. Me'n Jaffsie'll come in from the Bluff zide and zee

if us can ketch that cable-end and hold un off for a spell, but for Christ's sake doan hang about, Maister. The scour's getting stronger every minute an' us'll have our work cut out as it is. Come on, Jaffsie, us'll launch in from the far zide o' the breakwater."

Before long, Paul could see without his binoculars "Jaffsie at the oars and the thick-set figure of Noah at the tiller," the mine a hundred yards offshore, and closing at a brisk pace. Remembering "Noah's expression the moment before he bent to lift the stern of the boat," Paul recognized that in the end they would be able to save Alf (288–89).

The work of locating the imperiled Willis and removing him to safety having been completed, Paul had leisure "to glance through the shattered framework on his left" and see Jaffsie "brace himself against the oars", forcing the skiff to "swing round in an arc and begin heading out to sea".

> It moved, Paul thought, with a terrible dragging slowness, so that he roused himself and shouted to the recumbent Noah, "Let her go and get ashore, man!" but Noah, if he heard, paid no attention to this advice but continued to sprawl with his face almost in the water and the splayed cable clutched in his hands. The mine, checked in its spiral-ling drift towards the end of the wrecked jetty, followed unwillingly, clearing the last beam by no more than a few yards. *Gauntlet*, 291–92)

As this last scene of the drama closed, Noah, "fifty yards seaward of the jetty," lowered the cable into the water and "rolled round facing his son who at once set a slanting course for the breakwater." Smut, following the operation with sure understanding based upon his own wide experience, said to Paul, "He's got zense as well as nerve," Williams has. "He's leaving her where the tide'll carry her 'way along the beach. Er'll blow off this zide o' the landslip and do no harm to nobody" (292). Paul and Smut are equally chastened by the astonishing competence of the man neither had respected before. The incident ends happily, but Paul has been marginally humiliated. His control over emergent situations has proved less competent than it had once been. The least they could do was done that night at The Raven. As they watched Noah's triumph, Smut expressed the intent of "standing him a pint if he shows up" that evening. But the Squire wanted to do the honors: "I'll do any standing that's to be done, and it'll be a quart if he can take it," and at this Smut's grin returned to him for the first time that afternoon" (292).

Outpost incident relates a second Valley episode that ends well after seeming to go badly. After Normandy, the Luftwaffe "was a spent force," and while V-bombs still kept Londoners "on the jump," the provinces were "groping their way back to a peacetime routine in that final winter of the war" (294). The Marine camp had shrunk, hit-and-run raids were never seen, Simon had been assigned an administrative job, Rumble was sailing slowly home across the Indian Ocean and Sergeant Morrisey, one of the few remaining Americans, would soon be sent to the States. Ed Morrisey had for long been enticing Prudence Honeyman towards sexual compliance by showering her with boxes and boxes of candy, towels and sheets, a canned turkey at Christmas, and "several pairs of nylon stockings, now accepted in the Valley as a kind of down payment on defloration." Not that defloration was the right term for Prudence Pitts-that-was, as she had "sampled most of the young men between the Whin and the Bluff before she settled on one in particular," Nelson Honeyman, because she thought she was in the family way by one or another of her admirers. At thirty-four, Prudence "still had a good figure, bold, snapping eyes, and a mop of red-gold hair," but she was now married to Nelson, the conscientious young man, "slight, earnest and unoriginal," who soon discovered that his good luck was due to her "false alarm" (194–96).

Prudence remained a flirt, but was careful not to put herself into the situation she had once feared, which is why "the prize eluded" her current admirers. All that Ed Morrisey got in return for his "time and capital invested" was her usual pay-out, "a kiss, a hasty fumble, a subdued giggle," period. By February of 1945, Morrisey came to the conclusion that "his manhood was at stake" and decided that push would come to shove before he was shipped back to the States. His visits were always "nicely timed" to avoid the husband, but Nelson was hanging about unseen when Eddy came this time and suggested that they go in the barn and climb to the hayloft, which was not unusual for them. Yet this time Prudence was unsettled, and "surprised to find herself trembling" as she said "Let's go up the ladder." Eddy was "getting on forty and his poor condition had been a factor in him being left behind when the Rangers moved out," but he was quick up the ladder. Yet Prudence was worried since she was putting herself in a position she wanted very much to escape from.

Nelson had spotted the jeep heading towards his farm, reversed, returned home and stood quietly to "plan his next move." The "stifled laugh" from the hayloft told him that Morrisey "had enlarged his bridgehead," so Nelton tightened his grip "on the mattock shaft and ascended the vertical ladder step by step, taking his time about it and testing each rung for creaks". Nelson's "gloomiest suspicions" were confirmed as he saw Prudence, so it appeared, "at last giving full value for money and from the glimpse he got of her in his rush across the floor she was not finding the discharge of the debt irksome." The heavy end of the shaft descended before either of them was aware of his presence. Morrisey disappeared through the hatch partly masked by the hay, plummeted with a terrible crash that broke his right leg and set him to screaming like a calf, while Prudence, also screaming, "embraced Nelson's gum-booted calves in the attitude of a drunkard's wife in a Victorian temperance print" (299–30). Nelson immediately phoned "ambulance and Squire" to do something about Eddy's leg and to inform Paul about his decision to leave the Valley for a farm in Dorset to which he would take his lascivious wife if she would go.

Nelson's phone call hastened the arrival of assistance to the farm and Prudence's screaming brought the hired help running, including "Nelson's aged pigman, Walt

Davey," who as an eye-witness was able to give a lively account of the tableau that night in The Raven. His narrative, a pungent Chaucerian Miller-and-the-Reeve fabliau, was reason enough for Nelson to leave the Valley or endure the contemptuous smiles of his neighbors evermore afterwards.

> "There 'er was," Walt was to declare, "screaming 'er ade off, like 'er was mazed! And ther was the Yank, hollering bliddy murder at the bottom of the ladder! You never zeed zuch a carry-on, and then down comes Young Maister, white as a vish-belly, steps right over the Yank like he was a bale o' straw, and runs out to the vone! Well, us straightened him out as best we could, and Bernard put a splint on his leg, and then down comes the missis showing all 'er's got, and not giving a damn neither for 'er was that scared. "Er stood looking at him for a minute without so much as a wink 'an then 'er zees us looking at her an' suddenly whips round and out and that's the last I zeed of 'er."
> It was the best story told in the bar for a generation. (*Gauntlet*, 301)

The Squire did his best to dissuade Martin from relocating but "his mind was made up by the certainty that the story had already passed into Valley legend".

Eddy's leg having been put straight for him, all that remained was for Paul to discuss the dust-up with Prudence, who is willing to "make a fresh start with him if he wants" but wonders why, after all her previous escapades, Nelson would raise "this kind of rumpus" after all those years. "It's very easy to explain," Paul said, the false pregnancy was a private matter,

> "but this makes him a Valley laughing stock and that's why he's determined to get out while he's got the chance." His resentment for her moderated as it always did when he was not faced with cant. These people in their early thirties were subject to pressures that had not been exerted on his own generation. The first war had damaged the structure of the old civilization but it had not rotted it, as had the Depression and the years of drift that had resulted in Hitler. Back in 1917 and 1918 one had always felt one was fighting to preserve something worth perserving, that once things had settled down everything would be much the same, but this wasn't true any longer. The whole fabric of community and family life was in tatters and there did not seem to be much hope of repairing it. Would it seem such a dastardly thing to her to betray a colourless husband like Nelson Honeyman, trading a few sweaty moments in a loft for an armful of household goods that no wife in the Valley would have wanted thirty years ago? He didn't think so. This kind of thing was in the atmosphere one breathed nowadays. It was in politics and business. It showed in the black-market traffic of men like Smut Potter and Henry, and in the business activities of his own son, Andy. Who the hell was he to condemn her for copulating with a Yank, when his own daughter-in-law had done the same thing with her brother-in-law and the passage of a year or so had resulted in his own wife's passive acceptance of the situation?

"Will you be happier among strangers?" Paul asks Prudence. "That's for Nelson to decide," she said. "One farm is as good as another for my money."

There it was again, this rootlessness, this yawning renunciation of tradition and the claims of a community, and even Rumble had been infected by it to some extent. It was frightening to a man who would be sixty-six in June. (*Gauntlet*, 303-04)

Conditional Surrender

The opening section of *Gauntlet's* second "Part," i.e., *Marchout with banners*, is a survey of the Craddocks from V.E. to V.J. Day, with special attention to Paul, Simon and Andy while they transition into their post-war situations. Paul observes that victory celebrations are very different in the Shallowford area than they had been. The Big House is no longer the fulcrum of events but Coombe Bay instead, there were "no Paxtonbury folk" present, and the coastal community of Whinmouth was conducting its own celebrations (312). An insular spirit has spread while the communal attitude so precious to Paul has atrophied.

Like his father, Simon, home from Brussels in time for the victory celebrations in London, "detected a false note in the orchestra." The festivities' sponsors were not the people of England spontaneously erupting with joy, but the bureaucrats "who had been handing down decrees" liberally for so many years that they had got into the habit, their "final edict" being "You will now celebrate." Walking in London, Simon felt, underlying some "strident laughter" and "uninhibited embracing", a sense of "compulsive enjoyment" (315). As for his own attitude, he was thoroughly bored with politics, the "disenchantment process" having begun in Spain ten years earlier. Politics lay in Simon's past, its demise being related to coming home, a sensation nourished by his "yearning for the remoteness of the Valley."

> Something akin to his father's extreme provincialism had seeded itself in him during [his earlier] leave and had been enlarging its hold all the way from Normandy to the Ruhr. The difficulty was to find a useful place in that withdrawn society, for he knew himself well enough to realize that whatever he would do would have to offer something creative.

Farming was not for him, nor the church, nor medicine, and he had been toying with journalism as a possible career when by chance he encountered on the London street "a party of schoolboys in charge of a dried out little nut of a man and a schoolmaster, catching his eye." The teacher proved to be his favorite faculty member at High Wood twenty-five years earlier (317-20). The teacher's job, Archie Bentinck tells him after they have renewed their acquaintance, is not to "cut boys to a pattern," which Bentinck would have had little hope of doing to Simon back then. The teacher's function is "to help them develop individual personalities within the terms of reference we call civilization" (323). This fires Simon's heart, being sufficiently abstract along with difficult enough to attract him. Bentinck challenges the former boy. "Pity about you, Craddock," he says, with the same I-take-you-seriously nonchalance that one guesses had made him magnetically attractive to Simon years before, "You've wasted a lot of time," as though even then Bentinck recognized in him the talent needed for effective teaching.

> "Still, you're better equipped to start fresh than I was. I never had a proper degree, whereas you have, plus a good war record. Put in for a teacher's training course and do what I did." (*Gauntlet*, 324)

And if he needs a letter of recommendation..., "Write that letter Archie" Simon blurts, without needing to dither about the decision. Simon's vocation has found him.

Though both of them would have denied it, Andy and his father were "more alike in essentials" than any of the family. "Both had a steadiness of vision that was strong, purposeful and could at times be brutally obstinate" (325). He had enjoyed the scrap-metal business, and flying fighter planes even more, but after his long stay in hospital Andy found the world had changed. "The Civil Service had moved in", and now "behind every rolltop desk and trestle table was a faceless man who worked from the book," one whose life was predictable and dreary (326). For Andy Craddock there was "no place in the present scheme of things" and he would go mad with boredom unless he could "make one" for himself. That was the personal-survival attraction of Ken Shawcrosse's "buccaneer commercial aggressiveness." He and Andy had joined forces and established "Romulus Development Incorporated" (327). Shawcrosse intuitively knew whether the right approach to a specific opportunity was "assault," "sapping and mining," or "bribing the garrison to open the gate at night." Andy had accompanied him into "a strange, higgledly-piggledly world, in its own way as bizarre as Zorndorff's world of scrap," and as exciting, although it required patience and long-term investment, perhaps as long as ten years. But in the end, Shawcrosse assures him, the profit will be not 10 or 15 per cent but "nearer a thousand per cent" (328-29). Paul's V.J. letter was a week catching up with Andy and when he had received it he pondered a long time before "passing it over to Ken," who was elated by its contents.

> "So old Dad has finally come round to it? He's handing over in advance, in the hope of doing the poor old Chancellor out of his death-duties! Well, good for him and good for you. Cash is nice to have but give me coastal land every time. It can't shrink in value like the poor old British quid. Nice little reserve, tucked away in the West." (*Gauntlet*, 330)

Delderfield delays informing his readers of Paul's adoption of the confiscatory-taxation-shield arrangement until after Shawcrosse has preemptively marked the Valley for his own enrichment. The shock of this shyster's massive theft of what Paul has spent his life fostering is that much the greater for the mouse's having been gobbled up without the least suspicion that the cat was nearby. Andy's abominable conduct is so stark that he cannot conceal it from himself, hence the long stall; he "pondered it a long time before passing it over to Ken," his "passing it over" articulating the delivery of his father's Estate into the pocket of his accomplice.

Paul's attitude towards money was a recoil from the "original source of his acres," the scrap-metal profits he had inherited as his father's heir.

> He had always been conscious of having profited by the death of Boer children in the insanitary concentration camps of the Veldt, and the murder of his own generation in Flanders. This was why, on his return to the Valley in 1918, one of his first acts had been to channel the whole of his wartime profits into the Valley and see most of it melt away in the agricultural slump of the 'twenties and early 'thirties." (*Gauntlet*, 332)

But the moment that agriculture picked up again, "taxation kept pace with its progress" and by the end of World War II "was galloping well ahead," such that "staggering amounts were demanded by the Inland Revenue" (332). This untenable situation determined Paul to set about crafting a plan that could cause his remaining children to "put down roots" in the Valley, roots that would "take hold of something," in the way every commemorative tree in French Wood "had rooted itself" (335). When Paul discusses that intention with a financial advisor, Edgar Wonnacott, the widely experienced fellow asks, "Before we go any further, can you trust you family?" Eager to put himself in King Lear's position of having given everything away to his daughters Goneril and Regan, Paul retorts "Now what a damned stupid question. If I couldn't I shouldn't be here, should I?" Quite true, but unfortunately, the Paul Craddock who had been utterly wrong about Noah Williams has lost a step or two. He is quick to *assume* what he thinks he *knows*. What is it Kent says about the King? "'Tis the infirmity of his age. Yet he hath ever but slenderly known himself" (*Lear*, Act I, Scene 1). Inadequate self-knowledge had not always been Paul's state, but it has grown upon him, the terrible power of the defect being the afflicted man's ignorance of his own ignorance. "All right, get cracking on it right away", Craddock tells Wonnacott (337), clearing the way for his cat's-paw son to proceed.

The first sale is that of the Coombe Bay properties, which are ancillary to the Estate proper.

> Neither Paul nor his agent ever met the purchasers. They were, it seemed, intermediaries who bought properties, did them up, and resold them immediately. Wonnacott, accustomed to the measured pace of provincial business, expressed disgust at what was going on now that the war was over and ex-servicemen were demanding living space. (*Gauntlet*, 339)

In the overall design, Shallowford Estates Limited would be administered by a Board of Directors, Paul as chairman, and Simon, Andy, Rumble [Mary's representative] and Whiz as the other members. Whiz "would serve more practical purpose on the board than her husband, for at least she had hunted the country" years ago; Paul does not know that she will be happy to take her cash and finally be done with the Valley. All in all, Paul left Wonnacott's office "feeling that he had achieved something lasting" (340). Indeed he had, but not what he had intended. His children wrote Paul letters, expressing their personalities and values, the crucial one being Andy's. "He had, he said, a number of ideas for increasing the estate income but he would not enumerate them until he had sounded out the others" (343). "Sounding out" means securing them as supporters of his advocacy on behalf of Shawcrosse's underhanded land-acquisition plans.

Routine reconnaissance

The next chapter, *Routine reconnaissance*, can be well summed up this way: Paul, having returned from a trip round the world with Claire, rides across the Valley finding some things familiar, yet other things rather different in some curiously disturbing way that is somehow connected to Andy. The Mediterranean cruise, the pyramids, the trip across the Rocky Mountains, all that was great fun, but Paul is happy to be back examining things again. He is concerned about the half-dozen families squatting on the abandoned Marine camp, needy people whose plight he recognizes, while Andy's advice is "to boot the buggers off" (351). Paul is sixty-eight now, and while not exactly living in the past, he is less aggressively committed to the future than Andy is. Remembering that David Pitts had "made an offer for the [Pitts] freehold and had been referred to Andy," Paul was surprised to learn that Andy had told David, "brusquely", that the Company "had no intention of selling more land"; this implied that the board "must have had a meeting during his absence." He asked Henry whether Andy had told him to "hold his horses until I got back." Paul presumes that he remains in charge, as does Lear, both of whom are painfully instructed otherwise. Henry says "*Your* boy's differ'ent. They doan zeem to be able to give an' taake zame as us did, backalong" (353). Paul is gratified to learn that Prudence Honeyman and her husband are back in the Valley, she much happier because "all she really looked for was security and to be admired and needed" by Nelson. Thus the Estate news is not uniformly disturbing, but his concern deepens again when he talks with Smut Potter, whose new landlord at the bakery is a company. "Your boy could tell you more about it than me," him and the "Chum of his who is the Chairman." Alerted, Paul recollected "Jumbo Bellchamber's hangdog look and his reluctance to chat" (364–65). Something is up. His reconnaissance ride across the Valley has given Paul information, though he lacks the key to the significance of the alterations he finds disturbing. Returning home, Paul learns that Claire had invited Andy to join them for lunch, but Andy had 'phoned saying "he had another engagement." Noting his frown, Claire asks is anything the matter, but Paul replies "no, or not that he knew of." That is exactly the truth (366).

Bastions for sale

Bastions for sale begins with a conversation between the Squire and his wife, Paul disturbed by an elusive worry that things are about to go very badly despite his attempt to solve the taxation problem. Claire poses a question.

"You mean you're sorry you formed the Company? But you told me only a month ago it was saving you two thousand a year in tax!"

"There are worse things than paying out half your income in tax."

"Tell me one."

"All right, I will. Seeing this entire Valley raped the way they've raped that village on the coast! It isn't parting with acres I resent—I'm advocating we sell Hermitage to David Pitts at today's meeting, but David is a farmer not a speculator. Suppose they got a real foothold and started a rampage on our side of the river?"

"How would they do that when we own the freehold?"

"I don't know," he said doubtfully, "but I do know that everyone associated with this Company except Mary considers me fossilized. Maybe if the money offered for sites was tempting enough..." (*Gauntlet*, 368–69)

The "post-war Andy" opened the Company's meeting by telling the members present about "the sudden popularity of farm land among business men seeking escape hatches for heavily-taxed profits." Clearly, Paul realized, Andy was the only one of them who "had really kept pace with the gathering momentum of the century" (372). The meeting broke up quite pleasantly, but a few weeks later the crisis came when Andy convened a special meeting. Bellchamber in Low Coombe is "very eager to buy his freehold" (375). Paul remembered Jumbo's "evasiveness" earlier on, along with Andy's "saying he was otherwise engaged" and couldn't come for lunch. He asked Andy, "carefully,"

"You've seen Bellchamber yourself? You've already discussed it with him?"

"That's right."

They were all watching now, sensing the tension between father and son.

"*When*, exactly?"

"Does it matter when?"

"Yes it does. Was it the day I came home from abroad?"

"It might have been."

"It damn well was. I saw your car. And you shot off like a bolted fox the moment you saw me riding down the Coombe on Snowdrop." (*Gauntlet*, 376)

Andy admits that Bellchamber wants to buy his freehold, and "certain people are backing an idea of his that will make money a good deal easier and faster than it's made by farming." It involved the expansion of Coombe Bay, "and if we block it in the north-west it will happen in the east beyond the Bluff, where there's an alternative site just as good as Jumbo's and even nearer the sea" (377). But Jumbo Bellchamber doesn't *have* the money to buy, and the matter would have to be "thrashed out" in a local and a County Council "before it could be approved." Not to worry, since Jumbo made a huge killing in black market food, and the Old Boys' network has already approved the project for building a camping site capable of housing "fifty caravans and probably twice as many tents," also latrines, incinerators, shops which sell milk, canned goods and other items (378). Claire [the "paid secretary"] and Simon raise objections, Paul simmers with anger, but to no avail. Andy states the blunt truth that none of them are prepared to understand.

> "Sooner or later we're going to have either housing or a caravan site on our eastern boundary. You can fend it off for so long but with everyone screaming for homes, and all this emphasis on youth clubs and outdoor activities that produce new industries— -caravan building for instance—the pattern of places like this has to change and it will change, no matter how far people like the Gov'nor dig their heels in. It's not change for the sake of change, either. It's made inevitable by factors like the population explosion, rising wages, and holidays with pay—especially holidays with pay. Places like this can't survive any longer on agriculture alone. They've got to develop as holiday centres whether they want or not and they're lucky if they can keep light industry at arm's length. Even as it is, with every coastal town expanding like mad, the younger generation are still moving out in search of jobs, in search of more sophistication if you like. I don't have to tell you how many men agriculture is losing every year. The figures are there in *The Farmer's Weekly*, for anyone to read. Well, that's point one—more housing and something less permanent and purely seasonal, like a caravan site. Point two, who makes a profit out of it? Us, or someone standing on the touchline, like that smallholder Lakeworthy the far side of the Bluff? We could let the site ourselves, of course, but the Gov'nor wouldn't stand for that in a million years and for once I'm with him, because Bellchamber doesn't know what he's in for with all the sanitary regulations and all the moonlight flits he'll have to cope with! My advice, for what it's worth, is to squeeze the last drop out of him while he's in a position to pay." (*Gauntlet*, 379–80)

An uncomfortable silence followed Andy's richly impressive crystal-ball description of the realistic options which lay before them. Consumed with anger, Paul bolts from the room while Claire, knowing that the problem will somehow have to be de-fused, tells Andy to "Get some kind of proposition on paper, and make sure that you put in that clause about leaving the timber on our side of the wood" (382).

In fact, however, Andy already *has* on paper everything that matters, and when that comes to light his chicanery is shockingly seen for what it is. Andy and Margie are living in a house near Whinmouth, "not a home but a plushy perch" with a "well-kept garden" and "between-the-wars" furniture. Looking for a blotter Andy sometimes used, Margaret opened a drawer of the "pseudo-Regency desk" where he did his work and "uncovered the plan," i.e., the "large, mounted tracing that she recognized as a detailed plan of the coastal belt between Nun's Head and Shallowford Bluff. Every farm, field and coppice was marked in and named". Along with the plan was a "memorandum sheet" which told her everything she wanted to know (384–95).

> This was the Shallowford Valley, not as Paul saw it, or as anyone else had ever seen it, but how it would look when Shawcrosse and Andy had finished with it. The ruthlessness of the exercise, already well started it seemed, stirred an indignation within her that made her feel physically sick. She sat back in his swivel-chair for a moment, closing her eyes and making a great effort to concentrate. Then, with deliberation, she compared key and plan, relating the initial capital letters—"A", "B", "C", etc. to coloured

twins on the map. "A", shown in blue, was property already acquired by one or other of the companies in Coombe Bay and there seemed to be a great deal of it. "B" was the holiday camp, absorbing one of the Shallowford farms and spreading, in the shape of a spur, to the cliffs east of the Bluff. "C" was labelled *"Proposed New Road"*...Suddenly the pattern became very clear indeed. Andy, as the dominant director of the family company, was the inside man operating on behalf of Shawcrosse, and perhaps some of the other vulpine characters who occasionally called at the house for a drink or left cryptic messages when Andy was out.

It was like finding oneself involuntarily caught up in a conspiracy to defraud or, even more frightening, witnessing a back-alley attack on an unsuspecting victim and being faced with the choice of intervening or looking the other way. (*Gauntlet*, 385–86)

There was more—correspondence between Andy and Whiz which told Margie that the Craddock daughter had already sold him her shares "more than a year ago". "But it didn't matter about Whiz. Andy was the central figure and behind Andy, like a puppeteer, was Shawcrosse, jerking strings to make the Craddocks dance" (387).

Margie took the plan to Claire, who "heard her out in silence" and asked some questions in order to integrate the plan she has just seen into the family she intends to save from destruction by what Andy has set going. Margaret had taken Vanessa to a dancing lesson when Andy's car "sent the gravel flying" before he came into the house with his usual brash officiousness, which did not slump appreciably when his mother reproached him. "You've rumbled it, then?" Andy asks. Yes, she has. "Well, I knew there would have to be a showdown sooner or later" and it will be "more civilized" with her than "with the Old Man," Andy having adopted the demeaning rhetoric of Shawcrosse along with the rest of his value system. But Andy's brutality and dishonesty aside, he has a powerful mind that is clear-sighted in predicting how events will play out; he recognizes tendencies that one ignores only at the risk of being left behind by history. Therefore, what Andy says here has to be considered one of the novel's shrewdest cultural-historical observations.

"An industrialised country doesn't stand still. It can't or it would go bust in a single generation. That was true when we stopped feeding Europe a century ago and it's even more true today. We live by importing food and exporting manufactured goods and we've been doing that for the last eighty years but there are still people like the Gov'nor who can't or won't admit it, and naturally they get hurt when it hits them between the eyes. I'm sorry about that—in a way I admire him, always have admired him, but for far different reasons than the middle-of-the-roaders like Rumble Patrick and Simon admire him...All I'm interested in is making sure that when he is taken for a ride he gets paid for it. That's been the general object of the exercise as far as I'm concerned. Do you think Shawcrosse would have paid twelve thousand for that tip of Bellchamber's if I hadn't twisted his arm?" (*Gauntlet*, 391–92)

Claire defends her husband's vision of the Valley, what he has tried to do. "He certainly doesn't deserve what you've done to him" and "it isn't your place to lead the stampede" to destroy everything he has worked for.

"I never did lead it," he said. "As a matter of fact, most of the time I've been trying to head it off."

"By ranging yourself with people like this man Shawcrosse, whoever he is."

This is the point at which Andy shifts from description of the complex factors which interact as nations move through time and adjust to emergent changes, to self-justification. He transitions from telling Claire how-things-are to a very different intention, i.e., attributing venality to one and all. "Loyalty", Andy says, "didn't survive the First War". But to insist upon that is to reshape personal choices into compulsive conduct. His advocacy of preemptive selfishness will be tacitly rejected by Claire and Margie, as shall be evident from their reactions.

> "Shawcrosse isn't anyone in particular," he said stubbornly. "Shawcrosse is just a symbol. There are hundreds of Shawcrosses, thousands of Shawcrosses, and most of them have eased themselves into places where they can call the tune! The departmental offices concerned with the future of places like the Valley are stuffed with Shawcrosses and there's a baker's dozen of them—half of them builders—on every sizeable town council. They've got dreams that he doesn't even know about and wouldn't understand even if he did know. But in ten years' time he'll find that out, and then it'll be too late, because the only power the Shawcrosses respect is the power of money. By then, unless he capitalises and reinvests the way I've been urging him to do, he won't have any money and not much land either. He'll have been bled white by tax and sewn up with legislative tape. They'll serve him with forms and requisitions and anything else they've got in their bloody pigeonholes. And even if he doesn't change the rest of the Valley will the moment they spot a chance of making big capital gains. You'll see a stampede then all right and who will be heading it? The Pittses, the Honeymans, the Eveleighs and the Bellchambers. The whole damned lot of them, one after the other, and they won't wait around to say good-bye either, because their kind of loyalty was spent long before I came on the scene. It didn't survive the First War and if you don't believe me ask any one of them how much they made out of the black market when I was in the Desert."
>
> He obviously believed every word he said. He was not, she decided, excusing himself, or softening her up in the hope that some of his arguments would be passed on to Paul when she got home. She said, distractedly, "You don't believe in anything, do you? *Nothing.* Nothing at all. When did you stop believing, Andy?" (*Gauntlet*, 393–94)

Just then a car door banged and Margaret was there with her "hat and coat and with a red suitcase in her hand," for she is leaving Andy. "It was not her words or her suitcase that disconcerted him but her act of addressing Claire as though there was no one else in the room." Margie will NOT take Vanessa when she leaves "on account of a damn silly family squabble," he insists. "You're not her father and have no say in what happens to her, Andy. Stop shouting at me and get yourself a drink" (394). The women have voted, and the posturing would-be cultural historian, who has left accurate description for tendentious self-justification, is tacitly informed that he is full of baloney. The lesson is not beyond his capacity, eventually, to see its truth. His allegiance to Lord Mammon ["the only power the Shawcrosses respect is the power of money"] will have to be broken for that to happen, and his affection-ate attachment to Vanessa is the faintest glimmer of the sun's breaking through.

That many of Andy's self-justifying predictions came to pass is true, yet the victory of greed in the guise of progress was not complete. Henry Pitts was rumoured ready to "sell a string of roadside plots for ribbon development but he never did" whether from "too much sympathy for Paul" or lack of a sponsor on the Planning Committee nobody knew. In any event, the estate was soon "a tight-waisted island" hedged in by the "new coastal road in the south and the new four-lane Paxtonbury road in the north" (398). During the mid-1950s a new threat emerged, since "longer runways" were needed for Paxtonbury's civil airport, which threatened the "north-ernmost clumps of Shallowford Woods." When Paul had "refused to fell a single tree" the battle was joined. But this time he found allies, "The Men of the Trees, and other rural preservation societies."

> But it was not until his youngest son John…made a close study of Green Belt legisla-tion aimed at protecting roadside timber, that victory seemed possible and the airport people drew off to ponder new strategy".(*Gauntlet*, 399)

About this time it was learned that Andy "had disposed of all his interests in Shawcrosse Enterprises and gone to live in the States." It became possible then "to persuade Paul that his son's equivocal attitude to local development did not quite qualify as perfidy". But that is hindsight, and the alternative explanation is that Andy grew weary of his prior perfidy, rejecting his "long apprenticeship among rascals". His affection for Vanessa may well have leaked over into candid self-eval-uation, and his move to another country might have been the strategy for distanc-ing himself from his usual habits of action. His father had begun to think of Andy as "someone who had contracted a skin disease whilst taking wholly unnecessary risks in a sewer" (400).

One of the compensations for Paul's losses on the land was the friendship he struck up with John, currently in his last year at High Wood. As they walked together one day, John told his father that he'd have been "far more at home in Elizabethan England" than in the 20th century, "not that I don't go part way with you, Dad" (403). His reflections are indebted to the High Wood history teacher, Menzies, who has a theory about the English that John now applies to his father's current situation. Here comes another interesting cultural-historical proposition to join the earlier ones.

> "He says that your kind of caution is so widespread among the English that it produces a steady percentage of inventive rebels in every generation and that's how the Industrial Revolution began, sons improving on their fathers' essentially sound methods and then, at about fifty, becoming conservative themselves and producing another reaction."
>
> "Interesting," Paul said, and meant it, for he had often thought along these lines himself when reading beside a winter fire. "Does this chap Menzies say where we got it from, or why it's peculiar to these offshore islands?"

"Yes, he says it's a racial accident, Celtic romanticism, Roman organization, Saxon preoccupation with agriculture, Scandinavian obsession with the sea and finally Norman know-how. Successive invasions produced a kind of five-decker sandwich and you're living proof of it. I suppose, knowing you, inclined me to take 'The Menzies Theory' on trust. What I mean is, you resent change like hell but you always end up by adapting to it and rescuing some of the pieces. The Valley's proof of it, proof of compromise I mean, and compromise—old Menzies again—is a basic English virtue. Two things could have happened to Shallowford under anyone else. It could have clung to feudalism and atrophied years ago, or it could have turned itself into a cash-register, like parts of the Lancashire and the Welsh coasts. But because you were there, directing the traffic so to speak, it didn't. In the end it not only kept most of its charm but its essential usefulness." (*Gauntlet*, 404)

John had sponsored the "victory that saved Shallowford Woods." After the university he chose a television career, and he made "a film of the entire Valley, including many of the items that passed as amenities." The half-hour feature "emphasized the changes that had already taken place and the importance of retaining what was left of the natural beauty of the Valley," which, we recall, was what had first attracted Paul the day John Rudd had ridden the estate with him. The feature would be called "*The Green Gauntlet*", for an aerial survey revealed that, from a thousand feet, that is what the Valley resembles: "a great, finger-shaped glove made of green and rust-coloured leather". The only jarring note in the fly-over footage was the new buildings around Coombe Bay. "There's a gimmick angle too", as John noted, "throwing down the gauntlet to the developers" (405–07). Paul was very impressed when he saw "the first run-through" of the TV special.

Somehow they had distilled the magic of the place into a pictorial potion, so that most of the elements that had contributed to his life-long love-affair with these few miles were there to be sipped. The ranks of the old timber marching down the ridges to the Mere. The Mere itself, enclosed by evergreens and starred with the islet and the ruin of the Folly. The rooted farmsteads of High Coombe, Deepdene, Four Winds, and Hermitage. The mellow look of the Big House with its steep, curving drive flanked by chestnuts. The winding Sorrel and its ox-bows. The open dunes, now confined between two busy roads. And finally the gentle curve of the coast from the landslip to Tamer's Cover, taking in the sandbars and the Bluff. It was all there. The only thing lacking was its colour. (*Gauntlet*, 407)

John's film was "a Westcountry topic for a week or so," and after it "there was no more talk of felling the Shallowford oaks". New runways were built "pointing east-west instead of north-south", so that, again, English compromise carried the day.

Cave-in

Cave-in's action begins to unfold soon after seventy-two-year-old Claire's heart had begun to fail. After the "fifth paroxysm of pain" in three months had travelled from her back to the left shoulder and down her arm, making her gasp and stagger, she sought Doctor Maureen. The diagnosis was angina, which could kill her tomor-row or bother her off and on for a decade. But Claire has duties that demand her attention. Margie will be planning John's coming-of-age party with Mary and Evie at the Big House, and Claire has promised to stay with Vanessa, immobilized in her plaster legcast following a hunting fall. Margie and Vanessa live in Mill Cottage, located below Potters' farm, i.e., between the Dell and the place where the Coombe, usually a rivulet or brook, empties into the River Sorrel near the houses at Coombe Bay. Mill Cottage is the place where Claire, after heroically preventing the flood waters from carrying away Vanessa, meets her own death-by-drowning. When the episode has ended, Henry Pitts recalls that it was just fifty years ago that they had saved the German mariners stranded off of Tamer's Cove, and because no men-tion of disastrous flooding can be found between then and Claire's drowning one might infer that Shallowford is experiencing a fifty-year-flood.

However, riparian alleviation had protected human life in earlier decades. As Smut points out, "Old Tamer knew a thing or two about the Dell. Woulden 'ave a bush trimmed yerabouts. 'Twas moren' our skins was worth to cut wood this zide o' the stream. Tamer always reckoned the on'y thing that stopped the bliddy hill shredding away was thicky tangle, reaching from the cliff fields to the river road" (410-11). Early in his tenure, Paul had directed him to remove all that useless foli-age to increase the arable portion of land on his farm, for at that time Paul knew no more than did the developers whose machines had ripped away what Tamer had valued. The developers could have solicited the services of a flood-control engineer during the design stages, but that advisor would have increased construction costs by recommending changes that would slow the building process, not to mention the time lost as local and county officials studied reports and dithered over things they but imperfectly understood. Paul now understands from his long experience in the Valley what he had once been ignorant of. He "noticed the weight of water coming down the Coombe and estimated that its volume had quadrupled" because so many trees had been removed along with "so much brushwood" where "the water had always been absorbed by thick undergrowth." For many years "the Coombe stream had been jumpable at any point between the Dell and Mill Cottage" (409). What Tamer had understood but the *young* squire had not recognized, the devel-opers do not learn from the *old* squire, although Paul had tried to help them see that problem before it was too late. Thus one of the cultural realities of the trilogy is the slippage of human understanding from one generation to another, in any number of areas. Had the developers been homicidal in their intention? No. Will those in authority learn from the disaster that takes Claire's life? Probably they will. If the airport people change the orientation of their new runways when they real-ize the wisdom of doing so, Claire's fate can be avoided in the future. Hindsight sees what foresight overlooks, or perhaps decides to ignore.

"The party was over Maureen had said and from now on she was a spectator" (418), but today Claire would prove to be a mover and shaker. She drove to Mill Cottage carefully because of the general flooding in the area, but arrived safely at Vanessa's and the two discuss the girl's literary enthusiasms, most recently John Betjeman. What she likes about him, she says, is that "he takes tiny, trivial things and tiny, trivial people who seem dull but aren't because he shows you the pathos about everything. Just listen to this" and she reads several poems by that writer and one of her own, about "Miss Adams, Miss Ball and Miss Parminter-Beach", three spinster schoolteachers whose lives, Claire thought, were wholly drab, having "never had an opportunity to weigh the disappointments of life against the bonuses of producing a family and having a husband." Claire praises Vanessa, who is about to reply when

> a long, rumbling sound reached her like the gust of an enormously powerful gale and the cottage shuddered and bucked like a horse frightened by the sudden flap-crack of a haystack tarpaulin." (*Gauntlet*, 424)

Having been raised at High Coombe Farm, Claire knew exactly what was happening. "The great hill behind the cottage had moved, sliding towards the road and the river," which she knew was the doing of "the cursed fools who had stripped the Dell of its vegetation" and made it vulnerable to the terrible destruction she was about to experience (425).

She saw the "means of survival" in "the trailing roots of a tree that had fallen on the cottage." If the roots of that tree "remained embedded in the ruins of the cottage," she had a chance of saving Vanessa. The tree was "angled" because its branches "must have been trapped in the granite outcrop on which the cottage had been built," and thus the trunk would "survive a great deal of pressure" (426). Her granddaughter was conscious, briefly, though her bad leg is caught. Assured that Vanessa remains alive, Claire begins securing her to the trunk using the webbing she tears from the underside of an upended sofa, wrapping eight feet of "the tough, fibrous fastening" around the girl and the tree—after first blinking "S.O.S" in morse code with her flashlight to the "distant lights" of a rescue vehicle, and seeing her message responded to by the car-lights which retreated up the road towards the ford, to return with more hands to assist in the rescue effort. When the "last knot was tied" securing Vanessa, she felt "the first exploratory probes of pain", which intensified "blotting out everything else" (428-30). Then the floodwaters carried her away.

Though Simon and Paul, Margaret and Evie arrive on the scene together, it was Paul who "took command" while the others deferred to him as he worked without haste or any hint of confusion. Upon entering "the chaos of the living room," Simon "sensed desolation" in his father and told him "Stay here, Gov, let me do the looking." Without waiting for paternal assent he "crawled through the roots", pushing his torch ahead until its beams rested on "the small figure lashed to the fork" of the tree "by strips of webbing". He called back then,

> "It's Vanessa. She's here, tied in a tree...It's okay, Gov'nor, she's fastened there." Then, despair lifting his voice an octave, "*Claire*. Where are you Claire?" as he edged out along the trunk and clawed at the fastenings holding the child in the "Y" of the lower branches.

Paul scrambled back "shouting to John to bring the ladder," excited when he realized that the girl was alive. "Hurry! Come over the roof!".

> Subsiding again, as though ashamed of his outburst, he said, "You say she was *tied* there? Out on that tree" and Simon, still chafing the child's hands, mumbled, "There's no one else out there, Gov. I'm sorry...sorry..." (*Gauntlet*, 437)

"Tied there," Paul muttered..."Must have dragged her there . . I couldn't have done it. Neither could you or anyone else, not with the place falling about her..."

Counter attack carries onward from Claire's victorious death. They recovered her body a mile below the landslide, where "flotsam was piled twenty feet high and the Sorrel, in its furious search for the sea," had turned aside to flood Coombe Bay's houses and shops. Nine people dead and thousands of pounds damage put the Valley on the front page and brought reporters "flocking in" from cities "to record the devastation and interview survivors" (440). Maureen, who understood Paul better than his sons, knew his silence covered a "complex and deepseated reaction" involving the whole Valley, for he "identified the Valley with his wife". She did not try to explain this to anyone, Mary being the only person capable of understanding it, and Mary had "her own grieving to do" (441). Simon and John told reporters little about their night sortie to Mill Cottage, which was easy since the reporters' attention turned to "Shawcrosse's stripping of the Dell and the supreme folly of cutting two new roads either side of an unpredictable watercourse" (442).

Knowing that in the weeks ahead Claire's death would fall upon Paul "like another landslide", Maureen decided to tell him the full truth. Claire "was almost certainly dead when the water closed over her," which startled Paul, whose blankness of expression pushed her into telling even more.

> "Well, Paul...it seemed to me you should know. What I mean is...she must have realized exactly what she was doing clambering up and down that tree trunk, getting those fastenings, and hanging on there in all that storm and wind. Perhaps a person in that situation with a helpless child would do what she did instinctively, or at least try to do it, but to me, knowing her heart condition, it was nothing short of a miracle. It was also a deliberate sacrifice." She paused. "Is that how you see it?" (*Gauntlet*, 444)

Yes, that's how he sees it, and that's "how it was." Paul has more to say, so Maureen waits. He continues, without looking at her.

"There's another way of looking at this business and it keeps returning to me. It's the curious completeness, almost *rightness* of that kind of death in that particular place. She was Valley-born and all her life she stood by me in a fight for and against the Valley but I don't mean by that a fight against outsiders. The Sorrel and all the soil that came down on her weren't outsiders. Neither was the heavy rainfall at the back of that landslide. These things have always been part and parcel of our life here. In a way we've always been fighting them, trying to tame them, trying to make them work for us. Somehow it doesn't seem so bad to go down fighting in an old cause. Hazel, Rumble Patrick's mother, was killed by a honking staff car near that cottage, and poor old Grace was killed in a foreign land by a foreign bomb. But Claire was luckier than either of them. If she had to go soon, then it was a wonderful thing to have a chance of doing something as useful as that at the final moment. I'm glad you told me. In fact, I'll never cease to appreciate it," and he pressed her hand. (*Gauntlet*, 444-45)

Soon after his discussion with Maureen, Paul called Simon and John into the library and, himself again, said that she should not be buried privately but instead be a part of the group burial which was likely to be televised. "This is a Valley occasion" and since she was "very much a part of the Valley", Claire wouldn't want to be buried alone. Further, she didn't die from exhaustion, but angina, and "I'd like that generally known". "You don't *mind* this sort of thing being broadcast?", John inquires. Why would he? "She did something astounding and why should it be passed over?" (445-46).

Turning from Claire's death to the Valley they tended together for so long, Paul opines to Henry that the cave-in could have a silver lining. They will "soon get around to clearing it up and rebuilding," and if we "raise the matter of replanting" someone might listen to us. Perhaps, Henry replies, "but I woulden bet on it, Maister" (447). Andrew didn't fly back from the States for the funeral, perhaps in tacit acquiescence to his responsibility for what happened. Paul sends Vanessa to Paxtonbury Convent School where, Mary assures him, her "creative impulse would be encouraged." Given Andy's reliable information about Valley events, Paul wonders if "Margaret herself had let slip that the disaster had been caused by stripping vegetation from that part of the Coombe" (448). In any event, when Andy returns after a five-year absence, he is eager to blackmail Shawcrosse into selling back the estate land he himself was instrumental in their Company's having purchased.

Andy is the more eager to correct the evil he has done when he sees the desolation that persisted despite non-stop work by bulldozers and "the dumping of hundreds of tons of soil and rock along the old course of the river" (449). Shawcross, still the same man he had been in the hospital where Andy came under his spell, is upbeat about what had happened. "We've had our teething troubles," baby stuff, "but we're over them now", ready to embrace wider horizons. Having a drink in Ken's home, Andy belatedly realizes that "everything he said and did was phoney," how he lifted his glass and "leered as he gulped," his desk, the curtains he had chosen, his wife Rhoda. "Every last thing about him was counterfeit," which makes

Andy's task that much easier. Knowing that his evidence of Shawcrosse's illegal conduct is sufficient ground to compel him to sign, Andy brings out the document his ex-partner glances over, watching to savor "the blood surge into his neck" as he reads the final page, which requires his signature approving the sale of Craddock land back to the family for (the stunned Shawcrosse wails) "*Twelve-five?* The price we paid for it?" No less, no more (450–51). Andy tells him

> "I'll give you two minutes to sign, and cut your losses, or I make a precis of everything I can prove about what went on between the time we were demobbed and the time we split up. I'm not putting the bite on you, not really. All I want is the Coombe farm, the rest of it, those places nearer the sea, aren't worth having any more." (*Gauntlet*, 453)

With the document in hand, Andy drove to the Big House and "slipped the bill of sale from his brief case," as he said "Prodigal's peace offering. I didn't squander all my patrimony on the husks that the swine eat" (456). Paul's response was to embrace his son, "holding him close for a full half-minute" (457). Andy needed to be more cautious approaching Margaret, who took Claire's death very hard and probably blamed him for it. But she greets him easily and without rancour. Andy saw her "as the girl of long ago," bluntly honest when the occasion demands it. "Let's face it, Andy", Margie told him, there was never much between them except "strong physical attraction". Yet when he went to the States she had thought about him "often enough," and wondered how he was doing, and what he was up to, which was as clear an invitation to make a personal statement as Andy was likely to get.

> He said, without looking at her, "You don't make anything more than casual contacts with people after the age of thirty or so. You lose the knack of making yourself matter, or finding something in them worth cultivating. It's been that way with me a long time now. I'm damned lonely and I'm going to get lonelier. I never found anyone or anything that came near replacing the old set-up. I suppose I took it for granted that you had by now." (*Gauntlet*, 458–59)

Margaret answers him this way: "You're sick of trapesing then, and I'm sick of making do, and living my life through Vanessa. I'm not that old yet," embracing him, and kissing him "in the way he had forgotten but now remembered" (460). Delderfield writes *comic* fiction, which gravitates towards reconciliation and embraces happy endings, which may be why academics have so little use for him. But that is their business, not mine.

Absorbing the enemy

Absorbing the enemy is the first of the three chapters that conclude the novel by presenting Paul Craddock as he reflects upon people and events during his last half-dozen years. At eighty, he is chiefly a spectator, the overall emotion of *Gautlet*'s closing phase being something between "Sleepy Time Gal" and "Sunrise, Sunset, Swiftly Flow the Years". Is Paul regretful? Not at all, and "in some ways these were the most rewarding years of his life." He has become a rich repository of cultural history, having fought in two wars and seen memorable events in England's history. That long view enables him to grasp what his children and grandchildren are too close to the present to see. "'I can recall all that European cackling at the time of the Boer war,' he would tell them, 'but in the end what happened? We had the Boers fighting for us against the Germans'" (463)—*cackling* being the noise raised by disturbed hens, the very paradigm of ignorantly plaintive outrage.

> Age, and enormous experience, enabled him to deal with people and problems more objectively than had been possible in his young and middle life, and although eighty on June 1st, he continued to enjoy splendid health. There was something else that mellowed him a great deal. He found that he could take the storms and triumphs and frustrations and controversies of the years and winnow them through a wry and retentive memory, setting the grain of commonsense and kindness on one side and discarding the chaff of prejudice and partisanship. It was his ability to do that that buttressed him against a prevailing mood of national pessimism and self-doubt, caused (so pundits assured him) by the effort and sacrifices of two world wars and the loss of an empire.
>
> Just as he had always seen the fruitfulness of the Valley reflected in the flesh of his wife, so he now saw the overall shift of pattern in national life adapt to the new pressures but without losing the more important of its basic values. Of course, he was very biased in this direction, and those who remained of his generation challenged the thesis, but he had the advantage of day to day contact with a horde of grandchildren and godchildren, and they nurtured his essential tolerance, so that he refused to join in the head-shaking of the over-sixties when pop art cut a swathe into culture, when the sputnik bleeped its way around outer space, and the cult of permissiveness rained volleys of custard pies at the Establishment across the television studios. He told himself that he had seen it all before, or something very like it, and reminded himself that, for all his anxieties, the Valley was still more or less intact and the British still the secret envy of other nations. His argument was simple. One did not, he would say, go out of one's way to mock an old lady who had been by-passed by the mainstream of life; one left her alone, or sniggered behind her back, but today, when almost everyone was busy abusing Britain, it was clear that they did so because they envied her her superb mastery of the art of compromise. (*Gauntlet*, 462–63)

The Valley had called him young Squire, then Squire, but now it was "Old Squire," and Paul accepted this as "an ironical compliment in days of coastal traffic jams, sonic booms, the Beatles, four-letter words, and hi-fi recordings of compositions that had been scored, he would remind them, in days when the creative impulse could get along without the help of gadgets" (463). Paul had developed "absorbing interests" that in earlier years he had lacked the leisure to pursue, although he had had a lifelong appreciation of "good china, old silver and moderately-priced oils" (464), all which now graced his home. This interest strengthened his attachment to Andy, who astonished everyone by opening an antique shop in Paxtonbury to which "he brought his aggressive initiative." His shop became a regular tourist stop, and a location which "The Trade" frequented as well. Margaret, whose reconciliation with Andy had "mellowed" him and helped reconcile him with his father, could always tell "whether or not he had had a good day at the auctions by his approach as a lover." One night after their energetic pursuit of their lost youth, he told Margie that it was no surprise that she and Claire had become such close friends, for they were "temperamentally as alike as he and Stevie had been." Moreover, "the only thing that ever mattered to either of you was to be needed and regularly man-handled...My guess is that all she was really interested in was the Gov, and the way he looked at her, especially when she took her clothes off" (465). Paul took Andy's advice about replanting the Coombe. A decade later, "the landslide scar had healed," detectable only as "a faint discoloration" on the estate's side of the Dell, "where a small forest of spruce, larch and Norwegian fir half covered the slopes" (466).

As for the other chief characters in the novel, Simon was given the headship of a new school in Whinmouth, along with "comparative freedom" to develop "theories about the processes of educating under-sixteens." He regularly took students on Bentinck-like trips to the local police station or out to examine "geological strata at the landslip" along with "an astonishing variety of object lessons" at various historial locations in England, enjoying himself immensely in the doing (471). John, the family's "eccentric," made a reputation for himself in television with programs such as "The Source and Course of the Thames," which were presented "with a whimsicality that softened a sharp social comment on John Bull's transition from farmer-industrialist to bankrupt ex-Imperialist." John made his living "the most entertaining way" he knew, for himself and for audiences.

Paul did not play favorites with his grandchildren and godchildren the way Claire had favored Vanessa. But he did sometimes "contemplate" the long list of their names and birthdays "in the old estate diary that was still clamped between the hinged covers of the Bible that old George Lovell, his predecessor, had used to camouflage his gallery of local nudes" (473). When Maureen Rudd died in Edinburgh at eighty-eight, her son sent her corpse to be interred in the Valley "among so many of her old patients." When he attended funerals, Paul reflected "without sadness" on the men memorialized at French Wood or buried in older parts of the churchyard.

Snow, and garrison alliances is our final look at Paul as the Valley leader, in the great winter of 1962–63, "the hardest, they said, since records had been kept." The snow continued to fall, covering everything to great depths that immobilized movement and made it impossible to get eggs out to market or food into the Valley, whether for residents or their livestock. "Rural isolation" no longer expressed the contrast between Shallowford and more populated areas, but the present threat to one and all, intensifying as the snow continued to fall.

It was as though, before he was quite through, the Valley gods, older and more capricious than Jehovah, were eager to show him everything in his celestial repertoire. (*Gauntlet*, 477)

This glancing deity-comparative remark begins Delderfield's ramp-up to Paul's death in French Wood. The novelist goes out-of-his-way to repudiate the Christianity he had endured from the age of six until almost twelve, during the Sundays wherein "Anglican, Wesleyan, Methodist, United Methodist, Primitive Methodist, Congregational, Baptist, Presbyterian and Plymouth Brother", all such denominations "went through the motions of a sullen resignation" (*Own Amusement*, 81-2). The Valley is *alive*, and Claire's body had participated in that life, and the "Valley gods" antedate "Old Moster," as Faulkner's Mink Snopes conceives of Jehovah: not as life's creator but as the brutal extinguisher of life; "Old Moster jest punishes; He don't play jokes" (*The Mansion*, 398). The Delderfield who still resents the experience of being forced to go to Baptist services many years earlier creates characters such as Paul Craddock, or such as Diana—who expresses her naturalistic convictions in her poetry, using the third person to express first-person beliefs. Here is Diana's belatedly 19th century poem *Senile Countryman*.

> He found his faith in the foxglove bell
> His creed in the clustered stars
> Of Ladies-lace, where dust-bent stems
> Played games with sunlit bars.
>
> In the moist, gold shine of the celandine
> He hunted Heaven's grace.
> Sermons he heard in every copse
> And many a gorse-grown place.
>
> He did not need the parson's plea
> To note a godly hand
> In the age of the oak or the blue-bell smoke
> On an April-stirring land.
>
> ...
> Thither he'll go when his time runs out
> And his loins have lost their swing
> No fear in his heart but sorrow perhaps
> In not outliving Spring.
>
> Senile? Perhaps, but less I think
> Than those who work by night
> Earning, yearning, tax-returning
> Under electric light.
> (*The Unjust Skies*, 284)

This deflection from an attack on Blake's "Old Nobodaddy" to the indictment of the desk-bound accountant could be the instinctive tact of a novelist who wants his characters to express their views about death without needlessly annoying his readers. The narrator of Diana's demise finds in her personal papers "some lines of Yeats' *Cold Heaven*" that she had highlighted by underlining.

> "...Ah, when the ghost begins to quicken
> Confusion of the death-bed over, is it sent
> Out naked on the roads, as the books say, and stricken
> By the injustice of the skies for punishment?"
> (Unjust Skies, 274)

I do not know if Mink's Old Moster and Yeats' "injustice of the skies" are identical but, to borrow Mark Twain's words once more, the difference between them is not spacious, and Paul Craddock's creed is theirs, to the extent Delderfield presents it to us. If the novelist wishes his characters' religious views to be made clear for readers, I am happy to oblige him.

It was in mid-February of that terrible year that Paul "conceived and organized" his last effort on Shallowford's behalf, a helicopter airlift that brought supplies into the Valley through the cooperation of "the County Agricultural Office at Paxtonbury." Choppers came sailing in "over the desolate slopes and dropping carefully packaged supplies" ordered in Craddock's name from suppliers with "snowplough access to the R.A.F. training base." Watching the activity unfold, Andy admitted that it was "absolutely fascinating to see all the threads leading back to that office of his, just the way it did when I was a kid growing up here." It was a pity that Henry Pitts had not lived to see it, for he would have given "his long whistle of surprise and his 'Gordamme, Maister, they vound a praper use for they bliddy ole contrapshuns after all, didden 'em now?'" (478–80).

Terms of capitulation

Terms of capitulation is the novel's ceremonial wrap-up, an ending that continues to assess the cultural history of England. Churchill's funeral is an appropriate occasion for bringing citizens together to memorialize the twentieth century within the context of British history. Craddock's attitude towards Churchill had been fluid across the years, but in his final analysis Sir Winston is "the embodiment of a number of essentially British characteristics" that taken together had "set him up as a tribal symbol, like the Union Jack, pre-First World War dreadnoughts, roast beef, Gilbert and Sullivan, and village cricket." Craddock and Churchill had been "born within five years of one another", and this fact alone "elevated" the Prime Minister in the eyes of "a man extremely reluctant to discard anything from the past that might prove useful in shoring up present and future" (487–88).

Paul found himself hankering to visit London and watch the funeral. That desire was enabled when Simon received a call from the editor of "a group of

Westcountry newspapers" asking him to witness the funeral and write an article "by someone with a sense of history." Simon and his father go there together. On location, Paul noticed that the orderly crowd "was not a gathering of mourners" but an assembly of citizens who were taking their place in the long chronicle of English history.

> The mood here was something he had never sensed among English people, a compound that defied accurate analysis, for it had about it elements of solemnity, good-temper, gaiety, inevitability, awe, and an overall sense of achievement, as though they were here to witness something half-way between the completion of an enormous national shrine and the pageantry that would attend the burial of a medieval king.
>
> It was, he decided, a very elusive mood indeed and the only constituent entirely absent on the streets was grief, even the pseudo-solemnity that passes for grief at the funeral of a paladin or a city father. (*Gauntlet*, 491)

Paul remained outside shivering with the rest of the crowd, "watching the history of the century unfold in a steady procession of V.I.P.s", DeGaulle, Eisenhower and the Royal party of the Queen, Princes Philip and Charles, along with the Queen Mother, who confirmed Paul's opinion that she was a woman who "knew instinctively how to radiate the good manners one expected of someone whose whole being was concerned with the mystique of ceremonial" (492). The passage of the cortege up the Cathedral steps was "the finale of an epic" that Paul himself had participated in, and he was happy that he had decided to wear his "gongs," the array of service medals which adorned him. Indeed, it was, as the taxi-driver put it, "Bloody marvellous" (494). Paul was

> engaged in piecing together impressions to form a whole and the process was familiar to him, the method smoothed by the sixty-three years he had spent in the Valley. What he sought, as he sat there musing, was a compendium of British virtues, some kind of justification for the intense national pride that brought a sparkle to his eyes, and he assembled it like a man building a utensil from odds and ends that had strayed within reach. There was dignity there, expressed in a pageantry that some might feel verged upon the ridiculous but it was not ridiculous because it was motivated by impulses worthier than pride—by respect and by an unconscious groping after traditions that had survived the passage of centuries. (*Gauntlet*, 495)

Paul's assessment brought to him "a sense of belonging" he had never felt in these London streets, and "a comfort that he had never found in religion or the promise of survival after death." He felt "at one" with that strange volcano of a man, Churchill, and "there was immortality enough in this fellowship and in the loins of his sons, daughters and descendants" (495).

Back in the Valley, Paul got the news a week or two after his eighty-sixth birthday that Vanessa had "won the great-grandchild race" by producing a nine-pound boy on her wedding anniversary. As he was recording the event in the estate diary, he "totted up" their descendants thus far and said aloud to Claire, as if she were present, "That's not so bad, old girl" (497). After his nap, feeling that the inside air was too "stuffy", Paul asks Rumble to drive him to French Wood where he can breathe more easily. Paul now had many descendants, whose company he enjoyed, "but they were not of his generation." All of them like Henry Pitts had died, "leaving him a Crusoe on an island of time". He was "filled with a great desire to see Claire, to reach out and touch her, to hear her voice and catch the sparkle of her eye as she looked over her shoulder at him while tugging a comb through her hair" (504). It's time for Paul to ship out, while contemplating the Valley that her body represented, and thinking that the Shallowfordians' lives had been "more useful and more enjoyable than they would have lived under the patronage of someone like that scoundrel Shawcrosse, or Sydney Codsall, who had also tried to usher in an era of ugliness and urban sprawl." On the whole, Paul reflected, he had succeeded, and when a man's eighty-sixth birthday is behind him, that's "a pleasant verdict" on his life (506). Then, as the blue haze of the Moor "began to advance like a long belt of clouds," and the Valley flowers expanded into "a gloriously prolific cascade of colour a mile wide" in a "kaleidoscopic miracle" before his eyes, Paul Craddock died in his favorite spot, French Wood. The expression found on his corpse when Simon and Rumble reached him was the "mute acceptance one might see on the face of an effigy on a tomb in an old church" (508). Wordsworth offers the appropriate epitaph:

> As in the eye of Nature he has lived,
> So in the eye of Nature let him die!
> (The Old Cumberland Beggar, lines 196–97)

WORKS CITED

Books By R. F. Delderfield

Napoleonic History/Commentaries

Napoleon in Love. (Simon and Schuster: New York), 1959.

The Golden Millstones. (Harper and Row: New York), 1964.

The March of the Twenty-Six (1962). (Pen and Sword Books: Barnsley, S. Yorkshire), 2004.

The Retreat from Moscow. (Atheneum: New York), 1967.

Imperial Sunset (1968). (Stein and Day: New York), 1980.

Napoleonic Novels

Seven Men of Gascony (1949). (Simon and Schuster: New York), 1973.

Farewell the Tranquil Mind (1950). (Pocket Books: New York), 1973.

Too Few for Drums (1964). (Simon and Schuster: New York), 1974.

The Avenue Novels

The Dreaming Suburb, 1919–1940 (1958). (Ballantine Books: New York), 1973.

The Avenue Goes to War, 1940–1947 (1958). (Ballantine Books: New York), 1973.

A Horseman Riding By

Long Summer's Day (1966). (Ballantine Books: New York), 1972.

Post of Honour, 1911–1940 (1966). (Simon and Schuster: New York), 1967.

The Green Gauntlet (1968). (Hodder and Stoughton: London), 1982.

Ancillary Books By Delderfield

The Unjust Skies (1962). (Hodder and Stoughton: London), 1971.

For My Own Amusement (1968). (Simon and Schuster: New York), 1972.

Overture for Beginners. (Hodder and Stoughton: London), 1972.

Books By Other Authors

Burke, Peter. *What is Cultural History?* (Polity Press: Cambridge UK), 2004.

Casey, Edward S. *Remembering: A Phenomenological Study.* (Indiana UP: Bloomington and Indianapolis), 1987.

Conrad, Joseph. *The Shadow Line.* (New York: Doubleday), 1926.

———. "The Secret Sharer," in *'Twixt Land and Sea.* (Doubleday: New York), 1972.

Doyle, William. *The French Revolution: A Very Short Introduction.* (Oxford UP: Oxford), 2001.

Erckmann-Chatrian. *The History of A Conscript of 1813* and *Waterloo.* Trans. R. D. Gillman, Everyman's Library (Dent: London and Dutton: New York), 1909.

Faulkner, William. *The Mansion.* (Random House: New York), 1955.

Franklin, Benjamin. *Autobiography and Other Pieces.* Ed. and Intro. By Dennis Welland. (Oxford UP: London), 1970.

Fussell, Paul. *The Great War and Modern Memory.* (Oxford UP: New York), 1975.

Heller, Joseph. *Catch-22.* (Dell: New York), 1955.

Hunt, Lynn. *The Family Romance of the French Revolution.* (U.C.Press: Berkeley and Los Angeles), 1992.

Macdonnell, A. G. *Napoleon and His Marshals.* (Macmillan: New York), 1934.

Marbot, Baron de. *Memoirs.* Trans. A. J. Butler, 2 Vols. (Longmans, Green: London and New York), 1892.

Remarque, Erich M. *All Quiet on the Western Front.* Trans. A. H. Wheen (Little, Brown: Boston), 1929.

Scott, Sir Walter. *Minstrelsy of the Scottish Border.* Ed. T. Henderson. (Thomas Crowell: New York), 1931.

Sternlicht, Sanford. *R. F. Delderfield.* Twayne: Boston), 1988.

INDEX